Roots Too

Roots Too

White Ethnic Revival in
Post–Civil Rights America

Matthew Frye Jacobson

HARVARD UNIVERSITY PRESS

Cambridge, Massachusetts

London, England

2006

Library of Congress Cataloging-in-Publication Data

Jacobson, Matthew Frye, 1958–
    Roots too : White ethnic revival in post–civil rights America /
Matthew Frye Jacobson.
        p. cm.
    Includes bibliographical references and index.
    ISBN 0-674-10898-2 (alk. paper)
    1. Whites—United States—Ethnic identity.   I. Title.

E184.A1J23 2005
305.809'073—dc22   2005050363

To my family, root and branch

Contents

Introduction: Beyond Hansen's Law   1

1. Hyphen Nation   11

2. Golden Door, Silver Screen   72

3. Old World Bound   130

4. The Immigrant's Bootstraps, and Other Fables   177

5. I Take Back My Name   206

6. Our Heritage Is Our Power   246

7. Whose America (Who's America)?   312

Coda: Ireland at JFK   389

Notes   399
Acknowledgments   465
Index   471

Roots Too

I am an Italian-American who doesn't speak Italian, just as I am a French-American whose French ranges from tremulous to nonexistent, as well as a Russian-American who barely recognizes the sound of Russian and has never seen a street in Russia. Because of all these complex combinations, moreover, I am an American-American who spent years denying being American, years inhabiting a country (or perhaps countries) of hyphenation—maybe even a hyphen nation.

—Sandra Gilbert,
"Mysteries of the
Hyphen" (1997)

Introduction:
Beyond Hansen's Law

The notion that the intense and unprecedented mixture of
ethnic and religious groups in American life was soon to
blend into a homogenous end product has outlived its useful-
ness, and also its credibility. . . . The point about the melting
pot . . . is that it did not happen.

> —Nathan Glazer
> and Daniel Patrick
> Moynihan, *Beyond the*
> *Melting Pot* (1963)

The leader of an antiracism workshop in the 1990s once noted a
disquieting inclination on the part of the group's white participants to dissociate themselves from the history and persistent reality of white privilege by emphasizing some purportedly not-
quite-white ethnic background. "I'm not white; I'm Italian," one
would say. Another, "I'm Jewish." After this ripple had made its
way across the group, the seminar leader was left wondering,

"What happened to all the white people who were here just a minute ago?"[1]

Such modifications of whiteness were not unheard of on the American scene: earlier generations had spoken of the Celtic, Hebrew, Slavic, or Mediterranean "races" even though these peoples had entered the country as the "free white persons" of American naturalization law. But the salience of these distinctions had largely faded away in the middle decades of the century. In the realm of self-ascription, such evasions of whiteness would have been rare—unthinkable, in some parts of the country—by the 1950s. In the late twentieth century the sense of a statement like "I'm not white; I'm Italian" rested on several historical preconditions, now loosely relayed in the term "ethnic revival": the Civil Rights movement had heightened whites' consciousness of their skin privilege, rendering it not only visible but uncomfortable (the more so, perhaps, because it was so hard to disown its chief comforts). The example of Black Nationalism and the emergence of multiculturalism had provided a new language for an identity that was not simply "American." After decades of striving to conform to the Anglo-Saxon standard, descendants of earlier European immigrants quit the melting pot. Italianness, Jewishness, Greekness, and Irishness had become badges of pride, not shame.

What the second generation wishes to forget the third wishes to remember, observed Marcus Lee Hansen before an audience of Swedish immigrants in the 1930s. According to Hansen, a typical member of the second (American-born) generation of Swedes "wanted to forget everything: the foreign language that left an unmistakable trace in his English speech, the religion that continually recalled childhood struggles, the family customs that should have been the happiest of all memories." At the time, Hansen's oratory was as much a jeremiad as it was a sociological lecture: nothing could "absolve the traitors of the second generation," who in their rush to become American "deliberately threw away what had been preserved in the home." But for Hansen the immigrants' grandchildren represented "a new force and a new opportunity": reversing the assimilationist trajectory of their parents, members of this generation strive to remember and to recover what has been lost. Hansen called this "the principle of third-generation interest."[2] His observation on the ethnic behavior of generations, thought to transcend ethnic boundaries and perhaps history as well, eventually achieved semi-official status as "Hansen's Law."[3]

Discussion of the ethnic revival of the 1960s and after must begin with Hansen's Law, not necessarily because of its explanatory power, but because, in the decades since, Hansen's Law has shaped Americans' very understanding of the new, resurgent ethnicity. As a matter of simple definition, Hansen's Law in action is in fact what the ethnic revival is widely presumed to have *been*. Ethnic traces and trappings that had been lost, forgotten, or forcibly cast off by prior generations in their rush to Americanize were now rediscovered and embraced by a younger generation who had known nothing but "American" culture. Polish and Gaelic language lessons; *The Joys of Yiddish;* klezmer records and folk dancing; a hunger for Old World history; the elaborate re-creation of family genealogies—take this individualized identity quest and multiply it by a few million, and there is the ethnic revival.

A few objections might be raised. When we cast a glance back across the ethnic landscape to texts like "Americans All—Immigrants All" (1938), Louis Adamic's *Nation of Nations* (1944), or

John F. Kennedy's *Nation of Immigrants* (1958), we get the feeling that, whatever death or slumber ethnicity was supposedly "revived" *from* in the ethnic revival, the hiatus could not have been very long. Perhaps "ethnic reverie" would be a better term. But indeed there *was* a surge in popular "ethnic" concerns in the 1960s and after, and the common focus on the personal dimension of identity is too limiting to accommodate the full circuitry of the new ethnicity and its social and political significance. It is not just that many, perhaps millions, of people became newly absorbed in the idea of their ethnic heritage at the same moment, but also that they received all kinds of support and direction from the key institutions that engaged their lives. Psychological dynamics undoubtedly played some part in the wish to recover Grandma and Grandpa's lost heritage. But missing from the standard Hansen's Law reckoning are the surrounding cultural, institutional, and political forces: trade presses and television networks, which produced mass paperbacks and TV shows like *Roots;* news agencies, like *Time* magazine, which turned the roots phenomenon into a roots craze by providing instruction in genealogical research; publishers, scholars, and universities, which produced studies like *World of Our Fathers* and offered college credit for *Roots*-inflected family histories; and politicians like Gerald Ford and Jimmy Carter, who sanctified a vision of "ethnic heritage" that had vast implications not only for individuals and families but for the nation itself and for reigning notions of "Americanness."

Ethnic pride and a newfound passion for genealogy are only part of the story. The culture industries—especially publishing, Hollywood, and television—lavished a new attention on ethnic particularity, at times actually generating ethnic interests *(Roots, Holocaust)* and at others merely reflecting them *(Fiddler on the*

1.   *A token of the new pride. Ethnic trinkets, memorabilia, and kitsch represented a growing cottage industry in the 1970s.* RICHARD CUMMINS/ CORBIS.

Roof). Academic commentators forged a new consensus, after Nathan Glazer and Daniel Patrick Moynihan, that America was less a "melting pot" than a "mosaic." Teachers and students across the country engaged in a series of institution-building movements on behalf of Italo-American, Irish, Jewish, or Ethnic Studies. Immigration history emerged as a subfield, revising the received national narrative and proliferating distinct "ethnic" histories. New ethnic merchandise and marketing practices appeared, ranging from the *kitsch* shamrock key chain to the tourism industry's "discover your homeland" touring packages across Greece, Ireland, Italy, or Lithuania. And perhaps most significant, the state itself became engaged in the construction and celebration of "immigrant heritage" in projects like the Ethnic Heritage Studies Program and the Statue of Liberty and Ellis Island restorations. Working-class whites who had never exactly lost their ethnic identifications now mobilized on the basis of this new public language of group cohesion, collective destiny, and, often, group rights under siege. "This is a Warsaw ghetto mentality," said one Jewish resident, describing a busing conflict in the Canarsie section of Brooklyn. "It's an uprising like the Masada."[4]

Taken together, these developments mark the emergence of a wholly new syntax of nationality and belonging—a change in personal feeling for some, perhaps, but a shift in public language for all. In the mid-1960s the sociologist Talcott Parsons could still assert with some confidence that Americans' "emancipation" from the "particularist solidarities" of ethnicity, religion, regionalism, and class was accelerating, and that the United States was adopting "universalistic norms." By 1975, however—even before *Roots* aired—Parsons had reversed himself, conceding that "full assimilation" in the sense of ethnicity's becoming "absorbed within the single category of 'American' is very little the case."[5] It was not the interiority but the *collectivity* of the ethnic revival whose reach in American political culture was most important—not the politics of "identity" for individuals, but the politics of "heritage" for the nation at large. Far more momentous than any individual's experience of that "single category of American" has been the shifting conception of America itself that attended this decades-long contest between "universalistic norms" and "particularist solidarities."

"The 1960s was the decade of gaps," reflected Peter Schrag in a piece for *Harper's* in 1970, "missile gaps, credibility gaps, generation gaps—when we became, in many respects, a nation of outsiders, a country in which the mainstream, however mythic, lost its compelling energy and its magnetic attraction."[6] Schrag called this "thinning" of the mainstream "The Decline of the WASP."

This shift in collective identities did not disrupt, but actually bolstered, the racial whiteness that had long held the key to American belonging and power relations, though it did generate a new
set of popular narratives about who these "Caucasian" Americans
were and where they had come from. It relocated that normative
whiteness from what might be called Plymouth Rock whiteness
to Ellis Island whiteness. In the years beyond the melting pot
there arose a new national myth of origins whose touchstone was
Ellis Island, whose heroic central figure was the downtrodden but
determined greenhorn, whose preferred modes of narration were
the epic and the ode, and whose most far-reaching political conceit was the "nation of immigrants."

"Ellis Island whiteness" conveys two ideological currents that
coexist uneasily and in tension: "Ellis Island *white*" (the long-
standing white hegemony of U.S. political culture has persisted
in somewhat revised form) and "*Ellis Island* white" (myths and
symbols of a distinctly *immigrant* whiteness jostled with the older
icons of WASPdom, radically revising the conceptions of American diversity and "Americanism" that had prevailed before). These
competing meanings, along with the tension they generate,
have lent a peculiar cast to the political struggles and the culture
wars that have raged in one form or another since the time of
the Moynihan Report. ("England out of Ireland—Niggers out of
South Boston"; "I'm not white; I'm Italian.")

The roots obsession, then, was not some quirky, momentary
identity quest; nor can its impact be measured by the attendance
at St. Patrick's Day parades, by box office receipts for *Fiddler on
the Roof,* or by the volume of visitors to the nation's genealogical
archives. Rather, in their loving recovery of an immigrant past,
white Americans reinvented the "America" to which their ances-

tors had journeyed. The ethnic revival recast American nationality, and it continues to color our judgment about who "we" Americans are, and who "they" outside the circle of "we the people" are,
too. As early as 1967 Martin Luther King, Jr., decried the notion
that the United States was a "nation of immigrants," and he cau-
tioned against the damning exclusions inherent in such a conception. Citing the line inscribed on the Statue of Liberty that
identifies her as the "mother of exiles," King exclaimed that it is
no wonder "the Negro in America cries, 'Oh Lord, sometimes I
feel like a motherless child.'"[7] As late as 2004, even though the
American political imagination was gripped by blue-state/red-
state warfare—and hence "white" political mobilization conjured
images of Protestant evangelicals more readily than Emma Lazarus's huddled masses—still the Republicans kicked off their national convention on the hallowed ground of Ellis Island. Amid
pious talk of how the site "represented the Republican Party's
commitment to cultural diversity," speakers appealed to Americans' populist conceptions of "the people" by enumerating the
many immigrant Bushes, Cheneys, Patakis, and Giulianis whose
names grace Ellis Island's "wall of honor."[8]

Ultimately the language, symbols, and logic of the white ethnic revival profoundly influenced those political movements, both
progressive and conservative, that are the legacy of the 1960s—
neoconservatism, the New Left, second-wave feminism, multiculturalism, and both pro- and anti-immigration coalitions.
Though clearly a political resource for progressives, as evidenced
in the ethnic awakenings of figures like Tom Hayden and Judy
Chicago, the net effect of the Ellis Island epic has pitched decisively toward the right: appeals to the romantic icon of yesterday's
European immigrant—downtrodden, hard-working, self-reliant,

triumphant—have shaped policy debates about everything from affirmative action and the welfare state to slavery reparations and contemporary immigration. The pervasive conceit of the nation of immigrants, as King recognized, blunted the charges of the Civil Rights and Black Power movements and eased the conscience of a nation that had just barely begun to reckon with the harshest contours of its history forged in white supremacism.   •

Quite aside from Marcus Lee Hansen's notion of interior, psychic, hyphenated identities, there is such a thing as hyphennationalism; and indeed ours has become a hyphen nation. Like those that came before, this mode of American nationalism is founded in large part on white primacy. However appealingly draped in a celebratory rhetoric of diversity and inclusion, however attentive to the "little people" of American history, it serves in part to protect that primacy. If hyphen-nationalism has articulated and celebrated one myth of origins for the United States and its white population, then it has effaced an older one. Ellis Island remembrance, that is, has perhaps entailed an even more portentous *forgetting* of the gradual and violent history of this settler democracy in the making long before the first immigrants of the Castle Garden–Ellis Island variety ever came ashore. Indeed, in order fully to understand how white primacy in American life survived the withering heat of the Civil Rights era and multiculturalism, we must understand the displacement of Plymouth Rock by Ellis Island in our national myth of origins.

Jennifer DeVere Brody writes that "the hyphen performs—it is never neutral or natural."[9] Early in the twentieth century the hyphen performed a kind of adopted Americanism that was largely rejected in the majority view. In the 1910s "hyphenated Americanism" amounted to *un*-Americanism, as far as some were concerned; it was the subject of much surveillance and worry. But two generations later, in that political era "beyond the melting pot," the Americanism performed by the hyphen has risen above reproach. Ethnic hyphenation, if not neutral, has at least become a natural idiom of national belonging in this nation of immigrants.

The prodigious performance of the hyphen is indispensable in assessing many of the political tendencies of the late twentieth century—both rightward and leftward—that remain largely unremarked and unnamed. Historiography, we know, is a presentist pursuit; the biggest game it is after is never simply "the past" but a *usable* past. If the period from the 1960s to the early 2000s is not yet distant enough to qualify as "history," then it is still worth highlighting some obscured political patterns and trying to crack some of the culture's unacknowledged codes, because a more usable *present* wouldn't be such a bad thing.

Chapter One

Hyphen Nation

Maybe the melting-pot idea was a bad one. Maybe it's bet-
ter to be a Corleone than a Loud, better to be tribal and
ethnocentric than urbane and adrift. We are like jelly fish
in the vast ocean, dropping our young into the waves and
immediately losing them because we are all merely
transparent.

—Anne Roiphe, *New York*
Times Magazine (1973)

In the summer of 1963, amid much fanfare on both sides of the Atlantic, John F. Kennedy returned to Ireland. Whether he had ever actually been there before was not the point (though in fact he had visited three times). Rather, the President's celebrated "re-turn" referred to his clan's century-long absence from the green fields of County Wexford, where Kennedy's great-grandfather had been raised. Ireland readied for the visit with all the excite-ment befitting the return of a favorite son. "Preparations were tackled with tremendous enthusiasm," according to one account. "The walls of thatched-roof cottages were freshly whitewashed,

choirs and bands in the towns and villages he would visit practiced incessantly, women bought new outfits, and altogether
throughout the country excitement reached fever pitch."[1]

The familial brogue of this state visit did not go unnoticed in
the United States. "President to Visit Home of Ancestors in Ireland," the *New York Times* announced in May; and on his arrival:
"President Kennedy arrived in Dublin this evening and in a sense,
he said, it was like coming 'home' . . . Mr. Kennedy was hailed by
President Eamon de Valera as the 'first citizen' of the United
States but also by the people of Dublin as the local boy . . . who
made good." Kennedy told a cheering crowd in New Ross that it
had taken him "115 years, 6000 miles and three generations to
make the trip."[2]

If Kennedy's ascendance to the White House seemed to denote
the absolute assimilation of the Irish in American life, his sentimental journey in the summer of 1963 suggested that perhaps "assimilation" itself was more complicated than many had assumed.
The election of an Irish-American president, remarked the *Irish
Independent*, symbolized "the closing of a chapter in our history
. . . After three generations a young man of fully Irish stocks [*sic*]
has reached the last point of integration into American life—the
chief executive post of the nation." And yet, as Kennedy himself
said in response to de Valera's welcoming address, Ireland's "sons
and daughters" scattered throughout the world "have been among
the best and most loyal citizens of the countries they have gone
to, but have also kept a special place in their memories, in many
cases their ancestral memory, [for] this green and misty island, so,
in a sense, all of them who visit Ireland come home."[3]

Kennedy had earlier defined the United States as "a nation of

2.   *Cork, 1963: John F. Kennedy's "return" to Ireland. Received by Irish throngs as a favorite son, Kennedy articulated a brand of hyphenated Americanism that became increasingly common in ensuing years.* BETTMANN/CORBIS.

immigrants," the title of his slim 1958 volume on the contributions of diverse ethnic groups to American life. In a 1957 address before the Irish Institute in New York, he had spoken at length about what that meant from an Irish-American perspective in the context of the Cold War:

> All of us of Irish descent are bound together by the ties that come from a common experience; experience which may exist only in memories and in legend, but which is real enough to those who possess it. And thus whether we live in Cork or Boston, in New York or in Sydney, we are all members of a great family which is linked together by that strongest of chains—a common past . . .

> Let us here tonight resolve that our nation will forever hold
> out its hands to those who struggle for freedom today, as Ire-
> land struggled for a thousand years.[4]

The President's Ireland visit lent this conceit a new stateliness, pomp, and circumstance; his appearances in Dublin and New Ross were thrilling embodiments of this newly articulated pluralism. It had only been a few years since the sociologist Will Herberg had asserted with an astonishing confidence that "the ethnic group . . . had no future" in American life, that "ethnic pluralists were backward-looking romantics . . . [who] were out of touch with the unfolding American reality."[5] Although the weight of social-scientific authority had concurred with Herberg in the 1950s, Kennedy's own Irish sentiments confounded such facile formulations.

The ethnic accent of Kennedy's Ireland speeches added two distinct notes to his Cold War homilies (which were, after all, the main point of his European tour: he had been to Berlin to peer over the wall earlier that same week). First, having benefited perhaps above all others from America's historic role as an asylum for the oppressed, the Irish understood and appreciated most readily the United States' role—not least, its anti-Soviet role—as a global savior. Second, "knowing the meaning of foreign domination itself," Ireland held a special place as both example and inspiration for those who engaged this freedom struggle against world communism: "how many times was Ireland's quest for freedom suppressed only to be renewed by the succeeding generation? Those who suffer beyond that wall I saw on Wednesday in Berlin must not despair of their future. Let them remember the constancy, the faith, the endurance, and the final success of the Irish."[6]

There was nothing "un-American" about Kennedy's Irishness, in other words. But his pronouncements and his wild Irish reception did indicate a new way of imagining Americanness itself. In his official state welcome, Eamon de Valera greeted Kennedy three times over as "the chief executive and first citizen of the great Republic of the West," as "the representative of that great country in which our people sought refuge when the misery of tyrant laws drove them from the motherland," and as "the distinguished scion of our race who has won first place amongst his fellow countrymen." In his speech before the Dublin Parliament, Kennedy responded that, if Ireland

> had achieved its present political and economic stature a century or so ago my great-grandfather might never have left New Ross and I might, if fortunate, be sitting down there with you. [*Applause*] Of course, if your own President had never left Brooklyn, he might be standing up here instead of me. [*Applause*] . . .
> . . . My presence and your welcome . . . only symbolize the many and the enduring links which have bound the Irish and the Americans from the earliest days.[7]

This emergent public language of "enduring links" between Americans and their many homelands—Kennedy's conceit of the "nation of immigrants"—was to become increasingly apparent in sociology and history textbooks, in Hollywood blockbusters, in the national passion for genealogical research, in the heritage industries devoted to "ethnic" merchandise and marketing strategies, in the public discussions of citizenship and social policy, and in the shifting racial politics of "we" and "they" at a moment when the wretched, tempest-tossed "we" of Ellis Island memory assumed the aura of national mythology. Kennedy had not single-handedly authored these developments in U.S. political culture, either in *Nation of Immigrants* or in his celebrated "return" to Ireland during what turned out to be the final summer of his life. But the symbolism of Kennedy's visit to Ireland proved the early stirring of a profound reorientation in American civic life. The visit was greeted with enthusiasm by Irish Americans; perhaps it was greeted with bemusement among those non-Irish Americans who had worried about Kennedy's Catholicism during the campaign of 1960. But people on all sides were astonished to hear the President say, as he did before an adoring crowd in Limerick, "This is not the land of my birth, but it is the land for which I hold the greatest affection."[8]

Kennedy's Irish awakening and his version of being at once American and Irish have become more legible, even natural, in the years since his "return" than they would have been anytime before. That same year William Shannon began *The American Irish* with the observation that, when referred to as "an Irishman," Joseph Kennedy had once lashed out in exasperation, "I was born here. My children were born here. What the hell do I have to do to be called an American?" Nineteen sixty-three marks an end to that particular variety of exasperation: both Kennedy's return and Shannon's pluralistic portrait of an unmelted Irish America signal an emergent understanding—soon to be widely shared—that to seize and celebrate the hyphen is not to diminish a given group's "Americanism," but rather, as Shannon put it, "to show what kind of Americans they are."[9]

By the time Ronald Reagan "returned" to Ballyporeen, County Tipperary, two decades later, such roots talk had become ubiquitous in American culture. When Reagan joined townspeople "to worship at the modest Church of the Assumption in Bally-poreen," where his great-grandfather had apparently been baptized in the 1820s, a marching band played a peculiar medley of Irish tunes and Hollywood themes—including the theme from *Rocky*, the "roots" era's greatest paean to an underdog-triumphant white identity. As the *Times* reported, presidential aides, meanwhile, "have not even tried to conceal their delight over the resonance that today's visit is expected to have with millions of Irish-American voters at home, and with many other Americans who lately have become fascinated with tracing their ancestry. The camera crew from the President's re-election campaign was here filming the scene for campaign commercials later in the year."[10]

The mid-1970s represented the consolidation of this new ethnicity; the heritage fest of the nation's bicentennial, followed immediately by the broadcast of Alex Haley's blockbuster *Roots*, denoted Americans' heightened self-consciousness about their own roots and about the new, pluralized idioms of national membership. In its editor's choice column for the best books of that year, the *New York Times Book Review* included Alex Haley's *Roots*, "a study of . . . how a people perpetuate themselves, how each generation helps to doom, or helps to liberate, the coming one"; Maxine Hong Kingston's *Woman Warrior*, portraying "the crises of a heart in exile from roots that bind and terrorize it"; and Irving Howe's *World of Our Fathers*, a study of "bedraggled and inspired" immigrants on the Lower East Side, "a complex story of fulfillment and incompleteness."[11] The concurrence and enthusiastic reception of these three landmark publications on the black, Chinese, and Jewish experience in the United States marked the maturation of a long-term development in American intellectual life and the entry into a new phase of cultural politics.

In its formative moments, "multiculturalism" was not the exclusive province of Afrocentrism, Ebonics, or Bilingualism, as is often supposed; nor does its genealogy simply run from *Roots* to *The Joy Luck Club* to *The Mambo Kings* and beyond. Irving Howe's work, for example, may have spoken to insular, specifically Jewish concerns of peoplehood, collective destiny, and memory, but the meanings affixed to the best-selling *World of Our Fathers* in the non-Jewish press may be more important. *Time* magazine set its review beneath the telling banner "Assimilation Blues," situating Howe's work alongside *Fiddler on the Roof* and *Portnoy's Complaint*, texts that spoke only imperfectly to the hungered past of those "many Americans whose non–English-speaking [forebears] were part of the huddled masses that funneled through Ellis Island at the turn of the century." *Business Week* mused on ethnicity's new status as "a literary and political buzzword," noting that "135 colleges have established ethnic studies programs, and recently President Ford appointed a special assistant for ethnic affairs"; *World of Our Fathers* is "the most impressive of the recent ethnic books." The *Christian Science Monitor* ventured that Howe's Jewish masses were "the archetypes of the immigrant (one wants to say American) experience." This reviewer went on to remark that the greatest Jewish successes in this promised land were reserved not for the immigrants themselves but "for their children and grandchildren, who moved into the professions and into the suburbs—diaspora." His equation of mobility and suburbanization with "diaspora"—a dispersion from the "promised land" of immigrant immediacy—says a great deal about the reveries of the second, third, and fourth generations at mid-century. As Marcus Klein remarked in *The Nation*, "Everybody wants a ghetto to look back to."[12]

Everybody. The story of the ethnic revival might begin with

psychic interiors—the villages and ghettos of family legend that Americans privately looked back to with strange yearning—but finally it leads outward to the political culture at large, to the revision of American history textbooks; to the massive, state-sponsored project of restoring and sanctifying Ellis Island; to wholly new ways of imagining the nation and articulating the individual citizen's place within it and relationship to it.

The Roots of the "Roots Phenomenon"

The "new ethnicity" sprang on the United States from many directions at once. The first, most politically potent source of the ethnic revival was the Civil Rights movement, which introduced a new and contagious idiom of group identity and group rights on the American scene. Of course, in the history of the Republic, white male property-holders had been enfranchised as a group; blacks had been enslaved, emancipated, and granted citizenship as a group, only to be disenfranchised as a group; Native Americans had been dispossessed and subject to slaughter and "removal" as a group; Mexicans had been conquered and annexed as a group; Chinese immigrants had been excluded as a group; women had been disenfranchised and later enfranchised as a group; Japanese immigrants and their children had been interned as a group; and now African Americans had fought for and won their civil rights as a group. But American liberalism has long cherished the notion that individual liberties reside at the very core of the nation's political culture and values, and that appeals to *group* rights and protections were profoundly un-American. Never was this insistence more powerful than during the Cold War.

Only with the Civil Rights successes of 1964 and 1965 did the dominant discourse of national civic life acknowledge the salience of group experience and standing. The effect of this acknowledgment was electrifying, not only for people of color, whose racialized experience with society, law, and the market in the United States suggested a political kinship with African Americans, but also for white ethnics, whose inchoate sense of social grievance required only the right vocabulary to come alive. There exists "an inner conflict between one's felt personal power and one's ascribed public power: a sense of outraged truth, justice, and equity," wrote Michael Novak, suggesting the limits of white privilege in "The New Ethnicity" (1974). If European ethnics were indeed white, they weren't *that* white. Howe himself wrote, "even in the mid-twentieth century many American Jews, certainly a good many of those who came out of the east European immigrant world, still *felt* like losers."[13]

The group-based mobilization of the Civil Rights movement, the group-based terms of its victories in 1964 and 1965, and the group-based logic of rising black nationalism all suggested a model for action. As Charles Hamilton and Stokely Carmichael wrote in *Black Power* (1967), "we have been oppressed as a group, not as individuals. We will not find our way out of that oppression until both we and America accept the need for Negro Americans, as well as for Jews, Italians, Poles and white Anglo-Saxon Protestants, among others, to have and wield group power." By 1970 the *Ukrainian Weekly* could comment, "The notion of 'Ukrainian Power'—a borrowing to be sure, from America's black community—is passing in Ukrainian circles from a mere phrase to a workable and quite feasible concept."[14]

These white movements modeled on Black Power could be quite studied; the founding manifesto of the Radical Zionist Alliance (1970) asserts:

North American Jews are a marginal people in a society of economic, political, and cultural oppression. The Jewish community has adopted a tradition of ignoring its own needs, and has structured itself in an undemocratic manner, geared toward assimilation and disappearance as a functioning nation. We call for the liberation of the Jewish people and the restructuring of our people's existence in such a way as to facilitate self-determination and development of our own institutions so as to control our destiny as a nation.

At a protest following the harassment of a Jewish recruit at boot camp in South Carolina (he had allegedly been ridiculed as "Jew boy" and "Bagel," and had a Star of David forcibly painted on his forehead), Radical Zionist Alliance activists echoed Muhammad Ali's famous observation, "No Viet Cong ever called me nigger," with placards reading, "No Viet Cong ever called me Bagel."[15]

The Civil Rights movement influenced the ethnic consciousness of nonblacks in another way, too. The sudden centrality of black grievance to national discussion prompted a rapid move among white ethnics to disassociate themselves from white privilege. The popular rediscovery of ethnic forebears became one way of saying, "We're merely newcomers; the nation's crimes are not our own." Reporting an exchange with a Native American speaker who was decrying "what our ancestors did to *his* ancestors," Michael Novak wrote, "I tried gently to remind him that *my* grandparents . . . never *saw* an Indian. They came to this country after that. Nor were they responsible for enslaving the blacks (or anyone else). They themselves escaped serfdom barely four generations ago." Similarly, commenting on the deep significance of the Holocaust and the Triangle Shirtwaist factory fire to American Jews, Melanie Kaye/Kantrowitz wrote, with a fully incandescent candor, that these are "images of greater persecution than most American Jews are subject to today. As Jews, afraid of the myth of Jewish power . . . guilty about our skin privilege, we are so hungry for innocence that images of oppression come almost as a relief."[16]

Such ethnic self-distancing from whiteness and privilege is open to critique, as Kaye/Kantrowitz suggests. Novak's comment on his newcomer status ("my grandparents never saw an Indian") is typical, in that it fossilizes racial injustice in dim national antiquity, and so glosses over more recent discriminatory practices in housing, hiring, and unionization, for instance, which *did* benefit these "newcomers," fresh off the boat though they were. This move to distance oneself or one's group from monolithic white privilege gave way in some cases to a politics of white grievance that pitted itself against unfair *black* privilege (as in the ensuing affirmative action debates), often, ironically, couched in a Civil Rights language poached from blacks themselves.[17] If the logic of *group* rights was so irresistible, as Carmichael had proposed and the Radical Zionist Alliance had concurred, nonetheless the idea of *white* group rights was uneasy in the wake of Montgomery, Birmingham, Jackson, and Selma. Even as various racialized struggles over busing, housing, or "community control" helped white ethnics "to complete their journey to unambiguous white identity"—as their *whiteness* became increasingly salient in the black-white conflicts of Boston, New York, or Detroit—a language of ethnic specificity, of not-*quite*-whiteness, became ever more valuable. Ethnic particularity provided a newly legitimate language for the "nervous provincialism" that stemmed from the era's social conflicts.[18]

Another impetus to ethnic revival was a powerful current of

antimodernism, the broadly accepted notion that ethnicity represented a haven of authenticity that existed at a remove from the bloodless, homogenizing forces of mass production and consumption, mass media, commodification, bureaucratization, and suburbanization. If antimodernism has been one of modernity's most potent legacies, a certain tribalism has been antimodernism's chosen idiom. History has "carried us away from the shtetls of Russia and Rumania, Poland and Hungary," wrote Anne Roiphe in *Generation without Memory* (1981),

> We were driven or we drifted onto the Lower East Side, out to the fringes of Flatbush and onto the streets of the Western world, to medical school, to condominiums in Boca Raton, to suburbs and exurbs. As a family we moved from the eleventh century to the twentieth in two generations. The speed has been dazzling. We are shaking like astronauts passing through dimensions of space and sound . . . We are in Sartre's terms "nonauthentic." We have escaped the night of ignorance, of superstition, of poverty, of the narrow streets of the Old World where science and technology had been beyond all reach . . . We escaped, but along the way we lost comforts, consolations, communities. We escaped, but we are more alone than ever before.[19]

As early as 1924, Horace Kallen had equated assimilation with absorption into an undignified and vacuous modern mass. "In these days of ready-made garments, factory-made furniture, refrigerating plants, boiler-plate movies and radio," he had lamented, "it is almost impossible that the mass of the inhabitants of the United States should wear other than uniform clothes, use other than uniform furniture . . . or eat anything but the same kinds of food, read anything but the same syndicated hokum, see anything but the same standardized romances and hear anything but the same broadcast barbarisms." In Kallen's view, pluralism—that insistent respect for and claim to one's "ancestral endowments"—ennobled the spirit and provided an oasis in the cultural desert of modern, mechanized, mass-consumed lifeways.[20]

With the advent of the postindustrial order, such misgivings about the modern would become more urgent still: as modern advances "lighten the family labor, they increase the futility of family life," wrote Harry Braverman; "as they remove the burdens of personal relations, they strip away its affections; as they create an intricate social life, they rob it of every vestige of community and leave in its place the cash nexus."[21] Like Kallen before them, many latter-day pluralists rebelled "against 'mindless' and 'soulless' modernism," in Michael Novak's words, by seeking refuge in the symbolic, "pre-modern" communion of ethnic identity. According to David Lowenthal, "we mourn worlds known to be irrevocably lost . . . We yearn for rooted legacies that enrich the paltry here and now." Heritage becomes strictly a "minority virtue, with mainstream 'progress' its regrettable antithesis." The radical rabbi Arthur Waskow wrote of a rising generation of anti-"establishment" Jewish students in the 1960s; many "whose parents had proudly assimilated themselves to the American Promise . . . find they do not want to be 'Americans' after all . . . Many of our youth began to celebrate, not mourn, the end of the melting pot, and to herald the creation of a real Jewish community. They began to criticize as assimilationists those Establishment elders who had triumphed in the triumphs of America." "Establishment" here implied the political arenas of the Cold War and

Vietnam, but it also evoked materialism, commercialism, the sub-urbs' interchangeable houses and manicured lawns, office work, impersonal bureaucracies, and sprawling "multiversities" of the kind championed by Berkeley president Clark Kerr. In short, ver-sions of community and authenticity cast in ethnic terms would be the salve to those postindustrial discontents that 1950s observ-ers like David Riesman and William Whyte had spelled out in *The Lonely Crowd* and *The Organization Man*.[22]

The ethnic revivalists' "rhapsody on history" involves not only an elevation of forebears to the status of giants but also a senti-mental journey to the harsh circumstances that those giants en-dured and overcame. If twentieth-century America has become "a nation of big business and little men," Henry Miller's "air condi-tioned nightmare," then Famine Ireland or the shtetl offer ready escape. Markers of this tacit connection among ethnicity, authen-ticity, and antimodernism include the Native American and peas-ant motifs of hippie fashion ("We are no longer die-cast parts of a national mechanism," commented the *East Village Other*. "We are a tribe."), as well as the explicit appeals to mighty, blood-coursing tradition in popular "mainstream" stage plays like *Zorba the Greek* and *Fiddler on the Roof*. "Sentimentally speaking," lamented Anne Roiphe, "I wish we could return to an earlier America when soci-ety surrounded its members with a tight sense of belonging, of being needed. Maybe the melting-pot idea was a bad one."[23]

In David Mamet's "Disappearance of the Jews" (1982), Joey tells Bobby Gould, "I would have been a great man in [pre-emi-gration] Europe—I was meant to be hauling stones, or setting fence posts . . . I should be working on a forge all day. . . . [I]t's good to harvest wheat, to forge, to toil." For many like Joey, the fire and storm of Old World hardship provide an antidote to the hollowness of modern masculinity no less than to the weightlessness of modern living.[24] More recently, Anthony Rotundo writes that *The Sopranos* "gives us values such as loyalty, rootedness, and interdependence—values that have provided a foundation for Italian American manhood and offered common manly ground to the Artie Buccos and Tony Sopranos. Part of Tony's humanity—and part of his tragedy—is that he knows America . . . is hostile to those values." In this respect the antimodernist accents of the ethnic reverie (as embodied by *The Sopranos* no less than by *Fiddler on the Roof*) update not only the pluralism of Horace Kallen's "Democracy versus the Melting Pot" but also the masculinism of Teddy Roosevelt's "Strenuous Life."[25]

Yet another source of the ethnic revival was the nationalist fervor of many ethnic subcultures in the United States, and the ways in which contemporary events in the Old World pulled for emotional involvement among those in the New. Soviet domination in the nations of the Eastern Bloc, the "Troubles" in Northern Ireland, the Israeli wars of 1967 and 1973, the "Prague Spring" of 1968, and the workers' movement in Poland all captured the attention and sympathy of overseas ethnic compatriots, whose diasporic cultures had invested Old World nationalist causes with a kind of mantric power. Such engagements in Old World affairs may have been symbolic in the sense that Americans had no intentions of actually returning to the homeland; but they were nonetheless organic in the sense that the logic and mythology of ethnic cultures often positioned immigrants and their descendants as "exiled" members of the homeland, uniquely placed to serve its cause.[26] In the wake of the Six Day War, for instance, Jewish Americans from across the country volunteered for Israeli military service, including more than 2,000 in New York City alone.[27]

3. *Members of the Irish Northern Aid Committee (NORAID) protest Prince Philip's visit to Lincoln Center, October 1980.* CORBIS.

4.   *Several thousand Polish Americans in Chicago's loop protest the imposition of martial law in Poland, December 1981.* BETTMANN/CORBIS.

In addition to renewed initiatives on the part of older associations like the Polish National Alliance, new organizations devoted to "homeland" politics also sprang out of the melting pot in these years: the American Committee for Democracy and Freedom in Greece (1967), the National Association for Irish Justice (1968), the Serbian National Committee (1968), American Students for Israel (1969), the Latvian Foundation (1970), and the Irish Northern Aid Committee (NORAID, 1970). Among the *New York Times Book Review*'s "best" books of 1976 were *To Jerusalem and Back,* Saul Bellow's portrait of an Israel "pocked with scars," and *The Damnable Question,* a compendium of "palatable and unpalatable" truths of Anglo-Irish relations from 1800 to 1922—a kind of *Roots* of the Irish "Troubles."[28]

5.   *New York demonstration in sympathy with Soviet Jewry, December
1987. The Star of David links the U.S. and Soviet flags.* PETER
TURNLEY/CORBIS.

Within this context of overdetermined ethnic consciousness, a stream of popular literary and cinematic texts charted the rise of the new pluralist sensibility. After languishing in neglect for decades, Abraham Cahan's *Rise of David Levinsky* (1917) found its way back into print in a popular paperback edition in 1960, followed soon after by new editions of Henry Roth's *Call It Sleep*, Ole Rolvaag's *Giants in the Earth*, Anzia Yezierska's *Bread Givers*, and many others. Fresh literary renditions of the ethnic saga, too, now found an eager audience: most famously, perhaps, Chaim Potok's *The Chosen* (1967) and Mario Puzo's *The Godfather* (1969). Audiences flocked to stage productions and films like *Fiddler on the Roof* and *Funny Girl*, and they reclaimed Old World cuisine with the help of "community cookbooks" like *The Badenfest Cookbook, From Zion's Kitchen, Shalom Y'all*, and *Czech Your Cooking*.[29]

Even television rediscovered diversity. The urban ethnic families of early television's *The Goldbergs, Life with Luigi*, and *Mama* had yielded in the assimilationist 1950s to the whitebread pedigrees of *Father Knows Best* and *Ozzie and Harriet* (the Goldbergs themselves became "de-Judaized" and moved to a homogenized suburb called Haverville). In American television from about 1954 to 1968, "ethnicity" was the exclusive preserve of a handful of culturally isolated—if lovable—oddballs: Lucy's husband, Ricky Ricardo; Danny Thomas's uncle, Tonoose; Rob Petrie's cowriter, Buddy Sorrell. Indeed, in the early 1960s Carl Reiner's pilot about an unmistakably Jewish comedy writer, based on his own experience with *Your Show of Shows*, became the ethnically "neutral" (read: WASP) *Dick Van Dyke Show*: Buddy Sorrell proved the only surviving trace of Reiner's original ethnic vision.[30]

But by the late 1960s and early 1970s, popular programming began to revel in ethnic particularity in shows like *Arnie; Bridget*

Loves Bernie; All in the Family; Welcome Back, Kotter; Rhoda; Kojak; and *Columbo*. (As Bernie Steinberg put it in *Bridget Loves Bernie* [1972], "I don't believe this. I've lived with you people all my life. Now why is everyone all of a sudden being so Jewish?") The advent of the miniseries and the made-for-TV movie generated "serious" treatments of ethnic subjects in *Holocaust* (1978), *The Triangle Factory Fire Scandal* (1979), *The Diary of Anne Frank* (1980), *Golda* (1982), *The Winds of War* (1983), *Ellis Island* (1984), *Evergreen* (1985), and *Escape from Sobibor* (1987). Such trends in "ethnic" programming extended through what Herman Gray calls "the Cosby moment" and beyond, a period of feverish attention to diversity in programming whose white ethnic exemplars include shows like *Chicken Soup, thirtysomething, Brooklyn Bridge, To Have and to Hold, Seinfeld, The Education of Max Bickford, Costello, Trinity, Legacy, The Sopranos, Will & Grace,* and *Everybody Loves Raymond*.[31] Television provided the shorthand for this entire complex of developments in U.S. culture, when the wildly popular 1977 miniseries *Roots* lent its name to the roots phenomenon. Decades later Fran Drescher's *The Nanny*, the most over-the-top 1990s ethnic sitcom, paid homage in an episode entitled "Fran's Roots," in which the Jewish nanny mistakenly supposes that her true biological mother is black.

Schooled in Pluralism

The new ethnicity was helped along by academia. Beginning in the early 1960s, standard academic conceptions of both the ethnic group and the nation underwent a sea change. Common understandings of group behavior and the national narrative came under drastic revision in these years, revisions which made their way into social studies and history textbooks at every educational level. Calls to alarm by Arthur Schlesinger, Jr., Dinesh D'Sousa, Lynne Cheney, or Richard Bernstein may seem overblown, but these critics are at least correct that a generation of American pupils has been schooled to look on matters of ethnic integrity, national composition, and American belonging quite differently from any previous generation.[32]

Although "ethnicity" is now invoked to emphasize particularity, when the concept ascended in social-scientific thought in the 1940s it carried quite the opposite connotation. In sharp contrast to the stubborn, biological, fixed inheritances of "race," "ethnicity" stressed culture: it represented an outlook rather than a condition of birth; a cultural affiliation rather than a bloodline; a set of sensibilities and associational habits that, however tenacious, were subject to the forces of assimilation and change. The ascendance of ethnicity as an analytic category was one element in a powerful tendency in American social thought at mid-century to revise away the concept of biological "difference" and move toward universalism.

The general movement in late-twentieth-century American thought has been a steady shift from a paradigm of human unity to one of ethnic particularity. The near consensus on universalism between World War II and the 1960s—as evidenced in Wendell Willkie's *One World* (1943), Joseph Campbell's *Hero with a Thousand Faces* (1949), Alfred Kinsey's *Sexual Behavior in the Human Male* (1948) and *Female* (1953), and Edward Steichen's *Family of Man* (1955)—was woven of many threads.[33] One was the ascendant "culture concept" in sociology and anthropology, beginning earlier in the century with thinkers like Franz Boas and Robert Park. Another, more urgent impetus was that events in Nazi Germany had rendered the race concept ever more unpalatable in liberal American social thought; figures like Boas, Ruth Benedict, and Ashley Montagu sought to expunge "race" from social analysis wherever possible. Montagu labeled race "man's most dangerous myth," and he self-consciously promoted the term "ethnic group" precisely because "the conventional stereotype of 'race' is so erroneous, confusing, and productive of injustice and cruelties without number."[34] As a corrective to race, the concept of ethnicity accomplished less as a term of distinction than it did as a partial erasure of "difference"—a universalizing appeal to the underlying sameness of humanity and to the assimilative powers of American culture.

Nationalist imperatives during World War II and the early Cold War also encouraged universalism. Neither the nation's touted "war against racism" in Europe nor the coming war against communism could tolerate anything that seemed to undermine the notion of unalloyed Americanism. Ethnicity, then, became a symbolic building block of American national unity. In popular culture the universalizing and nationalizing gestures of ethnic diversity come through most clearly in the multiethnic platoon of the Hollywood war movie. The Irish soldier, the Jew, the Pole all working together and defending one another—*this* is America. One popular wartime song expressed impatience for the day "When Those Little Yellow Bellies Meet the Cohens and the Kellys."[35]

Lloyd Warner and Leo Srole's *Social Systems of American Ethnic Groups* (1945) was among the first studies to advance ethnicity as an alternative to what had earlier been America's white "races." Warner and Srole did not entirely escape the biologizing concept of race in this discussion: their delineation of ethnic groups conspicuously breaks down along the line of "light Caucasians" (like the South Irish and English Jews) and "dark Caucasians" (like Sicilians). But even if the traces of race remain in this conception of ethnicity, the book shares a universalizing perspective with other works of the period. Any group whose differences were "minor" (meaning "ethnic" rather than "racial") could expect to be fully assimilated into the nation's core culture; and indeed, Warner and Srole close with the prediction that the future of white ethnic groups as self-conscious groups was "limited," and that European immigrants and their children would be absorbed speedily and completely. This was the view Will Herberg endorsed when he asserted that national or cultural minorities in America were but "temporary, transitional phenomena," and that ethnic pluralists were "out of touch with the unfolding American reality."[36] If this prevailing view of the 1940s and 1950s spoke to a generation whose ethnic differences were waning in salience (as English-language proficiency increased, for instance, and as suburbanization broke up the older ethnic neighborhoods), so did it neatly answer the imperatives of the moment.

But scarcely had the ink dried on such pronouncements when both scholarly and street-level assessments of ethnic particularity underwent a revolution. By 1963, Glazer and Moynihan were matching Herberg's confidence in assimilation with their own confidence in pluralism—the melting pot "did not happen." A year later, in *Assimilation in American Life*, Milton Gordon noted that while ethnic particularity in the realm of *culture* might be fading, "structural pluralism"—the force of ethnicity in shaping residential, occupational, economic, institutional, and organizational life—still prevailed. By 1971 Michael Novak could celebrate *The Rise of the Unmeltable Ethnics;* and by 1981, Thomas Sowell could remark, "The massive ethnic communities that make up the mosaic of American society cannot be adequately described as 'minorities.' There is no 'majority.'"[37]

In the years since the 1940s, race has been the larger body around which the concept of ethnicity has quietly revolved, as a moon around a planet. Each turn in the one has caused an adjustment in the other. In the early years of World War II, the culturally based concept of ethnicity may have seemed an alternative—a *solution*—to the biologically based "race concept," as Montagu and others suggested. But race and its inheritances have been stubborn indeed: the mid-century's ethnic revision of race stopped at the color line, universalizing *whiteness* by lessening the presumed difference separating "Hebrews," "Celts," and "Anglo-Saxons," but deepening the separation between any of these former white races and people of color, especially blacks. Ethnicity was born precisely when the American color line was sharpening in new ways—the "Negro Problem," as Stephen Steinberg puts it, "had migrated from South to North."[38] By the 1980s and 1990s, not only had ethnicity failed to displace race as an analytic category, but—since race had been so thoroughly etched into social practice and encoded in law—no conception of ethnicity could explain much if it failed to reckon with the undergirding structures of race. This has been apparent in both street-level politics (where ethnic particularism has been among the idioms of white backlash—"Niggers out of Boston, Brits out of Belfast") and scholarly discourse (where the most sophisticated recent analyses of ethnicity have taken up the term in conjunction with racialized categories like white, black, Asian, or Latino).[39] The concept of ethnicity has become—not the "race concept's" replacement, as Montagu and Boas had once hoped—but its inseparable sibling.

The burgeoning literature on ethnicity between the 1950s and the 1970s was almost exclusively about "white ethnics," though the full significance of the modifier "white" remained invisible for some time. In *Ethnic Options* (1990) Mary Waters warned that whiteness lent a certain flexibility to ethnic identity for Jews, Italians, or Poles in the United States—they *do* choose their grandparents, to a certain extent—which in turn led many of them to misconstrue the experience of their counterparts across the color line. Those who presume that African-American identity is just like Irish or Italian in its cultural basis and its sentimentality are not likely to grasp the structural, juridical features of race that come into play around questions of blackness. In *Ethnic Identity* (1990), Richard Alba traced the gradual formation of a "European American" identity among those for whom conceptions of Old World origin—romances of departure, arrival, and resettlement—are fundamentally defining. The normative status of this European-American experience, in Alba's view, may ultimately determine "the rules of the game" in American discussions of things like class, mobility, opportunity, discrimination, and welfare.[40] But in any case, by the end of the twentieth century "ethnicity" evoked specificity, not universalism; Jewish or Irish or Greek ethnicity represented a *distinguishing from*—either people of color or other "whites," depending on the circumstance—not a *merging with*.

As the social sciences reshaped conceptions of the ethnic group, U.S. historiography was also revising the national narrative, reintroducing "underdog elements"—like immigrants—who since the early Cold War years had vanished as historical actors. Kennedy's *Nation of Immigrants* (1958) was one of the first such works, depicting ethnic diversity as the nation's greatest strength and its good fortune. Here American culture is not a melting pot but a smorgasbord (to borrow a term from our Swedish fellow citizens). Each ethnic group arrived bearing its own particular brand of the work ethic, and each brought a unique dish to the national banquet—the Irish their political genius; Danes, the talent to establish America's dairy industry; Germans, their orchestras, glee clubs, and martial valor; Jews, the requisite skills to develop "the clothing industry as we know it today."[41]

Kennedy's was the multiethnic vision that would triumph over the course of the next generation. In an apocalyptic speech before the American Historical Association (AHA) in 1962, the historian Carl Bridenbaugh decried the professional impact of the shifting demographics of the university in the postwar period, particularly as a result of the GI Bill. "Many of the young practitioners of our craft, and those who are still apprentices," he worried, "are products of lower middle-class or foreign origins, and their emotions frequently get in the way of historical reconstructions."[42]

Indeed, historiographic focus shifted over the next decades, giving rise to the "new social history," Black Studies, immigration history, women's history, and Ethnic Studies. But the national narrative was already under significant revision. An early signal was Oscar Handlin's famous remark, "Once I thought to write a history of the immigrants in America. Then I discovered that the immigrants *were* American history." By the time Bridenbaugh stood wringing his hands at the podium of the AHA, the universalism of the early Cold War was already on its way out. Along with *The Uprooted* and *A Nation of Immigrants,* John Higham's *Strangers in the Land* (1955), Barbara Miller Solomon's *Ancestors and Immigrants* (1956), and Maldwyn Allen Jones's *American Immigration* (1960) had established beachheads for a new subfield;

the founding of the Immigration History Society in 1965 was but a stone's throw away; and a generation of social historians was just over the horizon.[43]

Among the quickest, most dramatic measures of the growth of ethnic or "immigration" history in the first full decade of the ethnic revival is the contrast between two state-of-the-field essays by Rudolph Vecoli, written in 1970 and 1979, respectively. In the first essay, "Ethnicity: A Neglected Dimension of American History," Vecoli remarked on Black Power's influence on student outlooks, and the unmet demand for courses in "minority" history. A survey of course offerings in 100 U.S. colleges revealed that only 38 offered some opportunity to study American diversity (including 20 courses in general social history; 19 in African-American Studies; 4 in Native American Studies; and 4 in immigration). The other 62 colleges offered no courses at all. At the graduate level, reported Vecoli, the United States had produced only 127 doctoral dissertations on immigration between 1893 and 1965 (or less than 2 per year), just over half of which had appeared since World War II. This paucity was due in large part, Vecoli thought, to the "powerful and pervasive grip of the assimilationist ideology" —elsewhere referred to as "the *blight* of assimilationist ideology"—in American scholarship: "Because of their expectations that assimilation was to be swift and irresistible, historians and sociologists have looked for change rather than continuity, acculturation rather than cultural maintenance. Since ethnicity was thought to be evanescent, it was not considered worth studying." He could discern a few signs that "the long winter of neglect of ethnicity is coming to an end," including AHA President John Fairbank's urging "a truer and multivalued, because multicultural, perspective."[44] But for the most part, the picture was bleak.

In a 1979 issue of *American Studies International*, however, Vecoli announced a startling reversal: "we are [now] inundated by a virtual flood of books, articles, and dissertations dealing with the roles of race, nationality, and religion in American history." Vecoli cited more than seventy-five book-length studies of immigration that appeared in the 1970s, many directly traceable to "the contemporary search for 'roots' among Americans," including studies of politics, religion, labor, and mobility, in addition to works devoted to particular groups or locales. More significant still, Vecoli demonstrated the astonishing pace of change in the "infrastructure of research facilities and resources," including "Research Centers and Collections," "Microfilm and Reprint Editions," "Reference Tools," and "Historical Societies and Publications." "Thanks to the 'new pluralism,'" he wrote, "the National Endowment for the Humanities, the Ethnic Heritage Studies Program . . . the National Historical Publications and Records Commission, private foundations, and ethnic communities have all provided generous funding for building collections, preparing reference tools, and sponsoring research." Publishing houses like Arno and R & E Research Associates had reprinted "several thousand volumes" pertaining to the history of immigration, including government documents like the Dillingham Commission Report, reformist tracts like *How the Other Half Lives,* and treatises in early sociology like E. A. Ross's *Old World Traits Transplanted.* By the late 1970s, as Vecoli had discovered, the new pluralism was a vested interest; the knowledge industries' apparatus was now in position; and America was poised to know itself anew.[45]

What was clear to Rudolph Vecoli by 1979 was that "a pluralistic perspective has transformed the basic paradigm of American historiography. Ethnicity has been generally accepted as a pervasive attribute which affected all areas of American life." This break with the scholarship of the past "presages a rewriting of the history of the United States which will be multi-ethnic, multi-racial, and multi-lingual in its interpretation of the American experience (or better yet, *experiences*)."[46] As a flyer appealing for donations to the Immigration History Research Center put it in the 1970s, "Your Ethnic History Is American History."[47]

The same year as Vecoli's second survey, Frances Fitzgerald's *America Revised* offered a detailed portrait of the textbook nation that had been presented to students from one generation to the next. According to Fitzgerald, whereas David Saville Muzzey's *An American History* (first published in 1911, but still in use in some schools into the 1960s) treated immigrants as an alien "they" whom "we" had better "mold into citizenship" lest they pose "a constant menace to our free institutions," later textbooks introduced immigrants in terms that were both more positive and more normative—in a word, more as "we." Clarence Ver Steeg and Richard Hofstadter, for example, averred in *A People and a Nation* (1971, 1974) that immigrants "introduced variety into American life, adding immeasurably to its color and interest"; "in time they showed their ability to enter the mainstream of American life without giving up either their identity or their distinctive qualities."[48]

By the late 1970s, Fitzgerald found, "most current texts" covered European ethnic groups in chapters on nineteenth-century industrialization, where a certain attention to poverty, injustice, and the brutality of working-class life was now allowed. In later passages on "modern-day life" the authors "describe . . . working-class families that came originally from Poland, Greece, or Russia, and they contend that the European culture of these families has not melted away." They insist—following Glazer and Moynihan—"that the 'ethnics' have not been assimilated but have separately added to the wonderful variety of life in America." Fitzgerald also notes that "a number of the authors of these American-history books are the children or grandchildren of such immigrants." In contrast to the melting-pot paradigm that had reigned supreme in school texts in the 1940s, by the late 1960s "most of the texts" had ceased "to talk about 'the immigrants' as distinct from 'us Americans.'" The "new orthodoxy," according to Fitzgerald, was the conceit that "we are a nation of immigrants."[49] School children today are far more likely to learn about Plymouth and Jamestown in the thematic context of Ellis Island—"America's First Immigrants"—than they are to learn about immigration in the context of settler democracy.

Among the greatest monuments to this pluralistic outlook on the nation (aside from Ellis Island itself) is the *Harvard Encyclopedia of American Ethnic Groups* (1980), a project undertaken with federal funding from the Ethnic Heritage Research Program. The *Encyclopedia* encompasses the work of 120 contributors over 6 years; it comprises 106 group entries, 29 thematic essays, 87 maps, and a number of statistical tables. As the editors wrote in the introduction, "It is generally assumed that maintenance of ethnicity is desirable, that preservation of differences is healthy, and that loss of group identity is to be deplored. The view that ethnicity is a social good became fashionable during the 1970s. The *Encyclopedia*'s underlying premise is that ethnicity, whether good or bad, has been and remains important in the American social fabric."[50]

This interest in refashioning the national narrative intersected with a widespread passion for genealogy and ancestral heritage in the 1970s, exemplified in Alex Haley's *Roots*. "I feel that [my ancestors] do watch and guide," Haley wrote in the closing lines, "and I also feel that they join me in the hope that this story of our people can alleviate the legacies of the fact that preponderantly the histories have been written by the winners."[51] American history in the years since has largely been rewritten by a previous era's downtrodden losers. Insofar as it was an institutional phenomenon—engaging publishers, universities, research foundations, federal granting agencies, scholarly organizations, and the disciplines themselves—the roots trip was as much a national phenomenon as a familial or personal one.

The Heritage Project

"After Haley's comet," *Time* magazine remarked, in reference to the best seller *Roots*, "not only blacks but all ethnic groups saw themselves whole, traceable across oceans and centuries to the remotest ancestral village . . . Americans have become like those adoptees who demand the long-denied knowledge of heritage." Although Haley himself had been concerned with recovering the "story of our people," by which he meant African Americans, readers from all backgrounds embraced *Roots* as a generic romance of ancestry lost and found.[52] Dell emblazoned its cover with the legend, "the saga of an American family," and the *New York Times* proclaimed that Haley "speaks not only for America's black people, but for all of us everywhere."[53] *Roots* is important as a national phenomenon not only because the book and the miniseries were so eagerly devoured by millions across the country, but because, over time, the roots idiom revised the vernacular imagery of the nation itself.

Roots speaks *to* all of us, certainly; but *for* all of us? The print and televised versions of *Roots* gave the history of slavery the broadest public airing it had ever received in American culture, and yet Haley's narrative was quickly appropriated as a moveable template for considering *anyone's* familial origins in *any* distant village. In the wake of the broadcast in January 1977 (seen by an estimated 80 million viewers, according to Neilson) hundreds of thousands of white Americans descended on local libraries and archives in search of information, not about slavery or black history, but about themselves and their own ethnic past.[54]

Although *Roots* sprawls across two centuries of history—seven generations—and across 729 pages of text, public attention was riveted on the final fourteen years, the final 27 pages. It is here that *Roots* addresses, not slavery and emancipation, but Haley's own work in sleuthing his family's saga. In these closing pages, Haley's detective work takes on a drama of its own: "When I had been thoroughly immersed in listening to [family stories] of all those people unseen who had lived away back yonder, invariably it would astonish me when the long narrative finally got down to Cynthia . . . and there I sat looking right at Grandma!"[55] If *Roots* brought black history to life, so did it bring an unusual dash of romance to the work of genealogical discovery. This narrative of Haley's quest represents an epic in itself, composed of trips around the world, encounters with the "exotic," and a moment of Old World celebrity.

In the author's journey *Roots* most forcefully relays its fable of American incorporation. *Time* characterized the book as "the story of the Americanization of the Kinte clan," a generations-long process whose completion is at once symbolized and in a sense *proven* by Haley's encounter with "authentic" Africa.[56] Here his unfamiliar sensation of being an "exotic" among his trans-atlantic kin underscores the extent to which Haley, as the final issue of the Kinte clan, has become not African American so much as simply *American*. "It embarrasses me to this day," he confesses, "that up to then my images about Africa had been largely derived or inferred from Tarzan movies and my very little authentic knowledge had come from only occasional leafings through the *National Geographic*."[57]

It was in part the narrative's powerful contrast between "assimilated Americanness" and an "exotic," premodern village past that gave *Roots* its appeal across lines of ethnicity and color, touching, as Haley saw it, "some deep pulse that transcends racial things."[58] In the wake of the miniseries' airing on national television, libraries and archives across the country experienced a run, not on books about slavery, but rather on materials relating to the genealogical search for roots in myriad "exotic," premodern villages—whether in County Cork, Abruzzi, Vilna, or Crete. Whatever narrative power Haley was able to generate regarding the specificities of the African experience in America, *Roots* was rather nimbly appropriated as a generic saga of migration and assimilation, not an African-American story, nor even an American story, exactly, but a modern one—a story that "speaks for all of us everywhere."

As *Time* pointed out, Americans' interest in "stalking their forebears" had been on the rise for some time: groups like the Chicago Irish Ancestry Workshop predated the televised *Roots*, as did how-to pieces like the one published in *Italian Americana* titled "Interviewing Italian Americans about Their Life Histories." But *Roots* added impetus to Americans' quest for an ethnic past. While specialists at the National Archives and the New England Historic Genealogical Society could point to a long-term increase in Americans' genealogical interests dating from the early 1960s, institutions with extensive archives all reported an unprecedented boom in 1977. Books with titles like *Searching for Your Ancestors; Finding Your Roots; Finding Our Fathers;* and *The Handy Book for Genealogists* suddenly found a massive audience.[59]

Within months of the first airing of *Roots,* widely circulating publications like *Time, Newsweek,* and the *Christian Science Monitor* were printing articles with titles like "Everybody's Search for Roots," complete with bibliographic guides to the genealogical literature and summaries of archival holdings. One archivist declared that, no longer the exclusive province of those in search of royalty or an otherwise notorious ancestor, genealogy had become "a small 'd' democratic phenomenon"—or, as *Newsweek* put it, a "National Parlor Game," "Better than Bingo." After the previous year's bicentennial, *Newsweek* reported, "Americans seem to be focusing not so much on their country's history as on their own. The names they are poring over like precious artifacts are not Yorktown or Valley Forge, but Grodno and Galway and Hallingdal." Pronouncing Hansen's Law in "full force," the magazine went on to describe the energy with which "younger hyphenated Americans are digging into their roots to reclaim a heritage denied them by assimilationist parents and grandparents—and in the process they are groping toward a redefinition of their Americanism." One observer later calculated that "millions of roots-seekers" had swamped the genealogical registries and that the "fallout from *Roots* and the national bicentenary by the mid-1980s spawned fifty thousand family-tree experts."[60]

For some, the search for roots entailed not only ancestor hunting in the local archives but "heritage tourism" in the "homeland" itself. Chicago's Poland Travel Agency doubled its charter bookings to Poland between 1976 and 1977, for instance, and Pan Am began promoting world travel with a series of "two heritage" commercials ("All of us came from someplace else"). The airline also produced an ethnic quiz and a board game called "Heritage Hunt." A major competitor later adopted Haley-esque advertising copy: "Roots: Trace Them to Ireland on Northwest Orient." Finer print would go on to urge readers, "Experience the land of your grandparents' past . . . Let Northwest Orient help you say hello to an old friend. Your homeland." As late as 1998, "Five out of six ancestry searches in Italy are made by Italian-Americans. Dublin is deluged with inquiries from Sons of Erin abroad . . . So many Jews today seek memories of *shtetl* forebears that East Europeans call them 'roots people.'"[61]

Such quests have generated a minor cottage industry over the years: Old World paradise regained, from *Portnoy's Complaint* (1969), to Michael Arlen's *Passage to Ararat* (1975), to *Madonna—Ciao Italia* (1988), to Michael Kalafatas's "journey home" from the Aegean diaspora in *The Bellstone* (2003).[62] Kennedy's return to New Ross in 1963 turned out to be the prologue to Richard Nixon's (rather strained) "roots" trip to Ireland in 1970, and Ronald Reagan's visit to Ballyporeen in 1984—all covered lavishly by the American press with continuing fascination, if increasing cynicism. Michael Dukakis's "odyssey of discovery" in Greece in 1976 provided the central theme of his presidential campaign in 1988. Even Tom Hayden, ex-president of Students for a Democratic Society (SDS), went to Ireland in 1971 "to explore my roots in county Monaghan." He later parlayed his attachments into two books, *The Irish Hunger* and *Irish on the Inside*.[63]

The discoveries in this "land of your grandparents' past," as Northwest Orient put it, tend always to be *self*-discoveries. As "an

6.   *Madonna Ciccone "returns" to Rome. The climactic moment of her 1988
concert film,* Madonna—Ciao Italia, *was when she paused in the
middle of the song "Holiday" to address the audience in her ancestral
language.* VITTORIANO RASTELLI/CORBIS.

Armenian American traveler returned from a voyage among the
Armenians," Michael Arlen saw himself "in some ways like the
proverbial Indian who has been brought up by white men and
who years later makes and returns from a visit to his old tribe.
Where do you stand now, sir? Are you with us or with them? Alas, by
then the alternatives are mostly rhetorical." If, like Alex Haley in
Africa, Arlen discovered on this voyage just how American he
actually was, he discovered a great deal else besides—what it
felt like to stop hating being Armenian, what it felt like to be
hated for being Armenian, what it felt like to be proud of being Armenian.[64] Even Howard Jacobson's *Roots Schmoots* (1993), a
self-conscious send-up of this roots tour phenomenon, ends in a
confession that the author-traveler has been moved after all. Ja-

cobson chases the roots trail and the elusive meaning of modern Jewishness from his native England, first to America, next to Israel, and finally back to the real origin (for him), the ancestral home of his Litvak ancestors. Jacobson had initially set out for America, where he could test his theory that "New York out-Jerusalemed Jerusalem," he could "eat Jewish, talk Jewish, fight Jewish, forget about being Jewish Jewish." Only at the journey's end, in Serhai, Lithuania, is his irreverence pierced. Jacobson's flamboyantly unsentimental journey comes to an end in a long-neglected, overgrown Jewish cemetery, where he finds himself with the feeling that "yes, I admit it . . . it is something, not nothing, that a Jew descended from this community has come back and for an hour or two on a wintry afternoon entertained a thought for those who lie here . . . it is ironic that it should be me of all people, the least familial, the least loyal, the least nostalgic of Jews, who has come . . . My presence is the proof, if anything ever can be, that no one should count himself forgotten and unvisited forever."[65]

But eclipsed in the emphasis on interior mindscapes and the psychic self-discoveries of the roots trip is the fact that the new ethnicity ramified outward through the larger units of social organization, from the individual, to the family, to the ethnic group, to the nation. A survey conducted by the U.S. Census Bureau among Polish Americans in the early 1970s found that over one million more people now identified themselves as Polish Americans than had done so in the census only a few years before.[66] This development may embody more than one million interior sagas of one sort or another, each a volume unto itself; but so does it portend something quite important for Poles as a group, and for those heritage industries organized around Polishness. Moreover,

as nearly moribund conceptions of group existence came spring-
ing out of the cauldron, "America" itself underwent drastic reconsideration. This was the *beyond* of "beyond the melting pot."

Ethnic organizations often stood in for the very heritage that
individual roots-seekers understood themselves to be rediscover-
ing. The new pluralism may not have been a boon to all such organizations, many of which had begun to falter in the 1940s and
1950s as a result of suburbanization, shifting demographics, and
the steady erosion of welfare and insurance functions that had
once been the site of "ethnic" responsibility. If some ethnic voluntary organizations did indeed receive a mild boost in these years
(the Polish Falcons experienced incremental increases in membership between 1970 and 1985; the Ukrainian National Association reached its high-water mark in 1974), others were plainly
in trouble.[67] But the appearance of new organizations did bespeak ethnicity's resurgence as an organizer of certain political
and social activities that in previous decades had become increasingly cosmopolitan and nonsectarian. Emergent ethnic organizations in the 1960s and 1970s included purely cultural endeavors
directed at recovering or preserving the ethnic past, such as the
Irish American Foundation (1963), the Byelorussian-American
Union (1965), the American Italian Historical Association (1966),
and the Polish Cultural Foundation (1972). They included conservative political groups like the Jewish Defense League (1968) and
the Ethnic Millions (EMPAC, 1975), as well as New Left groups
like Breira (1973). They included organizations borne of a new
self-recognition within nonethnic institutions, such as Italian Ex-
ecutives of America (1964) and the Harvard Jewish Law Students
Association (1977); antidefamation groups, like the Conference of
American Polonians (1972); groups devoted to particular events,

like the Westchester Columbus Committee (1970); groups devoted to social life, like the Armenian Churches Sports Association (1967) and the Albanian Social Club (1972); and groups borne
of a renewed dedication to the homeland, like NORAID.[68]

The impulse toward cultural preservation also resulted in a
range of local efforts of commemoration and ethnic exhibition.
In their *Guide to Ethnic Museums, Libraries, and Archives* (1978),
Wynar and Lois Buttlar identified local museums around the
country devoted to Czech, Dutch, German, Hungarian, Jewish,
Lithuanian, Slavic, Slovak, Swedish, Ukrainian, and Welsh life in
the United States, all dedicated between 1965 and 1978. Typical
mission statements not only pay tribute to *preservation* as a guid-
ing value—to "preserve the artifacts of Czech and German origin
used in the local community," "to preserve Dutch-American artifacts," "preserving the Welsh experience and heritage"—but often
speak of some wider civic aim as well: "to develop awareness of
the Jewish experience in America," "to unify the Lithuanian community," "acquainting Ukrainian-Americans and the community
at large with [Ukrainian] cultural contributions."[69]

The most spectacular ethnic preservation project was the National Yiddish Book Center, a drive begun in the late 1970s by a
twenty-three-year-old McGill graduate student to "rescue" the
thousands of old Yiddish books that sat neglected in basements
and attics across North America. Aaron Lansky had no idea at
the outset just what lay in store, though he did come to appreciate
how impeccable his timing turned out to be: "If I had tried to do
this fifteen years earlier, there would not have been sufficient interest. Fifteen years later, it would have been too late." The center
collected not thousands but millions of Yiddish volumes. By the
1990s Lansky had a new, eight-million-dollar facility and a fleet
of trucks; and the National Yiddish Book Center had so success-

fully stocked U.S. libraries that Lansky now turned his attention to reestablishing Yiddish collections in Europe. "It is a new day in America," Lansky later declared, "a day when we can begin reclaiming our baggage, our luggage, our cultural specificity, and bring it back into the American whole."[70]

If ethnic reclamation tended toward the academic in one direction, it shaded toward the commercial in the other, as perhaps Lansky's empire indicated. *Fortune* magazine reported in 1984 that "the ethnic sell" had become popular not only among candidates for political office—notably Geraldine Ferraro and Mario Cuomo—who had "decided that the immigrant experience is a good sell," but also among big business: "Thirteen corporations, including Coca-Cola, Eastman Kodak, and Kellogg, have launched ad campaigns tied to the 1986 Statue of Liberty centennial celebration." CBS, too, was to begin a series of one-minute specials "about America's lesser-known heroes and heroines, including Emma Lazarus, the poet whose words appear on the Statue of Liberty," while Joe DiMaggio now "leads viewers nostalgically around Ellis Island in a commercial for the Bowery Savings Bank." There is no small irony here, given the antimodern impulse of the roots phenomenon. As Vincent Brook notes, "The construction of ethnic particularism in the interests of privatized consumerism served a postwar U.S. economy and commercial televisual institution better than it served ethnic particularism itself." Perhaps this is why *Fortune* was able to draw glowing commentary on "the ethnic sell" from a creative director at Ogilvy and Mather, while the Harvard historian Stephan Thernstrom, editor of the *Harvard Encyclopedia of American Ethnic Groups*, skeptically dismissed the ethnic revival as "a fad that may go the way of mahjongg and macrobiotic diets."[71]

The most popular symbolic site for ethnic reclamation projects was the Lower East Side, represented as a literal way station in the history of Jewish migrations and deployed as a cultural shorthand for the generic "immigrant experience." As the historian Hasia Diner has amply documented, between the 1960s and the 1990s a veritable Lower East Side *industry* arose—a scholarly, institutional, and commercial infrastructure that generated and catered to ever heightened levels of interest. Early on, *The Jewish Catalog,* "one of the key documents to emerge from the Jewish counterculture of the 1960s," captured the antimodern flavor of the late-twentieth-century's ghetto yearnings, even as it promoted an unabashedly modern "consumption of Jewishness." *The Jewish Catalog* defined the Lower East Side as "American Jewry's sacred place," where "a Jew could engage with authentic Judaism . . . [and] a suburban Jew could sensually imbibe the residue of a more traditional past."[72]

This rising industry ultimately produced a vast library, from Howe's *World of Our Fathers* and Ronald Sanders's *Downtown Jews,* to novels like Gloria Goldreich's *Leah's Journey* (1978) and Meredith Tax's *Rivington Street* (1982), to exhibition catalogues like Allon Schoener's *Portal to America* (1966), to genealogical guides in the true roots tradition—*Orphan in History: Retrieving a Jewish Legacy* (1982) and *Tracing Our Jewish Roots* (1993). It produced films about immigrants, like *Hester Street* (1975), and about their meaning-seeking descendants, like *Crossing Delancey* (1988). It produced serious historical projects such as the Lower East Side Tenement Museum (1988) and the Eldridge Street Synagogue restoration (1991); and it produced Lower East Side walking tours—pilgrimages, really—like the Big Onion tours, as well as do-it-yourself guides like *Six Heritage Tours of the Lower East Side* (1997). And it produced kitschy and commercialized time-travel experiences, like Sammy's Rumanian Restaurant (1974), where bottles of *schmaltz* on every table quickly answer the question of why "the world of our fathers" came to an early end for so many of them. In 1976, inspired by the nation's bicentennial, one rabbinical student devised "Lower East Side Games" as a simulation for children at a Jewish summer camp: the children reenacted the immigrants' arrival in America, had their papers inspected and their names changed, and were forced to learn American manners.[73]

Among the most complete fossilized records of this impulse to recover ethnic heritage is Martin Scorsese's 1974 documentary *Italianamerican*. Like the many college students of the 1970s whose assignments included a heritage hunt, Scorsese sits in his parents' Little Italy apartment, prompting them gently as they recount their families' Sicilian-American odysseys and reminisce about the neighborhood in the old days. Mrs. Scorsese disappears to the kitchen occasionally to stir a pot of "authentic" Italian sauce, the complete recipe for which is finally revealed in the closing credits. In the meantime, in a mildly competitive but loving banter, the couple weaves a rich tapestry-in-memoir that encompasses their families' harrowing Atlantic crossing; work in the shipyards, failed ventures in fruit and vegetable retail and sewing homework in the garment industry; winemaking at home; the communal spirit of the old neighborhood ("Anybody talks bad about this neighborhood—forget it"); a return visit to Italy; a symbol-laden fable about one relative's "splendid" Staten Island bungalow and its fall into disrepair with the passing of the older generation; and the mournful disappearance of an entire world.

Along with the sauce recipe, the closing credits of *Italianamerican* also reveal that the film was funded in part by a grant from the National Endowment for the Humanities, a detail worth pursuing, as Scorsese was scarcely alone here. Significantly, many activities on behalf of ethnic particularity and cultural pluralism in this period received official state recognition and public funding. Among the signal developments in the state's mounting interest in pluralism was the Ethnic Heritage Studies Program of 1972, an amendment to the Elementary and Secondary Education Act of 1965. Authorization for the Act spelled out in some detail the perceived relationship between "ethnic history" on the one hand and the state's vested interest in patriotism and domestic harmony on the other: "In recognition of . . . the fact that in a multiethnic society a greater understanding of the contributions of one's own heritage and those of one's fellow citizens can contribute to a more harmonious, patriotic, and committed populace," and that "all persons in the educational institutions of the Nation should have an opportunity to learn about the differing and unique contributions to the national heritage made by each ethnic group," the title afforded students opportunities "to study the contributions of the cultural heritages" of their own and other ethnic groups. At the rate of about $2 million per year, the Ethnic Heritage Studies Program contributed to the development of ethnic studies courses, the collection of oral history material, and the compilation of various neighborhood histories.[74]

The nation's bicentennial observances in 1976 demonstrate the mutual engagement of grassroots ethnic activity and state-sponsored "heritage": massive events that were funded and staged by the state harnessed the street-level energies already at play around ethnic pride and the nation's mosaic heritage. For instance, the Festival of American Folklife evolved precisely during the years that the new ethnicity was in ascendance. The first festival, in

1967, had celebrated "democratic art" and the grassroots impulses of American creativity. But by the bicentennial celebrations of 1976, the festival had become a self-conscious tribute to ethnic diversity and American cultures—in the plural. One of the festival's stated aims was now "to stimulate cultural self-awareness and inter-cultural understanding." Similarly, in the 1970s festival exhibitions in Washington on "old ways in the New World" sought to "reflect accurately one of the principal facts that has made the U.S. so unique in world history, that America is the first unified yet genuinely pluralistic civilization in the history of mankind."[75]

Indeed, in trying to explain the boom in genealogical research in 1977, one archivist in Fort Wayne, Indiana, called it "bicentennial fallout." It was not just that Americans were hoping to discover a revolutionary soldier in their family's past (though some were, just as they had during the centennial celebration a hundred years earlier), but that the images conjured in this national celebration adopted ethnic diversity as a central motif. In an atmosphere in which "American folklife" was defined as "old ways in the New World," and presidential candidates were trumpeting "ethnic heritage" as "the living fiber that holds America together," the tempest-tossed ancestor from Grodno, no less than the minuteman, became newly interesting in both personal and civic terms.[76]

The candidates' pronouncements on ethnic heritage, like the festival's celebration of old ways, embody two highly significant strands in American civic life in these years. One is the presentation of the problematic notion of "heritage" itself, as if the authenticity of this "great treasure" were self-evident and could be pinpointed and named with reliability. "Heritage is not lost and found, stolen and reclaimed," writes Barbara Kirshenblatt-

Gimblett. "Despite a discourse of conservation, preservation, restoration, reclamation, recovery, re-creation, recuperation, revital-
ization, and regeneration, heritage produces something new in
the present that has recourse to the past." In fact, heritage is best
understood not as memory but as "a mode of cultural production
in the present."[77]

Second, then, is the confluence of the ethnic revival with U.S.
political culture, that is, the emergence of heritage as an idiom of
American nationalism. The ethnic contributions model of American nationality may have been a significant departure from the
homogenizing model of the melting pot, but it did share with the
waning paradigm an almost absolute erasure of power relations
that made for a fairly sanitized and happy national narrative: diversity as feast, the nation as smorgasbord. The harsher realities
of power that are most often hidden in the celebratory rhetoric of
heritage became exposed unexpectedly in the spring, when Jimmy
Carter endured a firestorm for using the unfortunate phrase "ethnic purity" in reference to historic city neighborhoods. Just where
did this Southerner stand on federal housing policy and residential segregation, many African Americans wanted to know? What
might "preserving our ethnic heritage" *mean?* Richard Pryor similarly punctured the heritage industries' pacific myths in a haunting monologue called "Bicentennial Nigger."[78] But by far the majority of bicentennial renditions of "old ways in the New World"
celebrated the nation's varied roots in such a way as to exalt the
hospitalities of U.S. political culture right alongside the fortitude
of its myriad adoptees, and to occlude the history of conflict, inequality, and violence that had attended the convergence of the
world's peoples at this global crossroad.

By the observance of the Statue of Liberty Centennial in 1986 the conceit of the "nation of immigrants" had become an article of civil-religious faith. As the *Washington Post* put it, 1986 was "clearly the immigrant's year—the year . . . of immigrant chic." New York mounted two separate centennial celebrations—one on the Fourth of July, and a second marking the anniversary of Grover Cleveland's October dedication of the Statue of Liberty. Even those who were not thrilled by the July Fourth festivities had to be impressed by their scale. Thousands camped in lower Manhattan as the weekend approached in order to ensure a visit to Liberty Island during the four-day celebration; some 30,000 vessels crowded New York's inner harbor by July 3. New York reportedly spent more than 11 million dollars on the four-day extravaganza, which included a fireworks display of 40,000 shells with more than 2 million people in attendance. Special photographic exhibits held in conjunction with Liberty Weekend included "The Ellis Island Experience" and "Liberty's Legacy" at local museums. Headlining musical performances included Frank Sinatra singing "The House I Live In," his 1940s paean to the diversity of the American folk, and Neil Diamond singing "America," his 1970s paean to the continuing tradition of immigration. Festivities also included a symbolic swearing in of 300 recent immigrants at Ellis Island, including Mikhail Baryshnikov, along with thousands of others in various U.S. cities via satellite. Baryshnikov later performed to the music of George Gerschwin, an irresistible piece of immigrant symbolism. "It's a circle," explained one of the producers: "Balanchine, an immigrant, fell in love with Gershwin and did this choreography. Now Baryshnikov, another immigrant, is dancing his choreography."[79]

The October celebration hit many of the same notes, minus the costly fireworks and the seven-digit attendance figures. The autumn commemoration included "The First International Immigrants' Parade" down Broadway. The celebration ended with Zubin Mehta and the New York Philharmonic's rendering of Richard Wilbur's cycle of poems "On Freedom's Ground," the last movement of which, "Immigrants Still," depicted American history as an unfinished process: "We are immigrants still, who travel in time, bound where the thought of America beckons."[80]

The circuitry is critical—ethnic clubs and associations, cookbooks, games and ephemera, festivals, roots tours, a rising genealogy industry, and, not least, an increasingly common brand of ethnic celebration and pageantry sponsored by the state. Each of the station stops on this national roots trip—Alex Haley's best seller, Northwest Orient's "homeland" advertisements, the Heritage Hunt board game, Jimmy Carter's diversity-sensitive oratory, the Festival of American Folklife, Richard Wilbur's "Immigrants Still"—assumed significance by its relation to the cultural tapestry as a whole. In its psychology, the roots trip served diverse functions for diverse individuals; heritage could resonate in many different ways. But it is the pervasiveness and variety of Americans' "heritage" quests, the collectivity and concurrence of these ventures, and their corresponding power to redefine not only the *self* but *the nation* that give the roots phenomenon its meaning. If many Americans were busily redefining themselves as "immigrants still . . . bound where the thought of America beckons," as Wilbur put it, so were they fundamentally redefining America as precisely such a beckoning land—a nation whose historic significance and political genius were best apprehended by the incoming immigrant from Europe. Presidential candidates' attempts at the "ethnic sell," and the participation of the state in the folklife of 1976 and the pageantry of 1986, hint at the civic reach of the ethnic revival. But as extravagant as they often were, none of these state-sponsored activities or installations could compare with what was taking place at Ellis Island itself between 1965 and 1990—the creation of "an official view of the American heritage of European immigration."[81]

Sanctifying Ellis Island

By the time John F. Kennedy was pronouncing on America's character as a nation of immigrants, the once teeming administrative buildings of Ellis Island had fallen into disuse, neglect, and increasing disrepair. Untamed bushes and weeds encroached on the grounds, finally engulfing buildings which themselves had become ruins of dilapidated brickwork, cracked plaster, peeling paint, and exposed lath. The island now served mainly as a refuge for huddled masses of wharf rats. As the *New York Times* had reported in late 1954, "Without ceremony, the career of Ellis Island as an immigration station came to a virtual close" after decades of declining use. Two years later a group searching for a suitable location for a proposed American Museum of Immigration rejected Ellis Island, because for many the site was "a depository of bad memories"; a fleeting reference in the *New Republic* in 1964 characterized the island's complex of medical and administrative buildings as "human stockyards."[82]

But fortunes turn: President Johnson designated the immigration station a part of the Statue of Liberty National Monument in 1965; the National Park Service began limited tours of Ellis Island in 1976; and after a costly restoration campaign, the refurbished buildings and a new immigration museum were opened to the public in 1990. By the century's end, the pilgrimage of "recreational immigrants" to Ellis Island numbered between ten and fifteen thousand per day—higher than the number of actual incoming immigrants during the peak immigration year of 1907.[83]

Nostalgic theme park, or sacred ground? There is a certain kitsch element to the ferry ride across the harbor from Battery Park, and the museum gift shop does offer a T-shirt depicting Mickey Mouse as an immigrant. But in their rituals and their contemplative hush as they pass through the exhibits, many of the visitors themselves resemble nothing so much as pilgrims at a holy shrine. As one citizen wrote to President Eisenhower way back in the 1950s, as controversy swirled around the federal government's plans to sell off the island, "To millions and millions of Americans Ellis Island was the nineteenth and twentieth century counterpart of Plymouth Rock. [T]his little piece of land has associations of deep affection."[84] The depth of this affection—even if second- or thirdhand—is daily in evidence as thousands of pilgrims gaze upward upon the vaunted ceiling or reach out to lightly touch the brickwork of the Great Hall.

In the symbolism it deployed and the narratives it generated, the project to restore and sanctify Ellis Island represents the most significant instance of state sponsorship at play in the ethnic revival. President Johnson initially annexed Ellis Island to the more popular and better-kept Statue of Liberty National Park as part of his public relations campaign on behalf of a liberalized immigration bill. "Our beautiful America was built by a nation of strangers," he intoned at the signing in 1965, in the shadow of the Statue of Liberty. "From a hundred different places or more they have poured forth into an empty land, joining and blending one mighty and irresistible tide. This land flourished because it was fed from so many sources—because it was nourished by so many cultures and traditions and other peoples."[85]

A familiar sentiment, more familiar now, perhaps, than at the time the words were spoken, but certainly at one with JFK's *Nation of Immigrants* and his celebrated homilies in Ireland. That this project to reclaim and restore Ellis Island unfolded against the backdrop of a mounting interest in ethnic history and a shifting language of national diversity is crucial, though these developments did not always make the efforts on behalf of the project any easier. If the ethnic revival boosted the project by providing a natural community of invested, energetic, and interested parties, so did it heighten the perceived stakes of the project to such an extent that an easy consensus on matters of form, style, or historical interpretation was unlikely. The enthusiasm for the restoration is yet another artifact of the ethnic revival, that is, but so is the raucous history of wrangling and disagreement over whose memories would be enshrined there.

One of the striking things about the Ellis Island restoration in retrospect is that the renown of "the isle of hope and tears" is relatively recent: there was a time not so long ago when the recognition factor of Ellis Island (the measure by which modern marketing departments gauge the public's familiarity with a particular brand) stood at only 20 percent. The first stirrings in what would become a vast restoration project were in 1955, when a group called AMI, Inc., was chartered to finance and execute an American Museum of Immigration. AMI began work at the pedestal of the Statue of Liberty late in 1961, in cooperation with the National Park Service, though financial problems plagued the project early on. Congress appropriated public monies in 1967 and 1968; and in the early 1970s, Peter Sammartino, founder and chancellor of Fairleigh Dickinson University, formed the Ellis Island Restoration Commission (EIRC), successfully lobbying congress for $8 million in appropriations by 1983.[86]

The ten-year period between the bicentennial year of 1976 and the Statue of Liberty Centennial in 1986 marked the escalation of the Ellis Island project in earnest, and the point at which the longer-term efforts of AMI, the resurgent interest associated with the EIRC, and the broader currents of the ethnic revival all converged. Barbara Duvall and Beverly Dolinski, among the first visitors to the island when tours began in 1976, sought permission to launch a fundraising campaign for the island's restoration. Their plan crystallized in the May 1982 establishment of the Statue of Liberty–Ellis Island Centennial Commission, whose figurehead was immigrant-cum-magnate Lee Iacocca, the CEO of Chrysler. The centerpiece of this fundraising effort, Iacocca's brainchild, was a plan under which donors could pay 100 dollars to have their immigrant ancestors commemorated on an American Immigrant Wall of Honor at Ellis Island. By 1990 "the wall" had generated $40 million. The numbers alone, from the initial congressional appropriation of $8 million to Liberty–Ellis Island's ultimate fundraising tally of $305 million (of which the Ellis Island installation finally cost $150 million), chart the meteoric rise of Henry James's "terrible little Ellis Island" in the national consciousness amid a collective fascination with heritage and roots.[87]

This was not a smooth process. By far the most difficult debates had to do with the message of the museum. Discussions took place just as American historiography took a distinct turn toward bottom-up social history, and when immigration history was taking shape as a distinctive subfield within the discipline. Discussions that had begun in the climate of melting-pot sociology and consensus history in the 1950s were now unfolding, not only in an intellectual cosmos dedicated to the new pluralism, but within a framework of interests represented by scholars such

7.   *Sacred ground, civic ritual: a visitor reads names on the American Immigrant Wall of Honor at Ellis Island.* TED HOROWITZ PHOTOGRA-
PHY/CORBIS.

as Rudolph Vecoli—whose research tended to overturn the older
melting-pot assumptions—and by new institutions such as the
Immigration History Research Center (1964), the Center for
Migration Studies (1965), and the Immigration History Society
(1965). The celebratory, assimilationist vision of the AMI's inaugural planning sessions did not sit well with this emergent gallery
of scholars whose own findings cut in a very different direction. More explosive still was the question of *who*, exactly, should
be depicted in the museum. As the project broadened in scope
from a modest immigration museum to a more ambitious gesture
toward American liberty and national character, the inevitable
questions arose: what of *today's* immigrants? And what of those
millions of Americans for whom Ellis Island was not the touchstone? One official on the board of directors candidly remarked

that "the most recent immigration . . . did not fit in line with [the board's] particular cultural perspectives and that this was going to be a white man's museum."[88]

Although not solely a "white man's museum" in the end, still Ellis Island *was* the point of entry for migrants who were overwhelmingly admitted as the "free white persons" of U.S. naturalization law; and so the iconic figure of the white immigrant has dominated all others. This goes not only for the site itself but for the considerable industry of Ellis Island remembrance that has emerged in recent years—trinkets, "ethnic" memorabilia, and T-shirts sold at the museum gift shop, as well as coffee-table books, children's books, popular histories, and TV documentaries. The largest single boost to this remembrance industry was the Statue of Liberty Centennial, whose festivities included the publication of *Liberty: The Statue and the Dream; In Search of Liberty; Ellis Island: A Pictorial History; Images of Liberty; Maiden Voyage; The Statue of Liberty Enlightening the World; Sam Ellis' Island,* plus several postcard books, Dover Press's *Cut-and-Assemble New York Harbor* and *Statue of Liberty and Ellis Island Coloring Book,* and, as one Random House official put it, "about a gillion" children's books.[89]

In constructing the prototypical, epic-heroic "immigrant," these artifacts also construct a very particular version of "the nation." In a 1963 review of Elia Kazan's film *America America,* the *New York Times* commented that the film was "not only a tribute, but also a ringing ode to the whole great surging immigrant wave. An ode—that is what it is, precisely, for the story conveyed in this film . . . is a minor odyssey that has major connotations of a rich lyric-epic poem." This notion of the immigrant saga as both ode and epic captures the spirit of much that goes on under the aegis of Ellis Island remembrance. In fact, it is striking just how hard it has been for people on all sides of the question to break out of that generic mold. The project on behalf of Ellis Island remembrance has been steeped in conservative politics of one sort or another ever since the idea for an immigration museum first surfaced in the 1950s. One dominant motif has been America's Cold War "leadership of the free world." As one proponent put it in 1951, the museum's depiction of the immigrants' search for "liberty and opportunity" ought to bolster the United States in its "worldwide struggle for men's minds and aspirations." In his overall assessment, National Parks Service historian F. Ross Holland credits the restoration with "bringing the country out of the Vietnam syndrome" and "healing the wounds the nation had inflicted on itself. The restoration was a patriotic effort that most Americans could rally around, and the celebration . . . marked the nation's emergence from the shadow of the Vietnam experience."[90]

But Cold War politics aside, the history enshrined at the Statue of Liberty–Ellis Island National Park exerts a quieter but more significant force when it comes to this country's domestic social relations. Richard Nixon sounded the keynote in his 1972 speech for the dedication of the immigration museum (then housed on Liberty Island). The immigrants "believed in hard work," he declared, encoding a racial comparison that could hardly have been lost on his listeners. "They didn't come here for a handout. They came here for an opportunity and they built America."[91] Nixon here annexes the European immigrants to the national legend of rugged individualism, even as he redefines the legitimate national community itself to exclude the supposed welfare-mongers of the present-day ghetto.

"Opportunity" and "liberty," both of which evoke individualism, are still the dominant themes at the site. The overall effect, in the words of the historian John Bodnar, has been to reinvigorate "the view of American history as a steady succession of progress and uplift for ordinary people." This self-congratulatory national storyline might have been particularly resonant in the 1980s, as anxieties surfaced over the nation's ability to deliver opportunity and progress. Insofar as it is the governmental, administrative dimension of the immigration saga that is evoked at Ellis Island, according to Bodnar, the site resurrects the republican trinity of liberty, equality, and fraternity as the best available explanations of the American experience, and thus "forges a link between the state and all of its citizens."[92]

Both the Ellis Island site and the experience of visiting and celebrating it perform a delicate but transformative maneuver on behalf of the national imaginary. The rituals and artifacts of Ellis Island remembrance might tap into the personal impulses of the ethnic revival, but ultimately they turn outward toward the nation at large. In a characteristic paean to both the immigrants and their adopted country, the preface to *Island of Hope, Island of Tears* explains,

> [This] is the story of all those tens of millions who came to America searching for peace and several kinds of freedom—and in the main found what they were searching for; the story of the wit, humor, irony and compassion of ordinary people made extraordinary in the process of braving an extraordinary time. In short, this is the story of our parents, grandparents, great-grandparents and neighbors; of their voyage to America and their passage through Ellis Island to freedom.[93]

The movement here between national affirmation ("in the main [they] found what they were looking for"), personal epic ("ordinary people made extraordinary"), and national redefinition ("*our* parents, grandparents, great-grandparents") recapitulates with wonderful economy the pivotal ideas of Ellis Island remembrance. In the first instance, the immigrants stand as proof of the goodness of the nation—of all the places in the world, they came *here* looking for peace and freedom, *and they found it*. In the next instance, the immigrants themselves are exalted for their hardiness, wit, and courage—they were deserving of the nation's greatness, in other words. And finally, by the end of the third sentence, the immigrants *are* the nation, just as the nation *is* its immigrants. If America is defined solely by the "freedom" the immigrants sought, so, finally, is America composed solely of these seekers and their descendants. The tremendous power of the mythic immigrant is threefold: the image of the immigrant "functions to reassure workers of the possibility of upward mobility in an economy that rarely delivers on that promise"; the "hegemonic myth of an immigrant America" obscures the nation's less flattering "foundings" (conquest, slavery, expansion, annexation, and more slavery); and finally the immigrant provides "a nationalist narrative of choiceworthiness."[94]

Here is one of the reigning ironies of the ethnic revival, and one of the mainsprings of our national political life in the decades since. If the project to restore Ellis Island initially took root in the soil of an ethnic-revival ethos of disquiet—even of outright protest against the homogenizing forces of modernity—it ended in an ancestral vision that has been made fundamentally nationalist. And if the "nation of immigrants" paradigm began as a push for recognition and inclusion, it ended in a vision of the nation that is strangely *ex*clusive, even in its celebration of diversity. As the African-American historian John Hope Franklin remarked of the centennial spectacle in 1986, "It's a celebration for immigrants and that has nothing to do with me." William Harris, president of Paine College, concurred: "If you can't communicate to blacks that when you talk about liberty you are talking about more than just European immigrants . . . then there just isn't much in it for me." Although the Centennial Commission made at least a few gestures toward broad inclusiveness—awarding the Ellis Island Medal of Honor to Muhammad Ali, César Chavez, Daniel Inouye, Rosa Parks, and Chien-Shiung Wu right alongside European recipients like Victor Borge, Zbigniew Brzezinski, Claudette Colbert, Joe DiMaggio, Martina Navratilova, and Michael Novak—still many black critics joined Franklin and Harris in their skepticism. The Schomberg Library in Harlem mounted a dissenting exhibition, "Give Me Your Tired, Your Poor . . . ?"; and Jesse Jackson urged that this "would be an excellent time to redeem and amend the Statue of Liberty just as we redeemed and amended our Constitution to outlaw slavery."[95] Such dissenting comments point to the potent ideological "accomplishment" of Ellis Island remembrance: if "liberty" is coterminous with what European immigrants sought and found in the New World, then most of U.S. history slips off the page and the legitimate range of our public discussion of both past and future narrows considerably.

Ellis Island remembrances of the sort tacitly but firmly encouraged by the National Park Service actually conflate two quite distinct themes: immigration as geographical movement versus immigration as legal standing, citizenship, and civic incorporation. It is only in the first sense that this country is really anything like "a nation of immigrants"—everybody came from somewhere, whether from JFK's New Ross, Alex Haley's Kinte-Kundah, or across the land bridge from Asia. But this meaning has eclipsed the second, more profound meaning when it comes to comprehending the body politic. To celebrate this as a "nation of immigrants," to construct "America" solely through the eyes of the incoming European steerage passenger, is not only to redraw a line around the exclusive white "we" of "we the people," but simultaneously to claim inclusivity under the aegis of commonly held "liberty." Steerage, chains, whatever. A collective gaze trained on the diverse avenues of civic incorporation (as well as the diverse obstacles) would result in a vastly different understanding of "liberty" and of "the American experience."

In 1963 a team investigating the possibilities for restoring the immigration station declared that "Ellis Island has been as important in fact as Plymouth Rock has become in fancy." Now, after decades of celebration and sanctifying rituals, the Ellis Island of popular fancy has come to rival the significance of either of these sites in fact. Vice President Dan Quayle once remarked, "What we celebrate in Ellis Island is nothing less than the triumph of the American spirit." The new, improved Ellis Island has become, as the performance artist Guillermo Gómez-Peña has written with considerable skepticism, "the mythical island of American genesis"—a creation of the ethnic revival, to be sure, but also the single most important site and symbol channeling the energies of the ethnic revival toward a very particular version of American nationalism.[96]

In a brilliant, ironic comment on the appeals of ethnic community, Vivian Gornick recalls accompanying her mother to a lecture at Hunter College in commemoration of the Warsaw Ghetto Uprising. When they arrive at the auditorium, they stand outside the open door for a time, listening to the proceedings. Inside, two or three hundred Jews sit

> listening to the testimonials that commemorate their unspeakable history. These testimonials are the glue that binds. They remind and persuade. They heal and connect. Let people make sense of themselves . . . My mother and I stand there on the sidewalk, alone together, against the sound of culturemaking that floats out to us. "We are a cursed people," the speaker announces. "Periodically we are destroyed, we struggle up again, we are reborn. That is our destiny."
>
> The words act like adrenaline on my mother. Her cheeks begin to glow. Tears brighten her eyes. Her jawline grows firm. Her skin achieves muscle tone. "Come inside," she says softly to me . . . "Come. You'll feel better."[97]

This is a version of "feeling better" that has become increasingly common on the American scene in the years beyond the melting pot. Such "culture-making" among the cursed and reborn peoples now in America has been made to carry a varied freight—respite from the "air conditioned nightmare"; symbolic reconstitution of life on a human scale, the "trusted interdependency" that seems to have been ploughed under and paved over by modernity; solace in a world of tamed masculinity; redemption from the class betrayals entailed in New World paths of mobility and assimilation; certification of underdog status (and hence of moral rectitude) in battles over urban housing and schools, in which whiteness might be taken as a marker of immense privilege (and hence of culpability).

Culture-making in the accents of ethnicity might be experienced as primarily emotional or intellectual; it can be interior and private, or social and self-consciously political; it can tend to the left or to the right. It represents a powerful idiom for the expression of meaning, not meaning itself. But in this decades-long heritage hunt, Americans' myriad identity quests and their articulations in civic terms have produced a portentous new image of the nation and its make-up. The phrase "middle America" long carried an unmistakable connotation of white Protestantism—one thinks of Sinclair Lewis's *Main Street*, the Lynds' *Middletown*, or television families like the Andersons or the Cleavers. But in 1976, around the time that American nostalgia discovered Arthur Fonzarelli and Detroit anchorman Tom Conrad reverted to his "lost" name, Korzeniowski, the *New York Times* pronounced "white ethnics . . . the largest segment of Middle America."[98] As the nation has held itself up to the media mirror in the decades since, the image of white America that reflects back looks less and less like the whitebread, Protestant world of Rob and Laura Petrie, and rather more like, well, a big fat Greek wedding.

Chapter Two

Golden Door,
Silver Screen

Everywhere around the world, they're coming to America.
Every time that flag's unfurled, they're coming to America.
Got a dream to take them there—they're coming to America.
Got a dream they come to share—they're coming to America.
. . . Today!

—Neil Diamond,
"America," *The Jazz
Singer* (1980)

Mass culture ratified the conception of the United States as a nation of immigrants many times over. Television was suddenly populated by characters with names like Arnie Nuvo, Bridget Fitzgerald, Michael Stivic, Rhoda Morgenstern, Vinnie Barbarino, Laverne DeFazio, and Shirley Feeny—a generation of ethnic characters whose descendants include Carla Tortelli, Joel Fleischman, George Costanza, Fran Fine, Tony Soprano, and Dharma Finkelstein. Sometimes ethnicity was exactly the point (as in *Bridget Loves Bernie*, a 1970s update of *Abie's Irish Rose*), but even where deeper ethnic significances were muted or entirely absent in plotlines, an Ellis Island saga was vaguely implied, as in *Kojak, Banacek, Baretta, Columbo, Toma*, and *Cagney and Lacy*. The new ethnicity on American television runs from *Arnie*, to *Saturday Night Live*'s Greek diner and "Jew/Not-a-Jew Game Show" sketches, to *Northern Exposure, Brooklyn Bridge, The Sopranos*, and *Everybody Loves Raymond. Sanford and Son* was initially conceived as a show about an Irish father and a son who took after his Italian mother; and today even *The Rugrats* get an occasional visit from their Yiddish-accented Grandpa Boris.

Ethnic accents have been even more pronounced in Hollywood film. Ethnicity had never faded entirely from the American scene, nor had it melted away in American film. Hollywood had segmented its audience according to narrow demographic surveys several years before television did, and was thus "industrially predisposed" to the cultural pluralism of the 1960s. The figures at the helm of the three television networks in these years—William Paley, David Sarnoff, and Leonard Goldenson—were cut from precisely the same assimilationist cloth as that generation of Jews in Hollywood who, oddly enough, had *invented* the standard images of a WASP Middle America earlier in the century. (Emblematic, perhaps, was CBS founder William Paley's judgment that *Fiddler on the Roof* was "too Jewish.") Whereas television was stuck for a time with a brand of "video assimilation" that diminished uniquely ethnic elements, throughout the same period Hollywood could depict the gritty ethnic enclaves of *On the Waterfront* and *Marty*, or suggest the multiethnic camaraderie of the Rat Pack.[1]

But the rise of the independents and the birth of the "blockbuster" coincided with the ethnic revival, and indeed many of the most successful films in the era beginning with *Funny Girl* (1968) have explicitly treated themes of immigration or ethnic particularity: *Fiddler on the Roof, The Godfather I* and *II, Rocky, The Deer Hunter, Raging Bull, Saturday Night Fever, Grease, Moonstruck, Fargo, Goodfellas, Titanic, Good Will Hunting, Angela's Ashes, The Gangs of New York,* and *In America,* just to name some Academy Award nominees.[2] This leaves untouched the quieter, more deeply embedded ethnic sensibilities that have informed the work of some of the nation's most celebrated filmmakers—Francis Ford Coppola, Martin Scorsese, Brian De Palma, Mel Brooks, Woody Allen, John Cassavettes, Paul Mazursky, Sidney Lumet, and Joe Eszterhas—and the ethnic tones and audience associations that many major screen actors carry with them to roles that are not otherwise ethnically marked, including Barbra Streisand, Marlon Brando, Robert De Niro, Al Pacino, Cher, Sylvester Stallone, Bette Midler, Alan Arkin, John Travolta, Olympia Dukakis, John Turturro, and Marisa Tomei.[3]

Whereas many studies have analyzed Hollywood's depiction of various groups in isolation, the cumulative effect of cinematic imagery, not of "the Jew" or "the Italian," but of the *nation,* remains unnoted: in the cosmos projected in American film in this era, the normative American social location has largely been recast from simple whiteness to a distinct brand of Ellis Island whiteness.[4] The "fabulous '50s" invoked by the All-American Dance Competition in *Grease* (1978), for instance, is populated almost exclusively by Zukos, Rizzos, Kenickies, and Bianchis. Even the figures of social authority at Rydell High, Principal McGee and Coach Calhoun, conjure something quite distinct from the usual WASPdom. The ethnic boundaries of the American norm in

Grease are marked off, at one end of the spectrum, by the indeterminately Latin "Cha Cha," and at the other, by the Australian immigrant Sandy Alston, played by Olivia Newton-John.

In the romantic fulfillment of the film's ending, the white-bread Australian assimilates to the norm of Italian badboy Danny Zuko; she now sports black leather, big hair, a cigarette, and an attitude. In the song-and-dance rendering of the melting pot (represented by a carnival ride called the "shake shack"), ethnicity *is* the assimilated norm: Danny Zuko *is* the America to which the Australian immigrant must conform. To a significant degree, the prevailing ethnic logic of Hollywood film in the final decades of the twentieth century is the ethnic resolution in *Grease* writ large. In its mounting iconography of European immigration, in its thematic rendering of ethnic incorporation as the American success story, and in its popular narratives of white grievance and white triumph—think *Rocky* or *Flashdance*—Hollywood has created an alternative social portraiture befitting the emergent hyphen nation. There was a time when ethnic representations in popular culture functioned as a cultural *transgression*, marking the limits of American (WASP) normativity and thus serving "as a sort of guardian of the values and structures which [were] being transgressed."[5] In the decades since the 1960s, however, a once transgressive ethnic presence has become a popular version of the American norm itself.

The Iconography of Immigration

Midway through Barry Levinson's film *Avalon*, the family patriarch tries to muster something meaningful to say at the Krichinskys' Thanksgiving dinner. "We give thanks . . . We give thanks . . . ," he struggles, blurting at last, "The pilgrims started it, whoever they were." This misplaced referent in the national narrative is a significant feature not only of the Krichinsky saga in *Avalon* but also of a more pervasive narrative line in American film since the 1960s. Just as, according to Krichinsky family lore, Baltimore's Fourth of July celebration, 1914, marks Sam's arrival in America rather than national independence ("The sky exploded; people cheered . . . there were fireworks. What a welcome it was"), so Hollywood's cumulative lore has supplied an alternative myth of origins for the nation, whose touchstone is Ellis Island rather than Plymouth Rock, and whose inception is roughly in the 1890s rather than in the 1600s.

The basic iconography of immigration has become so pervasive in American film that not only does a single image carry with it the entire history of European immigration, but the theme of immigration in turn becomes a stand-in for the national narrative and for the nation. Consider the following, highly conventional cinematic images: Tevye the dairyman, his family, and fellow villagers slog across the mud of Eastern Europe on their way to "New York, America" (*Fiddler on the Roof,* 1971). Newly disembarked Stavros Topouzoglou kisses the ground at Ellis Island (*America America,* 1963). As he makes his way through the immigration station's administrative process, Vito Andolini's progress is conveyed in a sequence of now mythic images—a crowded maze of immigrants waiting in line, the dreaded trachoma (eye) exam, a peasant woman with a basket, a rag-tag group of Italian musicians, an indecipherable English-language interrogation by uniformed bureaucrats. Young Andolini's name is changed by an indifferent administrative recorder, and the ensuing shot of the boy gazing on the Statue of Liberty from his detention cell bears the legend, "Vito Corleone, Ellis Island, 1901" (*The Godfather,*

Part II, 1974). Amid the same Ellis Island mayhem, a sallow, anxious young woman in Old World dress and an orthodox wig scans the throngs on the other side of the wire mesh divider. Her gaze passes over a smartly dressed young man several times before she recognizes him as her own husband. A Yiddish exclamation is rendered in English subtitle, "My God, he shaved off his beard!" (*Hester Street,* 1975). A gentle, young Russian Jewish man sits amid the squawking chickens and the general hubbub of a Lower East Side marketplace selling his silhouette lanterns. He will resurface in the next reel as the immensely successful film director Baron Ashkenazi (*Ragtime,* 1981). The narrative of Frank McCourt's hope is plotted in four glimpses of the Statue of Liberty—once on leaving New York for Ireland in despair; twice as he gazes hopefully on a replica at the Our Lady of Liberty Pub in Ireland; and once, wordlessly but triumphally, as he indeed does return to America in the film's closing moment. Each time, Frank's physical proximity to the statue expresses his relationship to the abstract ideal of Liberty itself (*Angela's Ashes,* 2000).

Doubtless certain truths about the great migrations are embedded in these scenes, but the most striking thing about such images is that, with marvelous economy, they fully contain Americans' vernacular knowledge on the subject of immigration: little that is known by nonspecialists in immigration falls beyond the pale of these mass-mediated icons. Such images do not resurrect memory, they have become it. Like the restored Ellis Island site itself, they successfully displace less pleasing national truths: no corresponding popular iconography of civic incorporation is either as extensive or as pervasive regarding slavery and emancipation, conquest, or the trans-Pacific saga of Asian immigration through Angel Island in San Francisco.

In creating this visual iconography of immigration, Hollywood was closely engaged with a newly popular photographic archive. "Drawing inspiration from the New York ghetto photographs of Jacob Riis," runs a promotional blurb for Sergio Leone's film *Once Upon a Time in America,* "Leone's cast and crew recreated period settings with meticulous authenticity."[6] The final credit in *Hester Street* conveys Joan Micklin Silver's thanks to the Jewish Museum of New York, undoubtedly for access to its photographic archive: virtually every frame of the film mimics period photography by its camera angle, settings, and dark black-and-white tone. Silver and Leone's meticulous re-creations or the literal reproduction of Riis and Lewis Hine photographs in *American Pop* may be unusually self-conscious, but still one cannot miss the references to the turn-of-the-century photographic tradition that pervade other cinematic treatments of the immigrant saga. Whether in *The Godfather, Part II; Ragtime; American Pop;* or *Titanic,* the aspect of the steerage passengers, the obligatory glimpse at the Statue of Liberty from above deck, the mayhem of Ellis Island processing, the ghetto street scenes and marketplaces, the grime of the tenement and the closeness of its interiors, and the tenement district's crush of children and chickens and goats and rag-pickers and men in prayer shawls—all pay homage to the photographs of Riis, Hine, Alice Austen, and Joseph Byron, which were themselves being reproduced and popularized as part of the burgeoning "heritage" industry.

The signal event in this recovery of the photographic record was "Portal to America," an exhibit at the Jewish Museum in New York that drew an estimated 150,000 visitors in 1966.[7] The exhibit catalogue appeared the following year, a compendium of photographs, letters to the *Jewish Daily Forward*'s (now) famous advice column, "Bintel Brief," and a grab bag of period newspaper articles, all arranged to represent New York's Lower East Side as "the epic first America for millions of immigrants." Among the photographs exhibited at the museum in 1966 are many that have become very familiar in the years since: Edwin Levick's "Immigrants on an Atlantic Liner," Joseph Byron's "Steerage Deck of the *SS Pennland*," Lewis Hine's "Italian Immigrants on Ferry" and "Carrying Work Home," Jacob Riis's "Street Arabs, Mulberry Street" and "Bohemian Cigarmakers Working in a Tenement," Underwood and Underwood's "Examining Eyes, Ellis Island," and Jesse Tarbox Beals's "In the Kitchen, 1915."

In exquisite revival fashion, curator Allon Schoener remarked that work on the exhibit "provided me with the opportunity to discover my heritage."[8] No doubt the exhibit provided the same for many of its 1966 visitors: Milton Hindus observed, "The majority consisted of suburbanites, who were descendants of the immigrants pictured in the exhibit."[9] But more significant, Schoener's exhibit granted this "vanished world" a newfound immediacy in visuality and inaugurated a new genre, the immigration photo-epic, within that ascendant mode of 1960s cultural production called heritage. True, Kennedy's *Nation of Immigrants* had reproduced forty-six photographs, and Moses Rischin's *Promised City* had contained fourteen (including period daguerreotypes and cartoons). But there had never before been anything on the scale of *Portal to America*—neither so many images gathered in one place, nor such aesthetic care taken in the effort, not simply to document this facet or that of "the immigrant experience," but to re-create an entire social cosmos. The genre grew in ensuing years to include Dover Press's popular reprint of Jacob Riis's *How the Other Half Lives* (1971) and Joseph Byron's *New York Life* (1985), as well as the photo galleries in books like Isaac

Metzker's *Bintel Brief* (1971), Howe's *World of Our Fathers* (1976), Brownstone, Franck, and Brownstone's *Island of Hope, Island of Tears* (1979), the Center for Migration Studies' *Pictorial History of Italian Americans* (1981), and Pamela Reeves's *Ellis Island* (1998). Exhibits at the Ellis Island site, too, stand as a monument not only to immigration but to the immigration photo-epic as a popular genre.

Throughout these years an unmistakable canon of immigration photography took shape. The most widely disseminated images have generally been those produced by celebrated photographers Jacob Riis, Lewis Hine, and Alfred Stieglitz. But among the commonly reprinted images are also many by less familiar figures like Joseph Byron, Alice Austen, Jesse Tarbox Beals, or contemporary photographers who remain anonymous. But so stark have the conventions of recirculation become, so clear the consensus on the emergent canon, that one reasonably expects to encounter one or more of the top ten or so images in any volume dedicated to immigration published after 1970.[10]

Cinema's engagement with this photographic revival and with the earlier visual traditions of a Jacob Riis or a Lewis Hine is plain but not simple. Before the 1930s most photographers of newly arrived immigrants or of the immigrant ghetto were interested in conveying an impenetrable exoticism and foreignness. The photographs of Riis and his contemporaries are characterized by "a physical and/or emotional distance from the subject." In line with the social work that was their aim, turn-of-the-century photographs were both inspired by "shock" and calculated to generate this shock anew within the viewer. Riis in particular was known for his "pictures of reeking, murder-stained, god-forsaken alleys and poverty-stricken tenements," as one contemporary put

8.   *Famiglia values. Vito and Carmella Corleone with their children in New York's Little Italy,* The Godfather: Part II *(1974).* JOHN SPRINGER COLLECTION/CORBIS.

it. These photographers sought "to capture the striking physical world [of the ghetto], including its poverty and alien cultures, for presentation to an outside audience"; the photographs were "brief but graphic lessons in the nature of poverty, in the ways and hows of immigrant life," which conveyed nothing of the worldviews or values of the people they depicted.[11] The immigrant of Jacob Riis or Alice Austen is a mere curiosity, a symptom of the rising social ills attending industrialization.

The cinematic treatments of immigrant life that build on this turn-of-the-century visual tradition in some respects retain its overriding sense of alienness and difference, though on film they register quite differently. Here, in the darkened theater and from the temporal remove of two generations, the outsider's gaze registers a historical distance rather than ethnological "foreignness." As Allon Schoener wrote in *Portal to America*, life in the immigrant ghetto was "a panorama of hardship, misery, poverty, crowding, filth, uncertainty, alienation, joy, love, and devotion." Turn-of-the-century photographers most often provided a rich portraiture of the hardship, poverty, crowding, and filth. They hinted at the misery. But the alienation, joy, love, and devotion—the immigrants' firsthand subjectivity, that is—had little place in the social work that was their photography.[12]

Film, by contrast, through its narrative advantages over still photography, restores "alienation, joy, love, and devotion" to the portrait, even while borrowing the visual power of Riis or Byron's poverty, crowding, and filth. The effect is to render a world no less alien and distant than the one rendered by turn-of-the-century photographers, but to portray the people themselves as a familiar *we*—perhaps even a *familial* we—rather than as an irretrievably exotic and alien *they*. "The important thing is to make a different world," Leone told an interviewer for *American Film*. "To make a world that is not now. A real world, a genuine world, but one that allows myth to live. The myth is everything." In fabricating this myth, Leone sought above all "to find the perfect visual setting for each event in his tale"—perhaps a cinematic equivalent of what Lewis Hine meant by the "added realism" of photography.[13]

There are, of course, several ironies here. One is that massmediated imagery—whether Dover Press's reprint of the Riis collection, *Fiddler on the Roof*, or *Once Upon a Time in America*—would be so eagerly seized on in Americans' feverish enthusiasm for heritage. Where a pervasive hunger for the "folk" resulted in a new visual vocabulary within the industries of mass media, mass-mediated images themselves gradually became "folk" knowledge. But another, more vexing and important irony is that a popular impulse toward ethnic specificity should have generated so *generic* a rendition of "the immigrant experience." The logic of the images was not to depict the specificities of an Italian, Jewish, or Hungarian experience or culture, but rather to convey the crushing circumstances of American poverty and to pace off the distance between the immigrant as an idealized type and the photographer's presumed American viewer.[14]

As filmmakers drew on the visual record bequeathed by these photographers, so did they reproduce this inclination toward the generic immigrant. As David Thomson wrote of *Once Upon a Time in America,* "Its would-be Jewish gangsters seemed very Italian." Reportedly, in response to the suggestion that he ought to hire some Jewish actors (De Niro plays the lead, Noodles Aaronson), Leone replied, "Jews, Italians, there is no difference." Although this generalizing narrative strategy also characterized written work like Oscar Handlin's book *The Uprooted: The Epic Story of the Great Migrations That Made the American People,* ultimately the notion of a singular, knowable "immigrant experience" owes most to the traditions of visual culture. This conception is neither a natural development nor a foregone conclusion: the power of this generalizing formulation derives from the power of images to capture and fully become our memory as well as from the cookie-cutter templates of conventional photographic and cinematic images, whether depicting Jews, Italians, Greeks, or the Irish.[15]

Two particularly striking images from 1980s and 1990s film demonstrate the mutual engagement of conventional immigration imagery on the one hand, and the broader imaginings of this "nation of immigrants"—a national "we" whose point of origin is the steerage deck of the European steamer—on the other. The first is the closing scene of *Yentl* (1983), in which Barbra Streisand strolls among the steerage passengers of the *SS Moskva* on its trans-Atlantic crossing, singing, "What's wrong with wanting more? / If you can fly, then soar." Whereas the rest of the scene recapitulates the turn-of-the-century steerage images of Alfred Stieglitz, Edwin Levick, or Lewis Hine with some precision, the central figure of Yentl herself stands out. Although the anachronism of her dress is not so pronounced as to be fully jarring, in contrast to those around her Streisand looks as though she might be sporting a retro fashion of the 1970s rather than period dress, and she bears no sign of the hardships of a trans-Atlantic crossing in steerage. Visually, that is, this scene melds Yentl's historical moment with Streisand's "assimilated" present a century later. Far from conveying the kind of exoticism and foreignness that were the hallmarks of period photography, this scene prompts a reading of the *Moskva*'s passengers as, quite recognizably, *us*—the very embodiment not only of a national pedigree originating in steerage, but also of the modern, assimilated "we" whom those steerage passengers have become over time.

Second, the patterns of sympathy and the layered, flashback narrative strategy in James Cameron's *Titanic* (1997) not only remake Rose DeWitt Bukater the native into Rose Dawson the immigrant, but also reinforce the view from steerage as a typical American experience. Over the course of the narrative, Rose's sympathies steadily and decisively shift from her first-class fellow travelers to the more decent and genuine folks—indeed, the "folk"—down below. Rose forsakes her fiancé for the immigrant

Jack Dawson; she flees an excruciating and stilted first-class dinner to take refuge in the lively drinking, music, and dancing down
in steerage ("So, you wanna go to a *real* party?"). Her sympathies
most powerfully become the viewer's when, as the *Titanic* goes
down, the crewmen and first-class passengers treat the steerage
passengers with a steadily escalating brutality (first locking them
below to keep them from the lifeboats; then jabbing at them with
ax handles to prevent their escape; finally shooting and killing one
young Irishman).

Although these matters are cast in class rather than ethnic
terms throughout most of the film, the resolution at once enfolds
Rose into the nation of immigrants and holds her up as an emblematic Ellis Island arrival. By the time the survivors reach New
York aboard the *Carpathia,* not only does the babushkaed Rose
look like the iconic immigrant of Byron's *SS Pennland* or Hine's
"Young Russian Jewess at Ellis Island," but, when asked by a U.S.
functionary, she identifies herself as an immigrant as well. The
young, 1990s researchers of the *Titanic* who are interviewing the
elder Rose "Dawson," then, become *Roots*-era genealogists climb-
ing all over the family tree; the elder Rose (Gloria Stuart) who
has survived to tell the tale narrates her own alternative myth of
origins. Rose the younger (Kate Winslet) becomes in memory her
own immigrant ancestor.[16] As in *Yentl,* the resolution of *Titanic*
layers the past and the present in such a way as to project an affiliation with steerage as the very soul of "Americanism."

Ethnic Incorporation, the Musical

In American cinema the genre of the musical in particular has
generated a powerful set of conventions for the master narrative

9.   *Barbra Streisand as Fanny Brice.* Funny Girl *(1968) inaugurated the roots era in Hollywood film.* JOHN SPRINGER COLLECTION/CORBIS.

of ethnic incorporation. Two features stand out in the historical trajectory of the Hollywood musical: one is that the genre went into a steep decline in the late 1960s; and the other is that whatever remains of the musical as a viable enterprise in the years since has relied heavily on the imagery, color, presumed charm, and plot-entanglements of ethnicity. The success of *Oliver* and *Funny Girl* in 1968 represents the last time two Hollywood musicals received Oscar nominations for best picture in the same year. Meanwhile, *Funny Girl* itself, a paean to the Jewish actress and singer Fanny Brice, inaugurated a new, "ethnic" era in the genre.

The ethnoracial storyline had its precedents in musicals of an earlier era—*South Pacific, Porgy and Bess, Flower Drum Song,* and *West Side Story.* But the number of post-1968 musicals that play on ethnic particularity is striking: *Fiddler on the Roof, Funny Lady, Grease, Yentl,* and the Disney cycle of multicultural animations, including *Pocahontas, Aladdin, The Lion King,* and *Mulan.* Indeed, in order to sustain the musical as a viable category in recent years, critics generally include a number of films that are not "musicals" in the classic sense of having scripted dialogues or monologues rendered in song, but whose *raison d'être* nonetheless is song and dance. These films, too, bear heavy ethnic accents: *Saturday Night Fever, Fame, The Jazz Singer, American Pop, Flashdance, Staying Alive, The Cotton Club,* and *Dirty Dancing.*[17]

This tight alignment between ethnic film and the musical was partly due to the tradition that remained intact within the musical even as the genre began to fade. The folk musical, for example, whose earlier exemplars include *Hallelujah, Annie Get Your Gun, Oklahoma,* and *The Music Man,* continued to emphasize the communal ethos of a bounded regional or cultural universe—often portrayed as a backwater—but now shifted its attentions toward a different version of the romanticized "folk." Perhaps earlier staples such as the middle-American musical comedy of manners or the African-American extravaganza (as seen, always, through white eyes) could not survive the withering political heat of the 1960s. A usable folk past was now sought and discovered in places like the shtetl *(Fiddler on the Roof, Yentl),* or in the charms of the Irish in mythical "Missitucky" (*Finian's Rainbow,* adapted in 1968 from the earlier stageplay).

The contemporary reception of *Fiddler on the Roof* suggests the ways in which the musical could at once feed on the emergent "heritage" industries and engage the more general antimodernist strains of 1970s American culture. Based loosely on the *Tevye* stories of Sholem Aleichem, *Fiddler* was a Panavision portrait of a

10.   Chaim Topol as Tevye the dairy man in Fiddler on the Roof *(1971). From its stage production in the 1960s, to its incarnation as Holly- wood's "big ethnic thing" in the 1970s, to its Broadway revival in the early 2000s, Fiddler has been one of the ethnic revival era's most popu- lar reclamations of the "folk."* BETTMANN/CORBIS.

typical Russian shtetl on the eve of the great Jewish exodus, and of the indomitable spirit of those driven from the land by Czarist edict. Like many contemporary critics, a reviewer for *Newsweek* compared the film unfavorably with the stage production, which had by then been popular for some years. But in praising the stage production, he perhaps hit on those virtues that many among the audience were willing to attribute to the film as well: "its charm lies in its intimacy," he wrote, in the "close rapport" that Tevye es- tablishes with the audience "as he ponders his predicament as one of many poor Jews living in a ghetto among hostile Russians, as he debates the raw deal he's been getting with his close personal friend, God." American audiences were evidently attracted to this rendition of "the folk," even in the inferior film version: popular tribute at the box office made *Fiddler* the third most successful film musical of the 1970s.[18]

But in its opening celebration of "Tradition!," its depiction of the mighty toils of everyday Anatevka, its stirring cinematic landscapes, and its *gemeinschaft* emplotments of courage, solidarity, faith, dissension, and fear, perhaps *Fiddler on the Roof* more accurately depicts a twentieth-century American hunger than it does a nineteenth-century folk reality. Although the intimacy of Anatevka and *Fiddler*'s ode to the ethnic past were appealing to a wide audience, many critics were wary of the film's very scale—its *bigness*—and its ethnic self-consciousness. "To call the movie an epic is really to define what's wrong with it," remarked Vincent Canby. Director Norman Jewison's main mistake was that he had made "a big ethnic thing" out of it. *Newsweek* decried *Fiddler* as a monstrous "Goliath of a musical" whose downfall was its "big-deal treatment" of Sholem Aleichem's modest stories. The film's portrait of "the exodus of the Jews from Anatevka," by this reviewer's account, was "choreographed with the pomp of Napoleon's retreat from Moscow." Canby saw in *Fiddler* the unmistakable evidence of the film musical's demise: "a new, mostly joyless tradition . . . of the safe, artistically solemn, presold musical behemoth adapted from the Broadway hit."[19] While audiences flocked to this presentation of "the folk," that is, some critics saw in *Fiddler* symptoms of the very modernity and crass commercialism that the folk epic was meant to redress.

The show musical, like the folk musical, is also a natural for ethnic storylines. Show business has always been heavily popu-

lated by immigrants and ethnic and racial minorities—from minstrelsy, vaudeville, and burlesque to radio, film, and television.
Moreover, the entertainment industries have also been among the
most celebrated avenues of mobility and ethnic incorporation. It
at least *seems* natural, then, that the generations-long American
odyssey of one Russian Jewish family in *American Pop* would be
charted according to the dominant styles and genres of American
entertainment—from vaudeville, through jazz, swing, and psy-
chodelic rock, to Lynyrd Skynyrd's "Free Bird." *Funny Girl* was
the first performance musical of the ethnic-revival era, followed
in subsequent years by *Funny Lady; Saturday Night Fever; New
York, New York; The Jazz Singer; American Pop; Fame; Staying
Alive; Flashdance; The Cotton Club;* and *Dirty Dancing.*

Whereas folk musicals like *Fiddler on the Roof* and *Yentl* harked
back to the past, thus measuring the distance that now separated Americans from their premodern roots, show musicals in
effect *explained* that distance by providing a standard narrative of
mobility and incorporation. The breakthrough moment in the
performance film, when the lead character crosses from the ethnic periphery into the wider, more cosmopolitan world, is the
performance itself: the exuberance of the well-executed performance and the exuberance of mobility—"making it"—are fused.
The climactic performance represents both the moment and the
means of social triumph, as in *Funny Girl, The Jazz Singer, Fame,
Flashdance,* or *Staying Alive.* Although powerfully implied by the
musical's very narrative structure, this fusion of performance and
mobility-incorporation often receives explicit comment as well,
as does the distance between the two worlds being traversed:
Jesse Robin's "Old World" wife's certainty, on seeing his smash-
ing rock performance, that she has lost him forever in *The Jazz*

Singer; Mrs. Manero's wonderment on the triumphant conclusion of Tony's Broadway debut, "Where did he learn to do *that?*"

Finally, the musical's conventional romantic plotline also adds to the currency of ethnicity within the genre. The musical is typically structured on an overdetermined narrative, visual, and vocal-melodic commitment to *coupling:* "The American film musical seems to suggest that the natural state of the adult human being is in the arms of an adult human being of the opposite sex. Pairing off is the natural impulse of the musical, whether it be in the presentation of the plot, the splitting of the screen, the choreography of the dance, or even the repetition of a melody."[20]

The couple *is* the plot, but the romantic tension of the musical requires the central couple to represent not a simple duet but a duality—they must be "different" from each other in terms that somehow call into question the final fulfillment of their love. This underlying convention itself promotes a "different worlds" or across-the-tracks quality to the romance, for which ethnicity provides a common shorthand. In earlier years this central trope of difference within the romantic duet was most often expressed in terms of the lovers' disparate ages, personal styles, or temperaments *(The Band Wagon, Silk Stockings, Carousel).* But by the 1970s ethnicity had become common coin in this construction of romantic duality: Brice-Rose in *Funny Lady* (1974), Doyle-Evans in *New York, New York* (1977), Zuko-Alston in *Grease* (1978), Rabinowitz-Bellangocavella in *The Jazz Singer* (1980), Finsecker-Garcy in *Fame* (1980), Owens-Hurley in *Flashdance* (1983), Manero-Revelle and Manero-Cole in *Staying Alive* (1983), Dwyer-Cicero in *The Cotton Club* (1984), and Houseman-Castle in *Dirty Dancing* (1987).[21]

The musical's tendency toward themes of ethnic "coupling,"

then, adds to the more generalized iconography of immigration and settlement in the standard Hollywood narrative of national incorporation. Not only does the culture industry surrounding musical entertainment prove an assimilative site in historical terms, from nineteenth-century minstrelsy, to tin-pan alley, to vaudeville; but by its ethnic plotlines, the genre of the film musical recapitulates this history, setting the central characters' advance from parochialism to cosmopolitanism firmly within a tale of cross-ethnic alliance in which assimilation and success are one and the same.[22] The performer's triumph is always assimilative, that is, but the materials that go into the narrative are always ethnic and undigested. The musical is *about* assimilation, but it *depicts* pluralism.

Like its 1927 ancestor, the 1980 version of *The Jazz Singer* is paradigmatic of the genre's tendency toward a narrative of ethnic incorporation. Not only is Jesse Robin forsaking the insularity of his orthodox Jewish enclave for the cosmopolitan world of the rock industry, not only is he exchanging his position as a cantor for the spotlights of rock stardom, not only is he leaving his Jewish orthodox wife in favor of an ethnic other, but the entertainment world he has chosen is itself populated by people who have similarly bartered away their ethnic birthright. Just as Jesse arrives at the airport in Los Angeles, he has the following exchange with the woman (played by Lucy Arnaz) whom the record company has sent to greet him:

MOLLY: I'm with Keith Lennox Productions. Molly. Molly Bell—that's what they call me. My real name is much longer.

JESSE: So's mine.

MOLLY: Bellangocavella?

JESSE: Rabinowitz?

MOLLY: [*Impressed*] Ooooh, that's not bad. Pleased to meet you.

Francis Ford Coppola's film *Cotton Club* (1984) combines the standard song-and-dance motif of the ethnic-assimilation narrative with another common Hollywood trope of immigrant mobility, gangsterism. Although the coronet player Dixie Dwyer is "not bad for a white kid," as we learn very early on, his musical career is hemmed in by the segregationist racial codes of Owney Madden's Cotton Club. "Too bad you ain't colored," Madden's henchman tells him bluntly. "We could book you here." Dwyer's racial marginality in the music scene of 1920s Harlem leaves him particularly vulnerable to the strong-arming and tacit extortion of the gangster Dutch Schultz, who becomes Dwyer's employer-benefactor-master in an arrangement that looks something like indenture. Dwyer finally escapes the Dutchman's clutches and "makes it" by combining both the performance and the criminal worlds: hand picked as an apt gangster by the mob-ruled film industry, he goes on to star in the fictive 1931 hit movie *Mob Boss*. But here again, Dwyer's social movement from Harlem musician to Hollywood star is charted by his romantic coupling with Schultz's Italian girlfriend, Vera Cicero—Dwyer's version of Molly Bellangocavella.[23]

This ethnic motif in the American success story spills well beyond the bounds of the musical, though that may be where it is still most pronounced. *Working Girl* (1988), for instance, purports to address women's liberation and working-class justice, though the markers of ethnic assimilation are ever present. Tess McGill is a corporate secretary who aspires to something bigger. Taking advantage of her boss's temporary absence, she poses as an executive and arranges an ingenious corporate deal on behalf of the financially troubled Trask Industries. She succeeds: the film's ending has Tess settling in at her own executive desk, talking on the phone to her (cheering) working-class friends back in the secretarial pool. As a narrative of liberation, *Working Girl* does not accomplish much in either the feminist terms or the class terms that its title seems to promise: the chief villain of the piece is certainly not "patriarchy"—nor even male privilege—but the despicable Sigourney Weaver character, Tess McGill's boss. Moreover, though Tess proves upwardly *mobile*, she leaves the wider arrangements of political economy very much as she had found them. (The secretarial pool's thrill at her triumph is the very picture of Gramscian hegemony, workers' "spontaneous allegiance" to the existing order.)

But as a narrative of symbolic assimilation, *Working Girl* actually has some sense to it. The film opens with a close aerial shot of the Statue of Liberty accompanied by Carly Simon's rousing anthem "Let the River Run." Against the familiar visual image of Liberty, the song is vaguely evocative of Emma Lazarus's "huddled masses yearning to breathe free." ("Let the river run / Let all the dreamers wake the nation / Come / The new Jerusalem.") Lest this connection remain too obscure, the camera pans down to capture the Staten Island Ferry chugging toward lower Manhattan, soon to disgorge a throng of newly arrived commuter-immigrants. Among the first things we learn about Tess McGill, in a comment to her friend Cyn as they disembark, is that—like so many "immigrants" before her—Tess is taking speech classes at night. ("Whadya need speech clee-ass fowah?")

The "two worlds" theme carries throughout the film, beginning with the contrasts between corporate, well-to-do Manhattan and Tess McGill's working-class neighborhood, a spatial distance that Tess traverses daily by steaming across New York Harbor. Tess is marked ethnically by little more than her surname (and, perhaps, the standard ethnic shorthand of her boyfriend's name, "Mick"), but the working-class spaces she inhabits are all populated by characters with names like Di Mucci, and the tone here mimics the familiar ethnic spaces of *Saturday Night Fever* or *Flashdance*. Tess's corporate rise as an ethnic-assimilation narrative is emphasized further when her transfer from one division of the firm to another is handled by a gruff personnel director, played very much in the mold of an Old World padrone by Olympia Dukakis. Tess may seem a social and cultural orphan—we know nothing of the McGill clan or of their coming to the New World. But her narrative, like so many other Hollywood renditions of "making it," is fundamentally an immigrant story whose triumphal moment is marked by the ethnic outsider's cross-ethnic romantic alliance (in this case with Harrison Ford). This is no musical, it is no performance narrative; but it is a version of American arrival that would be familiar to the likes of Jesse Robin and Molly Bellangocavella, Dixie Dwyer and Vera Cicero—no less to Doris Finsecker than to Fanny Brice.

Cinema of White Grievance

As refracted through the Ellis Island saga, this narrative line of ethnic incorporation is incapable of resolving the social complexities of a nation that is not merely multiethnic but multiracial. The dominant version of the American success story moves from the ethnic margins toward the mainstream, but it is nonetheless a *white* story. Race is thus the spectral presence that haunts much ethnic film. When the presence of people of color is acknowledged at all, it is in either a problematic or a fully troubling way. In *Flashdance,* for instance, Alexandra Owens's ethnicity is unnamed, though it is marked by her economic location (she is a welder in Pittsburgh), her religion (she is a practicing Catholic), and her vaguely articulated familial ties (she periodically visits a grandmotherly Old World figure named Hannah). Both her romance with Hurley and her success in dancing promise to remove her from this enclave, as is the standard promise of the genre itself. But though Alex insists on making it in the dance world without anyone's help (as she tells Hurley, throwing a shoe at him in a rage), the unacknowledged fact is that she finally wins the admiration of the Dance Conservatory board, and so gains admission to that august institution, by virtue of the dance moves she has copped from some nameless black breakdancers—played by The Rocksteady Crew in an uncredited cameo—on a Pittsburgh streetcorner. This narrative is symptomatic of the wider, troubled politics of ethnic film, which rests on a kind of white primacy in its very insistence that we are all immigrants fresh off the boat.

A major subplot of Oliver Stone's film *Any Given Sunday* (2000) explores the question of whether a young, talented, black, third-string quarterback can make it in a world dominated by owners named Pagniacci, head coaches named D'Amato, first- and second-string quarterbacks named Rooney and Cherubini— a world made and still very much ruled by glorious ghosts named Lombardi and Unitas. As the veteran quarterback Cap Rooney puts in some extra time lifting weights in fear that he may be losing his job to the black back-up, his wife quips, "Yo, Rocky, you've had enough." The *Rocky* reference is particularly apt in this context of black-white competition, calling up a decades-old film that originally appeared at a crucial juncture not only in the ethnic revival but in the backlash dynamics of post–Civil Rights race relations. (*Flashdance* itself was originally haled as "*Rocky* in toe shoes.")

Any given film has its own distinct historicity, an engagement with salient questions and public discourses of the moment—*The Producers* with a new, frontal reckoning with the meaning of the Third Reich; *The Deer Hunter* with questions of national decline in the wake of Vietnam; *King of Comedy* with an emergent, critical recognition of the perversions of the culture of celebrity; *Working Girl* with 1980s pink-collar feminism and critiques of American business culture during the Reagan era. In this sense film is inherently political. It is therefore worth considering at closer range the ideological work that certain ethnic films have accomplished within a more tightly delimited historical moment. As Cap Rooney's wife instinctively acknowledged with "Yo, Rocky," Sylvester Stallone's boxing films of the mid-1970s embodied a powerful set of ideas about black-white competition and the ethos of the white (ethnic) "underdog." As the Civil Rights era gave way to the post–Civil Rights era, white resentments surfaced over the ameliorative policies so recently won (notably affirmative action and busing); new stories were told about power relations and justice on the American scene—who had what, who deserved what, and who held power over whom. If the "post" of post–Civil Rights indicated to some the premature and disappointing demise of a noble movement, to others it suggested that a new social order had indeed been established. The margin-to-mainstream trajectory of the white ethnic saga became entangled in precisely such questions.

On September 16, 1976, the California Supreme Court held that the UC Davis Medical School's affirmative action program was unconstitutional, and that the rejected (white) applicant Allan Bakke had to be admitted. A few weeks later Stallone's *Rocky* opened in theaters across the country, garnering astonishing box-office receipts and much popular acclaim. The *Bakke* case and the boxing film shared more than a historical moment: they shared an ethos, a way of understanding the respective meanings of "whiteness" and "blackness" in post–Civil Rights America. If the white applicant had unjustly become an underdog under Title VI admissions practices, as the California court held, Rocky Balboa dramatized precisely that underdog status in his titanic struggle to unseat the flashy and arrogant black champion, Apollo Creed. Indeed, so united were the legal case and the film in their ethos of white grievance, and so successful were they in confounding common conceptions of victimization, that many now misremember the outcome of both: Bakke has become the symbol of the unjust loser (he won), while Rocky Balboa stands for the underdog's just triumph (he lost). The *New York Times* headline that characterized Bakke as "White/Caucasian and Rejected" seems to have stuck, as have the triumphal images of Rocky Balboa, surrounded by adoring fans, raising his fists in exhilaration on the steps of the Philadelphia Art Museum.

Allan Bakke was born in Minnesota in 1940. After a tour of duty with the U.S. Marine Corps in Vietnam, in 1967 he secured a job as a research engineer for NASA in California, though his fondest hope was to study medicine. He worked for a time as the lone male figure among a group of hospital volunteers called the "pink ladies" and applied to medical school. When Bakke was turned down by UC Davis, he felt sure that he owed his misfortune to a Civil Rights–era admissions policy that reserved sixteen of the school's one hundred slots for minority candidates. Once denied, he sued the university for discrimination.

By the early 1970s, admissions and hiring policies of the sort that Bakke was challenging already had a bit of history behind them. By an Executive Order in 1961, Kennedy had mandated affirmative action by government contractors to recruit and promote minorities; the principle was then strengthened by the terms of the Civil Rights Act of 1964. As Lyndon Johnson famously put it a year later, "you do not take a person who, for years, has been hobbled by chains and liberate him, bring him up to the starting line of a race and then say, 'You are free to compete with all the others,' and still justly believe that you have been completely fair."[24] By decade's end, affirmative action policies were in place in a wide variety of institutions.

The issue vexed the courts. "[Since] the persons normally stigmatized by racial classifications are being benefited, the action complained of should be considered 'benign,'" a Washington judge had written in *DeFunis v. Odegaard* (1974), a similar case involving a Sephardic applicant to the University of Washington Law School. "However, the minority admissions policy is clearly not benign with respect to non-minority students who are displaced by it."[25] The California courts concurred in *Bakke*. A lower court first found the Davis admissions policy unconstitutional but issued no injunction on Allan Bakke's behalf, judging that this particular applicant would not have gained admission, even absent the flawed affirmative action policy. But in the fall of 1976, the state Supreme Court issued a ruling that was regarded on all sides as "a complete victory for Bakke": UC Davis had denied access to whites "solely because of their race"; this constituted a violation of the equal protection clause of the Constitution; the university had demonstrated no *necessity* of such a program to achieve its stated goals; and there was insufficient evidence in the first place that UC Davis had "discriminated against minority applicants in the past." In effect, Davis had unjustly created a class of victims in order to redress a prior injustice that had perhaps never even occurred.[26]

The legal principles behind *Bakke* achieved nationwide notoriety and took on a politically explosive character. As the case reached the U.S. Supreme Court for review, the justices were deeply divided. Judge Rhenquist found Davis's admissions policy to be "as difficult to sustain constitutionally as one conceivably could be." Justice Brennan, by contrast, had no legal doubts that "states are free to pursue the goal of racial pluralism in their institutions in order to afford minorities full participation in the broader society." As he explained in justification of his position, "If I thought that Davis' failure to admit Bakke represented a governmental slur of whites . . . 'whites are too dumb to be good doctors,' or because 'Bakke is Mick Irish, or Jew, or Hungarian, or Englishman'—then I would not hesitate to apply the strictest of scrutiny." Justice Marshall, too, lamented that the principle of "color-blindness" had not been accepted by the majority in *Plessy v. Ferguson* way back in 1896. "For us now to say that the principle of color-blindness prevents the University from giving 'special' consideration to race . . . is to make a mockery of the principle of 'equal justice under the law.'" But in a tortuously worded decision, the Court upheld the state court's decision in favor of Bakke. As the *Amsterdam News,* an African-American paper in New York, summed it up, "Bakke—We Lose."[27]

The narrative line of *Rocky* presents an uncanny cinematic ana-logue to the politics of black-white and advantage-disadvantage in the *Bakke* case. The only position of real power depicted in the film is inhabited by the reigning black champion, Apollo Creed, a brash, vocal, theatrical, arrogant fighter cast in the unmistakable mold of Muhammad Ali. Not only is Creed in the position to call all the shots when it comes to selecting his opponents and thus charting his career, but he is inclined to call those shots according to a logic of race. Demanding that his promoters find him a "snow white" opponent—presumably for both the social drama and the personal satisfaction this will afford—Creed settles on Rocky Balboa, an obscure neighborhood fighter from one of Philadelphia's grittiest working-class wards.

From the outset, then, this is an ethnoracial battle: Rocky's ring moniker is "The Italian Stallion," while the name "Creed" can only evoke the other figures in the American triumvirate, "race" and "color." But notwithstanding the "snowy whiteness" that Creed attributes to his challenger, the tone and logic of the narrative finally dismantle the very notion of white privilege. If the Italian Stallion is indeed white, the film suggests, he is not *that* white. Rocky's powerlessness in the boxing world as compared with Apollo Creed's omnipotence, the camera's lingering gaze on scenes of crushing poverty and squalor in (white) working-class Philadelphia, and the stark contrasts between the two fighters' surroundings, lifestyles, and modes of dress, all work to efface or invert the historical white-over-black power dynamics of American society.

This smoldering sense of Rocky's white *under*privilege ignites into full-fledged grievance in the closing sequence, the fight footage at the Philadelphia Spectrum. Not only does Rocky manage to go the distance with the champion (his own modest aim), but

11. The poster boy for white victimization. Sylvester Stallone and Talia Shire as Balboa and Adrian in Rocky *(1976).* JOHN SPRINGER COL-LECTION/CORBIS.

12.   *Philadelphia statue of Rocky Balboa, 1982. By the 1980s Rocky had become a chief symbol of the triumphant white underdog.* LEIF
SCOOGFORS/CORBIS.

the crushing body blows he delivers—some of which lift Creed momentarily from his feet—break one of the champion's ribs and cause him to spit blood from some internal wound. This is one extraordinary fighter; and even a pounded and bewildered Creed himself says at the final bell, "There ain't gonna be no rematch." But in the closing seconds of the film, as Rocky declares his love for his girlfriend, Adrian, amid the postfight mayhem of the ring, the drowned and barely discernible voice of the ring announcer declares what can only be interpreted as an *unjust* split decision in favor of Apollo Creed. Rocky himself does not comment on the decision—indeed the commotion of the scene offers no evidence that he is even aware of it. But his very silence, along with the jarring abruptness of the freeze-frame and the suddenly rolling credits, generate a kind of dismay in the viewer that is more powerful than anything the script could have delivered with words. It is a poignant dismay; it is a dismay that, in the context of the racial climate of 1976, carries a potent political charge.

Rocky II—the rematch—begins with this aggrieved white dismay and develops it much more fully than the first film. Both the ethnoracial dimension of the Creed-Balboa rivalry and Rocky's fundamental entitlement are played up more forcefully here. The film opens by recapping the fight sequences of the first *Rocky* film, but this rendition is edited in such a way as to clear away the ambiguities and to highlight the injustice of the judges' decision. Directly afterward, as the two fighters and their cornermen address reporters in a hospital corridor after the bout, Mick exclaims, "I don't care what the hell them judges said, this [indicating Balboa] is the man that won the fight."

The plot of *Rocky II* derives much of its tension from Rocky Balboa's crisis of masculinity. Warned away from boxing because of the injuries he has sustained in the Creed fight (he is in danger of going blind), Rocky wrestles with questions of unemployment, productivity, and the stakes of masculine pride involved in accepting or declining a "hand-out." But at the center of this gendered narrative is his relationship with Adrian. When they marry and Adrian becomes pregnant, Rocky's public masculine duty to fight Creed a second time is suddenly at odds with his private masculine duty to guard his health so that he can care for his family. Although he does reluctantly "allow" Adrian to take a job, he chafes at her insistence that he give up boxing for good, especially when Creed begins to taunt him. Faced with the choice of either betraying his wife or enduring the humiliation of retiring from the ring under this pall, he pleads, "Adrian, please, don't ask me to stop being the man." Only when Adrian commands him to "do one thing for me—win!" are the masculine imperatives of Rocky's public and private lives aligned, and the rematch narrative can proceed in the epic mode.

Although *Rocky II* derives much of its tension from this gender trouble, the plot is actually set in motion and propelled by racial conflict. Creed has said that "there ain't gonna be no rematch"; we have forcefully been led to suppose that Balboa is the better fighter and that Creed knows it. Rocky's vulnerable health should provide Creed the easiest of outs. So why *is* there talk of a rematch? Whereas the first fight originated in Creed's desire to defeat some "snow white" chump, the second originates in his sense of imperiled stature within the African-American community. Ensconced amid the conspicuous comforts of his beautiful home (a far cry from Rocky's dismal flat), Apollo Creed is obsessed with the reams of hate mail he is receiving—from blacks. As one disparaging writer wants to know, "How much did you get to carry

that bum for fifteen rounds? You're a disgrace to your people."
Now there *will* be a rematch, if Creed has his way. This second
bout will be as much a battle for the pride of "the race" as for
Creed's personal pride.

Creed flushes Rocky out of retirement through an orchestrated
campaign of public humiliation. In Creed's high-profile television interviews, and even in leaflets that begin to appear around
Rocky's neighborhood, the Italian Stallion has become "the Italian Chicken." (This in itself represents a significant inversion of
recent social history: how often, in the annals of Civil Rights
struggle or the busing wars, was *black* supremacist literature disseminated through a neighborhood by mimeograph?)[28] Rocky's
humiliation momentarily intersects the established plotline of his
masculinity crisis—both have him chafing to return to the ring.
But even after the gender conflict is resolved and Rocky has
Adrian's blessing to fight, the "Italianness" at stake in the taunt of
"Italian Chicken" remains. Rocky, too, will be fighting for "his
people."

As a worldview, an ethnic ethos, Rocky's Italianness is accentuated in several scenes in a Roman Catholic Church, and when, on
his way to the arena, he stops outside his priest's window and asks
him to "throw down a blessing." As a set of social associations, his
Italianness is conveyed when a member of the mob finds Rocky
doing menial chores at the gym shortly after his layoff. "You don't
need a job like this," remarks Tony. "Besides, you're Italian—now,
you come back and work for me." And as a matter of self-ascription and pride, his Italianness is conveyed in Mick's many, spir-
ited peptalks: "You're gonna be a greasy-fast Italian monster";
"You're a greasy-fast, two hundred pound Italian titan." Scanning
the Philadelphia Spectrum just before the bout, a TV announcer

observes, "I've never seen so many Italians in one place in my life!" Rocky Balboa is a five-to-one underdog, representing "his people" in the ring against the black "Master of Disaster"— a reigning champion who has shown no restraint in using his considerable power and status publicly to demean the Italian fighter. The inclusion of a black cornerman seated prominently in Rocky's corner might soften the racial animosities of the narrative line, but it cannot efface them.

Despite the racialized logic of the *Rocky* films, Rocky Balboa himself is no outspoken white supremacist. On the contrary, he is depicted as a loving, gentle, decent, and remarkably modest man. These essential traits are showcased in many ways, big and small—in his tender affection for Adrian; in the image of the children of Philadelphia following him, in Pied Piper fashion, on his training runs through the city; in his unremitting humility ("I was wonderin' if you wouldn't mind marryin' me very much"); in his wishlist of things to buy with the purse money from the rematch (including a statue for his church and a Kermit the Frog doll for his son); in his good-natured stoicism on being laid off (by an African-American foreman) at the meatpacking plant.[29] Prodded by a reporter to say something derogatory about Creed as the rematch approaches, he says simply, "Derogatory? Yeah, he's great." Whether his answer reflects a misunderstanding of the word "derogatory" or a principled refusal to engage in trash-talk we cannot know, but it is characteristic of his simple decency.

Ultimately, it is precisely because Rocky is no klansman, nor even an outspoken advocate of "white rights" like Pixie Palladino, that the early *Rocky* films generate such power as narratives of white grievance. Rocky Balboa is nothing if not deserving. He is not a spokesman for white backlash; he is a poster boy for white victimization. As the legal scholar Mary Ten Thor commented after the California decision in *Bakke*, "there is simply no way you can possibly equate the typical racist suffering that minorities of color have to endure almost every day of their lives in our white racist society with the occasional, incidental surrender of an advantage of the sort that a Bakke experiences once or twice in his lifetime."[30] But the narrative logic of *Rocky I* and *II* is precisely that, yes, you *can* equate downtrodden whiteness with downtrodden blackness—that the deck has been reshuffled since the 1960s, and now the Apollo Creeds of the world hold all the social power to be found anywhere in Philadelphia.

Although the *Bakke* case represented a critical moment in the emergent national discourse of "black privilege," this conception did not disappear—either from public discussion or from cinematic imagery—in the ensuing years. Indeed, the notion of black privilege has existed uneasily with the contrary notion of the underclass ever since, and both have exerted a considerable regressive pull in civic debate and social policy from the 1980s onward—having come together and crystallized, perhaps, in the figure of Reagan's mythic "Welfare Queen." For a nation in which the very concepts "slum," "ghetto," and "poverty" typically conjure distorted images of American *blackness,* American film has actually devoted a surprising amount of screen time to *white* slums, ghettos, and poverty. If the plight of the downtrodden white ethnic in such films is supposed to claim the audience's sympathy, that plight—like Rocky's—is often accented by some reference to blackness.

In *Raging Bull,* for instance, Jake La Motta's downward spiral, though a demise of his own making, is punctuated along the way by his devastating losses to black fighters: the Reeves fight (1941), which the black fighter wins by unanimous decision even though

13.   *Jake La Motta and Sugar Ray Robinson, February 1951. In* Raging Bull *(1980) director Martin Scorsese rendered La Motta's losses to black fighters as the very emblem of white tragedy.* BETTMANN/CORBIS.

La Motta has knocked him down three times; the second Sugar Ray Robinson fight (1943), which this black fighter also wins by unanimous decision, again despite having been knocked down; the Billy Fox fight (1947), in which La Motta takes a dive to appease the mob; and the final Robinson fight (1951), in which La

Motta is crucified by the black fighter in the thirteenth. A string of bouts with white fighters, meanwhile (Zivic, Basora, Kochan, Edgar, Satterfield, and Bell), are glimpsed in rapidfire succession only in brief still shots, or in fleeting scraps of slow-motion footage intercut with La Motta's home movies from the same period. "The narrative of boxing," observes David Remnick, "requires oppositions as broad as slapstick"—as true in the boxing film, evidently, as in the sport itself.[31] *Raging Bull*'s racialized black-white fight sequences indicate Scorsese's reflexive judgment that nothing will articulate La Motta's woes quite so well as spacious cinematic attention to the Italian fighter's demise before various black opponents.

But then consider the Jews of mid-1950s Baltimore in Barry Levinson's *Liberty Heights* (1999). At first glance the film seems another nostalgic lovenote to the old ethnic neighborhood, much like Woody Allen's *Radio Days,* Neil Simon's *Brighton Beach Memoirs,* or Levinson's own *Avalon.* The wistful last line of the film encapsulates much that has come before: "If I knew that things would no longer be, I would have tried to remember better." But beneath the soft surfaces of this charming lament burns a quiet rage of ethnic grievance. In one of the opening scenes, seventeen-year-old Ben Kurtzman and his friends puzzle over a sign posted at the swimming pool of a local club: "No Jews, Dogs, or Coloreds." After turning this over a few times among themselves, the boys reason that no one has ever seen dogs or "coloreds" swimming, "so this is definitely directed more at the Jews, then." The scene is disarming in its charm: third-generation midrashic minds, humorously at work on a problem of minute interpretation. But the boys' conclusion—that Jews are *really* at the bottom of the social heap—informs the script in a thousand ways. Finally, like *Rocky, Liberty Heights* pits white ethnics against blacks in a contest for supreme victim's status, even in spite of some touching moments on black-white relations among young people who, unlike their parents, are not averse to "the other kind."

The script for *Liberty Heights* began, for Levinson, with the theme of anti-semitic injury and a sense of moral rage. He was fuming over an *Entertainment Weekly* review of his science fiction film *Sphere*, in which the critic irrelevantly commented on Dustin Hoffman's Jewishness, throwing in a few Yiddishisms like "menschlike" and "noodge." "The movie has nothing to do with religion!" Levinson objects. "Why would that be mentioned? I mean, you wouldn't say that Mel Gibson in *Ransom* is a Catholic businessman whose son is kidnapped."[32] After pacing and raging around the house for a few days, by his account, Levinson locked himself in a room and wrote *Liberty Heights* in three weeks.

In the screenplay, Levinson's experience is retained in a brief exchange after one of the Kurtzman boys' friends gets in a fight with someone at a party who had asked whether he was Jewish:

YUSSEL: When's the last time you wanted to know if someone was Catholic? Or Episcopalian, Methodist, Protestant? Who gives a shit?

ALAN: What's the difference between all those groups? They all pray to Christ.

YUSSEL: It's okay to have a Jew on the wall, just don't have one come through the door.

ALAN: A dead Jew is okay. I think that's the operative word here.

But the overarching social equation in *Liberty Heights* ultimately becomes far more complicated than this simple morality play of anti-semite versus Jew. The narrative unfolds in three embraided subplots, two of which involve the relationship between blacks and Jews, all set against the backdrop of school desegregation in 1954: the story of Ben Kurtzman himself, who gently falls in love with Sylvia, the only African-American girl in his class; the story of his older brother, Van, who falls under the spell of a gentile woman whom he has briefly met at a costume party; and the story of their father, Nate, whose illegal numbers racket leaves him unexpectedly in debt and beholden to a smalltime black drug dealer called Little Melvin.

Aside from Levinson's own public statements and an occasional mention in a film review, the anger at the core of *Liberty Heights* passed largely unnoticed at the time of the film's release. Perhaps it lies hidden beneath the texture of the three plotlines, veiled by the thick nostalgia for a Baltimore of old, sweetened by the young love between Ben and Sylvia. But even more striking than the critical silence on the force of Levinson's polemic on anti-semitism is the critical acclaim for his multicultural vision: *Liberty Heights* focuses on "the dreams, diversions and disappointments of an increasingly multicultural America," according to the *Los Angeles Times;* "the movie emerges as an accurate memory of that time when the American melting pot, splendid in theory, became a reality," writes Roger Ebert; "Barry Levinson has moved the ball forward beyond stereotypes," applauds the New York *Daily News.*[33]

But just what *is* the implied "reality" in Levinson's melting pot? In its paradoxical combination of antiblack insult with black power and Jewish powerlessness, the Nate Kurtzman subplot is symptomatic of the film's tacit politics. On the one hand, Nate spends most of the narrative uncomfortably under the control of

Little Melvin. Nate's fortunes run aground when, after he has sweetened the pot of his numbers game by adding a "bonus" digit, Little Melvin plays what turns out to be the winning number—plus the bonus—not for the usual one dollar or two, but, on a lark, for fifty. Nate now owes him one hundred thousand dollars, and much of this subplot is taken up with how in the world Nate will pay him his due. The black-over-white power relations here are accentuated when the Nate-Little Melvin narrative briefly intersects the Ben-Sylvia love story: the kids have gone out to a James Brown concert at the Royal in Nate's car; when he spots the familiar Cadillac, Melvin waits and then kidnaps them at gunpoint in a final effort to recover his money. Melvin wields his fundamental power not only by extorting a favorable deal from Nate, but also by playing sadistic games with his young Jewish hostage while he has him in custody.

But on the other hand, though Melvin holds all the cards—or tickets, or hostages—throughout the film, he is nonetheless depicted as Nate Kurtzman's unquestionable inferior. Nate easily outwits him in ploys designed to buy some time; and finally, when Nate cedes his entire numbers racket to Melvin as a payoff, Melvin proves incapable of running the business. So badly does he mismanage things that Nate is finally able to bully his way back into the racket, extracting an 80 percent cut just to save Melvin from his own gross incompetence. Disrespect toward African Americans glares in an exchange between Ben and Sylvia's father, a prominent black doctor who has driven the white boy home after finding him hiding in his daughter's closet. As the car pulls up to the Kurtzman house, Frank Sinatra happens to be playing on the car radio. Ben refuses to get out of the car—even after the doctor firmly tries to rush him along—because "You don't walk out on Frank, sir. It would be too disrespectful." This plays for laughs; *Liberty Heights* has no vocabulary for acknowledging Ben's remarkable disrespect for Sylvia's father, even if Sinatra was known at that time for his racial liberalism.

Nate Kurtzman's woes do not end with the recovery of his business: his dealings with the black drug dealer have attracted the attention of the FBI, who charge Nate with income tax evasion and violating the Mann Act (one of the dancers at his burlesque club, it seems, was a former prostitute). Although one of Van's well-connected gentile friends sums up the FBI's case in an even-handed analysis of race and persecution—"they just love to go after the Jews and the coloreds"—Little Melvin and Nate's sentences say it all. The African American responsible for the debacle is sent up for eight-to-ten months, the Jew, for eight-to-ten years.

Despite the sweetness of the Ben-Sylvia storyline, then, the political moral of *Liberty Heights,* however subtle, is unmistakable: set against the backdrop of *Brown v. Board of Education,* the film not only trivializes the politics of desegregation but in fact upholds the logic of *segregation.* Nate's downfall, cast as tragedy, is attributed to his unwise dealings with Little Melvin. Despite their feelings for each other, Ben and Sylvia fairly quietly accept the judgment that they must go their separate ways—a judgment articulated not only by both sets of parents but even by Little Melvin in the kidnapping scene. In the political cosmos of *Liberty Heights,* the desegregationist politics of 1954 finally boil down to one late scene at a restricted swimming pool, where Ben and his friends stride in and sit down at poolside, chests bearing the proud legend "J-E-W." If *Rocky* argued that one *can* equate the indignities faced by a Rocky Balboa with "the typical racist suffering that minorities of color have to endure almost every day of their lives," then *Liberty Heights* at once pays homage to—*and displaces*—the history of Civil Rights struggle with the defiant image of three Jewish youths "desegregating" a country club swimming pool. The sign prohibiting "Jews, Dogs, or Coloreds" really was "directed more at the Jews," a thesis mostly veiled and thus rendered all the more powerful by the film's light tone, thick nostalgia, and self-conscious racial "poignancy."

Such black-over-white depictions of American society have not gone unchallenged, of course. Spike Lee's Italian-American trilogy of *Do the Right Thing* (1989), *Jungle Fever* (1991), and *Summer of Sam* (1999) intervenes in exactly this cultural conversation about white ethnics and white privilege. A loving but too public sparring match between interracial lovers in *Jungle Fever*, for instance, ends with an NYPD cruiser screeching up and two white cops enforcing at gunpoint the "proper" relationship of black and white. Flipper and Angela's playful competition over whose "folk" can claim the better fighters (Patterson, Liston, and Ali? Or La Motta, Marciano, and Graciano?) evokes the realm of Italian-black relations that framed ethnic-revival films like *Rocky* and *Raging Bull.* Here, however, as Flipper stares down the barrel of the white policeman's pistol, for the crime of horsing around with his white girlfriend, there is no mistaking where the real power lies, nor the awesome weight of race in this equation. *Saturday Night Fever,* too, challenges the politics of the white underdog, when Tony Manero refuses first prize in a dance competition, recognizing that his whiteness, not his dancing, had dispatched the Puerto Rican competition: "Stephanie, that was rigged," he says, disgusted by his unfair advantage. But dissent notwithstanding, for thirty years and more the national cinema's wide universe of downtrodden white ethnics—from Rocky Balboa, to Sergio Leone's two-bit immigrant criminals, to Nate Kurtzman, young Frank McCourt, and the gangs of New York—constitutes an important part of the cultural context within which Americans have articulated and grappled with social questions of equality, virtue, and justice.

Ethnic Awakening

Although evident in cinema's visual iconography, cast of characters, and melting-pot dramas, the ethnic revival has been strangely absent from Hollywood storylines. There is one fleeting moment in *American Pop* when Little Pete, now generations removed from the Russian shtetl and from any sense at all of his origins, pauses in an alleyway to listen to the plaintive spiritual tenor of a chanting Hassid. The brief but prominent image of a Star of David visually emphasizes the momentary arrest of Pete's attention. He takes notice, seems moved or inspired, then goes straight to his piano to compose a song (Bob Seger's "Night Moves"!). But even such a minor gesture stands out for its direct reference to the inner stirrings of ethnic identity. Most common are texts like *The Godfather, Yentl, Moonstruck,* and *Mystic Pizza* that speak *to* the ethnic revival but not *about* it, that tap the resurgence of ethnic interest without ever depicting ethnicity itself as an interest whose intensity and salience are changeable at all. In this respect Hollywood film is the prototypical reifying medium: its masquerades at once create and depend on a set of social categories that must come across as self-evident and immutable. Ethnic-revival audiences, that is, have been presented cinematic Italians or Poles who are so naturally and completely Italian or Polish that they could never be members of an ethnic-revival audience themselves. Their ethnic identity is too "real" for that.

The most self-conscious exception here is David Mamet's film *Homicide* (1991), the story of a tough city detective who rediscovers his Jewish identity and passions while investigating a seemingly anti-semitic murder. Joe Mantegna plays Bobby Gold, a hard-boiled isolate on a big city police force, who happens onto a crime scene while working another case. An old woman has been murdered during an apparent robbery attempt at a corner convenience store in the city's black ghetto, and when Gold notices that she is wearing a Star of David, his relationship to this routine case gradually begins to change. Over the course of the film Gold will come to question the very meaning of the phrase "my people"— cop first, or Jew?—as the imperatives of these alternate tribal memberships increasingly conflict with one another.

Gold's world is roiling with hatred—blacks against whites, blacks against Jews, straights against gays (a high-ranking black official calls Gold a "kike" in one of the opening scenes, to which Gold's comrades quickly shoot back, "faggot!"), and even locals against feds ("FBI could fuck up a baked potato," sneers Gold). This general atmosphere of tribalism and hatred constitutes the backdrop against which Gold will sort out his identity, and against which Mamet himself will explore the meaning of self-ascription and allegiance. (*Homicide* is perhaps the first installment of Mamet's 1997 novel *The Old Religion,* an aggressively philosemitic treatment of the Leo Frank case.)[34]

Gold begins as a complete naif in matters Judaic. He certainly is not religious; even when on the receiving end of the epithet "kike," Gold seems to react to it, not as an ethnoracial slur, but as a kind of generic affront that requires a heated response.

("Motherfucker called me a 'kike,'" he says, dismayed, perhaps, but not seared, as though the fellow had just called him, for example, a motherfucker.) He may know what the Star of David is when he sees it, but he does not seem to know much else. "It never stops, it never stops, does it?" remarks the victim's grown son at the murder scene. "What never stops?" wonders Gold, to which the victim's granddaughter replies, simply, "Against the Jews."

This is soon to become Gold's case, in more ways than one. He is at first furious to discover that he has been reassigned to this case at the request of Dr. Klein, the victim's son, who reasons that since it involves "his people" Gold will be more thorough than another detective. "I'm 'his people?'" Gold protests. "I thought I was *your* people, Lou [that is, a cop]." Later Gold elaborates the point during a phone call to the station from the Kleins' house: "Hey, [they're] not *my* people, baby. Fuck 'em. So much anti-Semitism last four thousand years, we must be doin' somethin' to bring it about." But Klein's daughter overhears him, and her sharp rebuke proves the first turning point in Gold's ethnic odyssey. "Have you any shame?" she challenges him. "Do you hate yourself that much? Do you belong nowhere?" Gold now vows to find the killer; and he quietly begins to rethink his relationship to "his people."

The investigation draws Gold into a complicated affair involving Zionist activism and organized Nazism. Gold's interest is piqued when he uncovers some old photographs and invoices that link the elderly Klein woman to an Israeli gun-running scheme back in 1946. When someone fires shots at the Kleins' apartment from a nearby rooftop and Gold goes up to investigate, he finds in among the pigeon coops and chimneys a scrap of paper bearing the cryptic legend "Grofaz." Even if its meaning is unclear, the word's foreign ring suggests to Gold that there is some kind of conspiracy afoot, and that it has something to do with the Klein woman's Zionist activities. A flyer discovered in the vicinity of the murder ("Crime is caused by the ghetto—The ghetto is caused by the Jew") convinces Gold that the murder was somehow related to organized anti-semitism.

As Gold follows up these baffling leads, his partner begins to wonder why he cares so much about this "routine pop" at a corner store. He asks, "Is there a broad in it? What's the thing?" He doesn't get it. "Maybe you don't want to get it," Gold snaps, endorsing Klein's original view that the Jewish cop would devote more to this case than would anyone else. What, "because I'm not a Yid?" asks his partner incredulously. "It's just not your thing, Tim. It's my thing," says Gold. His thing, indeed. The intrigue draws Gold ever further into Jewish history and ever closer to his own desire to do something meaningful for "his people."

"Grofaz," it seems, is an arcane German acronym referring to Hitler—"the greatest strategist of all time"—and both the murder and the gunshots at the Klein house appear to be Nazi reprisals for the Kleins' political activities during the fight for Israeli independence. Jewish defense association members in the neighborhood fear that a list of names from the gun-running days of 1946—now in a file at the police station—maps these Nazi attacks, and that the document must be destroyed. Here Gold's tribal associations as "cop" and as "Jew" come into conflict. Although he balks at the violation of police values that his destroying the list—state's evidence—would represent, he does redeem himself as a good tribal Jew by consenting to plant a bomb in the local print shop that serves as a neo-Nazi headquarters.

But the denouement of *Homicide* passes ambiguous judgment on Gold's ethnic awakening. The final scenes recross the plotline of the drug case that Gold had been investigating before his reassignment to the Kleins, and the parallel plots both end on a note of kinship and betrayal: the drug dealer has been turned over to the police by his own mother (and he brutally shoots Gold in the chest for telling him so), just as Gold has been betrayed by his resurgent affinity for "his people" and their "Jewish" interpretation of the Klein case. When he returns to the stationhouse after recovering from his gunshot wound, a sneering police chief hands him an advertisement for "Grofazt" pigeon feed—the true referent of the partial scrap marked "Grofaz" that he had found among the coops on the roof. The true perpetrators of the "routine pop" at the corner store are being led away in cuffs. Israel, gunrunning, anti-semitism? Irrelevant. "The greatest strategist of all time?" A misreading. Gold is off the force.

It is tempting to read this ending as pure nihilism, to say that Gold speaks nothing but the plain truth when he says in agony, "It's all a piece of shit." But there is a more complicated statement here on ethnic identity and the nature of ethnic belonging. Facile comparisons are often drawn between Gold in *Homicide* and Detective Emily Eden, who goes undercover in Brooklyn's Hassidic community in Sidney Lumet's film *A Stranger among Us* (colloquially known as *Vitness*, a faux Yiddishism identifying the film as a knock-off of the Amish-country thriller *Witness*). Emily Eden is not Jewish herself, but like Gold she travels along an arc of personal discovery that begins with her hard-boiled incomprehension and bafflement at a tight community of Jewish "Others." Offering one young Orthodox man a non-kosher éclair, she prompts him, "Go ahead, cheat a little . . . What, you never break the rules?"

"Of course not."
"Never ever?"
"No."
"Wow. You guys got a lot of rules?"
"Actually there are 613 rules or commandments . . ."
"No shit."

Like Gold, Emily Eden does find herself drawn to the spirit and communal values of a community that she had at first derided (in her case, as looking "like an ad for Laura Ashley"); and like Gold, she redefines herself along the way—not converting, exactly, but *going native*. The final scene has her outside the precinct station on Knickerbocker Avenue talking about "waiting for my *bashert* [my intended—in this instance, a God-given soulmate]," appropriating both a word and a concept from the population of distinct, premodern "Others" whom she has come to know during her investigation.

Bobby Gold, on further reflection, is more closely akin to Emily Eden's Hassidic Others than to Emily Eden herself: despite the hard-boiled crudity of his language, Gold actually remains much closer to the young scholar's 613 commandments than to Emily Eden's secularized unbelief. In discussing the agile intellectual moves of anti-semitic thinking, Dr. Klein had derided the common logic by which Jewish alertness to anti-semitism is "always a fantasy" according to the non-Jew, an ethnic paranoia. If such paranoid fantasies prove true, then it is merely a coinci-

dence—the Jew is *still* a hopeless paranoid, in popular estimation. Klein's lament provides the interpretive legend for *Homicide,*
though Mamet casts the plot of the film as an inverse of Klein's
commentary: here, even if the Jew's fears prove *untrue,* still the
Jew is *not* a paranoid. If the ending seems to suggest that Gold's
"roots trip" has been either misguided or fully delusional, the fact
remains that neo-Nazi forces are on the loose in Philadelphia,
that neo-Nazi print shops are churning out anti-semitic literature, and that none of the non-Jews on the force seem to care as
much about it as Jews—including Gold—*naturally* do. Indeed,
Klein's initial estimation of the importance of having a Jewish detective on the case may prove mistaken when it comes to finding
the true perpetrators, but it is fully prophetic when it comes to
larger social questions of neo-Nazism and the activity of hate
groups.

Gold's Jewishness is not changeable after all—there is no ebb
and flow to his ethnic identity; rather it is essentialized and stable
throughout. Even Gold's former detachment from "his people"
had been, not a matter of cultural isolation or ethnic naivete, it
turns out, but an ethnic outsider's willful strategy for getting
along in Christian America. His was the revival not of a *lost* ancestral connection but of a defensively *suppressed* one—the suppression itself, here, representing just another sort of ethnic accent. "They said I was a pussy all my life," he explains in a
moment of ethnic confession that echoes the masculinist imperatives of Stallone's *Rocky.* "They said I was a pussy because I was a
Jew. And the cops, they'd say, 'send a Jew—might as well send a
broad on the job.'" Gold had become the department's hostage
negotiator precisely because of his unique angle of vision as the
perpetual ethnic outsider, "because I knew how the bad guys felt."

"You have your own home," he now rhapsodizes to an Israeli acquaintance. "Now what can that be like? To have your own country!"

In this respect *Homicide*—one of the few "ethnic-revival" films seemingly *about* ethnic revival—exemplifies the most important ideological work that celluloid ethnicity performs: there can be no "roots trip" in Hollywood, only genuine "roots"; there can be no heritage industries, only authentic heritage itself. Film's commitment to a realist ethos is radically inhospitable to the notion of social constructions of any kind, even as the medium traffics in images and narratives that themselves are nothing if not constructs. Cinema is a big put-on, as every audience member knows, but its put-on identities—like minstrels' masks—authenticate the very categories that it fabricates with such ease and with which it plays so mirthfully. (The role of Gold, it should be noted, is played by Joe Mantegna, an Italian.) Here is where motion pictures' aesthetic attributes ("cinema") become social and political attributes ("film"): "ethnic options," to take Mary Waters's formulation, are depicted as being anything but optional, just as the historical mutability of race becomes frozen and naturalized.[35] This reification of ethnoracial categories represents perhaps Hollywood's most portentous contribution to vernacular American discourses of peoplehood and difference.

If Erin Brockovich had not been the woman's real name, doubtless some screenwriter would have come up with it, or something like it—Tess McGill, Daisy Arujo, Mona Lisa Vito, Pearl Kantrowitz, Marge Gunderson, Molly Bellangocavella.[36] Ethnicity has become common currency in American film realism, a reliable cornerstone of "authenticity," sometimes in spacious and grandly conceived social tableaux, such as the ethnic wedding *(The Godfa-ther, The Deer Hunter)*, other times in throw-away narrative details as minute as a character's surname *(V. I. Warshawski)*. As a consequence, the cosmos of American film has increasingly become peopled with European immigrants and ethnics, even in the era of self-conscious "multiculturalism" (which, in Hollywood, has generally been taken to mean films about people of color). Despite a lengthy list of high-profile "multicultural" productions beginning with *The Color Purple, Dim Sum,* and *Glory* in the 1980s, Hollywood film has quietly constructed and reinforced a normative American subjectivity whose white ethnic accent was prefigured in *West Side Story*, where the Polish, Irish, and Italian youths of the Jets represent "an anthology of what is called 'American.'"[37]

Ethnic references assume many shapes: the cultural accents of ethnicity can be deployed in the name of comedy *(My Cousin Vinny)*, dramatic effect *(A Walk on the Moon)*, tragedy *(The Deer Hunter)*, or drollery *(Fargo)*. Ethnicity can conjure the exotic *(Sophie's Choice)* or the everyday *(Mystic Pizza)*; or film itself might mediate the contest between these two competing visions of a people ("We are not cute little characters, quaint or exotic," one Hassid tells Eden in *A Stranger among Us*). By the conventions of cinematic shorthand, ethnicity might communicate the constraining parochialism that one longs to escape *(Saturday Night Fever)* just as easily as it represents the communal warmth to which one yearns to return *(Crossing Delancey)*. But quite aside from the specifics of any one film, it is also worth contemplating celluloid ethnicity's cumulative effect—the totality of the cinematic cosmos, and the social portraiture of the nation that these ethnic references, multiplied by the hundreds, have created.

There is considerable political significance to public visibility—the parade, the street fest, or the carnival—as a means of staking a claim on public space, and so on civic belonging. On the Caribbean and American Indian spectacles of carnival and powwow, for instance, Rachel Buff writes, "Grass Dancers and Midnight Robbers, jingle dresses and steel bands: all arrive in an urban landscape that offers Indian and Caribbean people only partial access to power and citizenship. These festival denizens, bearing their complex and potent historical legacy, signify richly about alternative notions of citizenship, nationality, and home."[38] Can the occupation of *cinematic* space advance similar political claims? Certainly the stakes are quite different for Ukrainians, Poles, Italians, and other white ethnics, whose civic incorporation has followed a very different trajectory than the populations about which Buff was writing. Far different, too, are the politics, processes, and representations involved when such a spectacle is authored and orchestrated by a director and a production crew rather than by a politically mobilized group of ethnic denizens.

But by repetition such visual statements of ethnic presence may add up to a politics that is equally significant, even where the intent is not political per se. In this respect, Hollywood's reoriented gaze on the nation of immigrants might share a great deal in common with the reorientation taking place within academic disciplines like sociology and historiography in the 1960s and after. According to Martin Scorsese, for example, *Mean Streets* (1973) was "an attempt to put myself and my old friends on the screen, to show how we lived, what life was like in Little Italy. It was really an anthropological or sociological tract."[39] The internal "sociology" of ethnic film can vary a great deal from one instance to the next, as a comparison of two films like *Rocky* and *Jungle Fever* will attest. So, too, can the politics of ethnicity in film incline one way as readily as the other. "I wanted to say to Americans, 'Look what people gave up to get here,'" Elia Kazan once said of *America America*. "'Look what this country meant to the world. People would give up their lives to get here.'"[40] In Joe Eszterhas's tale of Hungarian immigrants, *Telling Lies in America* (1997), by contrast, a savvy Karchy Jonas warns his father, "This place is different, Papa. It's not like the old country. . . . This place isn't fair." But in either case, film has conjured an assemblage of Italians, Armenians, or Hungarians on American soil, and the resulting claim on national attention is not altogether different from the ethnic claims on civic space that annually take place on St. Patrick's, Israeli Independence, or Columbus Day; at the Feast of San Gennaro; or during powwows or Caribbean festivals.

The ethnic vision of cinema need not unfold on such a grand scale, however; nor is the significance of a group's New World presence necessarily diminished when the cinematic tableau is domestic and intimate rather than public and disruptive. With far more economy than Scorsese's Feast of San Gennaro, directors have frequently sought to convey a given character's entire life-world through one scene at the family dinner table, for example— domestic interiors, cuisine, kinship arrangements, patterns of familial authority, conversational styles. The dinner-table scene was a staple of televised ethnicity in shows like *Bridget Loves Bernie*, and in film, perhaps beginning with the split-screen dinner in Woody Allen's *Annie Hall* (1977). Having been forewarned that "you're what Grammy Hall would call 'a reeeeaaaal Jew,'" Alvy Singer nonetheless joins Annie and her family for Easter dinner. The Hall family's conversational style is reserved to the point of strangulation; topics of conversation range from a genteel appreciation of the meal itself ("dynamite ham," Singer has to concede) to "the swap meet." Through the eyes of Grammy Hall, Singer appears as an Old World, rabbinical, Orthodox Jew; while in a stage whisper to the camera, Singer remarks, "they look very American . . . nothing like my family." The screen then splits to depict the two family dinners: the Halls continuing on the left, the Singer family gesticulating, arguing, and overwhelming the staid silence of the Halls by their dinner-table commotion on the right.[41] Depictions of the family meal also hold a significant place in the action and, as it were, the sociology of films like *Saturday Night Fever*, *Brighton Beach Memoirs*, *Radio Days*, *Moonstruck*, *Avalon*, *Polish Wedding*, and *Kissing Jessica Stein*.

At stake here is not merely the ethnic presence but vernacular conceptions of the familiar, the normal. The split screen in *Annie Hall* derives its humor primarily from the extremity of the contrast: by their stark juxtaposition, both the Singers and the Halls become comic. But by the time Nia Vardalos was writing *My Big Fat Greek Wedding* (2002), the sensibility of the culture had shifted decisively toward the Singers. The WASPs have become the butt of the joke in a nation of immigrants for whom Greekness, here, stands in for the generic Otherness that is "us." This message is carried most forcefully in two dinner scenes: one, the deathly quiet dinner at Ian Miller's parents' house (during which, in their privileged ignorance, the Millers betray a ridiculous confusion among Armenians, Greeks, and Guatemalans), and the other, the feast at the Portokalos home, in which the WASPs' stiffness quickly gives way to an ouzo-inspired torpor. Tula Portokalos laments the oddball standing of her unassimilated family in an otherwise "normal" suburb; but by the logic of the film, in fact, Greekness assumes a kind of generic, fill-in-the-blank ethnic feel (indeed, in the television advertising for *My Big Fat Greek Wedding,* the word "Greek" in the film's logo rotates with an endless succession of alternative ethnicities—Jewish, Russian, Italian, and so on). This ethnically marked subject position becomes the normative "American" one. As Chaim Waxman has written of American Jews, "Paradoxical as it may appear, [heightened ethnic consciousness] was not a manifestation of the *rejection* of assimilation," but proof of its fulfillment. Ethnic difference *is* the assimilated norm.[42]

In his 1996 introduction to the screenplay for *Fargo,* Ethan Coen opens with a Coen family story about his Jewish immigrant grandmother's encounter with an African-American thief. Though perhaps puzzling at first, the anecdote finally goes to the heart of the Coen brothers' artistic vision, including their vision of Scandinavian *Fargo:* "picture the world as Grandma might have," Coen writes,

> as a great ball thinly crusted with oceans, soil and snow. People crawl across this thin crust to arrive at some improbable place where they meet other crawling people. Some of these people are Red Russians, some of these people are White Russians, some of these people are not Russians at all. They do various improbable things with and to each other, and later tell stories about the things they did, stories having greater and lesser fidelity to truth. The stories that are not credible will occasionally, however, turn out to be true, and the stories that *are* credible will conversely turn out to be false. Surely young Grandma . . . would not have believed anyone telling her that she would never in her life see Kiev, but *would* see

The Jolly Troll Smorgasbord & Family Restaurant in Minneapolis.[43]

Notwithstanding the Coens' unusual cinematic signature, there
may be no better brief on the shared sensibility that textures our
cinema in this nation of immigrants: the iconography—now posing as memory itself—of the various peoples who have crawled
across the earth's crust to arrive at this improbable place; the pervasive sense that the name "American" refers chiefly to this congeries of Red Russians, White Russians, and others, and that their
convergence in the New World necessarily reads something like
the musical emplotments of the Zuko-Alston or Rabinowitz-
Bellangocavella storylines; and the bedrock certainty that there
really is no such thing as waxing and waning ethnic "interest,"
only primordial attachment, even if white ethnicities tend to
meld into one another in a generic, "Euro-American" formation.
*Funny Girl, The Godfather, The Jazz Singer, Jungle Fever, Homicide,
Telling Lies in America, My Big Fat Greek Wedding, The Gangs of
New York*—the "improbable things" that people do "with and to
each other" in these stories are all cut from this cloth. Nothing is
made to seem quite so foreign as the perfectly ordinary, which,
like The Jolly Troll Smorgasbord & Family Restaurant, more often than not turns out to be "foreign" after all. Ethnicity has become one of the chief idioms by which American film, as Coen
said of *Fargo,* "aims to be both homey and exotic, and pretends to
be true."[44]

Chapter Three

Old World Bound

*I wanted to know only one thing of Italy: could I have
her back?*

—Robert Viscusi, *Astoria*

(1995)

The ethnic revival in American literature commenced in or
around July 1960.[1] That summer Harper and Row rescued Abraham Cahan's novel *The Rise of David Levinsky* (1917) from a
decades-long oblivion. In his introduction to the reissue, the historian John Higham instinctively invoked Hansen's Law of third-
generation interest in addressing a new readership. "Since 1950
the problems that weighed so heavily on the second generation
have ceased to be oppressive," he wrote:

> Discrimination has vastly diminished. The strains of extreme
> mobility have let up. A third generation, more self-assured,
> has come on the scene, and it is willing to recall what its fa-
> thers tried to forget. Once again we are reading about the old
> East Side . . .

Before writing *David Levinsky,* Abraham Cahan had completed the whole cycle of alienation and return that has separated the perspectives of succeeding generations. Perhaps we
are ready at last to read him, and to possess, through his di-
rectness and immediacy, a part of our national past.[2]

Although neither a literary critic nor a Jew himself, Higham
proved correct in his sense that American readers were newly
prepared to look back to the East Side immigrant ghetto. The
twenty years beginning with the 1960 reprint of *David Levinsky*
saw the meteoric rise of an American literature steeped in ethnic
sensibilities and interests—best sellers like *Portnoy's Complaint,*
The Godfather, Fear of Flying, and *Ragtime;* classroom standards
like Chaim Potok's *The Chosen* and *The Diary of Anne Frank;* and
popular reprints of long-neglected works like Henry Roth's *Call
It Sleep,* Anzia Yezierska's *Bread Givers,* Ole Rolvaag's *Giants in
the Earth,* Mike Gold's *Jews without Money,* Pietro DiDonato's
Christ in Concrete, and James T. Farrell's *Studs Lonigan.*

Abraham Cahan must be *plotzing.* Although he enjoyed modest success in his own lifetime, for the most part he lived in an age
when immigrant writers published immigrant stories in immigrant penny papers for an immigrant readership. Cahan was "discovered" and brought before a wider American audience in the
1890s by the "dean of American letters," William Dean Howells,
who was captivated by Cahan's first novella, *Yekl.* A bare handful
of other immigrant writers similarly achieved some New World
notoriety—Mary Antin, Morris Rosenfeld, Finley Peter Dunne,
Israel Zangwill.[3] But until the 1930s most immigrant writings
were confined to the pages of journals like the *Jewish Daily Forward, Zgoda, Irish World, Staats Zeitung,* or *Il Progresso,* where

they remain—mostly unknown—to this day. In later years, between the late 1910s and the 1950s, a second handful of immigrant and second-generation authors—now writing in English—
published their work in discrete volumes and found a modest
audience of both co-ethnics and "Americans." One thinks here
of proletarian novels like Mike Gold's *Jews without Money* or,
later, the social consciousness literature of the 1940s—Jo Sinclair's
Wasteland, Laura Z. Hobson's *Gentleman's Agreement,* or Farrell's
Danny O'Neill stories.[4]

Only as the ethnic revival verged toward multiculturalism would
ethnic narratives attain a certain cachet and occupy a celebrated
niche on the American literary scene. Series like Ballantine's "One
World, Many Cultures" would become commonplace, as would
the unbounded popularity of works like *The Joy Luck Club,*
Dreaming in Cuban, Native Speaker, When I Was Puerto Rican, or
Caramelo. Though the most widely acclaimed authors in this vein
are men and women of color, this wave carried along a number of
Euro-American authors, too: "rediscovered" writers like Anzia
Yezierska and Henry Roth, and contemporary writers like Mario
Puzo, E. L. Doctorow, Philip Roth, Erica Jong, Annie Proulx,
and Jeffrey Eugenides.

A comprehensive rendering of the ethnic revival in literature
would encompass volumes. Instead, here we seek to peer beneath
the surface of America's changing literary tastes, to map some of
the portentous uses of the "usable past" that the ethnic narrative
has made available. Like American film, much American literature began to traffic in a new currency of ethnic particularity as
"Americanness" itself. But, though its visuality might grant film
the greater ideological power, by its very commitment to the
word, fiction may be more revealing of the political and social
ideas attaching to "ethnic" themes.

In Samuel Ornitz's ghetto novel *Haunch, Paunch and Jowl* (1923, reprinted 1968), one stubborn and aspiring immigrant insists, "I don't need ancestors . . . I'm going to be an ancestor myself." Ancestral tradition and its disruptions are in part what novels like *Haunch, Paunch and Jowl* were about to begin with, but all the more when vintage explorations of the immigrant ghetto now resurfaced in popular reprint editions aimed at precisely those assimilated progeny for whom Ornitz's characters expected to "be ancestors." The peculiar ebb and flow of "ethnic" publication history gives the genre of immigrant fiction some unexpected layers and convolutions. It hails distinct audiences who might be separated by a generation, by decades, or by an immeasurable social distance, but who are yet united by powerful sentiments of collective destiny. The cover of the 1968 reprint characterizes *Haunch, Paunch and Jowl* as "an unsentimental classic about the ghetto that was the Lower East Side." But perhaps for that 1968 audience, the features that mark the novel as "unsentimental"—its unflinching portrait of the ghetto's ugliness, its harsh rhythms, its grittiness—represent sentimentality itself. As Cahan had written at the close of *David Levinsky,* "I can never forget the days of my misery. I cannot escape from my old self. My past and my present do not comport well."[5] Past and present collided anew in the rising phenomenon of popular ethnic literature. The 1920s business of "being ancestors" spoke in powerful, complicated ways to those late-century readers who were so engaged in the business of *finding* ancestors.

Assimilation Blues

The most significant ideological work of the ethnic literary revival included a rescripting of the culture's standard assimilation narratives. The bargain into which immigrants had entered on becoming "American" was not an altogether pleasing one, this newly popular genre suggested, nor was the immigrant's success an occasion for unalloyed celebration. This lament could take many different forms—an antimodern yearning for the earthier ways of the old country; a disquieting suspicion that the New World success ethic violated the more human and humane impulses of Old World tradition; or a worry that perhaps too much had been bargained away as the price of admission to this "blasphemous" new homeland, as Mario Puzo put it. Novels like Puzo's *Fortunate Pilgrim* (1964) or Harry Mark Petrakis's *A Dream of Kings* (1966) played the theme of American assimilation, not as a triumphal march, but in the unaccustomed mood of the blues. But their celebration of heroic ancestors and past ethnic grandeur could tend toward an ethnic chauvinism that nonetheless carried some triumphalist strains, especially in the context of Civil Rights–era discourses of group identity and social reward. Puzo's later best seller *The Godfather* (1969), for instance, may have argued that there was an ethnic past that was nobler than the present, but in the context of the times so did its loving depiction of *famiglia* values imply a preference for past ghetto dwellers over present ones. This is the dual malady of the assimilation blues: not just the blues the white ethnics felt, that their better days lay behind them in an imagined past before Americanization, but the blues they inflicted, as their antiassimilationism now played out across the backs of non-European Others in a tacit politics of invidious comparison.

A Dream of Kings is a keen expression of the common midcentury lament that the Old World may have represented a better, mightier place after all. The novel's controlling metaphor is

Leonidas Matsoukas's certainty that a dose of Greek sunshine will cure his desperately ill American son, Stavros. "The sun has risen but you cannot see or feel it . . . It is pale and without strength and beneath it even the weeds wither and die. But soon now, my beloved, we will leave this place of dark and rot, soon you will feel the sun of the old country, the sun of Hellas . . . You have never seen a sun like that . . . It warms the flesh, toughens the heart, purifies the blood in its fire. It will make you well, will burn away your weakness with its flame."[6]

Like Horace Kallen's view of "ancestral endowments" as a refuge from the modern world's "broadcast barbarisms," Petrakis thinks of Greekness largely as a haven from the modern. In a characteristic diatribe on "the curses of modern life," he catalogues "the tax collector, the bikini, the cinema, the television" among "the foul plagues of our horrendous age." Matsoukas's friend Cicero comments that "the old scourges were pestilence, the desert, and the wilderness . . . Today they are fear, boredom, hopelessness, and despair."[7] Even the worst that olden times had to offer was somehow nobler than the slings and arrows of today.

But this theme of antimodernism is not simply temporal. It is mapped geographically (mighty Greece and the pale United States), and then ultimately ethnologically, as ancestral endowment (mighty Greekness, pale Americanness). In addition to his faith in the sun of Hellas, Matsoukas finds a talismanic power in the sod of the old country, a jar of which he keeps on his desk, "pressing it in his palm at times of anguish and receiving great strength from the fierce black earth, kneaded with the tears and blood of centuries." He cherishes it "as if it contained some vibrant seed."[8]

Locale and personal endowment—Greece and Greekness—are

never altogether separable by Petrakis's narrative logic, and so *A Dream of Kings* establishes a powerful equation between the premodern, the Old Worldly, and blood-coursing Greekness itself. "We live in a dark age," comments Matsoukas, "a time of dwarfs afraid of life. A time of robots who cannot laugh or cry." Greeks, by contrast, represent "a race of mighty men." "We are living men, you and I, in a world of timid shadows," he tells Cicero. This magnificent bodyscape is finally inseparable from the landscape that reared it, Matsoukas contends, as he reflects on Stavros's lineage and on his prospects for revival:

> For [Matsoukas] knew the roots were strong, the ground was fertile, his seed was part of the olive, the myrtle, the honeycomb, and the huge luscious grapes. His heart contained the wind and the stars. The stream of his blood ran through the enchanted caves where nymphs played, over jagged promontories on which wild shepherds danced, into valleys stained with the blood of heroes and giants.[9]

Both the vintage of Matsoukas's migration (post–WW II) and the setting of the novel (a declining urban enclave rather than a bustling immigrant ghetto) set *A Dream of Kings* apart from the classic immigration saga. Nonetheless, Petrakis's contention that "to dance to a Cretan lyre is to invade the domain of the gods" echoes many other texts and reprints of the ethnic revival, in the terms by which it at once critiques the American present and identifies a singular power in ethnic heritage.[10] Like *Fiddler on the Roof, The Godfather,* and many others, *A Dream of Kings* measures and celebrates the distance between a particular ethnic tradition and the presumed properties of the mainstream New World. In offering up a portraiture of ancestral giants—not unlike Rolvaag's "giants in the earth"—such texts reinvented an ethnic Otherness for Euro-Americans on the New World scene, but now an Otherness worth embracing. Though finally a story of *hubris* in the Greek tradition, *A Dream of Kings* at once voices antimodern discontents *and* articulates their remedy in a newly discovered ethnic pride—a conception of selfhood rooted in a mythic genealogy of the ancients.

Mary Doyle Curran's novel *The Parish and the Hill* is a related treatment of this anti-assimilationist theme. The book originally appeared in 1948 and was reprinted in 1986, the year of the nation's lavish Statue of Liberty Centennial. The text's most direct resonance for readers of the 1980s was its proto-feminist narrative line (indeed, the reprint edition was published by The Feminist Press) and, one might say, its multicultural political sensibility. In her will, in fact, Curran provided that "proceeds from any publication after my death shall go to any creative project in the arts for American Indians, American Chinese, American Blacks and Puerto Ricans."[11] This political impulse toward cross-ethnic allegiance is very much in evidence in the text itself, a literary dirge on the ravages of Americanization.

Curran's anti-assimilationism registers on two planes. One is the mournful tone of the narrative itself, a keening for that world lost not when the Irish left the Emerald Isle but later, as America's "shanty Irish" became the "lace curtain" Irish of more "respectable" neighborhoods. The novel is structured as a wake (each chapter begins with the melancholic, "I remember . . ."), echoing not only the social ritual of waking the dead, but also the "American wake," in which those left behind in the Old World had lamented the passing of the emigrants to the New.[12] The novel wakes the bygone, not-yet-American world of the shanty Irish in a New England mill town.

The formal significance of the wake is announced as early as page two, when the narrator describes the wakes she recalls from girlhood: a room would be filled with "relics from the past," and the family Bible would be "carefully inscribed" with "all the names of the living and the dead." The novel itself will now evoke those relics and inscribe those names. "Only for a death or a birth was the Bible ever opened," Curran reports, after beginning the novel with an epigraph from Job. Later she explains more fully, "People went to wakes, not to mourn the dead, but to comfort the living. The function of attendance was to give tongue to the dead and say to the living the consoling things the dead could not say."[13] This figure-and-ground of consolation and mourning is at the very heart of the quotation from Job: "For there is hope of a tree, if it be cut down, that it will sprout again, and that the tender branch thereof will not cease." The sprout must have seemed uncertain indeed to Curran's generation in 1948; it probably seemed even more so to readers of the reprint in 1986.

But what precisely is this "tree" whose revival is so devoutly wished? Here is the second plane of anti-assimilationism in the novel. If the waning of the shanty Irish world provides the novel its wistful tones, then the narrative details of just how, exactly, that world passed away provide the novel its moral voice. Time alone did not ravage that bygone world, and the tree did not simply wither away; it was cut down. A rampant, soulless Americanization did the cutting. Curran introduces the encompassing villainy of the host culture on page two (one paragraph before the earliest reference to the wake), when the Irish emigrants "found that they had exchanged the English landlord for the Yankee mill owner." But though cold Yankee ways remain a chief evil throughout the tale, it is above all the *allure* that Yankee ways and self-satisfaction hold for certain emigrants that proves the most deadly New World poison. "You will never see those days again, for they are gone, all of them, and it's the Hill that did it," says Mary's grandfather, referring to Money Hole Hill, the area of second settlement for the emergent lace-curtain crowd, "the Hill with its pot of gold and Irishmen fighting Irishmen to get at it . . . trying to outdo the Yankees at their own game."[14]

Narrator Mary O'Connor is in a precarious position as this tempest brews: her father has been reared to despise the marks of his Irishness, but her mother is among the community's most vocal critics of lace-curtain aspiration. The family eventually does move to the Hill, and so the social tensions between the Parish and the Hill play out daily within Mary's own self-conception. Her grandfather and mother emerge as the moral voices of the novel, and as Mary's ardent defenders against the corruptions of this divisive New World. "We moved," Mary comments, "and I grew up on the Hill, with my grandfather and then my mother protecting me as well as they could against the misery and shame of being shanty Irish on Money Hole Hill. All of us . . . were introduced to an insecurity and an isolation that has not lessened during the years."[15]

But perhaps Curran's sharpest analysis concerns not the besieged *identity* of the Irish but their besieged social conscience. As Mary's mother remarks, "Put an Irishman on a spit and you'll find a lace-curtain Irishman to turn him." "Assimilation" in this view is mostly a gleeful and mean-spirited degradation of the one further down. "This country has plenty of room for all," argues Mary's grandfather, "but not enough if there's to be bitterness between those who have nothing but their hands to sustain them. There's enough bitterness between the Hill and the Parish as it is, with the Yankees looking down on the lace-curtains and the lace-curtains looking down on the shanties, and here now we have the shanties thinking themselves better than someone else so they can have someone to look down on. It's a disease, I tell you, and if you catch it you're done for."[16]

What is lost, ultimately, is the communal "oneness" that characterized the old Irish community. For Mary's grandfather, this tragic rage for hierarchy is rooted in capitalism and its acquisitive contagion: "It's the sense of ownership that divides people," he explains, as he urges Mary to share a bag of candy with some newly arrived Polish children. "It's happening in the Parish the same way as on the Hill. It's an evil that spreads, you will see. There will soon be no oneness there either." Mary's mother, too, sees an economic basis to this social rot: she hated the Irish of Boston even more than those of the Hill, for "it was to Boston that the lace-curtain Irish . . . moved when they rose in the hierarchy; that is, when they acquired more money and more intolerance."[17]

Like *A Dream of Kings*, then, *The Parish and the Hill* critiques the American present, whether Curran's present or that of her newfound audience of 1986. And like Petrakis, Curran offers up some towering figures to cling to in ancestral memory. Like the ritual of the wake itself, the narrative both mourns a loss (in this instance the loss of a communal spirit) and consoles the living (by recalling the possibility of a better, more generous Irishness). In doing so the work becomes strangely double-edged: it makes the plea for a more catholic social sensibility, but also marks that sensibility as unmistakably—perhaps parochially—*Irish* through its embodiments in the "parish" sensibilities of Mary's mother and grandfather. In this respect the reprint may have represented a "left" cultural agenda. But like other works by "unmeltable" white ethnics, it could also mesh with the more exclusive Eurocentrism that by 1986 had begun to mourn the passing of the traditional (and traditionally *white*) literary canon, Curran's intentions notwithstanding.

This counter-revolutionary aspect of the ethnic revival is more apparent still in the best-selling novels of Mario Puzo. Indeed, there is no better map to the ethnic literary revival than Puzo's 1964 novel *The Fortunate Pilgrim*, one of the earliest immigrant sagas addressed to the presumably "assimilated" generations of the mid-twentieth century. The novel chronicles the epic struggles of Lucia Santa Angeluzzi-Corbo in her resettlement from Italy to America. Mother of five, twice widowed, Lucia Santa survives countless New World travails in the squalid canyons of Manhattan's West thirties by the sheer force of her Old World spirit, before resettling her family to the suburbs of Long Island.

Much of the narrative lingers over the contrast between Old World and New, and especially over the fate of Italian ways and ideals in the face of what seems at times the magic, and at other times the corrosive power, of the American setting. "America, America, blasphemous dream," sighs Puzo. Chief among its blasphemies are a steady turning away from parental authority—"that lack of a sense of duty which flourishes in children brought up in America"—and an unbridled materialism whose effects neither generation can escape. Italian fortitude amid New World struggle and the history of this people as a tale of decline provide the running continuities in the novel's narrative. But even despite Puzo's emplotment of decline, America does not always come out the loser in comparison with Italy; the picture is mixed: "America was not Italy. In America you could escape your destiny. Sons grew tall and worked in an office with collars and ties, away from the wind and earth. Daughters learned to read and write, and wore shoes and silk stockings, instead of slaughtering the bloody pig and carrying wood on their backs to save the strength of valuable donkeys."[18]

Even more than the social and geographical distance separating America from Italy, the novel dramatically marks the distance between Manhattan's Italian colony and the suburban climes of New Jersey or Long Island. This epic of immigration opens in a harsh urban canyon "formed by two great walls of tenements" and closes with the family's arrival on suburban Long Island—*this* is the most portentous resettlement in a novel all about resettlement. Traversing the urban ghetto and the classic American suburb more thoroughly than *The Parish and the Hill*, *Fortunate Pilgrim* makes more explicit the social geography that was most salient to that upwardly mobile generation of the ethnic revival. The urban ghetto, not the Old World, represents the "premodern" —an equation Puzo emphasizes in a continual trope of the urban pastoral or "rooftop idyl."[19] Modernity itself is mapped onto the suburb, and it is a modernity with which many of Puzo's readers were surely familiar. If Puzo's West 30s are harsh in their squalor, their angular geometry, and their piercing metallic sounds, they are nonetheless the site of considerable romance (Larry Angeluzzi, the figure upon whom the narrative's cinematic opening "shot" lingers, rides a horse down this urban "canyon" "as straight and arrogantly as any western cowboy"). Puzo finds neither romance nor epic heroism in the suburbs, meanwhile, though everyone in the urban canyon seems eager to get there.

As in Curran's work, the most significant distances here are not spatial but socioeconomic—even, one might say, moral. Money "was God" in this world. "Money could make you free. Money could give you hope. Money could make you safe . . . Money was a new homeland." Ultimately it is this "new homeland" of modern comforts and suburban securities, not the more general homeland of blasphemous "America" as embodied by the Italian west side, that claims narrative attention. "Nobody is going to disgrace this family name," Octavia, the oldest of Lucia Santa's children, warns her brothers in a sharp lecture on education and discipline, "and you're not growing up ignorant guineas to live on Tenth Avenue the rest of your life." Lucia Santa herself objects to Octavia's harsh judgment of "ignorant guineas," but nonetheless adds, "At your age I was chasing goats and digging vegetables and shoveling manure. I killed chickens and washed dishes and cleaned houses. School to me would have been like moving pictures . . . So: know your good fortune."[20]

But the "fortune" of mobility, as Lucia Santa knows, is not simply "good." Those "more fortunate relatives who had achieved success and moved to their own homes on Long Island or in Jersey" usually appear as a cautionary tale, both in Lucia Santa's consciousness and in the narrator's running commentary.[21] This is sometimes a matter of modern loss, echoing the antimodern sensibilities of Petrakis and Curran. "In a few years," remarks Puzo, "the western wall of the city would disappear and the people who inhabited it would be scattered like ashes—they whose fathers in Italy had lived in the same village street for a thousand years, whose grandfathers had died in the same rooms in which they were born." More often, though, the blight of the suburb is a matter of moral decay. Gazing on the suburban dwelling of a villainous relative who, in the guise of family succor, had attempted to steal Lucia Santa's son through a disingenuous, "temporary" foster arrangement, Lucia Santa reflects, "Ah, what a pretty house it was for the devil to live in." Nor is such devilry unusual in the suburbs. On the occasion of a wedding, "everyone on Tenth Avenue came to pay respects, and even those proud relatives who owned their own homes on Long Island come to gossip and lord it over the poor peasants they had left so far behind." Silvio Barbato, an upwardly mobile and ever-aspiring doctor, exhibits a similar lack of compassion for those he has left behind in his family's flight to the suburbs. He considers himself "too intelligent in his own right to be sentimental about these southern Italians who lived like rats along the western wall of the city."[22] It is in this promised (waste)land that Lucia Santa and her children will finally arrive, when they move to Long Island in the novel's closing paragraph.

Lucia Santa's thoroughly entwined hope and lament for a more comfortable world—her wish for healthful ease, and yet her pride in the strength and morality that derive from adversity—constitute a kind of myth of origins for Puzo's now assimilated, mid-century readership. The dance step is a complicated one, and the ambivalences involved are themselves emblematic of the contending political logics of the ethnic revival. The narrative may deplore the modern suburb, and so resonate with the antimodernism of so many other texts of the ethnic revival; but so does it celebrate the fortitude of those who made it there, offering up a gallery of epic-heroic forebears as solace to a now-suburban readership. Thus in the context of a postindustrial, rapidly suburbanizing America, *The Fortunate Pilgrim*, like *A Dream of Kings* and *The Parish and the Hill*, tacitly argues that, though their "modern" lives be pale and bloodless, present-day white ethnics nonetheless descend from a bold and admirable pedigree—as Petrakis put it, from "a race of mighty men."

But in a hint of the ethnic revival's rightward tilt in ensuing years, such texts implicitly compare the "mighty race" of yesterday's ghetto dwellers with the ghetto dwellers of today. This myth of ethnic origins, so soothing in a bureaucratized, mass-consumed, postindustrial world, might be readily re-packaged and redeployed as a slur on the character of contemporary black, Asian, and Latino city dwellers, particularly a few years after *The Fortunate Pilgrim* appeared, in the wake of the 1960s urban rebellions and the 1965 Immigration Act. If the myth of immigrant origins created and popularized an appealing white Otherness for ethnics to occupy, it also suggested a quite *un*appealing racial Other for them to attend to in public discussion and policy debates.

One year after *The Fortunate Pilgrim* appeared, in an "Afterword" for a reprint of Mike Gold's *Jews without Money* (originally 1930), Michael Harrington delineated the distinctions between the "old" and the "new" poverty, quite frankly taking up America's newfound romance with the old. Amid the "rediscovery" of poverty in the United States in the 1960s, it was easy to see the "distinctive, and in many ways hopeful, misery" that had reigned in the immigrant ghettos earlier in the century. The "old" poverty was the experience of "an adventurous poor" seeking "streets paved with gold." Disillusioned though many may have been, "there was still an expanding economy and the possibility of battling one's way out of the ghetto." "For all the sadness of Gold's Lower East Side," Harrington contended, "many of its people prevailed over the environment . . . and perhaps today they suffer from a middle class hunger of the spirit rather than from the old impoverishment of the body."[23]

Despite his recognition that "the poverty of 1960 is not like the poverty before World War One," Harrington notes one element in Gold's narrative that perhaps left a deeper impression on American discourse: "even in [Gold's] dark view of the slum there are those moments of collective action and self-help which ultimately made the old poverty so dynamic."[24] The imaginative leap from "dynamic poverty" to "dynamic people" has been fairly thorough, as witnessed throughout the post–Civil Rights era, both in discussions of the "underclass" and in debates over the newest immigration. A widespread romance with more persevering, and more "assimilable" and "dynamic," European immigrants of a bygone era has been critical to both. Perhaps the present-day status that derives from this mythology has over time been the greatest fortune of all for Puzo's "fortunate pilgrims." The ideological portent of this revision is more visible still in Puzo's best-selling novel *The Godfather* (1969).

The Godfather is rarely considered a specimen of ethnic literature in quite the same vein as *Christ in Concrete* or *Mercy of a Rude Stream*. Too popular, perhaps; too ugly. But by stamping new meanings on Italianness just as the ethnic revival was cresting, Puzo creates "ethnic literature" par excellence. Among Italian Americans, *The Godfather* is best known as a slander sheet responsible for the widespread and stubborn legend of Italian criminality.[25]

But in sharp contrast to "that lack of a sense of duty which flourishes in children brought up in America," as depicted in Puzo's earlier novel, "family" itself—*famiglia* values—seems one of the keys to the titanic success of *The Godfather*. Strangely, for many non-Italians, criminality drops out of the picture altogether, notwithstanding Italian Americans' well-founded apprehensions. As the sociologist Mary Waters discovered in her 1990 investigation of white ethnic identity, like the Italian-American respondents, "the non-Italians mentioned the warm, happy extended family, which they viewed as a source of support for individuals. No one mentioned a drawback to this strong family . . . In fact, 'Italian' was the most common response by people to the question, 'If you could be a member of any ethnic group you wanted, which one would you choose?'"[26]

There is no small irony here, as Puzo himself held an unromantic view of Italianness and the Italian family. "As a child and in my adolescence," he wrote in "Choosing a Dream," "None of the grown-ups I knew were charming or loving or understanding. Rather they seemed coarse, vulgar, and insulting." Later in life, when he was exposed to "clichés about lovable Italians, singing Italians, happy-go-lucky Italians, I wondered where the hell the moviemakers and storywriters got all their ideas from."[27]

The Corleones, of course, are not exactly "singing," "happy-go-lucky" Italians, but many Americans saw them in a romantic vein. The compelling notion of *famiglia* that Americans took away from *The Godfather* is no doubt borne partly of what *Time* called "the assimilation blues"—the atomization of American social life; the isolation of the nuclear family; the malaise of late-twentieth-century suburban culture; the ravages of geographic mobility to the upwardly mobile, college-going family. Even Gambino suspected as much: Americans "yearn for a sense of security that comes from belonging. As a result the ordine della famiglia of Italian-Americans is most appealing to them, even though they see it almost exclusively in its corrupted form in the media splashings of Mafia stories."[28] Thus the romance of the family—especially the Italian family, and even the "crime family"—represents a second cousin to the antimodernism that characterized Petrakis's novel *A Dream of Kings.*

But there is another, profoundly political significance to "family" in this period: beginning in 1965, the notion of the ethnic family was intimately linked to the Moynihan Report and all it implied about social health and fit citizenship. That Moynihan characterized the black family as "a tangled web of pathology" is well remembered.[29] Forgotten is how quickly this line was taken up, and how it influenced national discussion not only of "blackness" but of "family" as well. In the second half of 1965 (Moynihan's report appeared in June), the *New York Times* ran fifteen articles on the report and on the black family—roughly one every week and a half. By the time *The Godfather* appeared in 1969, the report had been broadly covered in the full spectrum of American print media, including *Time, Newsweek, Life, Look, The New Yorker, Harper's, The Nation, The New Republic, Christian Century, Commonweal, America, Science News, The National Review, New York Times Magazine, Dissent, The Wall Street Journal,* and the *New York Review of Books*.[30] This is the context within which Americans became acquainted with the Corleones, and within which we must interpret the allure that the "crime family" has had for many non-Italians.

Lest this reading of *The Godfather* against the Moynihan Report seem far-fetched, consider the sentiment of Puzo's fictional Don of Detroit during a heated discussion of the drug trade: "In my city I would try to keep the traffic in the dark people, the colored. They are the best customers, the least troublesome and they are animals anyway. They have no respect for their wives or their families or for themselves. Let them lose their soul with drugs." The narrator soon explains that "Negroes were considered of absolutely no account, of no force whatsoever. That they had allowed society to grind them into the dust proved them of no account."[31]

The purpose of this discussion is not to assign racist intent to Puzo, but rather to underscore the currency of Moynihan's reasoning on "blackness," and to point up the ways in which the saga of European ethnic fortitude was built in close conjunction with a particular—if often tacit—understanding of African Americans. Whatever other ingredients might go into this vision of Italian fortitude in *The Godfather, famiglia* values are crucial. Whereas African-American culture presents a picture of tangled pathologies, Puzo's crime family offers up a strict code of honor, patriarchal authority, familial loyalty, and sense of duty, and—perhaps above all—self-help: "A man who is not father to his children can never be a real man"; "Tell the old man I learned it all from him . . . He was a good father"; "it had never occurred to him to desert his wife and children. He was too Italian"; "now she belongs to her husband. He knows his duties"; "The Bocchicchios' one asset was a closely knit structure of blood relationships, a family loyalty severe even for a society where family loyalty came before loyalty to a wife"; and "things went bad and I had to fight for my family."

> "And what do you believe?" Kay asked quietly.
> Michael shrugged. "I believe in my family."[32]

Puzo's familial romance, it is worth noting, differs only in degree, not in kind, from many other texts of the ethnic revival. One thinks of *Fiddler on the Roof*, for instance, whose famous musical paean to "Tradition!" includes separate verses on "the papa," "the mama," "the son," and "the daughter"—not only the division of labor governing the family's daily existence, but also the undying devotion each holds for the others. This construction of an Italian (or, more broadly, a European) "us" drew much of its power from its narrative trappings as a recovered memory. Over the decades it could be deployed as an invidious comparison between white ethnics and blacks or between white ethnics and the new immigrants, just as surely as it found its earliest articulation as an invidious comparison between "we" who took care of our own and clawed our way up and "they" who "have no respect for their wives or their families" and who have "allowed society to grind them into the dust." Here, then, is a striking example of what the sociologist Richard Alba meant by a romanticized European ancestral script defining "'the rules of the game' by which other groups will be expected to succeed in American society."[33]

Private and Public

If ethnicity textured the dominant discussion of citizenship and public virtue, so in the realm of literature did it lend a particular cast to an emerging discussion of *private* morality. Philip Roth's novel *Portnoy's Complaint* (1969) and Erica Jong's novel *Fear of Flying* (1973) are two best sellers that chart the mainstreaming of the sexual revolution. But while most will remember Alexander Portnoy's "extreme sexual longings" and Isadora Wing's fantasies of "the zipless fuck," fewer will recall the extent to which both novels represent extended and quite intimate meditations on the meanings and the sorrows of Jewish identity. The link here is not coincidental; nor is it coincidental that both novels unfold in a cosmos defined by psychoanalysis (Roth's novel takes the form of a monologue delivered on a psychiatrist's couch; Jong's is set at an international psychoanalytic convention in Vienna). The general opening up of the culture that resulted in increasingly frank discussions of sexuality, frank admissions of neurosis, frank explora-

tions of desire, and frank lamentations of familial failing represented the same dissolving of barriers between public and private
that also characterized emergent discussions of personal, "ethnic"
experience. Having "poured into Gentile territory as the Scotch-
Irish had poured through the Cumberland Gap," Roth put it in
Goodbye, Columbus, Jews—like other white ethnics at the time—
were now ready to reveal the ethnic impulses that had been re-
pressed inside their closed, seemingly "assimilated" mid-century
homes. In publicly rendering the private, then, these acts of ethnic testimony in *Portnoy's Complaint* and *Fear of Flying* have a
great deal in common with the stand-up routines of Joan Rivers
(who cracked *The Tonight Show* in 1965); the films of Woody Allen (who first developed his psychocomedy of Jewish neurosis in
The Sleeper in 1973); the novels of sexual-political awakening by
Alix Kates Shulman, Marge Piercy, Mary Gordon, or Marilyn
French; and even the ethos of self-revelation in *The Sopranos.*[34]

In her study of the sexual revolution in middle America, the
historian Beth Bailey posits a number of long-term developments
beginning in World War II that might usefully link the "pluralism" represented by a relaxing of moral codes on the one hand,
with the pluralism represented by ethnic reverie on the other.
The altered cultural geography of postwar America—accelerated
mobility, changing relationships between "local" and "national"
customs, enforced cosmopolitanism, and Americans' increasingly
besieged "local certainties"—was a vital precondition for the dramatic revision of sexual mores in the 1960s. "The fact that people who had never traveled more than a hundred miles from
their homes [now] moved across the country or across the world,
where they lived in close proximity to people from vastly different backgrounds, fundamentally altered the nation's cultural

landscape," she writes of the war. This jarring loose from tight, local moorings transformed the postwar world: the "new awareness of different ways of life precipitated by the war destabilized local certainties, whether about some small point of etiquette or about unexamined prejudices." The resulting postwar "conflicts over cultural authority and control" represented the opening battles of the sexual revolution.[35]

Students of American ethnicity, however, might also note that the erosion of the "local" is precisely what the insistent, antimodern rootedness of the roots phenomenon promised to redress. Beth Bailey's postwar world would be entirely legible to the likes of Harry Petrakis and Mario Puzo, for instance, and so it follows that the public articulation of emergent sexual sensibilities (the harvest of rootlessness, in Bailey's scheme) might share a vocabulary with the ethnic reverie's fixation on roots. This is at least part of what is happening in *Portnoy's Complaint* and *Fear of Flying*.

Bailey further argues that, as "more Americans than in any previous era found themselves in close and enforced contact with others not like themselves," standards of sexual custom and morality became yet another of the ways—alongside race, ethnicity, religion, or class—that people might define one another as being "not like themselves."[36] It is not just that Americans invented a new, postwar pluralism out of an emergent and increasingly frequent necessity of building bridges across lines of "difference"; but indeed in matters of sexuality as in other matters, "difference," not sameness, gradually became a more common baseline assumption. As Margot Adler prefaces her memoir of the 1960s, "the sex, the drugs, and the rock and roll were but the outer trappings of a rich world of ideas." For Adler, whose own trek led from a Jewish progressive upbringing on the Upper West Side, to

Berkeley's Free Speech Movement, to the feminist-antimodernist accents of neopaganism, among these ideas was the recognition that "the world is infinitely varied and that variety is to be cherished; that there are an infinite number of ways to live, to love, to create structures of society and government and community; that change is the only constant and if there is a 'prime directive,' it is to respect difference, to let others choose their own path in freedom, and to assume that there are always more possibilities than one can assume."[37]

A secularized language of the social sciences—and especially psychiatry—replaced the moral absolutes of religious discourse when it came to sexuality. This ascendant therapeutic culture posited a gray area between the "normal" and the "deviant," introducing "criteria for judgment about sexual behavior that made it difficult to draw clear distinctions between 'right' and 'wrong.'"[38] The moral relativism of this rising regime was closely aligned with the cultural relativism of ethnoracial experience. Moreover, psychiatry's emphasis on individuated—and narrated—experience itself ensured that a secular epistemology of diverse sexualities would be intimately connected to a social-scientific epistemology of plural ethnic cultures. Psychiatry's "talking cure" *is* ethnic autobiography. This, too, is part of what is happening in *Portnoy's Complaint* and *Fear of Flying*.

So inseparable is Alexander Portnoy's psychosexual condition from the ethnic past from which he has sprung, for instance, that there seems a natural analogy between the wailing of the tortured son and the wailing of the seasick steerage passenger: "look in through the portholes and see us there, stacked to the bulkheads in our bunks, moaning and groaning with such pity for ourselves, the sad and watery-eyed sons of Jewish parents, sick to the gills from rolling through these heavy seas of guilt—so I sometimes envision us, me and my fellow wailers, melancholics, and wise guys, still in steerage, like our forebears—and oh sick, sick as dogs."[39]

Ultimately, of course, the "Jewish parents" of this passage will give way to the towering figure of the Jewish mother alone. Indeed, the figure of Sophie Portnoy was to become the most powerful negative icon for a rising generation of Jewish feminists.[40] "What are they, after all, these Jewish women who raised us up as children?" Portnoy asks, in what is perhaps the most misogynistic of his many misogynistic reveries. Only in America "do these parents, our mothers, get their hair dyed platinum at the age of sixty, and walk up and down Collins Avenue in Florida in pedalpushers and mink stoles—and with opinions on every subject under the sun . . . think of them as cows, who have been given the twin miracles of speech and mah-jongg."[41]

For Alexander Portnoy, then—as, in fact, for Abraham Cahan's Yekl before him—the psychodrama of Jewishness and the multifold interpretation of its meanings will be played out on the sexualized field of women's bodies, beginning with the figure of his mother, Sophie.[42] Unlike Cahan, however, Roth can articulate this realm of ethnosexual desire in an imagery and a lexicon unprecedented in their frankness. It is not just that Portnoy will cast his musings on Jewishness according to a logic of coupling: the *goyim* "go bouncing off in their bouffant taffeta dresses to the Junior Prom with boys whose names are right out of the grade-school reader, not Aaron and Arnold and Marvin, but Johnny and Billy and Jimmy and Tod . . . These people are the *Americans.*" Nor is it merely that he peers across this chasm of perceived "difference" and wonders, with both shame and desire, how non-

Jewish women got "so gorgeous, so healthy, so *blond?*" Rather, Portnoy's every thought on the outsider status of the Jew and the aspired world of true belonging will finally come to rest on some ethnoracial trope of sexuality: "O America! America! It may have been gold in the streets to my grandparents, it may have been a chicken in every pot to my father and mother, but to me, a child whose earliest movie memories are of Ann Rutherford and Alice Faye, America is a *shikse* nestling under your arm whispering love love love love love!"[43]

Thus his quest for American self-fulfillment will take the form of a sequence of relationships with non-Jewish women—first, a coalminer's daughter whom Portnoy affectionately calls "the Monkey," and later a stand-in for "middle America" itself in the person of Kay Campbell, an "exemplary person" of the sort that TV taught a generation of Americans to view as "normal." Thus, too, both sexual relationships will be heavily influenced by Portnoy's attention to issues of "difference," rootedness, and belonging. Among the pastimes shared by Portnoy and the Monkey is an effort on his part to tutor her in literacy, in history—ironically, in her "roots"—an informal lesson plan imagined under the title "Humiliated Minorities, an Introduction" or "The History and Function of Hatred in America," whose purpose is "to make this daughter of the heartless oppressor a student of suffering and oppression." Portnoy's momentary hope is that such a course will result in the perfect Americanness, which is to say, the perfect *coupling:* "she puts the id back in Yid, I put the *oy* back in *goy.*"[44]

As for Kay Campbell, "*this* is what it means to be a child of *goyim*, valedictorian of a high school in Iowa instead of New Jersey; yes, this is what the *goyim* who have something have got!" Kay was "*rooted,* that's what I'm getting at! Joined by those lineman's legs to this American ground!" Ultimately Portnoy's personal essay in conquest is every bit as geopolitical or ethnoracial as it is sexual: "What I'm trying to say, Doctor, is that I don't seem to stick my dick up these girls, as much as I stick it up their backgrounds—as though through fucking I will discover America. *Conquer* America—maybe that's more like it. Columbus, Captain Smith, Governor Winthrop, General Washington—now Portnoy."[45]

Portnoy's quest ends on his trip to Israel with an invigorated understanding of the Jewish "folk," but also, ironically enough, with a bout of impotence and a romantic rejection. Here he comes to grips with the "implausible fact" that he is "in a Jewish country." "Who ever heard of such a thing?" asks this would-be Columbus, having suffered the longings of the outsider in the United States solely *because* of his Jewishness. In Israel he experiences the thrill of seeing "the faces of Eastern Europe, but only a stone's throw from Africa!" He realizes that here, "hey, here *we're* the WASPS!" But his "final downfall and humiliation" come in the form of a tough Israeli woman named Naomi, whom Portnoy picks up hitchhiking near a kibbutz at the Lebanese border. As ever, Portnoy expects to play out his Jewish identity quest on the body of this "admirable and brave girl": "Why don't I marry her and stay?"[46]

But this tough Israeli has ideas of her own. To Naomi, Portnoy's entire social bearing represents a "ghetto" whose very existence the nation of Israel was meant to overcome. She gives Portnoy to understand "that I was the epitome of what was most shameful in 'the culture of the Diaspora.' Those centuries and centuries of homelessness had produced just such disagreeable men as myself—frightened, defensive, self-deprecating, unmanned and corrupted by life in the gentile world." Diaspora Jews like Portnoy "had gone by the millions to the gas chambers without ever raising a hand against their persecutors . . . The Diaspora! The very word made [Naomi] furious."[47]

Tired of "never being quite good enough for The Chosen People," Portnoy decides to exact a revenge of sorts by raping Naomi, but he discovers that he "can't get a hard-on in this place." "Where other Jews find refuge, sanctuary and peace, Portnoy now perishes!"[48] Alexander Portnoy's personal sexual history is mapped out from assimilationist suburb to Israeli kibbutz; his trajectory from tortured Jewish son, to experimental interethnic lover, to impotent "ghetto" Jew is defined by sexuality all along the way. The self-revelations of the psychoanalytic monologue link the ethnic with the sexual at every turn. The publication of this monologue as a best-selling novel demonstrates just how far the public discussion of these private realms had been made to stretch under the twinned regimes of sexual revolution and the new ethnic consciousness.

Although Alexander Portnoy is certainly depraved, Roth's intertwining of ethnic and sexual yearnings in *Portnoy's Complaint* is hardly as idiosyncratic as his chief protagonist's predilections. Isadora Wing's "quest of joy and her own true self" (as the *New York Review of Books* had it) in *Fear of Flying* was similarly parsed out along lines of sexuality and Jewish discovery. Erica Jong herself identified Saul Bellow and Philip Roth as the "gods of my literary pantheon," and Isadora Wing further marks Jong's relationship to Roth as she reflects on her own unsettled childhood: "When I think of my mother I envy Alexander Portnoy. If only I had a *real* Jewish mother—easily pigeonholed and filed away—a real literary property."[49] On the one hand, Wing's Jewishness enters the narrative in conjunction with her feminism: as "men have *always* defined femininity as a means of keeping women in line," it becomes significant indeed that "in the most paranoid societies (Arab, Orthodox Jewish) the women are kept completely under wraps (or under wigs) and separated from the world as much as possible." A decidedly *Jewish* femininity is at least part of the question to which Wing's feminism—including its emphasis on liberated sexuality—is the answer.[50]

On the other hand, the complex of ethnicity and sexuality in *Fear of Flying* becomes yet more deeply emplotted in the psycho-analytic fabric of Wing's self-exploration. Precisely like Portnoy, Wing will trace the threads of her disaffection back to her Jewish home, and especially to the figure of her mother, Judith Stoloff White: "Of course it all began with my mother . . . My love for her and my hate for her are so bafflingly intertwined that I can hardly *see* her." Wing could not rebel against Judaism, exactly, "because I hadn't any to rebel against"; nor could she *simply* "rail at my Jewish mother because the problem was deeper than Jew-ishness or mothers."[51] But both Jewishness and mothers have an awful lot to do with it, and so Wing's journey too is charted ac-cording to the increasingly public coordinates of ethnicity and sexuality—a tale of ethnic revival and sexual revolution for an au-dience so recently revived and revolutionized.

That ethnic revival and sexual revolution are entwined in the novel are telegraphed in Wing's first example of the "zipless fuck": the imagined scenario takes place in a "grimy European train compartment" between "a pretty young widow in a heavy black veil and a tight black dress which reveals her voluptuous figure," and a "tall, languid-looking soldier" who has boarded the train "in a town called (perhaps) CORLEONE." The balance of the narrative suggests that it is no coincidence: if *Fear of Flying* is a postrevolution treatment of sexual freedom, so is it a pre-*Holocaust* (the miniseries) meditation on the timetables and trajectories of Jewish history. Wing's ethnic awakening occurs on a sojourn in Heidelberg, as her own Jewishness and the spectral presence of Germany's Nazi past collide in her consciousness at every turn. "Before I lived in Heidelberg, I was not particularly self-conscious about being Jewish," she explains. Wing had had "a fairly ecumenical childhood," having "learned the phrase 'Family of Man' before my training pants were dry"; she had learned a few scraps about Jewishness from reading *Goodbye, Columbus,* and Bernard Malamud's *Magic Barrel.* But she had been distant enough from her own Jewishness that her grandfather, "a former Marxist who believed religion was the opiate of the masses," later "accused me (in his sentimental Zionist eighties) of being 'a goddamned anti-Semite.'"[52]

"But like it or not," Wing recognizes, "[Judaism] was the only religion I had. We weren't really Jewish; we were pagans and pantheists . . . And yet with all this, I began to feel intensely Jewish and intensely paranoid (are they perhaps the same?) the moment I set foot in Germany." At bottom she was "every bit as Jewish as Anne Frank." Wing had been living in Heidelberg "almost as if it were a second home . . . as if I had spent my childhood in Germany, or as if my parents were German. But I was born in 1942, and if my parents had been German—not American—Jews, I would have been born (and probably would have died) in a concentration camp—despite my blond hair, blue eyes, and Polish peasant nose. I could never forget that either." In Germany, "For the first time in my life, I became intensely interested in the history of the Jews and the history of the Third Reich."[53]

While in Heidelberg, Wing began to entertain the fantasy that she was "the ghost of a Jew murdered in a concentration camp." She began to look on her German neighbors and strangers in the marketplace through a very particular lens: *"But we knew nothing about what was happening to the Jews,* they told me again and again . . . And I believed them, in a way. And I understood them, in a way. And I wanted to watch them all die slow and horrible deaths." In Germany, even in the simplest movements about the city, Wing admits, "I was tracking down my own past, my own Jewishness in which I had never been able to believe before."[54]

As with Alexander Portnoy in the homier climes of suburban North America, for Wing these themes of history and identity are deeply entwined with issues of love and sex. "I would have followed him anywhere," she says of one lover. "Dachau, Auschwitz, anywhere." In an exchange with this same man, he chances to ask,

"Where are you from?"
"New York."
"I mean your ancestors."
". . . Polish Jews on one side, Russian on the other."
"I thought so. You *look* Jewish."
"And you look like an English anti-Semite."

Moments later she confides to him, "You're the only person I've ever met who thought I looked Jewish"; she confides to her readers, "His thinking I looked Jewish actually excited me. God only knows why."[55]

In matters ethnic as in matters sexual, Wing wishes to be true and to be known. The question of "looking Jewish" comes back, not only to the issues of sexuality and Otherness that have been brewing throughout the narrative, but, quite explicitly, to the issues of identity, history, and violence that have haunted Wing throughout her sojourn in Heidelberg. My nose, she reflects, "betrays the genetic contribution of some pigfaced Polish thug who raped one of my great-grandmothers during some long-forgotten pogrom in the Pale." However different the two narrators may be, Isadora Wing, like Alexander Portnoy, finds the realms of sexuality and ethnic identity inseparable in the modalities of self-narration. But whereas Portnoy tends to turn inward in self-absorption or self-pity, Wing gestures outward, toward the sweep of Jewish history, concentration camps and all. Wing's declaration that "sex was no final solution" resides somewhere in the same psychic realm as Alexander Portnoy's identification of America as "a *shiksa* nestling under your arm" (and, for that matter, Betty Friedan's feminist protest that the suburban American home was "a comfortable concentration camp").[56]

The new ethnicity and postrevolution sexuality have converged in myriad ways in the decades since *Portnoy's Complaint* and *Fear of Flying*—in the work of "sex-and-shopping novelist" Judith Krantz; in more serious coming-of-age narratives such as Kate Simon's *Bronx Primitive* or Alix Kates Shulman's *Memoirs of an Ex-Prom Queen;* in the public debate over Geraldine Ferraro's Italian Catholicism and her stand on abortion; in the sexual personae of Madonna Ciccone and Camille Paglia; in the Sheepshead Bay Yiddishisms of Harvey Fierstein's *Torch Song Trilogy* or the Italian roots element of Michelangelo Signorile's *Queer in America;* in the pornographer Adam Glasser's nice-Jewish-boy demeanor in Showtime's *Family Business;* in the "Jewface"/"gay-face" formula of *Will & Grace* or *Kissing Jessica Stein;* in Calliope/Cal Stephanides's ethnosexual odyssey in *Middlesex*.[57] This stands to reason, given the commercial imperatives of cultural production in an age of multiculturalism, and given, too, the narrative conventions of self-disclosure at a moment when "coming of age" necessarily conjures ethnic social location just as surely as it does sexual awakening.

These entwined legacies of sexual revolution and ethnic pluralism have been made deeper still by the fact that the liberatory model of the Civil Rights movement provided the template, not only for white ethnic pride movements, but also for the later political movements around issues of sexuality, including reproductive rights and gay rights. This rights-conscious dimension of both sexuality and late-century ethnicity came into rare focus in the early 1990s, when groups such as the Irish Gay and Lesbian Organization (ILGO) and Queer Ireland demanded a place alongside more traditional ethnic groups like the Ancient Order of Hibernians (AOH) in the New York St. Patrick's Day parade. The gay Irish Americans were initially refused; then they were admitted to the 1991 parade as special guests of Division 7 of the AOH (of Manhattan); but later Division 7 was itself expelled. The fracas continued in New York, Boston, and other cities throughout the early 1990s.[58]

Although public discussion of the St. Patrick's Day controversy has focused mostly on the fact that a group of Irish Americans insisted on the right to publicly proclaim their gayness, an equally significant dimension of this moment was that a group of gay men and women were also insisting on their right to publicly celebrate their Irishness. The history of Irishness, indeed, provided the common liberal vocabulary—"tolerance"—for recognizing their rights as gays. Setting aside the question of whether being gay was an acceptable way of being Catholic, that is, being

*14.   Sexuality and ethnicity converge as civil rights protest, New York's St.
Patrick's Day Parade, 1996. JAMES LEYNSE/CORBIS SABA.*

tolerant was held up as the *only* unimpeachable way of being
"Irish." "We have heightened sensitivity . . . to the rights of those
in Northeastern Ireland," declared Pat Clark, a Division 7 member. "We should make sure that we have the same sensitivity right
here at home." Anna Quindlen noted the similarities between
the anti-Irishism of the nineteenth century and the homophobia
of the twentieth; and unsigned *Times* editorials argued that the
AOH would be "doing . . . their history proud" by making St.
Patrick's Day a more inclusive event for all Irish Americans. Exclusivity, they insisted, would be "a tawdry tribute to a proud people who themselves have surmounted centuries of discrimination."[59] The postwar discourse of sexuality has largely been a

discourse of pluralism; and as both Philip Roth and Erica Jong indicated, the politics of sexuality is deeply enmeshed with the politics of heritage.

Next Year in Jerusalem

The experiences of both Portnoy and Wing hint that the ethnic reverie is more complicated than just a unilinear fantasy of emigration and return. The emotional relationship between Old World and New is never precisely unidirectional, for one thing; the past is never simply past. The heritage project leads, not only back in time to ancestral antiquity, but also, in *persisting* kinship, across the ocean to contemporary events and concerns—thus Pat Clark's "heightened sensitivity . . . to the rights of those in Northeastern Ireland." Moreover, the diasporic sensibility may lay symbolic claim to more ethnic "homelands" than just the abandoned Old World village. The figurative geography of the "roots" trip for American Jews expanded to include both Nazi Germany (as for Wing) and the nation of Israel (as for Portnoy), even in the case of those whose literal family histories had been touched by neither.[60] The ethnic reverie among American Jews, though closely related to that of other Euro-American groups, was thus set on an altered course by the general reckoning with the Holocaust in the 1960s and after and by events in the Middle East in 1967. After the Arab-Israeli war, Israel at least partially displaced Ellis Island as American Jews' touchstone of romantic peoplehood. Though the Jewish ghetto of New York's Lower East Side remains *the* most popular symbol of the immigrant experience, and though there has been no shortage of literary or cinematic treatments of Czarist oppression and Jewish flight, after 1967 Is-

rael assumed the emotional charge that other ethnic groups reserved solely for their countries of origin, and the Holocaust became a central element in Jews' urgent attachments to Israel. The
depth of meaning is clear even in Portnoy's "implausible" discovery of a Jewish country in which, "hey, here *we're* the WASPS!"

The founding of Israel represented not only independence for
an existing populace but also an invitation to a potential populace
drawn from all corners of the Jewish Diaspora. What of those
who have refused the invitation? On the one hand, they are presumed in some quarters to imperil the nation by holding aloof. "It
is not pleasant to contemplate the wondrous perversity of over
99% of the major post-Holocaust remnant of the world's Jews
choosing *not* to dwell in the Jewish state," writes Haim Chertok,
an American emigrant to Israel; a danger exists that the national
dream will dwindle to "a sort of extended, holyistic Jewish com-
mune."[61]

On the other hand, because of Israel's value as a safe haven for
Jews, and because of its liberal immigration and citizenship laws
for all Jews, voluntary "exiles" from around the world are also presumed to enjoy a special relationship to the nation, replete with
both obligations and privileges. Amid the tempest occasioned
by the Pollard spy case, for instance, the Israeli scholar Shlomo
Avineri remarked of American Jews, "you, in America, are no different from French, German, Polish, Soviet and Egyptian Jews.
Your exile is different—comfortable, padded with success and renown. It is exile nonetheless." America, he concluded, "may not
be your promised land."[62]

The Jewish-American sense of obligation and belonging to Israel has received its starkest expression from extremists like Meir
Kahane of the Jewish Defense League. "Exile," he wrote, "even to

the most temporarily beautiful of all lands . . . has always been a curse for the Jew. It remains so." Regardless of his or her present circumstances and citizenship, the Jew's ties to Israel remain ever "unbroken": "the Jewish people and the land of Israel are involved in a dual relationship that is eternal."[63] Gentler acknowledgments of the tie to Israel have ranged from Haim Chertok's charming assertion that Zionism is "the only seaworthy dream afloat," to Morris Janowitz's certainty that the defense of Israel remains "the paramount task of the Jewish community" in the United States. In his suggestively titled study *We Are One! American Jewry and Israel,* Melvin Urofsky characterized the relationship as *mishpachah*—family—with all the tenderness, irritation, resentment, contentiousness, and devotion implied by the word.[64]

One dimension of this family feeling has been an angry defensiveness among American Jews about perceived instances of unwarranted Israel-bashing.[65] A second is the tendency among many others, as Alan Dershowitz noted during the first Intifada, "to speak out against Israel *as Jews*." Philip Roth aptly notes, "Disillusionment is a way of caring for one's country too." The very depth of Jewish-American disillusionment with Israel in many cases betrays the extent to which Israel is tacitly being embraced as "one's country."[66]

This "family" relationship with Israel, in all its ambiguity, is depicted, critiqued, and embodied in works of fiction by a range of Jewish-American writers. Melanie Kaye/Kantrowitz's short story "In the Middle of the Barbeque She Brings up Israel," for instance, recounts an impassioned backyard debate over Israel among several American Jews representing various generations and diverse political outlooks. "I know you think Israel is a tiny brave miracle," says Nadine Greenbaum, a twenty-two-year-old, spike-haired college student who is currently studying Islam. "You know what it's doing, our Israel? . . . It's breaking the hands of kids for throwing rocks."[67]

During the passionate debate over "our Israel" which follows, someone insists that "the Jewish people will never give up Jerusalem," and a second chimes in, "We refuse to negotiate with terrorists." Here the narrator pauses to wonder, "What does he mean *we?* He lives in the Bronx." Throughout Kaye/Kantrowitz's stories this conflict between those who see world Jewry as indivisible ("we refuse to negotiate") and those who do not ("what does he mean *we?*") constantly asserts *and* critiques the nationalist posture of the American Diaspora.[68]

Zionism itself is the controlling metaphor of Philip Roth's novel *The Counterlife* (1988), described by Letty Cottin Pogrebin as the "quintessential novel of Jewish-American identity conflict." Indeed, the book derives its title from the Zionist movement's normalizing logic: "a highly conscious desire to be divested of virtually everything that had come to seem . . . distinctively Jewish behavior." The establishment of a Jewish nation thus amounts to "the construction of a counterlife."[69]

Through his gallery of characters and the frankly polemic exchanges between them, Roth offers an impressive tableau of Jewish political and social consciousness. The novel reflects and explores various positions along the spectrum of Jewish political identity, from American assimilationism to the most vociferous Israeli Zionism, allowing each to comment on the complex, late-twentieth-century relationship between Zion and the Diaspora. As these polemics accumulate over the course of the novel, the issues of Jewish toughness and violence, anti-semitism and the threat of anti-semitic violence, the Diaspora's dependence on Israel as a haven, and Israel's dependence on the Diaspora for security, all become entwined.

At the center of this mesh of rivaling political commentaries, however, and indeed central to the portion of the novel devoted to Judea, is the question of identity. The plot focuses on the Zionist awakening of the narrator's brother, Henry Zuckerman, and on the narrator's attempt to come to terms with this inexplicable departure from the habits of a lifetime. The narrator visits Henry in Jerusalem in an effort to discover just how and why he, "a Jew whose history of intimidation by anti-Semitism is simply non-existent," had suddenly become a Zionist firebrand.[70]

Zuckerman's visit to Israel becomes the occasion for unceasing polemics on the Jewish Question. But bounded by Nathan Zuckerman's stolid assimilationism on the one hand and Henry's ethnic revivalism on the other, and refracted, moreover, through Nathan's own consciousness, broad political comment ultimately serves the highly individualized question of psychology and private "anti-myths." For Roth, in other words, the political is primarily personal: Zionism is less a political program than, as Zuckerman puts it, a mode of "self-analysis."[71]

The primacy of psychology is made plain when, in a dizzying whirl of self-reflexivity, Nathan Zuckerman's account of Henry's *aliyah* turns out to be a manuscript novel-within-the-novel—a fiction, moreover, that is angrily refuted by the *real* Henry. Railing at this fictive turn by which his older brother has depicted him as being "under the tutelage of some political hothead" in Israel, Henry remarks, "Another dream of domination, fastening upon me another obsession from which *he* was the one who could never be rescued." The earlier passages—the trip to Israel, the rantings of (Kahanite) Mordecai Lippman, the Zionist and anti-Zionist banter—are simply the fevered dreams of Nathan Zuckerman himself; they reveal an obsessive concern for Zionism, Israel, and all manner of Jewish Questions on the part of this ostensibly "normalized" American Jew. "The poor bastard," in Henry's words, "had Jew on the brain."[72]

For Roth, as for many writers who in one way or another "have Jew on the brain," Israel remains at the center of the ever-problematic Jewish-American identity. A few years later, in *Operation Shylock* (1993), Roth took the theme of the nationalistic nature of Jewish ethnic identity even further. In this flight of feverish ethnic angst, the plot revolves around the figure of a Philip Roth double (nicknamed "Moishe Pipik" by the "real" Roth) who has appeared in Jerusalem, and, in the guise of the famous novelist, has begun to preach a new political credo of anti-Zionism known as "Diasporism." Israel, his argument runs, is bad for the Jews. A militarized and perpetually embattled state is the last thing in the world the Jews ever needed; Israel is endangering Jewish lives and corrupting the Jewish soul. Pipik proposes to lead the Jews out of Israel and back to the ghettoes of Europe: "*Last* year in Jerusalem! Next year in Warsaw! Next year in Bucharest! Next year in Vilna and Cracow."[73]

The central reference points for the novel's convoluted plot are the Pollard spy case and the Israeli trial of John Demjanjuk as Treblinka's Ivan the Terrible. On the one hand, Pipik feels that Israel threatens to turn world Jewry into a mass of Jonathan Pollards—spies for (in his view) a vicious regime. Pollard becomes in this vision a victim of the Jewish state, and Israel is now "deforming and disfiguring Jews as only our anti-Semitic enemies once had the power to do." "What the Dreyfus case was to Herzl," Pipik explains, "the Pollard case is to me."[74]

On the other hand, the action of the novel unfolds in Israel, against the backdrop of the trial of John Demjanjuk. This trial becomes the occasion for competing commentary on the centrality of both the Holocaust and Zionism in the construction of late-twentieth-century Jewish identity. Much of the commentary plays on the tender distinction between Israeli *justice*—the Jewish state will hold Ivan the Terrible accountable for his crimes against Jews—and Israeli *justification*—the enormity of the Holocaust (embodied by Demjanjuk) overshadows, and so excuses, the Israeli response to the first Intifada.

Operation Shylock is perhaps the supreme expression of the diasporic imagination in the late twentieth century. Pipik's "Diasporism" takes as its unspoken premise, not only the centrality of the Jewish state to Jewish existence, but a Zionism so triumphant that it has transformed (disfigured, in Pipik's estimation) Jewish life everywhere. Pipik's program of Diasporism is the most extreme articulation of the point, but the entire novel revolves on this axis. The novel, subtitled "a confession," ends with a flurry of complex political exchanges between the "real" Philip Roth and a (fictional?) Israeli official. Roth himself turns out to be, in the words of that official, "no less ideologically committed than your fellow patriot Jonathan Pollard."[75]

These works rearticulate ethnic identity as an internal geography of national center and diasporic periphery, deeply embedded nationalist mythos and social codes of enduring obligation—or, in the case of Roth, enduring ensnarement. As one of Kaye/Kantrowitz's characters asks, "What does Jewish mean now anyway except fussing for holidays and arms for Israel?"[76] Perhaps no other ethnic group in the United States shares the conflict and emotional depth of American Jews' engagement with an overseas "homeland." But this is a difference of degree, not of kind: one thinks of Irish-American passions during the "Troubles," Polish-Americans' flaring interests in the fate of their "compatriots" in the shipyards of Solidarity-era Gdansk, or the feverish activities of groups like the Serbian National Committee and the Latvian Foundation. This sense of America-as-diaspora is not only a symbol of ethnicity but one of its engines as well. As works like *A Dream of Kings* no less than *Portnoy's Complaint* or *The Counterlife* indicate, the diasporic imagination is in close dialogue indeed with the antimodernist and psychosexual sensibilities that also characterize the ethnic reverie.

If Abraham Cahan's career was not timed to win the celebrity of the "ethnic" author in the era of multiculturalism, then Henry Roth's could have been timed no better. Like Cahan, Roth had written long before the ethnic revival—his first novel, *Call It Sleep*, appeared in 1934—and, like Cahan's *David Levinsky, Call It Sleep* was reissued in 1960. Although the enthusiasms attending the recovery of *Call It Sleep* tended to emphasize the literary over the historical, one still presumes Hansen's Law to have been in action. The opening pages deliver "the immigrants from the stench and throb of the steerage to the stench and the throb of New York tenements" before moving on to the ghetto portrait of David Scherl's boyhood—tenement, street, *cheder,* coal cellar.[77]

Unlike Cahan, however, Roth was still alive to enjoy the spectacular success of this "rediscovery" (the novel had gone through twenty printings by the early 1970s).[78] Further, he was poised to resume his literary career for a generation of readers whose tastes had been primed by a national ethnic reverie and by the emergence of multiculturalism. More telling, finally, than the "rediscovery" of *Call It Sleep* in the 1960s is Henry Roth's literary come-back, after decades of silence, in the 1990s. The four volumes of *Mercy of a Rude Stream* (1994–1998) tell the spliced stories of young Ira Stigman's coming of age in Harlem in the 1920s, and the older Ira Stigman, decades later, perched at his computer, writing the young Ira's tale, but also reliving that bygone era, re-flecting on past choices and shifting meanings, and reckoning with the passage of time. Like *Call It Sleep*, the *Mercy* quartet does capture the rhythms and grit of immigrant life early in the twentieth century, and so might assuage the hungers of a late-century readership that yearns for a ghetto to look back to. But in its dialogic movement between experience and memory, between youth and age, between immigrant desire and American despair, between the geography of experience and the topography of feel-ing, *Mercy of a Rude Stream* says as much about the ethnic present as about the immigrant past.

The four volumes chart the relationship between ethnic pe-riphery and "American" center in two distinct dimensions: in young Ira's efforts to navigate the distances between what is "Jewish" and what is "American," and in the elder Ira's running commentary on the 1980s ramifications of 1920s choices. Ira has felt the sting of American natives' disdain, and, idealizing all that is "American," he has begun to yearn for a kind of psychosocial self-transforma-tion that can only remain unrequited. In the stories to which the boy was drawn, "everything beautiful was Christian, wasn't it? All that was flawless and pure and bold and courtly and chivalric was *goyish*." Ira's defining attraction to the courtly and the *goyish* tends in two distinct but complementary directions. On the one hand, it becomes a bitter rejection of Jewishness. His Bar Mitzvah, for instance, "brought the realization he was only a Jew because he

had to be a Jew; he hated being a Jew; he didn't want to be one . . .
he was caught, imprisoned in an identity from which there was
no chance of his ever freeing himself."[79] On the other hand the
attraction becomes a deeply felt longing to be at one with an
idealized "America" that is every bit as fantastic as the storybook
pictures themselves, and equally unattainable:

> America, flourishing, prosperous, where modish women in
> picture hats pulled on long white gloves as they walked to
> their automobiles. Almost without benefit of words, as if
> thoughts were clouds imbued with meaning, he would mull
> on the imponderable gulf that separated him from everything
> he beheld—and was enchanted by—that separated him, the
> immigrant, from the American-born, the Jew from the
> gentile.[80]

In his quest for Americanization, Ira becomes, "not assimilated, alienated," not "American," but merely emotionally removed from other Jews. Ultimately it is neither the immigrant
experience in all its grit nor the wistful later attempt at recollection that occupies the center of the *Mercy of a Rude Stream* quartet, but rather the social and psychic distance between the two.
The "first American-born generation of Jews," the elder Stigman
now realizes, constitutes "the bridge between the poor East European immigrants who landed here and the American Jews their
offspring became."[81] Though Stigman's own lifespan indeed represents that very bridge, his extraordinary longevity—like Henry
Roth's—aligns him with the historic generations on either shore:
the elder Ira Stigman in the 1980s *becomes* an identity-questing
descendant, rooting around in the attic for all that the younger Ira

Stigman had abandoned six decades earlier. As the elder Stigman now recognizes of his earlier assimilationist choices,

> *when the revolt against the parochial world succeeded, and the individual . . . cast off the restrictions that were part and parcel of his formative milieu,* he simultaneously abandoned his richest, most plangent creative source: his folk, their folkways, *his earliest, most vivid impressions,* the very elements of his formation. *Hence, the price of success in his best work was to condemn him to discontinuity. What a paradox!*[82]

Therein lay both the literary and the psychic contradictions, for Stigman as, perhaps, for Roth: *"He might have returned to his source, he might have continued to write about a dwindling, a crumbling away of life, once lusty and flourishing, and—how unbelievably soon!—disintegrating."* But how could he do so *"with any validity and conviction—after he had rejected that life, after he had been infected by association with the cosmopolitan, the larger world in which he now functioned and moved freely?"* Looking back across the chasm created years ago by his own youthful assimilationism, an empty and aching Stigman now sees that *"history may have been a nightmare, but the ones who could have awakened him were the very ones he [had] eschewed: his folk."*[83]

Like Henry Zuckerman in *The Counterlife* and so many American Jews before him, Stigman partially resolves this dilemma through the internal geopolitics, as it were, of Zionism: *"Even though at times it seemed to him that reunion might be reunion with a lost cause, that history and social change might overwhelm the small nation to which his spirit had fused in hope and pride, nevertheless, he*

clung all the more loyally to the midwife of his rebirth: Israel." But it
is less the political Zionism than ethnic rebirth that ought to
claim our attention here. Rebirth not only aligns Stigman with
writers like James Joyce, whose own suspension between the "universal" and the "folk" Roth reflects on throughout the quartet, but
also charts his course comfortably within the main currents of
America's ethnic reverie. As Roth's friend Mario Materassi commented, the quartet represented a "monumental effort" on Roth's
part to "come to terms with the pattern of rupture and discontinuity that marked his life."[84] It is a variation of the same social
and psychic discontinuity that Cahan glimpsed and began to give
voice to through David Levinsky in 1917; it is a meditation on discontinuity that—from around the time of John Higham's musing
on the "cycles of alienation and return"—has been a fairly prominent feature on the national landscape, in the form of Philip
Roth, Mario Puzo, and Erica Jong best sellers, Hollywood's efforts "to be both homey and exotic," and roots trips and heritage
hunts of every description.

The wistfulness of this ethnic romance glides easily into the or-
bit of the political, as the muted racial politics of *The Godfather,*
the class politics of *The Parish and the Hill,* and the gender politics
of *Portnoy's Complaint* and *Fear of Flying* demonstrate. The white
ethnic revival may have been a lament over "assimilation," but so
was its literature a pan-European ethnic celebration of white *assimilability.* A close reading of the celebrated "us" and the implied
"them" in European ethnic sagas of this era suggests that the
bootstrap homilies of neoconservatism and the victimology of
multiculturalism may actually share an intellectual ancestry. But it
is worth emphasizing just how fertile a political ground had been

prepared on both sides by the psychic yearnings and ethnic reso-
lutions articulated in works like *A Dream of Kings*. The politics of
the 1960s and after found expression in a language that is at once
the blessing and the curse of a people whose present and past do
not always "comport well."

Chapter Four

The Immigrant's Bootstraps, and Other Fables

Who was I to be anything but grateful to this country that had taken in an impoverished and much oppressed family of former serfs from Slovakia, and that had given to me and countless others opportunities unprecedented in history?
—Michael Novak, "Errand into the Wilderness"
(1988)

Few people today would identify Glazer and Moynihan's book *Beyond the Melting Pot* as an inaugurating text of the recent "culture wars," but it does embody the critical elements that would characterize American discussions of diversity—left *and* right—over the ensuing decades. "This is a beginning book," the authors wrote portentously in 1963, and indeed it was. On the one hand, their fundamental premise presaged a number of key intellectual and political developments in the United States for the balance of

the twentieth century—the centrality of ethnic and racial differences to our conception of the nation, the tenacity of ethnic identity among the descendants of earlier European immigrants, and
the evolution of what would later be called "multiculturalism."
The notion that American diversity was "soon to blend into a
homogenous end product has outlived its usefulness, and also
its credibility," they declared. "The point about the melting pot
. . . is that it did not happen." Indeed, the homogenizing trope of
the melting pot soon fell from grace in public discussion, though
only a few years earlier sociologists had confidently dismissed
pluralists as "backward-looking romantics" who were "out of touch
with the unfolding American reality."[1]

On the other hand, the tenacious Eurocentrism of *Beyond the
Melting Pot* also predicted the tenor of the *anti*multicultural right.
Here Glazer spelled out what he later called the "ethnic pattern"
of American social development, a presumed group-by-group succession of "newcomers" for whom the voluntary European immigrant stood as the prototype. Like Kennedy's rendition a few years
earlier, this America was "a nation of immigrants," with all the celebrations and erasures the image entailed. The historical weight of
incorporation by conquest or by slavery, for instance, was of little
account in this model, as *all* groups could expect to proceed along
roughly the same lines of acceptance, mobility, and success as had
the great waves of immigrants from Europe beginning in the 1840s.
If the black experience in New York looked markedly different
from the Italian, it was only because "the Negro immigrant" had
not been there as long.[2] This Eurocentric formulation of American pluralism—neatly summed up in Irving Kristol's essay "The
Negro Today Is Like the Immigrant of Yesterday" (1966)—was to

leave a profound imprint on American conservatism, though neither Glazer nor Kristol had yet taken his turn toward the right.[3]

If the romantic narratives of European immigration established a renewed, non–Anglo-Saxon "we" for the so-called white ethnics, so did they establish an invigorated "we-and-they" that has informed the antimulticultural agenda. The Ellis Island epic has exerted real power in the discussion on both sides, and a paradoxical kinship ties many "multiculturalists" to their more conservative foes. Recent political contests over social policy, education, and nationhood itself—refracted on both sides through the prism of "diversity"—represent but one installment in a much longer, high-stakes competition between two fundamentally opposing models of American nationality: "civic nationalism," which rests on principles of inclusivity and unfettered, egalitarian political participation; and "racial nationalism," which rests on the principles of white primacy, hierarchy, and exclusion.[4]

For the "multicultural left" of recent decades, the perceived task has been to revitalize civic nationalism not only by trumpeting U.S. diversity, but also by naming and documenting the historical trajectory of racial nationalism, thus opening it up to public scrutiny and critique; hence what some deride as "oppression studies." In some segments of the right, meanwhile, this new pluralism has become a means of disguising racial nationalism *as* civic nationalism. Like the political logic of the Statue of Liberty Centennial, which ignored the many millions of Americans whose history did not pass through Ellis Island, much polemic actually reinvigorates ideologies of hierarchy and exclusion even as it celebrates "diversity" as a singular national virtue of this "nation of immigrants." At stake in this widely joined culture war is the very tenor of

American nationality—whether or not, at the end of the day, the nation of immigrants is still a "white man's country."

Ethnic Reverie and Conservative Rebirth

The new ethnicity emerged amid a dramatically shifting public discourse on "difference" and hierarchy: a shift from the "prejudice" model of mid-century concern (prejudice is a matter of individual bigotries and erroneous "attitudes"; it can be overcome by education) to the "racism" model of the post–Civil Rights era (racism is a matter not of attitudes but of *power;* it is not individual but institutionalized; mere education will never root it out).[5] Within this context of shifting explanatory languages white ethnic commentators like Nathan Glazer, Irving Kristol, and Michael Novak interpreted their own group histories. While they rightly noted the extent to which the "prejudices" of the past had largely been overcome in the case of white ethnics, they rarely considered the ways in which the successful incorporation of these groups might have been part of a broader pattern of racialized, structural power relations—an intractable American dynamic of "white" over "nonwhite."

Attention to the *structures* of inequality, in fact, remains one of the most potent distinctions separating the contemporary right and left. Structural factors such as Jim Crow unionism, government housing and loan policies, or the GI Bill have generally had little place in conservatives' rendition of the immigrant success story that constitutes the prototype of "the American experience"—the encounter between "newcomer" and "free market." It is not just that neoconservatives, like many other white ethnics, have conflated ethnicity with race and have taken their own ethnic options for a universal American principle.[6] They have generally stuck with the interpretive model of prejudice that many of them grew up with and that *seemed* to speak to their group experience. A major lesson from "the immigrant experience" that recurs again and again in conservative writing is that in America, discrimination can and will be overcome with hard work and the passage of time—a conviction whose corollaries include myriad assertions about bootstrap self-help and the impropriety of state intervention in correcting for the injustices of racial stratification.

This view of America's essential inclusiveness was hard won for a certain generation of white ethnics, and so it tends to die just as hard, when it dies at all. As late as 1998, Glazer argued that in America it has indeed been "possible for persons and groups operating under the enormous constraints of not being white, or not being considered white"—he was talking about Jews—"to make progress independently of [this racial] image." This presumption of American openness, proven again and again by "the immigrant experience," feeds directly into the widely held view that, as Irving Kristol put it, "the real tragedy of the American Negro today is not that he is poor, or black, but that he is a late-comer" to the American city.[7] Since what is needed in the realm of social policy must hinge on perceptions of what is possible in the realm of social experience, the sanitized immigrant saga has proven indispensable to the antistatist populism of the right.

The ethnic revival thus intersects the recent history of American conservatism in three crucial ways: first, white ethnic votes have contributed to the conservative electoral majority that handed the presidency to the Republican Party in five out of eight elections from 1968 to 1996 (and which rendered George W. Bush the narrowest of losers in 2000); second, unmeltable white ethnics

are prominent among the *personnel* of the New Right coalition—
particularly neoconservatives like Michael Novak, Irving Kristol,
Norman Podhoretz, and Gertrude Himmelfarb, who brought to
conservatism both an insider's critique of the left and an ethnic
memory of the ghetto; and third, the European immigrant saga is
made to carry tremendous symbolic freight in conservative arguments concerning the amelioration of poverty, the role of the
state, the importance of the family, and the perversity of policies
such as welfare and affirmative action.

Neoconservatives are "old liberals," remarked Michael Novak,
"but they are old liberals in a Burkean sense: they believe in the
importance of liturgy, community, ethnicity, and roots, not atomic
individuals. They have a sense of community, prayer, religion."[8]
Reading American conservatism this way lends a new kind of coherence to the moral vocabulary of the right, and to its antistatist vehemence, whether arrayed against the domineering "New
Class," the "Civil Rights Establishment," or the "pathological"
underclass itself. For some people on the right, this argument
from the immigrant experience originates in a literal, personal familiarity with the old immigrant ghetto; for others, the immigrant saga is a matter of symbolism rather than of memory. But in
either case, yesterday's European immigrant becomes not only the
typical but the *exemplary* American citizen.

Like "the left," the phrase "the right" is a misnomer in that it
imputes monolithic standing to a variety of disparate outlooks.
The building-blocks of the right, as it is now constituted, include
the "paleoconservatives" who arose in opposition to the New Deal
state and galvanized around the Cold War's domestic and international questions; the largely white, middle-class, fiscally conservative "populists" who put Goldwater and Reagan on the polit-

ical map in the 1960s; fundamentalist Christians, who have made their presence felt most forcefully since the 1980s; former partisans of the "solid" Democratic South, whose swing to the Republicans was presaged as far back as the Dixicrat defection of 1948; disgruntled white ethnics, largely of the Northeast and Midwest, who joined Nixon's "silent majority" in 1968 and who became known as "Reagan Democrats" in the 1980s; and the contending conservative "publics" associated with *The National Review, Chronicles, Commentary, First Things, Reason,* and with Fox Television and conservative talk radio. Recent years have also witnessed the rise of "multicultural conservatives," women, gays and lesbians, and people of color like Thomas Sowell, Dinesh D'Sousa, and Linda Chavez, whose ties to minority communities have granted them moral authority and a certain celebrity.[9]

The fault lines dividing these diverse conservatisms run deep on issues like immigration, anti-semitism, and the Middle East. But the conservatives' electoral coalition has been very important if not definitive in American politics since 1968, and for at least two of its constituencies—the Reagan Democrats and the neoconservatives—the ethnic revival has been pivotal. As the Republican strategist Kevin Phillips noted in *The Emerging Republican Majority* after Nixon's 1968 victory, Democratic defectors "stretched from the 'Okie' Great Central Valley of California to the mountain towns of Idaho, Florida's space centers, [and] rural South Carolina," but they also included "Bavarian Minnesota, the Irish sidewalks of New York and the Levittowns of Megalopolis." He continued, "In New York City the party is becoming the vehicle of the Italians and Irish . . . The new popular conservative majority has many ethnic strains, and portraits showing it as a white Anglo-Saxon Protestant monolith are highly misleading."

Among Phillips's "Republican trending groups" were "Germans, Scotch-Irish, Pennsylvania Dutch, Irish, Italians, East Europeans and other urban Catholics . . . who were principally alienated from their party by its social programs and increasing identification with the Northeastern Establishment and ghetto alike."[10] "The whole secret," Phillips said of Nixon's electoral strategy, "is knowing who hates who."[11]

Phillips did not quite foresee the electoral significance of the Christian Right, but he provides a prescient roadmap of the conservative patchwork in the late twentieth century. Although he emphasized the shifting party allegiances of the white South and national demographic shifts toward suburb and sunbelt (both of which expanded the "natural" base of the Republican Party), his attention to the volatile allegiances of white ethnics was well placed. As gross indicators of white ethnic behavior in the ensuing electoral cycles, the Catholic vote and the blue-collar vote tell an important story (though, obviously, neither represents white ethnics exclusively): in 1972 Nixon won with 61 percent of the blue-collar vote and 60 percent of the Catholic vote; in 1976 Democrats recaptured the White House with significant percentages of these voters (59 percent blue-collar and 55 percent Catholic); in the three-way race of 1980, Reagan won with pluralities of 47 percent of the blue-collar vote and 51 percent of the Catholic vote, figures that he stretched slightly in 1984; in 1988 Bush the elder won with 49 percent of the blue-collar vote and 52 percent of the Catholic vote; and the Democrats regained the presidency only when they once again built solid pluralities in these areas in 1992 (44 percent of the Catholic vote compared with Bush's 36 percent in a three-way race that included the billionaire "populist" Ross Perot).

In other words, beginning in 1972, majorities in the blue-collar and Catholic vote predicted every election with the exception of 1988 (when Dukakis edged Bush in the blue-collar vote by a slim 1 percent). Throughout these years both groups departed from the patterns of New Deal allegiance that had prevailed until 1968. A few snapshots suggest some of the particulars of this realignment: Italian-American support for Democrats nationwide, to take a case, dropped from 77 percent in 1964 to 50 percent in 1968, and later bottomed out at 39 percent in 1984.[12] In Macomb County, a white, Catholic working-class suburb on the northeastern edge of Detroit, Kennedy carried an overwhelming 63 percent of the vote in 1960. By 1976, after a period of much rancor on the issue of busing, Gerald Ford carried the county with 52 percent of the vote; four years later, Reagan defeated Carter by a vote of 56 to 44 percent. (It was in Macomb County, legend has it, that the term "Reagan Democrat" was coined.) Or again, the eight mostly Irish and Polish working-class wards of south Chicago had supported Democrats by an impressive margin in 1960; but in the 1966 elections, in the wake of Martin Luther King, Jr.'s, activism on behalf of open housing in Chicago, six of the eight wards voted Republican. As Democratic Representative Roman Puchinski put it, "Go into any home, any bar, any barber shop and you will find people are not talking about Vietnam or rising prices or prosperity. They are talking about Martin Luther King and how they are moving in on us and what's happening to our neighborhoods."[13]

There are two ways of understanding this emergent conservatism among the unmeltable white ethnics, and ethnicity itself is critical to both. The first explanation lies in the realm of moral and religious sensibilities, ideas that have aligned many Catholics with their Protestant counterparts of the religious right and that come into play most forcefully on issues like abortion, "family values," and gay rights. The conservative strategist Ralph Reed argued in 1993 that "the pro-family movement's inroads into the African American, Hispanic, Catholic and Jewish communities may be the most significant development since its emergence in the late 1970s." Indeed, the political historian Angela Dillard suggests that, given the low political cost of rhetorical assaults on homosexuality, "traditional notions of gender and sexuality have been more overt fixtures in the ideological glue of the [conservative] movement" than even race.[14]

The second explanation for white ethnic conservatism lies in the realm of social *status*—ideas about economics, opportunity, mobility, the work ethic, and the state, which have been easily mobilized around issues such as welfare, busing, and affirmative action. Here the salient "ethnic" lens has less to do with religious sensibility than with group standing and the accepted narratives of a particular group's history. Seymour Martin Lipset has identified those most receptive to the appeals of "status politics" (the quest to either maintain or improve one's social standing) as members of groups that "have risen in the economic structure and who may be frustrated in the desire to be accepted socially by those who already hold status," but also those "already possessing status who feel that rapid social change threatens their own high social position."[15] In the context of late-twentieth-century U.S. politics, white ethnics qualify on *both* counts: as non–Anglo-Saxon Protestants, they may indeed be "frustrated in their desire" for full acceptance into the mainstream. Yet as *whites* in a white-over-black political economy, they are stakeholders nonetheless in a privilege that has been under siege since the early Civil Rights era.

As important as the religious dimension of these ethnic subcultures may be in matters like abortion, feminism, or gay rights, then, the electoral swing of the so-called Reagan Democrats cannot be fully understood without reference to race. As Dan Carter has remarked, the segregationist George Wallace's "appeal to ethnic voters in the urban Northeast and Midwest initially confounded political observers . . . [But] the often blue-collar neighborhoods of Boston, New York, Philadelphia, Cleveland, Gary, and Chicago had borne the brunt of social transformation as the black community spread into these once stable sections. Many, though certainly not all, such ethnic voters saw in Wallace a kindred spirit: a man despised and dismissed by distant social planners all too ready to sacrifice working-class families on the altar of upper-middle-class convictions."[16] In pulling together a new Republican coalition, according to Carter, Kevin Phillips "emphasized the essential conservatism of the first- and second-generation ethnics," a conservatism rooted in questions of economic and social standing. Moreover, he "bluntly recognized the critical role that white fears would play." Phillips himself had asserted that "given the immense mid-century impact of Negro enfranchisement and integration, reaction to this change almost inevitably had to result in political realignment."[17]

Black Niggers, White Niggers

The writings of prominent white ethnics in this period gave voice to the grievances implied by this electoral swing, contributing significantly to the intellectual project of recent American conservatism. Michael Novak's book *Rise of the Unmeltable Ethnics* (1971) was the most thoroughgoing discussion of white ethnic sensibilities to appear in the Civil Rights years. Novak set out to articulate concerns that up to that point had received public notice only in piecemeal, haphazard fashion. Perhaps more important, he sought to lend *legitimacy* to white ethnics' outlook, both by rendering their inchoate sensibilities in a compelling and rational line of argumentation, and by critiquing that liberal American "mainstream"—largely WASP, but also Jewish, in Novak's view— that was so prone to dismiss groups who were "born outside what, in America, is considered the intellectual mainstream."[18]

The Rise of the Unmeltable Ethnics is woven of many themes, some of which pitched decidedly leftward: a fierce antimodernism in opposition to the "vapid 'true Americanism'" and "odorless 'modernity'" of the WASP mainstream; a vague anticapitalism, which identified big business as more corrosive of traditional values than anything radicalism had yet dreamed up; an antiintellectualism that decried the educated elite as a class prone to its own bigotries and antidemocratic impulses; and predictions of a profound electoral realignment, should the left of the Civil Rights era persist in its failure to distinguish "middle America" from "unionized America."[19] Indeed, appearing well before Novak's own conversion to conservatism, *The Rise of the Unmeltable Ethnics* was explicitly written to warn the left away from such a sad mistake, and to provide the basis for a renewed progressive coalition that could sustain the allegiances of both blacks and white ethnics on the basis of their shared victimization at the hands of arrogant WASPdom.

Race thus resides at the very core of Novak's lament for then-current polarizations separating working-class white ethnics from African Americans. "It is almost as if polarization were deliberate," Novak wrote, "as if the Left intended to condemn one social group and glorify another, assist one and penalize another, as if America had to choose between the two: black niggers, white niggers." White ethnics "have legitimate reasons for economic, social, and cultural anxiety about the black revolution," he insisted. "It is not 'racist' to have such anxieties. The ethnic will not say 'nigger' and the black will not say 'pig,' when the two decide that they are not each other's enemy . . . The *enemy* is educated, wealthy, powerful . . . The enemy is concentrated power."[20]

The composite "white ethnic" of Novak's portrait replies to the Black Power movement that had so captured public attention between 1965 and the publication of *Unmeltable Ethnics* in 1971. The salient feature of the white ethnic experience, by this account, is not the ethnics' share in historic "white privilege," but, on the contrary, the *mistaken* attribution of such privilege to peoples who had never fully possessed it. In the context of post–Civil Rights political discourse, this mistaken attribution had become so ironclad as to be fully defining: "Racists? Our ancestors owned no slaves. Most of us ceased being serfs only in the last two hundred years." "Couldn't [blacks] distinguish a fellow sufferer under Nordic prejudice from a WASP?" Novak wondered. "Black militants tend to perceive whites as if they were all WASPs, and that may be their most egregious political error."[21]

Novak based this lament on the bitter history of Slavic, Italian, and Greek immigrant pariahs under the regime of Nordic supremacy that had reigned from the mid-nineteenth century to the mid-twentieth. His argument, however, carried no acknowledgment that "whiteness" had been reconfigured in the intervening years—that "white" supremacism, not "Nordic" supremacism, was the more salient feature of U.S. political culture by 1971, or that yesterday's pariah groups had perhaps found a measure of acceptance and even privilege under more recent, modified conceptions of "Caucasian" whiteness.[22] White ethnics thus find "two forms of bigotry arrayed against them," according to Novak: one is the continuing regime of "Nordic" supremacy, and the other is the bigotry of America's educated classes against the allegedly "unenlightened," an elitism whose chief weapon is the charge that *white ethnics* are "racists."[23]

Novak did admit that white ethnics had complicated feelings about African Americans, but such feelings bore the marks of their own complex history as American pariahs. "It must be said that ethnics think they are better people than blacks," Novak wrote with candor. "Smarter, tougher, harder working, stronger in their families. But maybe many are not sure . . . [O]ne can understand the immensely more difficult circumstances under which the blacks have suffered . . . How much of this we learned in America by being made conscious of our olive skin, brawny backs, accents, names, and cultural quirks is not plain to us." But plain to many was blacks' illegitimate impatience: "The ethnics believe they chose one route to moderate success in America; namely, loyalty, hard work, family discipline, and gradual self-development. They tend to believe that some blacks, admittedly more deeply injured and penalized in America, want to jump, via revolutionary militance, from a largely rural base of skills and habits over the heads of lower class whites."[24]

Novak was scarcely alone in invoking the white ethnic ghetto in these early articulations of what would become the neoconservative view. "I came from Brooklyn, and in Brooklyn there were no Americans," writes Norman Podhoretz. "There were Jews and Negroes and Italians and Poles and Irishmen. Americans lived in New England, in the South, in the Midwest: alien people in alien places." The particular angle of vision from the old ethnic ghetto was critical to emergent neoconservatives in their discussion of the characteristics that differentiated today's ghetto dwellers from those of an earlier era. "It is almost a century since the majority of Jews arrived on these shores," Irving Kristol reflected in 1991, "but the memories remain fresh—memories of economic hardship and economic success; of acculturation, assimilation and the accompanying generational tensions; of triumphs and disappointments." A statement like this one was rarely far behind: "It may be noted in passing that . . . discrimination did not prevent Jews from acquiring wealth, education, and influence. It created hurdles, but not impossible barriers."[25]

Not only did many of the most influential conservative thinkers of the era trace their roots to the ethnic margins of American culture, but their own sense of place, their notion of history and belonging and right and wrong, too, was heavily inflected by the various immigrant ghettoes to which they now looked back, literally or figuratively: Irving Kristol, Nathan Glazer, Norman Podhoretz, Martin Peretz, Michael Novak, Midge Decter, Gertrude Himmelfarb, Milton Himmelfarb, Daniel Patrick Moynihan, Daniel Bell, Albert Shanker, Michael Medved, John O'Sullivan, Ben Wattenberg, Peter Viereck, Jude Wanniski, Aaron Wildavsky, and Ruth Wisse.[26]

Nor, for that matter, was Michael Novak alone in his inclination to interpret the immigrant experience and the black experience only in contrast to each other. Indeed, such contrasts became the hallmark of neoconservative writing. Having discovered the new pluralism in *Beyond the Melting Pot*, Nathan Glazer in 1964 reflected on the divergent historical trajectories of white ethnics and African Americans. For that brief moment around the time of the Civil Rights Act, black demands for "integration" looked to Glazer like an "assimilationism" that in fact had never operated on the American scene. "The force of present-day Negro demands," he wrote, "is that the sub-community, because it either protects privileges or creates inequality, *has no right to exist.*" Such demands were ultimately unrealistic, in Glazer's view, in that they seemed to rest on a set of false melting-pot assumptions: "The Negro now demands entry into a world . . . that does not exist, except in ideology. In that world there is only one American community, and in that world heritage, ethnicity, religion, race are only incidental and accidental personal characteristics." Such a world might be desirable, but it is quite different from the world in which "most of us who have already arrived" now live.[27]

But as the focus of the movement shifted from South to North, and as the movement's "unrealistic" integrationism gave way to a Black Power movement, this preference for the integrity of "sub-community" over "one American community" evaporated rather quickly. No longer were black demands insensitive to the realities of group cohesion on the American scene; on the contrary, they were predicated on a fundamental misunderstanding of the historic patterns and the institutional bases of *assimilation.* What did remain constant, however, was the comparison between African Americans on the one hand and "most of us who have already arrived" on the other. As the Reform Rabbi Jakob Petuchowski wrote of Jews' "poor and destitute" forebears, "those recent ancestors of ours did not riot," they "did not loot and they did not burn."[28]

If the comparison tended to paint an unflattering portrait of African Americans, less flattering still was the common depiction of the ameliorative programs associated with the Great Society and Title VII (the "affirmative action" clause) of the Civil Rights

Act. As Irving Kristol later wrote in a critique of welfare and its unintended effects, it is probable "that if the Irish immigrants in nineteenth-century America had had something comparable to our present welfare system, there would have been a 'welfare explosion' then, and a sharp increase in Irish family disorganization, too."[29] What was most striking was no longer the incompatibility between black "assimilationism" and the persistent pluralism of various white groups, but, on the contrary, the extent to which blacks' ameliorative demands on the state ignored the real lessons of white ethnic incorporation—the "ethnic pattern."

Norman Podhoretz's confessional "My Negro Problem—And Ours," which appeared in *Commentary* in early 1963, was one of the foundational texts in this neoconservative equation. Podhoretz began by calling into question the common "truths" that "all Jews were rich" and that "all Negroes were persecuted." One cannot "gainsay the evidence of [one's] own senses," he wrote, invoking his own childhood experience in the multiethnic ghetto of Brooklyn, "especially such evidence . . . as comes from being repeatedly beaten up, robbed, and in general hated, terrorized, and humiliated." To be blunt—as Podhoretz was—not only were Jews in America persecuted from time to time, but "it was the Negroes who were doing the only persecuting I knew about":

> Why, *why* should it have been so different as between Negroes and us? . . . How could the Negroes in my neighborhood have regarded the whites across the street and around the corner as jailors? . . . What share had these Italian and Jewish immigrants in the enslavement of the Negro? What share had they—down-trodden people themselves breaking their own necks to eke out a living—in the exploitation of the Negro?[30]

Podhoretz went on to confess his own tangled hatred, fear, and envy toward the blacks in his neighborhood. If they were the authors of his "persecution," so was it true that they were "free, independent, reckless, brave, masculine, erotic," "they were *tough;* beautifully, enviably tough." Extrapolating from his own ghetto experience, Podhoretz asserted that "all whites—all American whites, that is—are sick in their feelings about Negroes . . . Special feelings about color are a contagion to which white Americans seem susceptible even when there is nothing in their background to account for the susceptibility," hence even Northern liberals often discover that "their abstract commitment to the cause of Negro rights will not stand the test of a direct confrontation."[31]

In a surprise ending to "My Negro Problem," Podhoretz calls for an end to racial antagonisms through—"let the brutal word come out—miscegenation." So firmly established is the color complex in the white American psyche, that "in my opinion the Negro problem can be solved in this country in no other way."[32] Like those nineteenth-century abolitionists before him who advocated the "colonization" of Africa by America's freed slaves, no matter how powerful his professed yearning for justice, Podhoretz was finally unable to imagine a smoothly functioning American polity in which discernible blacks continued to exist.

This essay appeared well before Podhoretz's own political turn to the right, and longer still before the term "neoconservative" was in circulation as a label for this post–Civil Rights conversion among former liberals. Nor, obviously, is Podhoretz's call for "miscegenation" representative of neoconservatism. But "My Negro Problem" is a preface to neoconservative thinking in at least four respects: the essay interprets the African-American experience through the lens of Ellis Island's huddled masses and bases its political authority on lab work conducted in the immigrant ghetto; it lays claim to a kind of just-off-the-boat innocence in its rendition of white-black social relations (indeed, its moral logic fully exchanges white-over-black privilege for black-over-white victimization); it adheres to an individualized, even psychologized notion of "prejudice" or "bigotry," strictly avoiding the structural features of race and political economy; and it voices a certain skepticism in ameliorative intervention that one recognizes as an incipient form of the antistatism of a slightly later moment. For Podhoretz, as for neoconservatism generally, the question, "What share had [immigrants] . . . in the exploitation of the Negro?" was never a serious inquiry, but a rhetorical device whose very articulation supplied the answer—"none."

The most elaborate treatment of U.S. political culture and diversity from this point of view was Glazer's book *Affirmative Discrimination* (1975). Here Glazer worked out both the comprehensive history and the policy consequences of the "ethnic pattern" of group incorporation he had first articulated in *Beyond the Melting Pot*. His resistance to the structural interpretation was quite explicit: having enumerated many features of the historical landscape that might lead one to conclude that the course of true pluralism never did run smooth (including "the enslavement of the Negro, anti-immigrant and anti-Catholic movements that have arisen again and again in American life, the near extermination of the American Indian, the maintenance of blacks in a subordinated and degraded position for a hundred years after the Civil War, the lynching of Chinese, the exclusion of Oriental immigrants, the restriction of immigration from Southern and Eastern Europe, the relocation of the Japanese and the near confiscation of their property, the resistance to school desegregation, and so forth"), Glazer conceded that, were one to seek a defining "direction" in America's intergroup relations, this sequence of events "might well be made the central tendency of American history." But, he concluded—and this is a mighty reversal—"I think this is a selective misreading of American history."[33]

The alternative reading that Glazer supplied derived from three principles that, he argued, have informed American political culture over time: (1) that the nation was open to all comers, (2) that any and all groups had to join the political life of the nation rather than espousing separatism, but (3) that in the realm of *culture* ethnic groups could maintain themselves, if they wished, on a voluntary basis. The result has been a thriving and open culture where "the ethnic group is one of the building blocks of . . . society," and in which "one is required neither to put on ethnicity nor to take it off."[34] The history of race in this paradigm presents a fairly constant irritant, but it has been neither decisive to the course of American history nor fatally disruptive of the "ethnic pattern."

In Glazer's scheme, European immigrants are the exemplars of this "central tendency in American history"—its openness, its premium on a diversity of participants, and its laissez-faire attitude toward group cohesion and personal identity choices. As he wrote in his introduction to the 1987 edition,

> We had seen many groups become part of the United States through immigration, and we had seen each in turn overcoming some degree of discrimination to become integrated into American society. What this process did not seem to need was the active involvement of government, determining the proper degree of participation of each group in employment and education.[35]

Like Novak's, Glazer's group portrait of European immigrants is highly sympathetic, stressing that from their point of view they "entered a society in which they were scorned; they nevertheless worked hard, they received little or no support from government or public agencies, their children received no special attention in school or special opportunity to attend college, they received no special consideration from courts and legal defenders." All, of course, in contrast to blacks. And like Novak, Glazer stresses *innocence* as one of the central motifs of the European immigrant experience: "These groups were not particularly involved in the enslavement of the Negro or the creation of the Jim Crow pattern in the South, the conquest of part of Mexico, or the near extermination of the American Indian . . . They came to a country which provided them with less benefits than it now provides the protected groups. There is little reason for them to feel they should bear the burden of redressing a past in which they had no or little part, or assisting those who presently receive more assistance than they did."[36] In other words, only the distant past needs to be redressed in American social policy, not the present: if slavery, conquest, and extermination are the only markers of historic white privilege—as opposed to persistent racial discrimination in hiring, housing, and education, for example—then the whiteness of the European immigrant is hardly worth remarking.

States of Empowerment

If the mythic figure of the immigrant serves to mediate white primacy in conservative renderings of American diversity in the making, it also plays a prominent role in abstract neoconservative theories of the state and state practices. Though their relationship to the history is quite different from Glazer's or Novak's, Peter Berger and Richard John Neuhaus's influential 1977 pamphlet *To Empower People* drew its primary lessons from the immigrant experience. As they explained in their opening chapter, Berger and Neuhaus sought to invigorate *"those institutions standing between the individual in his private life and the large institutions of public life."* Like Novak, they harked back to Burkean liberalism: "To be attached to the subdivision, to love the little platoon we belong to in society," as Burke had written, "is the first principle . . . of public affections." *To Empower People* focuses on those "little platoons" in society that do battle with the abstract, universalistic, "geometric" tendencies of modernity: "As a consequence of this 'geometrical' outlook, liberalism has had a hard time coming to terms with the alienating effects of the abstract structures it has multiplied since the New Deal."[37] Berger and Neuhaus shared in Novak's antimodernism, but unlike the Novak of 1971, they saw the state itself as modernity's most menacing "large institution of public life."[38]

Though himself a Viennese immigrant, Peter Berger owed his antimodernist conservatism not to any wistful image of the ghetto but to "stories he had heard of the vanished glories of Habsburg Austria."[39] But in the context of critiquing the American welfare state, immigration history's "small platoons" were indispensable. It is no accident that, in enumerating the prime examples of mediating structures between the meaning-seeking individual and the soulless megastructure of the modern state, Berger and Neuhaus named the four staples of the European immigrant saga: the neighborhood, the family, the church, and the voluntary association. (By "church" they had in mind not that moral institution later invoked by the Christian Coalition, but rather *a gemeinschaft* social institution like the old Polish parish church.)

White ethnic neighborhoods, Glazer had written, were "scenes of a marked social order: stable neighborhoods, with children succeeding parents in the same area, strong organizations centered around the church, formal ethnic associations or patterns of informal ethnic association, the local political organization, the trade union, the local small businesses of members of the group, which serve as much for socialization as for ordinary business."[40] At key junctures in their own discussion of the interaction between the heroic, "small platoons" of Burkean thought and the "geometrical" designs of the modern state, Berger and Neuhaus, too, were drawn to social zones like "the community centered in the St. Stanislaus American Legion branch of Hamtramck, Michigan." Moreover, they argued that "the tribal patterns evident at an Upper West Side cocktail party"—presumably among the "New Class"—"are no less tribal than those evident at a Polish dance in Greenpoint, Brooklyn." "It seems to us," they wrote, in defense of the small, that "there is nothing wrong with an elderly Italian Catholic woman wanting to live in a nursing home operated and occupied by Italian Roman Catholics. To challenge that most understandable desire seems to us, quite frankly perverse. Yet challenged it is—indeed, it is made increasingly impossible—by depriving such a 'sectarian' or 'discriminatory' institution of public funds."[41]

But the link between Berger and Neuhaus's "mediating structures" and either Glazer's "ethnic pattern" or Novak's ethnics who had advanced by "loyalty, hard work, family discipline, and gradual self-development" represents nothing so vague as a mere intellectual affinity. In "Empowerment through Pluralism," the final chapter of *To Empower People,* Berger and Neuhaus laid bare what had to that point remained only a half-articulated analogy:

> Beyond providing the variety of color, costume, and custom, pluralism makes possible a tension within worlds of meaning ... the paradox is that wholeness is experienced through affirmation of the part in which one participates. This relates to the aforementioned insight of Burke regarding "the little platoon." In more contemporary psychological jargon it relates to the "identity crisis" which results from an "identity diffusion" in mass society.

The "national purpose indicated by the *unum,*" that is, "is precisely to sustain the *plures.*" Finally, in enumerating the "five characteristics of American society that make it the most likely laboratory for public policy designed to enhance mediating structures and the pluralism that mediating structures make possible," Berger and Neuhaus set "the immigrant nature of American society" at the top of the list (ahead of affluence, stability, the spirit of tolerance and the democratic idea, and strong institutions). "America has a singular opportunity to contest the predictions of the inevitability of mass society with its anomic individuals, alienated and impotent, excluded from the ordering of a polity that is no longer theirs."[42]

The most famous articulation of this antistatist principle of "mediating structures" came, not from the ethnic margins, nor even from a proper neoconservative, but from the Connecticut-reared and Yale-educated George Bush the elder at the Republican Convention of 1988:

For we are a nation of communities, of thousands and ten thousands of ethnic, religious, social, business, labor union, neighborhood, regional and other organizations, all of them varied, voluntary and unique.

This is America: the Knights of Columbus, the Grange, Hadassah, the Disabled American Veterans, the Order of Ahepa, the Business and Professional Women of America, the union hall, the Bible study group, LULAC, Holy Name—a brilliant diversity spread like stars, like a thousand points of light in a broad and peaceful sky.[43]

Here, then, is where the Moynihan Report, Novak's antimodernism, Burke's "small platoons," Glazer's "ethnic pattern," and the antistatist Reagan-Bush promise to "get government off our backs" all come together and enter the mainstream; and it is the bootstraps fable of European immigration history that binds them. As Glazer would write in *The Limits of Social Policy* on the eve of Bush's election (1988), "every piece of social policy substitutes for some traditional arrangement, whether good or bad, a new arrangement in which public authorities take over, at least in part, the role of the family, of the ethnic and neighborhood group, of voluntary associations. In doing so, social policy weakens the position of these traditional agents and further encourages needy people to depend on the government for help rather than on the traditional structures."[44] The historic immigrant ghetto thus supplied the prototypical "mediating structures" of conservative thought; and the presumed contrasts between the white immigrant ghetto and the contemporary black ghetto at once demonstrated conservatives' antistatist, laissez-faire model for success *and* proved the evil of large policies and institutions. Scaling back the welfare state would reinvigorate black *gemeinschaft* institutions, break black dependency, and allow blacks to follow the "natural" path of mobility and incorporation taken by Italian, Irish, and Jewish immigrants before them.

Neoconservatives exerted a tremendous influence on policy debate in the late 1970s, at once redefining and "domesticating" American conservatism.[45] This domestication partly meant incorporating the language and logic of diversity, in the form of the conservative view-from-the-ghetto offered up by writers like Kristol and Glazer. Neoconservatism did not pit a monolithic whiteness against an insurgent blackness in American political life, but rather paid homage to the little folk of the former (and some enduring) white ghettos, whose group experience no less than that of African Americans had lessons to teach about aspiration and justice on the American scene.

More striking than even blue-blooded George Bush's articulation of a governing principle drawn largely from the example of the white immigrant ghetto is the extent to which—during local battles over busing, housing, or multiculturalism—street-level discussion among white ethnics has replicated the central tenets of the conservative argument-from-analogy. From Boston to Brooklyn to Philadelphia to Detroit, renditions of Glazer's "ethnic pattern" resonated in grassroots articulations of white ethnic interests.[46] Thus it was that local movements opposed to liberal policy often mobilized a distinctly *ethnic* sentiment of group solidarity and grievance: those limousine liberals responsible for busing, argued the Italian-American activist Pixie Palladino, always look down on "people of color like me." "A lot of things went wrong for us, you know, for the Jewish people," said one embattled resident of the Canarsie section of Brooklyn. "What happened to the blacks happened to us too. We had to push hard in the beginning too." "It's all a matter of fairness," said another. "I believe in black pride, but don't step on my white Italian pride. We've all been discriminated against." Others seized the most potent ethnic symbols available to express both their sense of injury and their will to fight: "This is a Warsaw ghetto mentality in Canarsie. It's an uprising like the Masada. When you can't do anything, when you're pushed to the wall, you fight back." "It's like we're the Israelis," another argued. "They are surrounded by fifty million Arabs, they have to fight, but there's no place to retreat."[47]

This resonance between neoconservative argument and the street-level sensibilities of white ethnics was also evident in one New York school's battle over bilingualism and multiculturalism. In assessing local Puerto Ricans' social and political claims, Euro-American parents drew on their own immigrant success mythology, "in which all groups start from the same point and are assimilated into the national fabric by dint of hard work, sacrifice, and a willingness to conform to 'American' norms." "Our oldsters remember how we made our own way and shouldered our own problems," said one white resident. "The Italians were called guineas and wops, so what's new, what's the difference?" wondered another. As one teacher reported of the white outlook, "They say their parents or grandparents came from Poland, Ireland, and that kind of thing, Italy, and when they came here they could not speak English either." Their grandparents "worked hard in these mills," they "did not go on welfare, they were not shown any special favoritism, they were not given anything . . . And they don't think the Puerto Ricans should be either."[48]

The immigrant saga has had a profound influence on American conservatism since the 1960s. It is not just that the tacit logic of the "nation of immigrants" paradigm has worked an exclusionary alchemy in civic discussions of "diversity," as we saw in the Statue of Liberty Centennial. The immigrant saga supplied the normative version of the family, against which the "pathologies" of Moynihan's black family might be highlighted. It supplied the "ethnic pattern" of incorporation and advancement, which became for Glazer and others the template against which all groups might be judged (despite recent attention to Asian-American successes, that is, *European* immigrants have been and remain the real "model minority"). It supplied the "mediating structures" for the antistatist conservatism expressed in George Bush's "thousand points of light" as well as the postslavery, fresh-off-the-boat innocents of the white ethnic ghetto, who have become the most potent symbol for the fundamental inequity of policies like affirmative action, busing, and, most recently, reparations. Consequently, both the immigrant myth and immigration's real-life descendants contributed to the swing vote that rendered the Republicans the majority party in the electoral realignment beginning in 1968.

As early as 1966 Bayard Rustin chastised an American Jewish Congress audience, "When Jewish people run about boasting about how we Jews made it because we were intellectual, and lifted ourselves by our bootstraps, and we have such extraordinarily beautiful family life that obviously we just went up to the top like cream in coffee—well, this is hot air." Ballplayer Curt Flood was even more direct: "I probably cannot influence those whites who complain that they are tired of feeling guilty about what their grandfathers did to my grandfathers, but I can at least suggest that they stop making idiotic comparisons between my people and European immigrants . . . To hell with your grandfather, baby. Just get out of the way."[49]

But this cream-in-coffee argument remains critical to conservatism. As Thomas and Mary Edsall argue, the strength of American conservatism has been its ability to exploit "the gulf between two contradictory currents in modern political life": "that aspect of liberalism committed to shielding the weak," and the traditional emphasis on "self-reliance, entrepreneurial individualism, and hard work." The underdog white immigrants and their descendants have done double symbolic duty in conservative rhetoric on both counts: in the conservative populism of the post-Wallace years, white ethnics represent precisely those little people so in need of protection from the excesses of liberal social policy; and their exemplary mobility—from steerage to ghetto to suburb—is deployed in a damning critique of both the welfare state and contemporary ghetto dwellers themselves. On the meaning of Irishness and the spirit of conservatism, House Speaker Tip O'Neill once charged that Ronald Reagan had "lost track of his roots." But Reagan Democrats would never have conceded this point. Indeed, had he lived to see the 1970s and 1980s, Malcolm X might well have relocated his famous quip about Plymouth Rock a few hundred miles southward down the seaboard: "We didn't land on Ellis Island, my brothers and sisters—Ellis Island landed on *us*."[50]

Chapter Five

I Take Back My Name

Not only did I discover that I am my grandmother and grandfather, but I began to see that in my blood are the values and beliefs of nineteenth-century Russia! Here I am— a modern, hip, radical yippie. But if you look close, what I really am is a nineteenth-century Russian orthodox religious Jew.

—Jerry Rubin, *Growing (Up) at Thirty-Seven* (1976)

For a brief time in the early 1970s, former Students for a Democratic Society (SDS) president Tom Hayden reclaimed his immigrant heritage and changed his name to Emmet Garity (combining his middle name with his mother's maiden name). Suddenly invested in his Irish roots, Hayden went to Dublin in 1971 only to be denied entry as an undesirable alien. "I began to feel that I'd been stripped of my identity by the American assimilation process," Hayden later remarked. "My government wanted to put me in jail . . . And now the Irish didn't recognize that I was their

son."[1] For Hayden, as for many others in the New Left generation, the pulse of ethnic identity was far stronger flowing out of
the 1960s than it had been flowing in. Although his middle name
recalled the rebellious eighteenth-century Irish martyr Robert
Emmet, his Old World pedigree did not seem to be much on
Hayden's mind in 1962, as he penned the inaugurating manifesto
of SDS, *The Port Huron Statement.* Such "usable pasts" were rarely
invoked by whites, as the movement was just gathering force.
And yet a decade later—a decade in which the language of black
nationalism ascended within the Civil Rights struggle; in which
"the Movement" itself fractured and multiplied along new lines
defined by a politics of "difference"—there stood Emmet Garity
at the Dublin airport, hat in hand, an Irish son.

Around the same time that Hayden was in Ireland, *Ramparts*
editor Sol Stern was reporting "all these strange Bob Dylan Stories passing around New York"—that Dylan was studying Hebrew
with some hip rabbi out on Long Island, that he had donated
money to the Jewish Defense League, that he had refused to support the Black Panthers because of their stand on Israel, that he
was spending his thirtieth birthday in Tel Aviv. Whether or not
the stories were true, their very circulation conveys the ethnic
tone of the fractured New Left and counterculture by the early
1970s. As Stern put it, "if Bob Dylan has a Jewish problem, there
are a lot of Jewish radicals newly concerned about their Jewishness and its relation to revolutionary politics who could be sympathetic."[2] These newly aroused "Jewish concerns," like Hayden's
embrace of Ireland, had much to suggest about what the left
would become on the far side of "the days of rage."

The contemporary left itself is ill-defined and little understood.
Indeed, the left today is a kaleidoscopic coalition of distinct but

overlapping publics: an environmental left, an anti-imperialist left, an antiglobalization left, a feminist left, a Third World left, a multicultural left, a queer left, a trade union left, perhaps even an academic left. Multiculturalism is the site where many key constituencies overlap, though the cooptation of the term by corporations ranging from Random House to Barnes and Noble to Disney has led many to wonder at its usefulness, indeed its *left*ness. Nonetheless, there is such a thing as a meaningful multicultural leftism, distinguished among other things by its sensitivities to identity-based groupings and to structural features of power. According to this brand of multiculturalism, pluralism can never be neutral or apolitical; nor can the political sphere be culturally neutral.[3] The development of this multicultural left owes much to the new ethnicity.

Ethnic Reverie and the New Left

The relationship between the ethnic revival and the emergence of a radically pluralist, multicultural left is more convoluted than it might seem. A few complicating factors are worth underscoring at the outset: one is that recent denunciations of multiculturalism by high-profile figures like Dinesh D'Sousa and even Michael Novak have effectively erased white ethnics' co-authorship of multiculturalism, which had been so evident in *The Rise of the Unmeltable Ethnics*. Multiculturalism is now widely associated with an exclusive, balkanizing passion among peoples of color, and so some excavation is required in order to recover the white ethnic presence within the ranks of the multicultural left.[4]

A second complication is that many people within the single white group that *is* most often associated with the New Left—

Sol Stern's "Jewish radicals"—seem largely to have been acting not as "Jews" at the time but simply as radicals. As Stephen Whitfield and others have pointed out, for instance, neither Andrew Goodman nor Michael Schwerner was given a Jewish funeral after his martyrdom in Mississippi. Moreover, for the New Left generation, the relationship between Jewish self-identification on the one hand and social activism on the other was rarely articulated, at least in the years before the Six Day War. In sharp contrast to those liberals in organizations like the American Jewish Congress, members of the New Left adopted a distinctly *Jewish* identification only later. But the secularized progressives of the Student Nonviolent Coordinating Committee (SNCC) and Freedom Summer—the New Left equivalent of Isaac Deutcher's "non-Jewish Jews," who had been so pervasive in various secular revolutions in Europe—have been swept into the discursive vortex of "Jewish history" or "black-Jewish relations" in the years since. Many of them have been written back into the historical record as the "Jews" whom they never felt themselves to be.[5] Under these circumstances, discovering the "ethnic" valences of the left is no easy task.

In delineating the links between the ethnic revival and the American left of the Civil Rights era and after, there is no better place to begin than, once again, with Novak's book *Rise of the Unmeltable Ethnics*. Although in retrospect the book has become a useful guide to the cultural critiques that were just beginning to crystallize as neoconservatism, Novak was still self-identified as a member of the left when he wrote it, and indeed the book conveys the *leftward* pluralism of those years quite forcefully. Though Novak the neoconservative would later decry the "perversions" of vintage 1990s multiculturalism, a close reading of the original text confirms Arthur Schlesinger, Jr.'s, characterization of Novak as "an early and influential theorist of multiculturalism." In *Unmeltable Ethnics* Novak called for "a multiform ideology and culture. Not a superculture with satellite subcultures, but a multiculture in which each group supplies pivotal ideas and methods. [The new ethnic politics] demands that 'the American way of life' be broken open like a cocoon giving way to the burgeoning wings of a butterfly."[6]

Writing in *The Nation* in 1968, Theodore Roszak described the counterculture as "the embryonic cultural base" of the New Left, a quest for "new types of community, new family patterns, new sexual mores, new kinds of livelihood, new aesthetic forms, new personal identities on the far side of power politics, the bourgeois home, and the Protestant work ethic."[7] *The Port Huron Statement* had decried the "loneliness, estrangement, [and] isolation" of American life, "the very isolation of the individual—from power and community and ability to aspire." This politics spun between the poles of "alienation" and "authenticity" has been called the "existentialist" character of the New Left.[8] Such philosophical searching could converge with "the new ethnicity" in myriad ways. Indeed, Novak's own protests against the hegemony of WASP culture provide a glimpse at the countercultural logic here—an ethnically inflected critique of the American mainstream, with its Nordic supremacism, its atomizing social values, its alienating economic pursuits, its bloodless modernity, and its bloody imperial wars.

Novak's greatest frustration lay with the left (both black and white) for its hand in authoring the big lie about white ethnics' racism and white privilege. A left coalition "based on divergent cultural consciousness and mutual real interests" would double the strength of the old union solidarity, he argued. "An Italian proud of being Italian, a Pole proud of being Polish, and a Black proud of being Black are three times stronger than just three more bodies in a union asking higher wages." But still, Novak's real venom was directed against WASP elites and WASP cultural values. The first premise in his critique focused on WASP domination of other groups on the American scene—not blacks alone, but all non-WASPs. American democracy, he protested, operates "to reinforce a WASP sense of reality, stories, and symbols." "WASPs have never had to celebrate Columbus Day or march down Fifth Avenue wearing green. Every day has been their day in America. No more."[9]

There were two dimensions to Novak's core resentment. One was his sense of dispossession; American political culture, he contended, enforced the WASP's styles and modes of thinking as the national norm at the expense of all other groups' cultural integrity and sense of worth. Education in America had become little more than "indoctrination" into WASP culture, or, as Novak put it, into the "superculture"; the WASP enterprise fully depended on "denying ethnic roots to others." Here white ethnics and people of color should find common cause, he argued, melding white ethnic grievance with a Third World outlook on the historic course and legacy of colonialism. White Anglo-Saxon Protestants fear "the dark passions" of those who are unlike them, whether "the huge populations of China," "the darker-skinned and less-than-Nordic immigrants," the "red-skinned savages," or the American people themselves, in all their multiethnic complexity. But "I am an American!" he insisted, bewailing the myriad humiliations that had been endured before "one could say those words and not be laughed at."[10]

Novak lodged a second, more radical protest against the very fabric of WASP culture as well: it was bad enough that so many peoples have been culturally dispossessed, but worse still, just look what they have been made to *possess* in place of their lost birthright. If WASPs fear every variety of national or racial Other, "the only thing they do not fear is cool rationality." Here Novak's Catholicism comes into full play, not as a badge of membership in a group aggrieved by existing power relations, but as a worldview affronted by the emotionally cool, coldly efficient, overly rational, alienating, atomizing, and ultimately dehumanizing character of the WASP "superculture." "It is, of course, part of Americanizing the Indian, the slave, or the immigrant to dissolve network people into atomic people," he explained. "Some resisted the acid. They refused to melt. These are the unmeltable ethnics."[11]

In Novak's leftward thinking, then, the familiar antimodernist strain of the new ethnicity becomes a full-throated diatribe, leading him into his most radical, anti-establishment pronouncements. He would later recant, as mere frustration with the left gave way to disgust. For the moment, though, he railed against the arrogance and the inequities of the American mainstream with a vehemence borne of both ethnic and class injury. "Like an iron pipe on the back of the neck," he wrote,

> ethnics feel the authority of the educated. Insistently, they are made to feel unenlightened, stupid, immoral, and backward. A new and alienating cultural style is pressed upon them. The schools undermine their families. Television beats upon them. In their eyes, it is hard to distinguish engineers and advertisers of General Motors from sociologists and literary critics—both seem to insist on the atomizing values of modernity.

If Novak's sense of injury at the hands of the "New Class" set him apart from the largely middle-class, white students of the campus-based movement, still his critique of "establishment" values had much in common with theirs. "Antipersonnel bombs were not invented by men on a construction gang," he pointed out; "guys on beer trucks did not dream up napalm."[12]

Novak's brand of ethnic, working-class grievance brought him to condemnations of the mainstream that echoed SDS pronouncements on the theme of capitalism, according to which the "hidden costs" lurking in the word "productivity" included "selfishness, pollution, envy, international conflict, and alienation." And of the Vietnam War as well: "It is ominous that the grandparents of so many ethnics endured forty days of seasickness to escape conscription into imperial armies in Europe; now their grandsons are conscripted to maintain the stability of American empire around the world . . . They did not intend their taxes to pay a million dollars for a fighter plane over rice fields far across the world (where villagers as helpless as their grandparents watch)."[13]

For Novak as for many others on the left, political activism, the quest to slake one's alienation, and a nascent sense of ethnic selfhood were never altogether distinct from one another, though among whites the ethnic accents were rarely explicit until the late 1960s. Antimodernism, ethnic consciousness, and religiosity are not strictly coeval; but in the context of the 1960s and early 1970s the three (or any two out of the three) often converged in anti-establishment protest. "America's socially acceptable identities are no longer fulfilling," wrote Jim Sleeper, then a Yale senior; "they feel pasted on, and they leave a growing personal dissatisfaction . . . The search for a deeper affirmation of life begins within the self and in basic relationships and small communities . . . [It is] at root, an existential and religious search, a raw renewal of the courage to be. As such, it is a search which drives us back into the history of our people." According to Sleeper, Jewish youths' rejection of traditional religion had been "less a denial of Judaism as such than . . . part of a more general rejection of the deficiencies and misguided priorities inherent in the American Dream their parents have pursued"; "the riches of the new world have failed to satisfy; the warmth and piety of the old community are not found on Main Street or in Suburbia."[14]

In this same vein Sol Stern derided the mainstream's "Sammy Glick and Spiro Agnew homilies" and Aviva Cantor Zuckoff scoffed at "the assimilation game." Despite its wealth, wrote Zuckoff of her parents' generation, "the Jewish community is suffering from a fantastic cultural and spiritual poverty . . . It is this gnawing spiritual hunger that drives young Jews to search for meaning in Zen, astrology, scientology, Hare Krishna, drugs, encounter groups—and sometimes, only sometimes, in Judaism." In accents of protest even stronger than Novak's, Robert Greenblatt wrote, "The frontier spirit and self-reliance, manifest destiny, laissez faire, free enterprise and the great melting pot: these are the tombstones of a people enslaved, another exterminated and the waves of immigrants neglected, exploited and digested. But some of the victims refuse to die."[15]

There are a few common variations on the theme of ethnic revival and left politics—alternate maps, as it were, of the route from one to the other. The first entails an ethnic self-ascription of high and relatively constant salience. Recalling her own involvement in SNCC, for instance, Constance Curry asserts, "I have been acutely aware of my Irish roots as far back as memory allows." Nor (as her memory serves, at least) was this awareness unrelated to Curry's political commitments as a student activist. She avidly read William Butler Yeats and other Irish poets and "embraced the words from 'The Rebel' by Irish revolutionary Padraic Pearse:

> *And I say to my people's masters:*
> *Beware, Beware of the thing that is coming.*
> *Beware of the rising people,*
> *Who shall take what ye would not give."*

Remarks Curry, "I have often thought that these lines could have come straight from the Freedom Movement of the 1960s. It is clear to me that the Irish struggle got planted deep in my heart and soul at an early age, and that its lessons and music and poetry were easily transferred to the southern freedom struggle."[16]

For others, the relationship between ethnic identity and left politics was less conscious though no less apparent in retrospect. SNCC activist Elaine DeLott Baker traces her relationship with Civil Rights politics to "the turn of the century, when my maternal great-grandfather left Russia for rural Georgia after his ten-year-old son was kidnapped and conscripted into the Cossack army." In contrast to Curry's, Baker's dawning progressive consciousness derived less from the narratives of a usable ancestral past—a keen sense of aggrieved and rebellious *peoplehood*—than it did from the hazier awareness of "otherness" and its implications. Experiencing anti-semitic slights firsthand, and puzzling over her grandmother's stark and equally unsettling division of the world into Jews and *goyim*, Baker was drawn to an egalitarian politics that would find expression at Tougaloo in 1964: "The notion of the 'other' has long cast shadows over my life."[17]

Jewish participation and the question of ethnic Jewishness within the New Left does not represent an entirely special case, as the comments of Tom Hayden, Michael Novak, and Constance Curry will begin to suggest. But Jews' relatively high profile both in the counterculture (Bob Dylan, Allen Ginsberg, Paul Goodman, Fritz Perls, Arthur Janov, Leonard Cohen, and Phil Ochs) and in radical politics (Mark Rudd, Jerry Rubin, Abbie Hoffman, Todd Gitlin, Robin Morgan, Marge Piercy, Al Haber, Howard Zinn, and Noam Chomsky) has elicited more discussion than the involvement of any other ethnic group. By the time of the Berkeley Free Speech Movement, Freedom Summer, and the community organizing and antiwar protests, Jewish students were widely held to make up between 30 and 50 percent of the movement. Richard Flacks, for instance, found that 45 percent of the participants in a 1966 antidraft sit-in at the University of Chicago were Jewish; Jonathan Kaufman estimates that more than half of the white Freedom Riders and nearly two-thirds of the Mississippi Freedom Summer volunteers were Jewish.[18] Civil Rights workers passed the time in Hinds County Jail (Jackson, Mississippi) by dancing the *horah*, a Jewish folkdance; the steering committee of the Berkeley Free Speech Movement was mostly Jewish; and though the Jewish presence was more pronounced on the coasts than in middle American bastions of radicalism, still one SDS activist could write that "the Madison [Wisconsin] left is built on New York Jews." Nor could one miss the ethnic inflection—or the ethnic insinuation—in "The Grand Coolie Damn" (1969), Marge Piercy's denunciation of the "machers" of the male chauvinist left. (*"I am a professional revolutionary . . .* No, Ma, I'm not a bum. I'm a professional, like a doctor or a lawyer, like I was supposed to be.")[19]

Three competing interpretations have emerged to explicate the Jewishness of these Jewish activists. The first, known as the "radicals-who-happen-to-be-Jewish" thesis, discounts the ethnic *content* of Jewishness as irrelevant, and focuses instead on the particular social location of this generation of Jewish students. While researching her dissertation on Jewish women's involvement in the Civil Rights movement, Debra Schultz encountered this self-understanding among activists, who wanted to know, "Why are you focusing on *Jewish* women?" or who insisted, "My being Jewish had nothing to do with it."[20] Richard Flacks, among the first to attempt a breakdown of "The Liberated Generation" (1967), advanced a "continuity hypothesis" of New Left activism: children who had grown up in families descended from "bohemians, cultural radicals and Progressives" were "likely to be particularly sensitized to acts of arbitrary authority [and] to unexamined allegiance to conventional values." Like the "red diaper babies" of the 1940s and 1950s, such children had been socialized into a tradition that held much in common with the alienated styles of the New Left; and like them, they were disproportionately Jewish.[21] Here the religious strains of Judaism or the power of ethnic self-identification are less significant than a particular variety of mid-twentieth-century progressive upbringing—the social education described, for example, by Vivian Gornick, reared in a world of political emotion which, she explains, "I understood in my nerve endings long before I could understand it in my mind."[22]

A second argument holds that, while the specific precepts of Judaism may have been incidental to Jewish radicalism, the secular baggage of Jewish history could not have been, especially for a generation coming of age in the shadow of Nazism. Vivian Rothstein recalls the Holocaust as "the defining fact of my childhood. I was raised totally in a community of refugees. That's what propelled me into oppositional politics. I was used to being outside the mainstream. That made it easier to be critical and to identify with the oppression of blacks."[23] Trudy Weissman Orris explains, "I knew what racism was because of being a Jew"; and Marilyn Lowen writes of her Civil Rights work, "we went to Mississippi to spit in Hitler's eye." "It seemed to me altogether natural," Paul Lauter agrees, "that so many of the white Mississippi volunteers were Jews. Where else should a Jew be, after the Nazis, but on the front lines in the struggle against racism?" This tendency to work from analogies to anti-semitism would influence critiques of the Vietnam War as well, once the trajectories of SNCC and SDS had run their course toward antiwar protest: "As long as there are 'gooks' there will be 'kikes.'"[24]

Even Todd Gitlin, certainly no fan of identity politics, sees something specifically Jewish in his early radicalism. The former SDS president reflects, "We were survivors . . . without having suffered in the flesh, thanks to our . . . grandparents' having journeyed halfway around the world to Ellis Island." For Gitlin, this haunting awareness in the 1950s, however dim, translated more or less directly into a radical politics in the 1960s: "to me and people I knew, it was American bombs which were the closest thing to an immoral equivalent of Auschwitz in our lifetimes"; "We were going to be active where our parents' generation had been passive"; "The Jews—but not the Jews alone—were not going to walk into any more gas chambers, or see any other good Germans go on about their business."[25]

Like many others, Melanie Kaye/Kantrowitz came alive to her Jewishness long after her engagement in New Left politics had begun. But she now sees that her "rebellion had been enacted simultaneously by thousands of young Jews; that it was in fact a collective Jewish rebellion." For Kaye/Kantrowitz, there is no radical-who-*happens*-to-be-Jewish: rather, the New Left was full of those "non-Jewish Jews" like Leon Trotsky, Rosa Luxemburg, and Emma Goldman before them, who demonstrated Isaac Deutcher's dictum, "The Jewish heretic who transcends Jewry belongs to a Jewish tradition." As Kaye/Kantrowitz sees it, Jews in the late twentieth century "are haunted—intelligently so—by spectres of cattle cars packed to the top with our people." There is something intrinsically Jewish—however secular—in the activism that arises from that collective burden.[26]

Finally, a third interpretation holds that, whatever secular Jewishness might have contributed in the way of a progressive milieu or the specter of the cattle car, the Jewish religious ethos itself actually has a distinctly progressive pull, even for those who seem to have fallen away from the Temple. As the progressive rabbi Michael Lerner has it, "Moses' genius was in being able to see through the most elaborate and powerful system of organized oppression that the world had yet known, to understand the lot of the oppressed, and to identify with them." "Does the Jewish tradition impel us," asked Arthur Waskow, the author of the Freedom Seder, in 1971, "to believe that *at this moment* we must become committed *as Jews* to the radical transformation of America and the world?" Waskow thought so. For Lerner, Waskow, and others, Jewish theology *is* liberation theology: "In its heart, Judaism is a proclamation to the world that the way things are is not the way things have to be."[27] Thus the story at the core of the Jewish tradition is one of bondage and liberation; and thus, naturally, when the nation came alive with a politics of liberation, Jewish youths disproportionately answered the call. In doing so they were enacting the Jewish principle of *tikkun olam*—the repair of the world—a religious obligation that might have seeped through at some preconscious level, even despite what Jim Sleeper called the "prostitution of Judaism to the status quo" in the 1950s synagogue.[28]

We need not choose among these interpretations; indeed, there is likely some truth to all of them.[29] It is clear that Jews were overrepresented among the ranks of young radicals, but at least initially their Jewishness was not salient to many of them, nor could they easily decipher its significance. "Jewishness becomes intriguing," wrote Sleeper, "when you try to make sense out of the fact that as a Jew on the current scene you are a slumlord to blacks, a civil rights worker to Southern whites, a well-heeled business school opportunist to hippies, a student radical to WASP conservatives, an old testament witness to Vermont Yankees, an atheist to Midwestern crusaders, a capitalist to leftists, a communist to rednecks." What did Jewishness mean? How did it matter? For his part, Jerry Rubin admitted to "personally [feeling] very torn about being Jewish"; "I know it made me feel like a minority or outsider in Amerika from my birth and helped me become a revolutionary." And yet, "Judaism no longer means much to us because the Judeo-Christian tradition has died of hypocrisy, Jews have become landlords, businessmen, and prosecutors in Amerika."[30]

Abbie Hoffman plays his Jewishness mostly for laughs in his autobiography (the principles of guerrilla theater would have been familiar to "any good Jewish comedian from Hillel to Don Rickles"), and yet he seems sincere when he identifies his Jewishness as both a target and a resource of his rebellion. If Hoffman expresses a certain disdain for the mid-century, assimilationist style by which "avoiding a scene" had become the apex of virtue for his parents' generation ("'Avoiding a scene' was a very common expression then. Over there, six million Jews were avoiding a scene . . ."), so does he admit that—from the radical's point of view—a useful "intellectual arrogance and moral indignation grow out of the [Jews'] ghetto history. For five thousand years, Jews always had the opportunity to rebel against authority, because for five thousand years there was always someone trying to break their backs."[31]

But whether the activists were radicals-who-happened-to-be-Jewish or Lerner and Waskow's *tikkun* legions, their Jewishness began to crystallize as a distinct sense of peoplehood in 1967, when the left witnessed "a political and cultural renaissance among young Jews," according to one study. With suddenness and ferocity, many Jewish radicals now became, quite self-consciously, *radical Jews*. Ensuing years saw the emergence of Jewish student organizations like the Youth Mobilization for Israel, the National Jewish Liberation Movement, and the Radical Zionist Alliance. Jewish alternative papers sprouted like psilocybin mushrooms from Los Angeles *(Davka)* to Berkeley *(The Jewish Radical)* to Chicago *(Chutzpah)* to Albuquerque *(Out of the Desert)* to Boston *(Response)* to New York *(The Jewish Liberation Journal; Herut; Columbia Jewish Free Press; The Other Way)*. By about 1970 both "Jewish left" and "Jewish counterculture" were current and widely legible phrases: Arthur Waskow's Freedom Seder, drawing parallels between Egyptian bondage and contemporary oppressions, attracted 10,000 participants at Cornell University in 1970 (and ended with a spontaneous draft-card burning); a Passover Exodus March to the United Nations on behalf of Soviet Jewry drew some 25,000 people a year later; applications to the

American Zionist Youth Foundation's volunteers for Israel program quadrupled between 1968 and 1971; and the *havurah* (fellowship) movement began to grow, representing an alternative Jewish quest for community in contrast to the "crass materialism of the larger society" and in protest against what Sleeper called the "spiritual Hiroshima" of mainstream Judaism's accommodations to middle-class American culture.[32]

This is not to suggest that Jewishness had had *no* purchase on activists' consciousness before this point (the Student Struggle for Soviet Jewry dated from 1964, for instance). But 1967 was a pivotal year in Jewish radical consciousness. The Arab-Israeli war awakened Jewish feeling even among many secularized Jews; as one SDS leader in Michigan put it, he was "frightened" by his own "chauvinism." "Two weeks ago, Israel was they," wrote one young woman in a letter to the *Village Voice;* "now Israel is we." (Paul Lauter identifies this as the moment that Israel "launched its quite successful effort to convert American-Jewish identity into Israeli nationalism.")[33] Nineteen sixty-seven also marked the heightened fragmentation of the New Left, as the language of Black Power ramified through the Civil Rights movement—a growing rift between blacks and whites which, for Jews, was exacerbated by diverging Jewish and African-American interpretations of events in the Middle East. At a Conference on New Politics in Chicago (August 1967), a number of Jews walked out when the black caucus demanded a resolution condemning Zionist imperialism.[34] The confluence was powerful: Jews in the movement were being told to go "organize among your own" at precisely the moment when Black Power itself was offering a new model of ethnoracial consciousness, and when events in the Middle East had suddenly made Jewishness matter in unprecedented ways.

Under these circumstances, Jewishness ceased to be merely a quiet leitmotif of the left and began to claim attention in and of itself. Many Jewish radicals now discovered just how Jewish they in fact were, either by their emotional reaction to Israel's peril and stunning victory, by their pained response to the ensuing radical condemnation of Zionism as racism, or by the depth of their very ambivalence. In the coming years the key Middle Eastern referent in much Civil Rights and New Left discourse would no longer be the liberatory legend of Egyptian bondage and Jewish Exodus, but rather the present-day drama of Zionist imperialism and Palestinian oppression. Not all Jewish radicals would come to the position of Itzhak Epstein, who in an "Open Letter to the Black Panthers" in the *Jewish Liberation Journal* declared, in response to their position on Zionism, "whatever justice there is in the Panthers' own struggle, I must view them from now on as my enemies."[35] But plenty would; and others would share M. J. Rosenberg's dilemma: how exactly to "reconcile my leftist proclivities with my now admittedly Zionist ones? Did I have to choose between the Fatah-supporting SDS and the ultra-middle-class lox-and-bagel breakfast club Hillel society? . . . The choice was an impossible one. I felt that there had to be a third route." There is indeed a nice irony—but also plenty of portent, as Riv-Ellen Prell points out—in the fact that many black and white radicals were becoming increasingly strident in their anti-Zionism "just as many Jewish students began to identify themselves as Jews through the rhetoric of the Left."[36]

At this juncture many Jewish activists felt caught between the anti-Jewish attitudes of black leaders in SNCC, CORE, or the Black Panthers on the one hand, and the basic conservatism of traditional Jewish leadership on the other. Some of the hitherto "uninvolved Jews," in Arthur Waskow's phrase, were now "thrust into Jewish life by the urging of the blacks to go home and organize their own community, and some were thrust into it by the denunciations of their own community's 'leadership.' Most often both." Later, when the anti-Israel, antislumlord rhetoric of some black leaders seemed to shade off toward outright anti-semitism, "radical Jews found themselves grappling with *that*—and becoming more Jewish, but no less radical, in the process."[37]

The most immediate effect was the "political and cultural renaissance among young Jews" that Porter and Dreier noted—the rise of Zionist student organizations, including many radical ones; the emergence of a recognizably "Jewish" counterculture, inflected by a romance with both kibbutz and shtetl; a new Jewish religiosity ("creative Jewing," as some called it), by which youths at once reclaimed and challenged the traditions of a lost birthright; and the *havurah*'s efforts to build "a participant community" attuned to the values of "authenticity" and "scale."[38] The distinctly *Jewish* stream of this post-1967 ethnic consciousness flowed down through later years in the form of left organizations like Breira and the New Jewish Agenda; left religious publications like Arthur Waskow's book *Seasons of Our Joy* or Michael Lerner's *Tikkun* and *Jewish Renewal;* ethnically and politically engaged fiction, poetry, and art, like Melanie Kaye/Kantrowitz's *My Jewish Face,* Judy Chicago's *Holocaust Project,* or Marge Piercy's *Art of Blessing the Day;* and the rise of a distinctly "Jewish" feminism.[39]

But the seismic conflicts on the left in 1967 went far beyond the isolated question of Jewish identity; dust settled across the political culture at large. As the historian Clayborne Carson writes, "For both African Americans and Jews, the 1967 Arab-Israeli war signaled a shift from the universalistic values that had once pre-

vailed in the civil rights movement toward an emphasis on political action based on more narrowly conceived group identities
and interests."[40] In the showdown over Zionism at the Chicago
conference (and, not incidentally, in the slights that women like
Shulamith Firestone felt *as women* at that same meeting), identity
politics was born.

In this post-1967 moment the left, including activists of all
backgrounds and colors, began to organize around what Robert
Greenblatt called "the revolutionary possibilities buried in and . . .
retrievable from vague cultural memories and almost instinctive
group loyalties." If black and Jewish activists at the moment of
Black Power and the Zionist controversy were the first to hunger
explicitly for "a past with which to interrogate and be interro-
gated," as one student put it, the emphasis on identity and heritage, on political lineage and a given people's *particular* legacies of
struggle, quickly consumed members of other groups as well.[41]

Only within the context of Black Power, the Zionist/anti-
Zionist conflict, and the rise of a specifically "Jewish" counterculture did the *Ramparts* story on Bob Dylan's Jewish awakening
have any traction. But more significantly, it is also within this
context that one must understand Tom Hayden's retrieval of his
Irishness during the "Troubles," or Michael Novak's call for an
ethnically composed left coalition ("an Italian proud of being Italian, a Pole proud of being Polish, and a Black proud of being
Black"). It was within this context that Debbie D'Amico, in her
"Letter to My White Working-Class Sisters" (1970), evoked her
family's immigrant past—"how they 'came over,' and how they
survived, the first Italians in an all-Irish neighborhood. That is
my history." And it was within this context that members of a
Catholic splinter group calling itself the Class Workshop broke

from the radical feminist Redstockings and began their work, according to Susan Brownmiller, by exploring their family histories.[42]

Tom Hayden now refers to his adoption of the name Emmet Garity as "a brief flirtation with Malcolm X's strategy," but the "romantic phase of [his] Irish identification" owed as much to those SDS radicals who seemed everywhere to be "coming out" as Jews. Assimilation, he wrote, "erased the memories that could link Americans with the struggles and sufferings of other people." Hayden now grasped why "Jews were the most liberal 'whites' in American society; it was because they remained the least assimilated, the most sensitive to the experience of oppression . . . what young Americans, and perhaps increasingly Americans of all ages, were looking for was a new, richer identity in life than just 'making it.'" If ethnicity is "as much a tactic as a definition," then after 1967 ethnicity would ascend as a tactic of the left no less than of the right.[43] Both the New Left's critique of U.S. power structures and its rejection of "mainstream" or "establishment" values tended toward a logic of "de-Waspization," in Paul Lyons's phrase—a project in which, for some, personal (non-WASP) identity choices would become ever more important.[44]

The Arc of Multiculturalism

Multiculturalism as a coherent phenomenon captured little attention until the 1990s: Nathan Glazer's database search in the mid-1990s found "no references to 'multiculturalism' as late as 1988, a mere 33 items in 1989, and only after that a rapid rise—more than 100 items in 1990, more than 600 in 1991, almost 900 in 1992, 1200 in 1993, and 1500 in 1994."[45] But by then multiculturalism had already been twenty years in the making. Insofar as this was a student movement rather than a workers' movement, insofar as it developed its critiques and its logic amid a race-based struggle rather than a class-based one, and insofar as it had embraced existentialism as early as Port Huron, the New Left had been ripe for such a turn for some time. Drawing inspiration from writers like Herbert Marcuse, C. Wright Mills, Paul Goodman, and the Beats, this left tended from the very beginning to focus more on "subjective conditions" than on the old left's "objective conditions." Richard Rorty characterizes the brand of dissent that is the New Left's legacy as a "cultural Left" for whom economic exploitation is less a matter of concern than "the 'politics of difference' or 'of identity' or 'of recognition.' This cultural Left thinks more about stigma than about money." By the late 1960s this cultural left required only a destabilized notion of center and periphery to become a fully "*multi*cultural left." The New Left's universalism had been "fragile from the outset," Todd Gitlin notes in retrospect, "the category of citizen, or even human being, had long felt like a weightless abstraction." This was the "alienation" of *The Port Huron Statement* in 1962. Within a decade "it was as members of a specific category—as a black person, a woman, or later as a Jew or a lesbian—that people increasingly insisted on being represented in 'the decisions that affected their lives.'"[46]

The initial relationship between Civil Rights–New Left activism, education, and multiculturalism was immediate and direct. The very language of multiculturalism, indeed, had arisen amid local Civil Rights battles over schools and education in the mid-1960s, as questions of desegregation, hiring, and the content of the curriculum collided. Just as the tensions that would later culminate in the battle for Ocean Hill–Brownsville were surfacing in

New York, for instance, a 1966 proposal for Intermediate School 201 in Harlem touted an education for "successful living in a democratic, multi-cultural and multi-racial city."[47] Civil Rights questions of school desegregation and hiring—who was to be taught and who would do the teaching—inevitably raised multiculturalism's basic question of *what* would be taught.

Such questions were germane at the university level, too. In November 1968, within an atmosphere of general Civil Rights and antiwar protest, students at San Francisco State College staged a strike in dissent against various university policies. Among the demands presented to the administration were open admissions, the establishment of a School of Ethnic Area Studies, and self-determination of curriculum and faculty for the different nationality groups within the new school. While members of the Third World Liberation Front (TWLF) disrupted campus operations, according to Karen Umemoto, "400 white students marched to President Smith's office in support of TWLF demands." In 1968 and 1969, similar protests erupted at 524 colleges and universities across the country, and more than half of these institutions established ethnic studies courses, programs, or departments as a result.[48]

The curriculum wars in ensuing decades, then—that site where "identity politics," student activism, disciplinary flux, and institutional transformation and resistance all converged—had their roots in 1960s Civil Rights protest. Knowledge itself became a Civil Rights issue, as students and less traditional faculty members began to theorize and contest the ways in which the "apartheid curriculum" of the liberal tradition reinforced the white supremacist patterns endemic to American life. SNCC's confrontational strategies supplied the models for redress. Small victories in minority hiring and curricular innovation, moreover, laid the groundwork for changes that were to become the grist for many polemic mills in the 1980s and 1990s, as the legitimacy of African-American Studies, Ethnic Studies, or later multicultural requirements dominated public debate on American education. Indeed, this particular Third Worldist strain of multiculturalism has eclipsed all else in public discussion, leading commentators like Michael Novak to denounce the (antiwhite) *exclusivity* of the multicultural vision.

Although there is a regional valence to these developments—a "west coast" ethnic studies model that has emphasized the Third Worldist critique versus an "east coast" model that has been slightly more hospitable to European ethnicities—still the structural features of race and inequality have become central to both. Since students' curricular demands initially arose out of a more general Civil Rights protest against racialized social relations, both the structural features of the national color line and the histories and cultural contributions of various peoples of color were highest priorities.

There is no question that multiculturalism's most influential voices have been men and women of color like Toni Cade, Armando Rendon, Frank Chin, Ishmael Reed, and Gloria Anzaldua. But much has been obscured in the common conflation of multiculturalism with "Third Worldism," in the spirit of the City College graffiti perhaps too vividly remembered, "Honkies: Attention—Your Time Has Come."[49] In their insistence that multiculturalism represents a hijacking of the curriculum solely on the part of peoples of color, critics like Novak distort the contours of multicultural aims, curricular changes, and the history of multicultural coalitions themselves.[50] Black Studies was the meteor in the academic firmament that most captured national attention in the early years (nearly five hundred programs were established between 1966 and 1972, however begrudgingly in some cases), and Black Studies is routinely singled out for attention even now, often misrepresented as "Afrocentrism." But recall that by the end of the decade the Italian-American historian Rudolph Vecoli, too, called for "a rewriting of the history of the United States which will be multi-ethnic, multi-racial, and multi-lingual in its interpretation of the American experience (or better yet, *experiences*)."[51]

Thus Mark Naison, the chair of Black Studies at Fordham, a radical-who-happened-to-be-Jewish, recalls that the enrollments for Black Studies in 1971 included thirty Italian-American students: "For the Italian and Puerto Rican students, who encountered little representation of their cultural traditions on the Fordham campus . . . African-American studies courses created a discourse on race and culture that resonated with their own experience, both as ethnic outsiders in a changing Catholic university and as products of a black-influenced New York street culture."[52] Jewish students—Jewish students on behalf of Jewish Studies, no less—were among the most vocal in their calls for curricular innovation in that first wave of radical student demands. By 1971, in response to student agitation, 185 colleges and universities in North America had begun to offer Judaic Studies courses, or to sponsor existing noncredit programs for credit. Hebrew Houses were established at colleges like Oberlin, while "free universities" established elsewhere offered courses with titles like "Jewish Mysticism, Chassidism, and Radical Theology," "Zionism and World Liberation," "The *Shtetl* Culture," and "The Oppression of Jewish Women."[53]

Multiculturalism carries the singular honor and burden of having become known primarily through the assaults against it. Such assaults have uniformly painted multiculturalism as an affair for peoples of color, not for all comers; as tribal and ceaselessly ethnocentric, never reaching for wider horizons; as a feel-good approach to the nation's heritage and its past, not the stuff of rigorous academic inquiry. But missing in most denunciations are the thousands of teachers and students for whom the study of diversity represents a civic matter of comprehending the nation, not an ethnocentric matter of "self-esteem" or "therapeutic" history. *Balkanization* is the critics' watchword, as Michael Novak made clear when he renounced the idea that there had been any connection between *his* ethnic revival and "that new beast called 'multiculturalism'": "Just as they were excluded before the early 1970s, the ethnics from Southern and Eastern Europe are again today given no place in curricula about 'diversity . . .' In this respect . . . multiculturalism as currently practiced in most universities is a fraud."[54]

If, in their zealous vigilance against "balkanization," critics are apt to miss the extent to which a person of color like Ronald Takaki has relied on the insights of Herman Melville in constructing his narratives of multicultural America, they are even more apt to miss the degree of white ethnic participation in that complex of pursuits that now goes under the name multiculturalism. Multiculturalism did not unfold on one side of the color line alone, nor have most manifestations of multiculturalism represented *separatist* impulses. "When I say multiculturalism," writes Barbara Ehrenreich, "I do not mean African American students studying only African American subjects; I mean African Americans studying Shakespeare . . . I mean Caucasian students studying African American history, Asian American history, and so on. That's my idea of a genuine multicultural education."[55]

Although they have become objects of derision for critics, the racial pride movements and the separatisms then developing among people of color were not neatly cordoned off from the ethnic revival. On the contrary, as Lawrence Levine points out, the dramatic changes in the American university derived in part from its *demographic* transformation in the postwar years—"the entry of new ethnic and racial minorities into the academic world as both students and teachers," including many second- and third-generation ethnics from what Levine (who numbers himself among them) calls "the 'wrong' parts of Europe." Early multicultural volumes like Theodore Gross's book *Nation of Nations* (1971) capture the catholic tone of the diversity project in its formation. Not only does the roster of the anthology convey the full variety of Americans' plural histories (including John F. Kennedy, James Baldwin, Emma Lazarus, Langston Hughes, Mario Puzo, Chief Standing Bear, Allen Ginsberg, Lin Yutang, James T. Farrell, Eldridge Cleaver, Muriel Rukeyser, Ole Rolvaag, Toshio Mori, Norman Podhoretz, Oscar Handlin, and Carlos Bulosan), but the brief preface conveys the inclusive and unifying philosophy of early multiculturalism:

> America is a nation of immigrants. No other land has been so informed with the myth of men creating their own futures from their individual attributes. The American dream is a collective dream, and it has haunted the sleep of every child in this country. This book is an expression of that dream and the ways in which it has possessed, liberated, and often frustrated the minorities in America.[56]

In 1975 a young Werner Sollors would present an Ethnic Studies initiative at Columbia University in these terms: "Since the 'new ethnicity' emerged in the course of the 1960s, the interpretation of Black cultural nationalism may offer one suggestion toward an understanding of ethnic culture as a broader concept, derived from—or in confrontation against—Black culture."[57]

Here is where the 1960s history of Civil Rights sensibilities, student radicalism, curricular demands, black nationalism, the transformation of Jewish radicals into radical Jews, and the rising white ethnic consciousness characteristic of the post-1967 left all come together. This convergence explains why so many of the most significant *white* participants in the various projects and struggles of multiculturalism bear the evocative surnames of Ellis Island and "the 'wrong' parts of Europe." This includes not only Novak, demanding that "'the American way of life' be broken open like a cocoon," but highly influential educators and writers with surnames like Lipsitz, Gabaccia, Mazziotti, Lauter, Vecoli, Kaplan, and Gerdje. And Levine.

Paul Lauter describes one route from Ellis Island to multiculturalism, in his autobiographical musings on the experience of being the Jewish professor whose responsibility it was to teach a course entitled "The Origins of Christian Civilization." In thinking about the seldom explored intertestamental period for his lecture set—trying to breeze through texts that were "neither canonical texts nor the classics of our civilization (whatever it was that defined 'our' or 'civilization')"—Lauter stumbled into the core insight of later "multiculturalism": "If so much of such interest was left out, what confidence could we have in the narrative we were presenting? . . . Were we really teaching [students] the best that had been thought and said or only the good news that seemed to fit? Some of it, after all, didn't seem to fit *me* that well." It came to seem "almost reasonable," Lauter continues, ". . . that I was omitted from the underlying cultural narratives that informed curricular structures. If I were here . . . why was I left out? By the end of the 1960s, of course, questions like 'Where are the blacks?' and 'Where are the women?' became central to rethinking the curriculum. And discomfort, a queer sense of malaise, was transmuted into demand, a politics of identity."[58]

Reflecting on her interest in Warner McGuinn, a black Yale student in the 1880s whom she had discovered in her researches of Mark Twain, the literary scholar Shelley Fisher Fishkin similarly writes, "Like Warner McGuinn, I knew that 'people like us' (people possessing the 'wrong' skin color or gender or religion or ethnicity) had somehow not really been a part of the story our culture told about who and what it was . . . Empowered by our education and training, yet disempowered by our awareness that mainstream American culture marginalized people and traditions we respected, we responded by channeling our energies into changing the structures themselves—desegregating American cities, desegregating the American literary canon." As Jews, she continues (though here she might have included all the other "wrong parts of Europe"), "we know what it's like to be written out of the story."[59]

A second route from Ellis Island to multiculturalism has less to do with who is "written out" than with the substance of group history. Like many earlier Civil Rights activists, white advocates of multiculturalism in the academy and the arts often drew on their own ethnic perspective in articulating sympathies or in formulating an understanding of the nation. "It's always a failure of ethical nerve to settle for compare-and-contrast-oppression competitions," writes Robin Morgan, whose efforts in the area of feminist multiculturalism ("global sisterhood") have been prodigious. Rather, "the challenge is to use one's own suffering as a skeleton key to gain access to the suffering borne by others." Such are the mainsprings of contemporary multiculturalism: Lillian Robinson traces her commitment to multiculturalism to her own "awareness of the existence of anti-Semitism as a form of racism"; Elizabeth Abel explains her attraction to black women's writing as "shaped by my Jewishness; there's some identification at work there that's only starting to become clear to me."[60] Maria Mazziotti Gillan's poetic memoir "Public School No. 18: Paterson, New Jersey," helps to situate her editorial work on two multicultural volumes, *Unsettling America* and *Identity Lessons:*

> *Miss Wilson's eyes, opaque*
> *As blue glass, fix on me:*
> *"We must speak English.*
> *We're in America now."*
> *I want to say "I am American,"*
> *But the evidence is stacked against me.*
> . . .
> *Without words, they tell me*
> *To be ashamed.*
> *I am.*[61]

In "Growing Up Italian" Gillan celebrated "my Italian American self / rooted in this country," casting her lot with "all those black/ brown/red/yellow/olive-skinned people" who "soon will raise their voices" and sing "Here I am." "Today," she announces, "I take back my name."[62]

Some Third World students chafe at the notion that European immigration constitutes an acceptable concern for "ethnic studies." The University of California defines "European Americans" as one of the five "racial and cultural groups" within the compass of multiculturalism. The multicultural requirements at the University of Wisconsin can be met with courses like "Community and Ethnicity among European Americans" and "Jewish Civilization in Medieval Spain." Some Jewish students, for their part, are dismayed to find themselves counted unproblematically among "European descended whites."[63] But if the inclusion of white ethnic groups may seem a watering down of the multicultural agenda, it is nonetheless also true that white ethnics played a significant role in the genesis of multiculturalism from the outset.

As the curricular debates raged throughout the University of California system, the forces of multiculturalism found an ally in Tom Hayden, now a U.S. congressman, who went on record in favor of multiculturalism "as a means of researching and restoring what has been lost or suppressed in history." The Irish ex-president of SDS felt that he knew a little something about "loss," "suppression," and retrieval. Tom Hayden–Emmet Garity's interest in Ireland had not ended with his brief interlude in Dublin during the "Troubles." In 1997 Hayden edited a collection of essays on the Famine called *Irish Hunger,* in which he contributed a highly personal memoir of the 1960s as refracted through his search for roots. This memoir, in turn, became the basis for his extended reflection in 2001, a book-length treatment titled *Irish on the Inside.* Cracking the assimilationist wall that his parents had erected between him and his Old World past, Hayden now narrates his 1960s activism in terms of an increasing engagement with things Hibernian. Although severed from his heritage throughout his childhood and youth, as he puts it, "the sixties made me Irish."[64]

When Kennedy's non-WASP heritage became an issue during the presidential campaign of 1960, Hayden recalled, "I was so assimilated, I simply dismissed the attacks . . . as obsolete, irrelevant echoes from a past that no longer mattered." But as the "authoritarian ice" of Cold War conformism began to thaw, Hayden's Irish blood began to flow. The ascendance of Bobby Kennedy, "a wild Irishman" whose identification with "non-conformists, resisters, farmworkers, ghetto dwellers, [and] the Sioux" suggested to Hayden that "there was such a thing as an Irish soul":

> The identity which I received from my parents continued to unravel during 1968, finally ending on the streets of Chicago. Assimilation led to emptiness. All around me others were realising new identities for themselves, as liberated women, black or Chicano nationalists, even gay people. They were leaving the melting-pot to regain their roots. But who was I?
>
> History tells of a "hidden Ireland," of a native character behind the Anglicised facade. I was beginning to understand that there was a hidden Irish-America too. There was not only Cardinal Spellman but Bobby Kennedy; not only Charles Coughlin, but the Berrigan brothers; not only George Meany, but Elizabeth Gurley Flynn. The figures in American life who most repelled and most attracted me, who warred for my soul, seemed all to be Irish.[65]

The thematic chords that Hayden strikes convey in highly personal terms the strict compatibility between the spirit of the New Left, of the ethnic revival, and of later multiculturalism. First,

Hayden's decrying the costs of the Irish emigrants' quest for American inclusion—"Assimilation led to emptiness"—recalls not only Novak's denunciations of "WASP hegemony" but SDS's poles of "alienation" and "authenticity." But over and above its authorship of that generalized "loneliness, estrangement, [and] isolation" in American life that *The Port Huron Statement* had so bitterly condemned, assimilationism was also responsible for the *specific* political crises that framed the New Left agenda. Having now reorganized his understanding of his early Civil Rights activities in the light of that "hidden Ireland"—famine on one side of the Atlantic and nativism on the other—Hayden can only remark with a drenching irony on his parents' disapproval of his radical politics.[66] Assimilationism led only to disinterest and complicity; *dis*similation, to justice.

A second prominent theme in Hayden's memoir, is the mythic power of the Old World to supply inspiring heroes for the New. If assimilationism lies at the root of all villainy, then renewed ethnic identity and an attention to Old World history will supply a redeeming heroism. "[T]he Irish tradition is filled with poets, and political leaders supportive of progressive, often radical, causes," Hayden discovers. "They were heavily involved in American labour radicalism, producing such personalities as Mother Jones and Elizabeth Gurley Flynn. They were stalwart supporters of the New Deal."[67] The lineage of rebellion descends, unbroken, from Robert Emmet, to Jeremiah O'Donovan Rossa, to Mother Jones and Elizabeth Gurley Flynn, to Bobby Kennedy and the Berrigan brothers—and Tom Hayden.

Finally, a third major theme is the discovery of this unremitting Irish heroism *in contemporary Ireland:* usable pasts and presents collided and fused in August 1968, when "several thousand civil rights marchers took to the streets in Northern Ireland, singing 'We Shall Overcome.'" Like those Jewish leftists who had formed the Radical Zionist Alliance in the wake of the Arab-Israeli war, or the young Polish-Americans who would later find inspiration in the dissident trade union movement in Poland, Hayden now saw political *sense* in his heritage. Irish ethnicity lent coherence to his life's path, making continuous and comprehensible the trajectory from his point of origins to his present commitments: "While the whole world may have been watching in Chicago [in 1968], now I was watching, for the first time in my life, *these Irish who seemed and looked so much like me.* Now I knew I was Irish too."[68]

These reflections underscore principles that are as significant as they are unremarked in the development of the multiculturalism that descended from the Civil Rights movement and the New Left: the extent to which particularism does *not* necessarily lead inexorably down a road toward "tribalism"; and the extent to which a salient white ethnicity is *not* the exclusive province of the right. As Hayden concluded in *Irish on the Inside,* "If Irish Americans identify with the 10 percent of the world which is white, Anglo-American and consumes half the global resources, we have chosen the wrong side of history and justice."[69] Notwithstanding the symbolic cachet of Ellis Island in the new right's bootstrap mythologies, the saga of European immigration continues to supply an energy, a social sensibility, and a gallery of political heroes that also nourish the "multicultural left."

The rivulets from vintage 1970s white ethnic consciousness are many: one led to the establishment of Jewish Studies or Italian-American Studies programs at universities across the country; one led to the social conservatism of the so-called Reagan Democrats in the 1980s; another, to the thin charms of *Crossing Delancey* (1988) or the keening for a bygone world in Barry Levinson's *Avalon* (1990); yet another, to green beer, the *faux* "authenticities" of *Riverdance,* and (as decried by Tom Hayden) the New Age "swooning over a Celtic spirituality."[70] But at least some were swept by these currents to the politics and concerns of contemporary multiculturalism.

"Little platoons," "loneliness, estrangement, isolation," "new types of community," "the search for authenticity," "a thousand points of light," "the warmth and piety of the old community," "liturgy, community, ethnicity, and roots"—since the 1960s the left and the right have perhaps shared more than they know. The New Left and the New Right were joined at the hip on the question of modernity and alienation, and a language of ethnic particularity has been crucial on both sides: as one Jewish student put it, "the myths of the melting pot" had amounted to no less than "America's plastic substitute for the rich experience of peoplehood."[71]

The ethnic motifs of anti-establishment protest initially inclined toward stylistic appropriations from the colonized world, such as peasant blouses, beads, and headbands. But the radical logic of Black, Brown, Red, and Yellow Power eventually led to a new understanding of America itself, not just as a demographic "nation of nations," but as a political structure so shot through with inequalities—so built upon the multiple, asymmetrical histories of conquest, slavery, exclusion, imperialism, and voluntary migration—that no political left worthy of the name could fail to take questions of diversity and "difference" into account. A more personal reflection on ethnic roots increasingly characterized the white student left in the wake of Black Power. This particularism has made significant contributions to the leftist critique, even if someone like Todd Gitlin can find a number of ways to disparage it—"the aggrandizement of difference," "the cant of identity," "the new identity orthodoxy," "the twilight of common dreams."[72]

On the right, meanwhile, the welfare state has become the chief villain in a morality play of megastructures and small platoons. The excessive, "disuniting" tendencies of the post–Black Power, "multicultural" left represent the dangerous perversion of an otherwise open and democratic pluralist ideal. Lost in most accounts of the antimulticultural right, however, is the extent to which the very critique of the new particularism is itself the product of a fierce but largely hidden particularism. The rules that both liberal social policy and multiculturalism are said to be breaking are rules derived exclusively from a national civics lesson supplied by the experience of European immigrants. The universalizing "ethnic pattern" of American history spelled out in *Affirmative Discrimination* represents a particularistic politics *par excellence*—"why can't everybody just be like us?"

Nowhere is the shared impulse behind contemporary multiculturalism and contemporary neoconservatism so pronounced as in the work of Michael Novak, and nowhere are the political stakes of this shared impulse so open to view. That the left and the right have shared to some degree in the particularistic romance of the ethnic revival must not be understood as a development without political consequence. On the contrary, though the ethnic lens has repaid progressivism by making visible many historical truths and themes, the *way* in which the "ethnic history" of various European groups is typically narrated has ultimately contributed to the nation's steady movement toward the right in the decades since the Nixon presidency.

Consider, briefly, *The Guns of Lattimer* (1978), Novak's treatment of a violent conflict between capital and (Slavic) labor in the mining region of 1890s Pennsylvania. The outward signs in the text of Novak's rising conservatism begin with his opening dedication: "This book is intended as a partial repayment for the gifts America gave." So is it woven into his narrative at key junctures, as a kind of patriotic reassurance that becomes the order of the day. "The American branch of our family has now been here just over a hundred years, and we still thank God for that every day," writes Novak. Even the protesting miners of the tale are "painfully aware that in the Austro-Hungarian Empire they could conduct no such open and peaceful protest as they did here."[73] This celebration of America's better way may have been fairly standard during the Cold War years, but it seems a strained introduction to a story in which—even "here"—many of the peaceful protestors will end up being murdered for their dissent.

But it is Novak's faithfulness to the historical record—his insistence, indeed, that the massacre at Lattimer become a *part* of the historical record—that aligns this work so completely with the wider project of multiculturalism. It is not just that, like other multiculturalists, he wanted his children "to have a history," as he wrote; but rather America itself cannot be properly apprehended without reference to these striking Slavic miners in 1897. "Whoever speaks of the 'American character,'" he averred, "must include theirs, for in significant ways they expanded its range and its depth." Despite his hardening conservatism, when it came to the plight of the downtrodden Pennsylvania miner, Novak also recognized the tragedy in American history. This tragic sense, too, has constituted one of the hallmarks of multiculturalism as it has resisted the easier, more celebratory formulations of consensus.

"The tragic destiny of America is hidden in its virtue," wrote Novak:

> Its founders, so noble and enlightened in countless ways, suffered from racial blindness in the largest sense: those of northern European culture have imagined themselves to be superior to others races of any color, including white . . . Every other race feels this whip. Were it no longer denied, such a flaw could be overcome.[74]

Most striking is not that such an account *could* have emerged from the left, but that precisely such an account *has* emerged from the left. Here is where the political stakes of this odd kinship of left and right becomes most evident: though an integral part of the genesis of multiculturalism at its inception, the narrative of European immigration—whether striking Slavic miners, ghetto-bound Polish meatpackers, or Yiddish-speaking ladies' garment workers—has largely been a narrative of down-troddenness, sometimes of pluck, often of revolt, but never, ever, of *privilege*.

It is no small thing that Americans were celebrating this brand of Ellis Island whiteness at the very moment that the Civil Rights–Third World critique of the U.S. social order was receiving its first full airing. In the absence of a recognized narrative of white *privilege* that could compete with the popular epic-romantic narrative of the downtrodden yet ever so resourceful immigrant, many principles of the militant antiracist critique never stood a chance. At the very moment that the "bigotry" and "prejudice" model of social analysis began to give way to the more systemic, structural model of "racism"—at the moment that discussion of "attitudes" waned and discussions of "power" and "privilege" ascended—a set of narratives was emerging to couch and conceal major elements of whiteness itself as a structural feature of the social landscape.

In the absence of a narrative of white privilege on a par with those narratives of white subjugation that have endlessly spun off the reels of the culture and knowledge industries—fashioned by figures as diverse as Irving Howe and Letty Cottin Pogrebin; Rudy Vecoli and Sylvester Stallone; Francis Ford Coppola and Helen Barolini; Tom Hayden and Daniel Patrick Moynihan— the most radical *structural* critiques developed from a Civil Rights or Third Worldist point of view could never quite get a purchase on the popular political imagination. Contributions like Stanley Lieberson's documentation of European immigrants' white privilege in *A Piece of the Pie*, Micaela di Leonardo's rendering of her own family history as a history of advantage in "White Lies, Black Myths," or Karen Brodkin's structural analysis *How Jews Became White Folks* stand out for precisely how far they depart from the norms of the conventional, "roots"-era narrative of immigration and mobility.[75] Having grown up with the Jewish ethnic wisdom "that we pulled ourselves up by our own bootstraps, by sticking together, by being damned smart," Brodkin now discovers some significant omissions: that not all Jews made it, first of all, and that "those who did had a great deal of help from the federal government," including a congeries of New Deal and postwar labor and housing policies, the GI Bill, and FHA and VA mortgages, which, though advertised as open to all, actually "functioned as a set of racial privileges."[76]

This bootstrap mythology, complete with its striking patterns of self-congratulation and erasure, has become standard fare as white Americans seek "to define themselves out of the oppressor class," in Micaela di Leonardo's phrase, "to construct a blameless white identity." "I wish I had a dollar," she comments, "for every time some paesan or Pole or Greek or Jew has started kvetching to me about how *his* ancestors didn't own slaves, *her* parents or grandparents worked their fingers to the bone, therefore he or she has no responsibility to fight racism." But this outlook on the "we" and "they" of American history is neither as simple as "the white ethnic's weasel," as some have called it, nor as plain as a case of trying to dodge "the old leftist insight that we all benefit from 'white skin privilege.'"[77] It is neither this simple nor this plain because, for one thing, this mystification of "the oppressor class" took place *not* in the isolated realms of family lore or hand-me-down identity, but within myriad institutions at the very heart of the political culture, including publishing houses, Hollywood studios, universities, and policy centers. For another thing, this "blameless white identity" was inadvertently a creation of the left no less than of the right.

Chapter Six

Our Heritage Is Our Power

Of course, ethnic revivalism need not inspire retrograde role playing or male chauvinism; it can empower a woman by linking her to her people, her history, and her resources.

—Letty Cottin Pogrebin,
Deborah, Golda, and Me
(1991)

As the rift between black and white radicals within the Civil Rights and student movements began to grow, the New Left also began to fragment along lines of gender and sexuality. Indeed, Shulamith Firestone raised the question of male dominance within left circles at the very conference that witnessed the split between black and Jewish radicals on the question of Zionism in 1967. As the New Left splintered, the "identity" left was born. Robin Morgan's piercing essay "Goodbye to All That" (1970) remains the most biting critique of New Left sexual politics as well as the most dramatic announcement that feminism was going to reshape the landscape of American progressivism. The "All That" of Morgan's title consisted of the myriad ways that the left itself had become no more than a "counterfeit, male-dominated cracked-glass mirror reflection of the Amerikan Nightmare."[1]

But like their brothers, friends, and lovers in the Civil Rights and peace movements, white feminists, too, found a powerful political resource in the legend of immigrant forebears. "Your grandmother might have been one of the 'huddled masses yearning to breathe free,'" wrote Debbie D'Amico in her 1970 letter "To My White Working-Class Sisters." That foremother might have been among those "who came to America and wound up in a tenement where free air never blew . . . made to feel alien and ashamed of an Old World culture infinitely more alive and colorful than the drab, Puritan, 'Mr. Clean' ways of America." The historic "huddled masses" were a living critique of America's broken promise. The immigrant past became suddenly and quite potently "usable," not only in further enumerating the nation's inequities, but in establishing a lineage that linked the 1960s generation with noble struggles of the past. "While Mr. Pullman was amassing his fortune," D'Amico said, "our people were fighting and dying for the rights of working men and women, our people were being shot and beaten for what they believed."[2]

D'Amico's chief concern was to conjure "the invisible women, the faceless women, the nameless women" of the white working class. In forging a new self-recognition and self-respect, she hoped to establish common cause with "Black and Puerto Rican, Mexican and Indian, Chinese and Japanese people," who had also "had their true history concealed and their faces scorned by TV and magazines."[3] But in returning to the tenement in search of a usable past, D'Amico gave voice to a significant motif within white second-wave feminism—a kind of world-of-our-mothers cultural politics that profoundly influenced later discussions of American diversity and the American past.

As Robin Kelley has written, American feminism draws from a deep well of "collective imagination," and so its best ideas and most brilliant texts are the products of "collective social movement[s]" in which unsung activists are often the ones who "produce new knowledge and open new vistas for inquiry." Vital to this process across the decades has been the radical imagination of women of color, whose feminism has often been inextricable from the race-based movements for liberation which sustained them and which they sustained.[4] To examine the workings of imaginative genealogy among white feminists, then, is not to venture a genealogy of American feminism itself. But a careful topography of white feminists' ethnic sensibilities restores a neglected dimension to the recent history of American feminism on both sides of the color line. The Jewish, Italian, or Irish accents of white feminism as it emerged in the context of the ethnic revival help to explain both the obstacles that arose and the alliances that were forged as white women and women of color reconfigured the personal and the political.

History and heritage were at the center of the white feminist project; thus ethnicity and white feminism articulated each other in meaningful ways. Feminists cannot afford an ahistorical stance, wrote Elisabeth Schussler Fiorenza in an essay titled "In Search of Women's Heritage," "because it is precisely the power of oppression that deprives people of their history."[5] As a Catholic theologian, Schussler Fiorenza meant "to reclaim early Christian history" and "to insist that women's history is an integral part of early Christian historiography." But her project was closely aligned with other feminist searches, both sacred and secular, "for roots, for solidarity with our foresisters, and finally for the memory of their sufferings, struggles, and powers as women." Of course "heritage" could mean different things to different women —an Italian-American childhood in Bensonhurst (Marianna De Marco Torgovnick), the Lower East Side at the turn of the century (Meredith Tax), the Italian countryside (Helen Barolini), early Christianity (Schussler Fiorenza), the mythic spaces of the Babylonian Talmud (the *Lilith* collective), pre-Hellenic Greece (Charlene Spretnak), or "Old" eastern and southern Europe between 6500 and 3500 B.C.E. (Marija Gimbutas and Riane Eisler).[6]

Feminism and ethnicity shared meaning and form. Esther Broner was speaking for all women, Jews and non-Jews, when in her feminist Seder she exhorted, "Who are our mothers? / Who are our ancestors? / What is our history? / Give us our name. Name our genealogy." Thus many feminist writings, including those only peripherally concerned with ethnic identity as such, are characterized at one point or another by an "ethnic moment." For instance, Shulamith Firestone's uncompromising critique of patriarchy in *The Dialectic of Sex* (1970) derived at least in part from Firestone's obligatory sojourn on an Israeli kibbutz. In sexual-political terms, she had to conclude, "the kibbutz is no radical experiment"; women at this particular "far left kibbutz were concerned with demanding private kitchens in addition to the communal one where meals were served six times a day."[7] A generation later (1997) and in a very different kind of book, Naomi Wolf cited *her* Jewish youth group's stay at a northern kibbutz as a pivotal moment in her own feminist awakening. Having fallen for an Irish laborer named Devin, Wolf found herself learning more about her identity as a *woman* than as a Jew:

> If to my trip counselors I was a miscegenating rebel, and if to [my friend] Ofra's uncle . . . I was a godforsaken secular

Jew, and if to Devin's mates I was that locker-room joke, the lubricious JAP, and if in the eyes of the Muslim men observing us while they played *sheshbesh* in the market cafes I was a representative of dissolute America, the country of women who are beyond whoredom, then the weight of all these clashing systems of control and expectation around female sexuality was just too much. In my mind, under the burden of all those dictates competing to stereotype rather than support me, the legitimacy of the notion of such control simply collapsed.[8]

In the years separating Firestone's kibbutz experience from Wolf's, many writers articulated their feminist outlook in the accents of an ethnic birthright either happily embraced or bitterly protested, consciously recovered or manifest by simple reflex: "one writes from one's skin," as Helen Barolini put it. In forging a renewed feminism, the daughters and granddaughters of immigrants now wrote from the "skin" of an *ethnic* experience of both women's lot and women's power. As Barolini recognized, the new ethnicity and the renewed feminist movement had converged, granting "permission to the young women of today to look deeply and closely at the family, to examine its values and its limitations."[9] Thus Vivian Gornick would reflect on the "immigrant home" of her childhood, and the ironic way in which her parents' mystification by American culture actually opened up worlds of possibility for her. Others came to just the opposite conclusion, as they parsed their experience of gender, ethnicity, and possibility: "A woman and a Jew," wrote Marge Piercy, "sometimes more / of a contradiction than I can sweat out."[10]

Still others found strength and inspiration in the Old World past, or interpreted their own political aspirations as an analog of

their forebears' hopes: Mary Daly acknowledged being particularly moved by "the work of the women of Ireland, that Treasure
Island which I recognize deeply as the wellspring of my Background, my ancestral home." Starhawk (Miriam Simos) likened
the egalitarian community she was envisioning to "the promise
the land whispered to my immigrant grandparents fleeing servi-
tude in the Russian army, the promise inscribed on the Statue of
Liberty." Others fancied that the critical edge of their feminism
opposed and so might counter the facile optimism of their immigrant predecessors. "Awakening from my immigrant Jewish family's dreams of America, I have had to reconfigure my own sense
of home," writes Laura Levitt.[11]

Symbols, metaphors, and analogies of immigration run through
American feminist writings throughout this period, as when
Adrienne Rich referred to feminist social space as "a place of emigration" or Gloria Steinem characterized the antifeminist Right
as "the kind of people our ancestors came here to escape." Elsewhere Steinem remarked that the "new ambitions nourished by
the rebirth of feminism may make young women behave a little
like a classical immigrant group."[12]

The most thorough discussion appeared in an essay by Elisabeth Schussler Fiorenza, herself an immigrant from Germany,
who proposed the metaphor of the resident alien as "an apt figure for a feminist movement and politics of liberation within the
context of Western societies and churches." She called on white
women, who in her formulation were "fairly recent 'immigrants'
in academy and ministry," to resist the pressure "to function as
tokens who are 'loyal to civilization'" as they found it. "Posi-
tioning ourselves as resident aliens, as insiders/outsiders in the
center of church and academy, calls for an ethos and ethics of pa-

15.   *Feminist rally in support of the Equal Rights Amendment, Liberty Island, 1970. As the ethnic revival and second-wave feminism dove-
tailed, the site may have held a special resonance for Edda Cimino (center) and others like her.* BETTMANN/CORBIS.

triarchal demystification, of common political struggles, and of multicultural visions for liberation."[13]

As her vision suggests, the ethnic secession implied in this insider-outsider formulation—whether literal or figurative for a generation of white ethnic second-wave feminists—hinted at the kinds of coalitions that were possible as ethnicity and feminism continued to inflect each other. By the time American feminists were rallying at the Statue of Liberty on August 26, 1978, to commemorate the battle for women's suffrage, the site had perhaps already assumed a special significance for many of them.[14]

Ethnic Feminism–Feminist Ethnicity

The link between nineteenth-century Castle Garden or Ellis Island on the one hand and second-wave feminism on the other begins, quite simply, with personnel. That many notable white feminists—including writers, artists, scholars, legislators, and activists from various wings of the movement—traced their roots to Emma Lazarus's "huddled masses" is well known. "Almost all the leaders of the feminist movement in North America were Jewish," comments Michele Landsberg. (Amy Kesselman of Chicago Women's Liberation goes further: "the very character traits that women's liberation had validated and freed were, well, Jewish.") A cursory list of Jewish feminists includes figures as influential and varied as Betty Friedan (Bettye Goldstein), Robin Morgan, Gloria Steinem, Shulamith Firestone, Andrea Dworkin, Susan Brownmiller, Adrienne Rich, Judith Butler, Carol Gilligan, and Miriam Simos (Starhawk).[15] But a proprietary claim and a certain Jewish exceptionalism has obscured the fact that, in overwhelming numbers, the prominent white feminists who are *not* granddaughters of the Jewish ghetto tend to trace *their* roots back through Ellis Island to Europe as well. This list, too, encompasses a wide variety of feminist ideologies, temperaments, and influences, including figures like Kate Millett, Marilyn French (Mara Solwoska), Anselma Dell'Olio, Eleanor Cutri Smeal, and Kathie Sarachild. A few among them were immigrants themselves, notably Gerda Lerner and Elisabeth Schussler Fiorenza (German), Irena Klepfisz (Polish), Marija Gimbutas (Lithuanian), and Anne Koedt (Danish).[16]

Identifying feminists' ethnicity, however, does not tell us the percentages of women within each ethnic group who identify as feminists, nor what portion of the movement comprised representatives from these ethnic groups. Indeed, as the northern, urban, and coastal biases of the U.S. media and knowledge industries match up rather comfortably with the historic geographies of European immigrant settlement, this scroll of prominent feminists may say more about the map of American notoriety than it does about the actual demographics of the feminist movement. (The picture in the South, where white ethnic identities have generally been less salient, is undoubtedly quite different, for example; but white feminists in the South have not claimed as much *national* attention as those in the urban North and West.) The development of feminist politics between 1963 (when both *Beyond the Melting Pot* and *The Feminine Mystique* appeared) and 1984 (when ethnicity and feminism came together in popular perception in the vice presidential candidacy of Geraldine Ferraro) becomes a dual story of how certain social locations engendered a feminist critique—and how, in turn, American feminism carried strong traces of the *ethnic* history that attended its birthing.

The precise relationship between ethnicity and second-wave

feminism, however, varies a great deal. For some, like Melanie Kaye/Kantrowitz, ethnic concerns became central to the left-feminist project. A poster child for Hansen's third-generation, "repatriated" daughters, this poet-activist reclaimed the "Kantrowitz" that her father had Anglicized to "Kaye," rooting her politics in a gender-insurgent understanding of Judaism and a specifically *Jewish* interpretation of "difference" and justice. (Developments to which her father, exemplifying his portion of Hansen's Law, could only respond, "So, Melanie, what's with all the Jewish?") Ratifying Rose Schneiderman's turn-of-the-century demand for "Bread *and* Roses," Kaye/Kantrowitz now argued that the "roses" of a preserved and unharassed Jewishness—including "our peoplehood, our culture, history, languages, music, calendar, tradition, [and] literature"—were crucial because these things "are beautiful and ours, and because the point of struggle is not bare survival but lives full of possibility." Her writing represents a radical, feminist update of Horace Kallen's early-twentieth-century stance, in which the *raison d'être* of true democracy is to grant a free field for the play of "ancestral endowments."[17]

For others, like Kate Millett, ethnic identity scarcely organized the scope and shape of feminist consciousness, but was rather an uneven and stubborn outcropping, only occasionally jutting from beneath the surface of a more universalizing political language. "Imagine all those years fighting the church," Millett writes, in a fleeting reference to the Irish Catholic radical Dorothy Day. "I grew up hearing her denounced from the pulpit as a dirty commie while still chained by Mother to my pew, cheering her on, another rebel." Or again, reflecting briefly on a friend she calls O'Rourke and on her own political pedigree, Millett marvels at "this prodigious Irish-talking lady scattering emeralds into the

sink and garbage can, waving her gold rings into desolate age unheard . . . I feel she is an aunt, a mother, a hag, a witch, a saint, a
fairy six feet tall—the old kind we had in Ireland before the English cut us down to size."[18]

Mary Gordon articulates a more self-conscious, more complicated relationship between her feminism and her Irish Catholicism, a political sensibility at the crossroads of attraction and re-
pulsion. On the one hand, as she put it to an interviewer in
1987, she felt a certain affinity for the rebelliousness of the Irish:
"There's something in the Irish not being with the program that I
like." And yet, on the other hand, if Gordon attributed her capacity for fury to her Irishness, she also recognized that the Catholic
Church supplied all too many occasions to let that fury loose.
"One of the truly depressing things," she explained, "is to look at
the early labor movement and see the number of Irish women
who were 'heroes.' Mother Jones was an Irish woman, as was
Leonore O'Reilly . . . So the heroes of the early labor movement were largely Irish and the church just stomped on them."[19]
Gordon's identity, not as an Irish–American feminist, but as an
Irish *Catholic* feminist, then, derives from the contradiction between her allegiance to these "heroes" and her relation to those
who "stomped them."

Adrienne Rich, for her part, articulates yet another variation of
the relationship between feminism and ethnicity. "It is feminist
politics," she wrote, "the efforts of women trying to work together
as women across sexual, class, racial, ethnic, and other lines . . .
that have pushed me to look at the starved Jew in myself; finally,
to seek a path to that Jewishness still unsatisfied, still trying to define its true homeland, still untamed and unsuburbanized, still
wandering in the wilderness."[20] If there were distinctly ethnic

paths to feminism, in other words, there were also distinctly feminist paths to ethnicity; and for women like Rich, feminism *was* an "ethnic revival."

Perhaps it was inevitable that, cradled as it was by the Civil Rights movement, second-wave feminism would fix on questions of ethnoracial particularity. But for many women, feminism grew organically from the social and cultural positions they occupied by virtue of their family histories. Like the men of the New Left, many feminists were not especially conscious of their own ethnicity as they entered the political fray, but nevertheless it was in part the social milieu and the angle of vision they inherited that brought them to a politics of dissent in the first place. Indeed, many of these women embraced their ethnic identity *as* ethnic identity only much later.

Betty Friedan was not a member of the New Left, "ethnic revival" generation, but her work was central to second-wave feminism, and her own case is instructive. *The Feminine Mystique,* the book most often credited with supplying a nomenclature for "the problem that has no name" and thus galvanizing the 1960s feminist resurgence, contains very little in the way of a recognizably "Jewish" outlook. The ethnic accent here is slight, with the possible exceptions of Friedan's passing reflection on the German phrase "Kinder, Kuche, Kirche" (the Nazi decree that women must "be confined to their biological role"), her comparison of those who "'adjust' as housewives" to "the millions who walked to their own death in the concentration camps," or her characterization of the suburban home itself as "a comfortable concentration camp."[21]

Not until long after the fact did Friedan attribute her feminist "passion against injustice" to her early "feelings of the injustice of anti-Semitism." In 1970 she took her first trip to Israel to "get in touch with [her] Jewish roots," and in later editions of *The Feminine Mystique* she included her 1983 essay "Thoughts on Becoming a Grandmother," in which she described awakening to "the religion of [her] ancestors." Her roots in an immigrant household in Peoria, Illinois, might have been quietly influential in her feminist politics, but her politics were not articulated as "Jewish" until the nation's more general ethnic revival. In this she had a great deal in common with many younger activists of the New Left generation. In her sardonic novel *Memoirs of an Ex-Prom Queen* (1969), Alix Kates Shulman, too, equates the important social lessons of being a girl with the important social lessons of being a Jew: "Prudently I gave up football, trees, and walking to school unaccompanied for acceptable 'girls' things,' until . . . like everyone else I unquestioningly accepted the boys' hatred of us as 'normal.' Just as the Cortney kids wouldn't play with me because I was a Jew, the boys wouldn't play with me because I was a girl. That was the way things were."[22]

Ethnic antagonism, anti-Catholicism, and anti-semitism were not the only "ethnic" factors influencing the feminists of the second wave. In *The Feminine Mystique,* Friedan noted that many of the discontented women in her Smith College sample "had come from 'the more restrictive ethnic groups' (Italian or Jewish)." Friedan later speculated that the tension at the core of *The Feminine Mystique* between personal ability and aspiration on the one hand and society's gendered horizons on the other might have been particularly extreme for Jewish women, who were among the most highly educated women in America and yet whose "legitimate" self-conception was based almost entirely on home and family.[23]

Indeed, during her keynote speech for the Women's Strike of 1970, Friedan found herself invoking "the religion of my ancestors," in which men had daily thanked the Lord "that I was not born a woman"—one of many ways in which, by religious dictum and cultural custom, traditional Judaism enforced women's second-class standing. "Today I feel, for the first time," Friedan said, ". . . absolutely sure that all women are going to be able to say, as I say tonight, 'Thank thee, Lord, that I was born a woman.'" A year later Vivian Gornick, too, would decry the Judaic codes by which an Orthodox man "may not look upon the face or the form of a woman—ever—and he daily thanks God that he has not been born a woman." (As Judy Chicago later put it, after an Orthodox man in Israel refused to shake her hand, "I said I couldn't accept that God wanted him to do something that made me feel like a piece of dirt.")[24]

Blu Greenberg, one of the first women to challenge the Jewish strictures on women's religious authority, seemed to be misreading this correlation between ethnic traditionalism and ethnic feminism when she noted, "Oddly enough, Jewish society—in which many pioneer feminists were nurtured—was one of the last groups to grapple with the challenges of feminism." Nothing odd about it. She later notes, "As I reviewed my education one fact emerged . . . the study of Talmud, which was a primary goal in my family and community, consistently was closed off to me. Beginning with elementary school, the girls studied Israeli folk dancing while the boys studied Talmud."[25]

The constraints of the ethnic enclave have been corroborated many times over, in terms both religious and secular, by the women who emerged among the most significant white voices of second-wave feminism. "A major theme in the literature on white ethnic families is their 'stability,'" writes Micaela di Leonardo. "Stability here is in part a code term for patriarchy: what is claimed is not only that ethnics remain married and care for their aged, but that women remain in the home and 'do their duties,' that parents discipline their children strictly, that [Christopher] Lasch's . . . nostalgia for the authority of the father is here satisfied." Louise DeSalvo, too, writes of women's hardships and narrow horizons as a feature of *ethnic* heritage: "in the land of my forebears, women sit around and wait for their men. Or they work very hard and watch their children and wait for their men. Or they make a sumptuous meal and they work very hard and watch their children and wait for their men. But they don't go anywhere without their men. Or do anything for themselves alone without their men. Except complain." (Beware, DeSalvo cautions—having learned a few things on her own personal "roots" trip—of "any recipe that begins, 'Take a mortar and pestle . . .'")[26]

In her memoir of Italian Bensonhurst, Marianna De Marco Torgovnick similarly remarks that "in an Italian American household . . . the boy comes first. Always did, still does." Elsewhere, Torgovnick speculates on feminist bête-noire Camille Paglia's solution to the same gendered conundrum: the brusqueness and the undercurrent of violence in Paglia's intellectual style result from her having "mastered typical Italian American male patterns." (Helen Barolini proposes a similar ethnic genealogy for the cultural rebellions of Madonna Ciccone: the singer may not "read" as ethnic Italian in any significant way—nor unproblematically as "feminist," for that matter—but within the context of a confining Italian Catholic womanhood, she may *perform* as such.) The strictures on "proper" womanhood could be doubly felt, of course, among lesbians in these communities. As Julien Murphy wrote, "A Catholic lesbian grows up learning that her body is destined to be heterosexual, and that *the body of every Catholic girl is marked as the breeding ground for the Church.*" Murphy critiques this oppressive "fertility ethic" as a "Catholic policy of birth-out-of-control."[27]

Many feminists, like Theresa Del Pozzo, later made quite plain the connection between the smothering enclave and their own political commitments: "It was my mother's unhappiness with that oppressive macho culture of the Italian American world," wrote Del Pozzo, "that initially propelled me in search of a different life."[28] Given the demographics of the student movement, such ethnically inflected masculinism is no doubt *part* of what the women of the New Left were up against here, too, as they began to confront the oppressive gender arrangements of SDS and SNCC.

Thus it may be no coincidence that Irish America, an ethnic subculture noted among sociologists for its "gender antagonism," reared Kate Millett, the author of *Sexual Politics.* "Our society, like all historical civilizations," wrote Millett,

> is a patriarchy. What goes largely unexamined, often even unacknowledged (yet is institutionalized nonetheless) in our social order, is the birthright priority whereby males rule females. Through this system a most ingenious form of "interior colonization" has been achieved. It is one which tends moreover to be sturdier than any form of segregation, and more rigorous than class stratification . . . [S]exual domination [is] . . . the most pervasive ideology of our culture and provides its most fundamental concept of power.[29]

Where Millett acknowledges her Irishness at all, it is most often as an indicator of her pedigree as a radical: "Remember the steerage," says her mother, whom Millett identifies as "a daughter of Galway whose favorite song and only composition for pianoforte during [Millett's] own childhood was a lively rendition of 'The Wearing of the Green.'" But consider Millett's analysis of "birthright priority" within the context of an Irish famine, exodus, and disproportionately female diaspora whose contours were determined precisely by "birthright priority"; consider the venom of her "interior colonization" model within the context of a culture for whom colonization was critical, sure, but for whom "social realities [had] created a pattern whereby marriage and the interaction between husband and wife was at best one of irritability and separate spheres and at worst one of tension and domestic violence." Indeed, Irish culture was so "enmeshed in an ethos of gender hostility" that one analyst commented, "Ireland is divided by a boundary even more pernicious than that between North and South—the boundary between the sexes."[30]

According to Friedan and others, ethnicity could also heighten the tyranny of the "host" or "mainstream" culture's social codes. If cultural retention or isolation posed a problem from the standpoint of gender equity, that is, so did assimilationism. Here in America, wrote one Slovak-American woman, "the male was the ruler in the home [and] a marriage a slave relationship at worst, a benevolent despotic sovereignty at best." Assimilation into *what?* But others have noted that the most stressful point in women's social sphere is not where the "despotic sovereignty" of the enclave and the host culture converge or collude, but where they *collide.* Recall, for instance, Naomi Wolf's identity lesson on her trip to Israel, when she was subjected to the conflicting but unforgiving expectations of her rabbi, her trip counselors, her friend's uncle, her boyfriend's mates, and the Muslim men in the market cafes. Like Wolf at this moment, women who simultaneously in-habited an ethnic enclave and the broader "American" culture—whether as immigrants or as children of immigrants—were sub-ject to "the weight of . . . these clashing systems of control and expectation around female sexuality." Moreover, for many of these ethnic women, as for Wolf, "under the burden of all those dic-tates . . . the legitimacy of the notion of such control simply collapsed."[31]

Maria Frangis was a Greek American who yearned to do many things that would render her "too Americanized" by Old World measures, "'lost' to my family, my parish, my community," as she puts it. "I was not pained by my ethnic origin as much as I felt re-stricted by it." Like Torgovnick and others, Frangis was most crit-ical of the enclave's patriarchy. But her oblique reference to those "pained" by their ethnic origin is telling. Sexuality was an area where the competing cultural norms of gender were most appar-ent and oppressive, but so was women's physicality itself, the body: part of what it meant to be "pained" by one's ethnic origin was to deviate from the physical ideal that defined American "beauty." As Frangis wrote, "The emphasis was on assimilation, on not looking or acting Greek. Girls dyed their hair blond to look more 'American.'"[32]

As the historian Elizabeth Haiken notes in her study of cos-metic surgery, American definitions of beauty have long been keyed to "Caucasian, even Anglo-Saxon, traditions and standards." Though perhaps only skin deep, such definitions are not merely superficial; rather, they "speak to questions of power, or the lack of it, and access to it." Power here is a term laden with both gendered and ethnic significance. Consider, for instance, Hazel Rawson Cades's 1927 assertion that "being good looking is no longer optional . . . There is no place in the world for women who are not," or plastic surgeons' routine references to certain kinds of aesthetic deviations as "racial or ethnic stigmata." It is no accident that the blond-haired, blue-eyed Barbie Doll has become a symbol of the oppressive norms of American femininity; nor is it incidental that Barbie herself—the "ultimate *shiksa* goddess," as Rhonda Lieberman puts it—was the invention of the *Jewish* toymakers Ruth and Elliot Handler.[33]

Thus by the Anglo-Saxon biases of proper Americanism and the gendered dimensions of assimilationism, ethnic women were doubly situated to suffer—and to critique—the tyrannies of feminine beauty ideals, Bess Myerson notwithstanding. As Shulamith Firestone wrote in *The Dialectic of Sex,* "in America, the present fashion vogue [1970] of French models, or the erotic ideal Voluptuous Blonde are modeled on qualities rare indeed." For Firestone, "the exclusivity of the beauty ideal serves a clear political function": not only does "social legitimacy" for women inhere in physical appearance, but notions of beauty turn women against themselves and against each other.[34] If to become American meant to become "white" for the generation that came of age in the mid-twentieth century, still, as Wini Breines comments, "the recent immigrant history and bodies many brought to the suburbs" carried the muted costs of a certain "otherness." "From Eastern and Southern Europe," she notes, "suburban assimilation took the form, for many girls, of aspiring to WASP beauty standards."[35]

Although their whiteness certainly exempted Jewish, Italian, and Greek women from the harshest exclusions of standard American beauty, still their outsiders' perspective on the physical imperatives of "proper" femininity may have guided them toward

a critique of beauty itself—not only its definitions, but its stran-
gling power as an imperative of female aspiration. The New York
Radical Women's protest at the 1968 Miss America pageant—
including the establishment of a Freedom Trash Can for the
disposal of bras, girdles, hair rollers, and various other "instru-
ments of female torture"—defined beauty as "an image that has
oppressed women."[36] On a small scale this protest is evident in individual women's vexed relationship to the American femininity
symbolized by Marilyn Monroe, the Barbie Doll, or the blonde
beauty pageant queen. From across the color line Barbara Smith
has written of women's "feelings of outsideness," "the self-hatred
about features and bodies that don't match a white, blue-eyed
ideal." Like Cherríe Moraga, who in this respect sees Jews as
"a colored kind of white people," Smith notes that "feelings of
shame and self-hatred affect not just Black and Jewish women,
but other women of color and white ethnic and poor women."
And so, for example, though Susan Brownmiller has never been
strongly self-identified as Jewish, there might be something both
politically dissenting and unshakably "ethnic" in her simple reflection in *Femininity*, "I have been at odds with the hair on my
head for most of my life."[37]

"Not looking Jewish was more important than being Jewish,"
Nancy Miller recalls of her 1960s youth. After a detailed discussion of her idealization of the "blonde, long-legged phys-ed ma-
jors" at her summer camp, of her pained recognition that being
Jewish "meant you would never look like Sandra Dee," and of
vainly ironing her hair in an attempt to achieve that glamorous
Carol Lynley look so prized in *Seventeen* magazine, Miller comments: "Despite my abject acceptance of these aesthetic norms,
whose historical significance I did not begin to suspect, like a

George Eliot heroine I also nourished a nameless and secret wish for some way of being in the world outside conventions altogether; it would take feminism for me to discover what that was."[38]

The "Jewish nose" as both fact and symbol has received by far the most attention in feminist writings on white ethnicity and beauty ideals. As Melanie Kaye/Kantrowitz writes, "We all knew Jewish noses were ugly. Never asking, 'why ugly?' or answering 'because Jewish.'" She recalls "setting and sometimes bleaching, sometimes straightening my hair. What I did to my eyebrows will be understood only by those women who also have black bushy eyebrows. I was not trying to look like a *shiksa*—I was trying to look pretty. (why ugly? because Jewish.)"[39] Second-wave feminism did not eradicate the beauty ideal or its Anglo-Saxon bias: "Locked in the family's bathroom," recalls Tali Edut, who came of age a generation after Kaye/Kantrowitz, ". . . [I] wasted precious teen hours staring at my reflection, wondering why I had been cursed." "Everything was too big. My nose with the bump on it was a trademark of my Jewish lineage (which I hated as a result)."[40]

Under this regime, it is no wonder that a certain set of *gender* imperatives should come under attack from an *ethnic* standpoint: feminism—the questioning and rejection of the culture's beauty ideals and its gender expectations—became one solution to the conundrum of ethnic self-acceptance. As feminists self-consciously dismantled the culture's Barbie ideal, the operative spectrum of judgment was not purely aesthetic but rather ethnic. As Teresa de Lauretis has noted, "The discrepancy, the tension, and the constant slippage between Woman as representation . . . [and] women as historical beings, subjects of 'real' relations . . . are motivated and sustained by a logical contradiction in our culture and an irreconcilable one: women are both inside and outside gender, at once within and without representation."[41] In this respect ethnic women were "without representation" in more ways than one.

But the tyranny of beauty represents only one edge of a much larger issue; namely, the extent to which many ethnic women endured a kind of double patriarchy. With their helpmate models of femininity, many ethnic cultures enforced a constraining set of choices indeed; and the dominant culture's unforgiving Anglo-Saxonism rendered its own harsh imperatives harsher still for non–Anglo-Saxon women. As Elly Bulkin observed, "Many Jewish feminists come from backgrounds of assimilation which continue to be a source of pain and potential tension."[42] That wider world conjured up by the word "Americanization" turned out to be narrow and unforgiving after all—an ethnic slur. Like Nancy Miller, many met these inherent contradictions and slights with a wish to be "in the world outside conventions altogether"; for many, "it would take feminism . . . to discover what that was."

The emergent feminism of the 1960s was seldom cast in "ethnic" terms. Indeed, writers like Kaye/Kantrowitz, Faderman, Brodkin, and Torgovnick did not explicitly link feminist consciousness to ethnicity until the ethnic revival.[43] The relationship between ethnicity and feminism before the 1970s was most often reflexive, in other words, rather than fully conscious or self-conscious. Betty Friedan's movement from oblique references to anti-semitism in *The Feminine Mystique*, through her "roots" trip to Israel in 1970, and finally to more explicit references to "the religion of my ancestors" and a re-narration of Jewishness and anti-semitism as foundational to her feminist education properly describes the general development of the *articulated* relationship between feminism and ethnicity during these years.

But that relationship was no less powerful for remaining unarticulated. Consider, for instance, the terms of debate as the generational and factional tensions played out within the women's movement. Ellen Willis's relentless 1981 critique of liberal feminism, "The Greening of Betty Friedan," casts a suggestive light on the ethnic textures of feminist discourse. Here Willis is writing not as a Jew but as a radical. Though her objection to Friedan is strictly ideological, she casts her argument in a logic that parallels the pluralist critique of assimilationism. "The rhetoric Friedan uses to describe the aims of 'first stage' feminism," chides Willis, "is all about getting *in*—in the mainstream, inside the party, the political process, the business world."[44]

Willis thus lodges the radical's typical objection to reformism, but here with an ethnic twist: the symptomatic moment is when Willis decries Friedan's fears "of alienating men, offending Peoria." Willis almost certainly intends *Peoria* here as a stand-in for "middle America" ("How will it play in Peoria?"); but both the phrase and the encompassing argument assume a different look when one recalls that Friedan in fact hailed from Peoria—it is to Peoria and its anti-semitism that Friedan herself points in describing the development of her own social conscience. Willis challenges that "to associate herself with radicalism [would mean] to exchange the marginality of a housewife for the marginality of a rebel" (a bargain Friedan refuses). Willis's challenge replicates Yiddishists' charge a generation or two earlier against German Jews, whose assimilationist sense of "arrival" in America had been threatened by the Yiddish-speaking hordes from Eastern Europe: the new immigrant masses would call too much attention to themselves, as far as the established German Jews were concerned. They would ruin it for everybody, as the phrase went, and yet they also threatened to *become* (and ultimately did become)

American Jewry. Reformists like Friedan now looked on radicals in much the same way, says Willis.[45]

American political culture posed precisely the same dilemma for feminists of the second wave that it had posed for the ethno-racial groups of the "new immigration": Should they stake their claim to civic participation on the basis of being the same as those already inhabiting the sphere of "we the people"? Or should they embrace their sense of "difference" and assert that it would enrich the republic? The dilemma held an ethnic resonance for many of the women involved, including Friedan and Willis. Both the safe "assimilationism" of Friedan's reformist politics and the dare-to-be-bad "*anti*-assimilationism" of Willis's radical feminism have a backstory; and that backstory runs from Czarist Russia, through Ellis Island, to the Yiddish ghettos of the New World.

World of Our Mothers

"How could a person, a woman not even five feet tall, change the world?" asks Rose Chernin. "I'll tell you. It's a good story." This preamble, first recorded in Kim Chernin's memoir *In My Mother's House* (1983) and later reproduced as the epigraph to Susan Glenn's book *Daughters of the Shtetl* (1990), conveys the ancestral impulse of second-wave feminism. If the women's movement had been energized by an angry rejection of The World of Our Fathers, so was it finally characterized by a loving devotion to The World of Our Mothers. The lives of the foremothers and foresisters, indeed, supplied both weapons and inspiration for the war against patriarchy, which explains why the feminist contribution was so central to the narratives of the ethnic revival (one thinks of reprinted novels like Anzia Yezierska's *Bread Givers;*

newly minted literature like Mary Gordon's *The Other Side,*
Meredith Tax's *Rivington Street,* or E. M. Broner's *Her Mothers;*
"women's" anthologies like Helen Barolini's *Dream Book;* historical monographs like Elizabeth Ewen's *Immigrant Women in the
Land of Dollars;* oral histories like Marie Hall Ets's *Rosa;* memoirs like Kate Simon's *Bronx Primitive;* and personal explorations
like Kate Millett's *Mother Millett* and Letty Cottin Pogrebin's
Deborah, Golda, and Me).

This attention to ethnic women also explains—counter-
intuitively, perhaps—why feminist energies have been so critical
to the project of multiculturalism. "In its demand for equality for
women," Katha Pollitt points out, "feminism sets itself in opposition to virtually every culture on earth. You could say that multiculturalism demands respect for all cultural traditions, while
feminism interrogates and challenges all cultural traditions."
Fundamentally, Pollitt concludes, "the ethical claims of feminism
run counter to the cultural relativism of 'group rights' multiculturalism."[46] This is a compelling line of reasoning, but it is flawed in
two respects. First, the feminist challenge to "cultures" can only
go so far; it cannot be an outright rejection, for without multiculturalism, how would one investigate the diverse history of patriarchal power arrangements and antipatriarchal struggles? As
Andrea Dworkin put it in the opening lines of *Scapegoat: The
Jews, Israel, and Women's Liberation* (2000),

> I repudiate all nationalism except my own and reject the dom-
> inance of all men except those I love. In this I am like every
> other woman, a pretender to rebellion because to break with
> patriarchy I would need to betray my own . . . [Jewish men]
> betray me through assertions of superiority intended to hurt

my human rights and my dignity. In this, too, I am like every other woman. Feminists try hard to fight for women at the same time maintaining special loyalties to subgroups of men. How could we not?[47]

Second, many of the templates, the inspirations, and the subversive tools for feminist *opposition* actually reside in the realm of "cultural tradition"—in the world of our mothers. Fully opposing "virtually every culture on earth," to take Pollitt's formulation, has been neither possible nor altogether attractive, not only because women are tied to their (patriarchal) communities in complex ways, but because the tradition of "a people" also includes its most inspiring (antipatriarchal) *counter*traditions—feminist "roots." Though ethnic cultures are all patriarchal, as Pogrebin puts it, "ethnic revivalism need not inspire retrograde role playing or male chauvinism; it can empower a woman by linking her to her people, her history, and her resources."[48]

The 1975 reissue of Anzia Yezierska's novel of the Jewish ghetto, *Bread Givers* (1925), was a signal intellectual event in the emergence of this world-of-our-mothers feminism. "In the light of the emerging women's movement," wrote Alice Kessler Harris in her 1975 introduction, "*Bread Givers* has become more meaningful than ever." If *Bread Givers* paints the Old World social codes of the immigrant ghetto in their harshest patriarchal tones, both the novel's protagonist and Yezierska herself stand as apt symbols of feminist dissent. Yezierska was "a revolutionary," wrote Kessler Harris. "Passionately convinced that her life was her own, she deliberately rejected traditional home and family roles."[49]

Similarly, Meredith Tax's historical work *Rising of the Women* (1980) represents the self-conscious effort to mobilize women's history for the sake of its modern-day lessons for feminism and for the left (recounting in epic tones the struggle of immigrant activists like Elizabeth Gurley Flynn, Emma Goldman, Fannie Kavanaugh, Clara Lemlich, Leonora O'Reilly, Margaret Sanger, Rose Schneiderman, and Rose Pastor Stokes). In the novel *Union Square* (1988), on the other hand, Tax emphasizes a far more constricting notion of "ethnic heritage." In answer to her daughter's question, "What does it mean to be Jewish?" Tax writes, "What was Rachel supposed to answer? To her, Judaism meant study for the men and drudgery for the women . . . it meant a father who could barely earn a living but thought he was better than everybody else, and a mother who was scared of her own shadow."[50]

The ancestral impulse in second-wave feminism shared in the same antimodernism found in nonfeminist ethnic revivalism, but to this it added resentment at having been written out of history and a quest to recover useful heroines for the renewed feminist struggle. In her 1969 "Letter to the Left," Ellen Willis theorized that "the American system consists of two interdependent but distinct parts—the capitalist state and the patriarchal family." It was "important for women to recognize and deal with the exploited position in the family system for it is primarily in terms of the family system that we are oppressed *as women*."[51] Once the patriarchal family was a focus of feminist theorizing, individual feminists would inevitably attend, not only to those patriarchs whom they knew best, but also to those women around them who had struggled and endured. If the personal was political, in other words, so was it historical: the examination of patriarchy and its challenges *was* a "roots" trip.

E. M. Broner's work is paradigmatic of the feminist investment in history. Her dramatic poem *Summer Is a Foreign Country*

(1966) tells of a Russian Jewish matriarch whose ancestors have bequeathed her magical gifts. As she lies dying, her American grandchildren gather around her in hopes of receiving the last gift themselves. Broner's first novel, *Her Mothers* (1975), is an exploration of mother-daughter relationships, literal and figurative. The "mothers" are not all biological; some are also historical and mythic, including Margaret Fuller, Louisa May Alcott, Emily Dickinson, Rosa Luxemburg, and various matriarchs from the Bible. Broner punctuates the novel with biting meditations on women's prospects in both Old World and New ("Mother, I'm pregnant with a baby girl . . ." "Does she have a date for the Senior Prom?" "No." "Then tell her not to be born.")[52]

But if the protagonist of *Her Mothers,* Beatrix Palmer, becomes Broner's vehicle for examining patriarchy's past as a garden of sorrows, Beatrix herself in turn authors a book, *The Pioneers,* which plumbs the immigrant past for its examples, inspirations, and heroisms. The pioneers of Beatrix's title are those "women who went from Kiev to Cleveland, Sevastopol to Staten Island." Having received "a small anthropology grant to work on the oral history of the dying-off immigrants" of the early twentieth century, Beatrix and a photographer friend set out to interview elderly couples, but make a discovery along the way: "out of the trappings of a patriarchal society, Beatrix and her friend discovered that it was a matriarchy that put the costume of dark suit, skull cap, and beard on their men . . . it was the women who held the families together when they were separated by the war . . . It was the women who invented ways to feed the family once they were reunited. Their book became one of pioneering women."[53]

Her Mothers conveys feminism's threefold interest in history. First, as only a study of history could reveal the roots of patriarchal arrangements, the present could be neither understood nor challenged without historical investigation. Second, as Beatrix's "pioneers" indicated, the past was also rich in examples of heroism. The past might be made up of layer upon sedimented layer of patriarchal power, but in its inspirational struggles, history could offer a blueprint for action. And third, the very fact that such struggles and such heroines were so little known pointed to the patriarchal practices of *historiography,* itself a condition to be resisted and overturned. Who knew anything about the ingenious ways that Beatrix's pioneers had invented to feed their families? Who knew about the strengths and triumphs of history's Emma Goldmans or Leonora O'Reillys? Who knew about women's everyday travails or, looking back further still, about the matrifocal societies of earlier epochs? There is no such thing as being "lost to history" without first *losing historically,* as Broner and others now understood: the patriarchy of lived history and the silences of written history were intimately related.

The development of the feminist historical project contains two distinct but entwined lines which, in their turn, were connected with the sentiments and yearnings of the ethnic revival. One originates in the praxis of group Consciousness Raising (CR) sessions, where through a collective process of recollection, testimony, and analysis, women's individual experiences became the basis for a systemic political critique. Beginning with the founding of radical groups like New York Radical Women, Redstockings, and Bread and Roses, as the movement was "oscillating between personal anecdote and grand theory," in Meredith Tax's phrase, personal history—including family history—became very important.[54] The "power of feminism," according to Vivian Gornick, "turned on the realization that social change had more to do with altered consciousness than with legislated law." In women's case, this meant "the necessity of squeezing the slave out of one-self drop by drop," a process of understanding one's life "in historical terms." As Ellen Willis noted, "Feminist consciousness-raising and analysis produced a mass of information about the family as an instrument of female oppression."[55]

The second line of feminist historical thinking originated in the academic disciplines, where campus struggles and the student left had already begun to challenge the received wisdom of what constituted "history." "American history will never be rounded until the lives of its women, immigrants or not, belong to the public," wrote the editors of a roots-era volume titled *Jewish Grandmothers.* "It will stand unfinished until the experiences of its minority groups complete it; it will flow shallow until the words of its elderly deepen it." The discovery of women's heritage in the disciplines was closely linked to the personal quest for a usable past, though here the pursuit found an institutional expression far beyond the ad hoc commentary and loose congeries of late-1960s and early 1970s CR groups. In 1969, on the heels of the San Francisco State strike over Third World issues, women at the University of California at Berkeley protested the "patriarchal" nature of their education, demanding women's studies courses along with other institutional changes that would recover the previously hidden history of women. On International Women's Day that year, fifty women marched through the city wearing turn-of-the-century garb.[56]

The institutional development of women's studies proceeded at an astonishing pace after 1969. *Female Studies,* a modest survey of American universities, documented 17 courses in women's history nationwide in 1969–70. *Female Studies II,* appearing six months later, included syllabi for 66 courses; and in late 1971 *Female Studies III* reported 17 *programs* in women's studies and announced receipt of syllabi for *300* courses and notice of 300 more. By 1973–74, some 2,500 courses were offered and 100 programs existed nationwide. "I wish some of our Women Libbers would do some homework and read history!" Vera Peterson Joseph wrote to her radical elder, Pauline Newman, in 1973.[57] But this indeed they had begun to do.

By 1975 enough work had been accomplished in the area of women's studies that Gerda Lerner could sketch a taxonomy of the different varieties of historical inquiry that made up the field. In "Placing Women in History" Lerner enumerated three basic endeavors, each in its way contributing to both the personal and the political dimensions of the feminist project as it came down from the movement itself: "compensatory" history (the recovery of "lost" women); "contributions" history (women's participation in male-centered spheres and arenas of traditional historical inquiry); and woman-centered history (a more fundamental reshaping of the discipline's conceptual schemes in the light of new discoveries). "Women's ambitions," Lerner later wrote, had been "lowered by the absence of heroines." History, "a mental construct which extends human life beyond its span, can give meaning to each life and serve as a necessary anchor for us."[58]

This feminist pursuit of "heroines" was a wellspring for the growing field of immigration history, as the personal, the political, and the historical—the ethnic revival and the feminist resurgence—converged in the work of scholars like Donna Gabaccia, Sydney Stahl Weinberg, Paula Hyman, and Elizabeth Ewen. "The new feminists hope to restore women to history," wrote Alix Kates Shulman in *To the Barricades: The Anarchist Life of Emma*

Goldman (1971). The Goldman biography itself opens with the frank, usable-past kind of assertion that "now, in the 1970s, new generations of radicals are taking up Emma Goldman's fight. Like her, they are willing to face jail, exile, and even death because they believe that the world must be made over according to a new vision. Emma Goldman's ideals and spirit are now very much alive. It is time that her story was heard again." Lest the dual, feminist-Jewish aspects of this radical past escape the reader, the author begins with the blunt description of Goldman's "four curses" from birth: "She was born Russian, Jewish, female, and unloved." "As a Jew she might be forced to live in a ghetto . . . But as a girl she was in danger of being given away to some man who would have absolute and permanent control over her entire life, even over her body." Goldman was fortunate, however, to learn about "another kind of woman," the "liberated Russian revolutionary women."[59]

Three decades after Alix Kates Shulman's retrieval of a usable past in *To the Barricades,* Karen Brodkin reflected on the personal, heartfelt dimension of her own scholarly engagement in feminist social science: "The story of the Triangle Shirtwaist Company in New York City has always been an important part of my (admittedly small) personal repertoire of secular Jewish identity. Together with stories about feisty young women garment workers, I've carried it with me to explain to myself why I feel connected to progressive causes." Elsewhere Brodkin deployed heroic stories of past (and largely obscured) activists like Pauline Newman, Rose Schneiderman, and Rose Pesotta, whose political lives were spent "in struggle with a sexist, recalcitrant, and fundamentally conservative, male, union leadership." Clara Lemlich, too, "is known in history books as the 'wisp of a girl' who ignited the crowd and the

1909 uprising of 20,000 women's garment workers in New York City. She later married and 'disappeared,' in much the same way that the political activism of mothers disappeared in Jewish men's histories of working-class politics—until feminist scholars unearthed it." Here again is the feminists' Double V: the exemplary lesson of women's past struggles, and the cautionary lesson of women's "disappearance" at the hand of conventional (male) historiography.[60]

As the personal, the political, and the historical came together in feminist writings, their intellectual import moved from the "compensatory" or the "contributive" (to borrow Lerner's lexicon), to the fully "conceptual," the forging of a women-centered history for the ethnic-revival generation. "Before 1965 most traditional American historians viewed immigrants as 'problems' to be solved by assimilation, while liberals emphasized discrimination, the ethnic American as victim," wrote Maxine Seller. "In the late 1960s and 1970s, however, the rise of the 'new ethnicity' and the revival of the women's movement changed the way that many scholars approached the history of immigration." Seller's own contribution, *Immigrant Women* (1994), self-consciously positioned "immigrant women as subjects rather than as objects and ethnic life as an enduring (and valuable) . . . feature of the American social landscape."[61]

Seller's reference to the "new ethnicity" is well placed here. Indeed, *Immigrant Women* itself, as the dedication proclaims, was written "In memory of my grandmothers." An intensely personal—which is to say, *familial*—investment runs as a constant leitmotif throughout the academic writing on immigrant women. This personal investment aligns such work, not only with writings like Kim Chernin's memoir *In My Mother's House*, but, ironically, also with the period's frankly masculinist works like David Mamet's book *The Old Neighborhood.* Elizabeth Ewen, for instance, begins her monograph *Immigrant Women in the Land of Dollars* (1985) with a memoir and a tribute to both her own Italian grandmother and her husband's Jewish grandmother. "In a sense," she writes, "this book began as an attempt to re-enter my two grandmothers' closets, to ferret out the fragments of a past when women made the journey from the fields of southern Italy and the market towns of Eastern Europe." Sydney Stahl Weinberg, too, writes that though she had only "fragmentary memories" of her immigrant grandmother, they were "connected with a sense of Jewishness that seemed exotic yet compelling to a child of assimilated parents." Weinberg eventually began to wonder about the many immigrant women who might have led lives of "quiet heroism." The result was *The World of Our Mothers,* one of the pioneering works in the literature on immigrant women.[62]

Nor has the ethnic-revival impulse necessarily faded among women's historians, even as *Roots* and the ethnic revival proper recede into the past. "This book has its roots in the memories and stories of my grandmother," writes Annelise Orlick in *Common Sense and a Little Fire* (1991), ". . . a sharp-tongued woman with a talent for survival and for dominating everyone she met . . . [S]he claimed to have led a strike when she was seventeen." When Orlick began to read about the immigrant work force, she noted that "women were nearly invisible in such accounts." In an introductory note titled "Starting from Home," Kathie Friedman-Kasaba attributes her interest in immigration to having grown up "in post-Holocaust suburban Detroit, a social climate dominated by a musical play about pogroms—*Fiddler on the Roof*—race riots, and anti-Vietnam War protests." In this setting, Friedman-Kasaba notes, "[I looked] in part to my grandmothers for help in sorting out my proper place in the world." *Memories of Migration* (1996) becomes a study of how women "tried to negotiate both the potentially empowering and corrosive aspects of transnational migration."[63]

Perhaps no one in these years was more deeply and publicly invested in the idea of women's heritage than the artist Judy Chicago. Chicago's father was descended from a line of twenty-three generations of rabbis, including the famed Goan of Vilna. He had rejected that tradition and become a communist and an organizer. "[L]ike many second-generation Jews," Chicago explains, "he (and my mother) basically rejected all things Jewish. As a result, I learned less than nothing about Jewish history and culture from my parents." Judy (Cohen) Chicago would take the standard Hansen's Law, "roots" route to "heritage." Interestingly, however, she ultimately identified the political judgments and values she grew up with, not as communist or progressive, but as Jewish: "even if I was ignorant of my Jewish background—knowledge that I would one day yearn for—with hindsight it becomes obvious that I was raised in a household shaped by what might be called Jewish ethical values, particularly the concept of *tikkun*, the healing or repairing of the world." If her father had rejected the rabbinical pulpit, still "he was, I now understood, Jewish to the core." This evolving sense of Jewishness and its importance both in her background and for her artistic work came to rest in "rage and despair at the distancing from our heritage embodied in the statement, 'We come from Lithuania and Latvia, but they don't exist anymore.'"[64]

Chicago's own brand of *tikkun,* a distinctly feminist one, was based on the notion of heritage itself—first "women's heritage," and only later, the Jewish heritage of which she had been deprived. Chicago's first big heritage project was an installation called *The Dinner Party*, an artistic rendering of the "compensatory" and "contributive" brands of women's history, even if radical feminist critics like Patricia Mainardi objected to the "age-old male imposed stereotypes such as pastel colors, womb shapes, [and] infolding forms" that characterized Chicago's work. The piece consists of 39 place-settings and iconic ceramic plates arranged at a huge, triangular table, each setting corresponding to some female "guest" hitherto lost to history—ranging from ancient goddesses like Ishtar and Kali, to "establishment" political figures like Eleanor of Aquitaine and Queen Elizabeth, to dissenters like Anne Hutchinson, Sojourner Truth, and Susan B. Anthony. The intent of the guest list, according to Chicago, is to symbolize "the whole range of women's achievements and yet also [to] embody women's containment."[65]

This three-dimensional field is unified by an underlying "heritage floor," on which appear the names and brief descriptions of 999 more "women of achievement," more or less corresponding to the categories established by the 39 guests—a raft of goddesses, rulers, dissenters, witches, martyrs, artists, writers, poets, athletes, and scientists compiled by a team of twenty researchers over the course of two years. Although *The Dinner Party* is "multicultural" by any measure (Amazon, Sappho, Saint Bridgit, Sacajawea, Sojourner Truth, Emily Dickinson), Chicago was little interested in her own Jewish or immigrant heritage. She did tip her hat to her Jewishness by seating Judith (sixth century B.C.), "a very devout and learned woman, [who] decided to take action against the enemy while most of her fellow Jews were bemoaning their fate." Margaret Sanger and Henrietta Szold, moreover, introduce an element of the immigrant past to both the table and the heritage floor. But *The Dinner Party* is primarily and quite self-consciously about heritage conceived in gender rather than in ethnic terms: "To make people feel worthless, society robs them of their pride; this has happened to women. All the institutions of our culture tell us—through words, deeds, and, even worse, silence—that we are insignificant. But our heritage is our power; we can know ourselves and our capacities by seeing that other women have been strong."[66]

While *The Dinner Party* was ecumenical in its conception of "women's heritage," *The Holocaust Project* (1993) was also invested in heritage, with the significant difference that Chicago had now discovered her Jewish roots. Along with husband-to-be, Donald Woodman, Chicago embarked in the 1980s on a personal research of the Holocaust. The two were overwhelmed "by our mutual ignorance about the enormity of this tragic event; and by the sudden realization of the preciousness of our shared Jewish heritage and the fact that it had been nearly wiped out. Moreover, this was the first time in my adult life that I felt bonded to another person, not by gender but by culture."[67]

Hers was a classic roots trip, in other words, but it also allowed her "to explore the whole notion of 'differentness' in human society." The result was a distinctly feminist attachment to Jewishness and a distinctly feminist interpretation of the Holocaust. Virginia Woolf had "described the rise of fascism and Hitler's march across Europe in terms related to 'patriarchy gone mad'"; Aviva Cantor had asserted, "What made the Holocaust possible . . . is the fact of patriarchy, and the fact that patriarchal values dominate our society." Such was the interpretive frame for *The Holocaust Project*. The Holocaust, for Chicago, was "one of the most graphic demonstrations of the injustice inherent in the global structure of patriarchy and the result of power as it has been defined and enforced by male-dominated societies."[68]

The Holocaust Project, then, is The Dinner Party with a Yiddish accent. From this standpoint, the most significant panels in the exhibit are Double Jeopardy, Lesbian Triangle, The Fall, and Rainbow Shabbat. Double Jeopardy, which depicts Jewish women in various scenes of labor, endurance, commiseration, bereavement, self-defense, and peril, represents Chicago's exploration of the "particular ways in which women suffered differently" from men during the horrific Nazi years. There had been "significant denial," in Chicago's view, "of the fact that Jewish women were the victims of a double jeopardy—as targets of both race and gender policies—and experienced a particularized form of suffering that illuminates the way racism and sexism frequently overlap." Framed by harsh black and white photographs of the camp's guard tower, barbed wire, and hardwood bunks, the pyramidic centerpiece of Lesbian Triangle depicts lesbianism as a lost freedom of the Weimar past, a coerced concession to Nazi power, and a healing gesture among captive women. "Lesbianism," writes Chicago, "seems to have manifested itself either as a function of the abusive power of female SS guards and kapos or, more positively, as a reaching out between women for comfort. Whatever it was, it was in marked contrast to the freedom that lesbians had enjoyed before the war."[69]

Chicago's panel The Fall, showing "how the Holocaust grew out of the very fabric of Western civilization," exemplifies the project's conceptual ambition. The mural narrates the Holocaust as but a late chapter in the much longer tale of "the historic defeat of matriarchy," the "rise of patriarchy," "the conquest of

women and nature and the gradual development of male-dominated religion and society," and thus the "historic relationship between anti-Semitism and antifeminism." Women's "fall" (the central barometer of *humanity's* fall, in this scheme) includes the
overthrow of the Egyptian goddess Neith (the goddess of spin-
ning), the reduction of women to wage-slavery in a factory system, and the burning of witches. Having come upon a medieval
volume "which explained how to identify a witch," Chicago was
"struck by how similar modern anti-Semitic writings seemed to
be to the rantings of these earlier texts." *The Fall* is an effort,
across the sweep of European history, to analyze and narrate "the
historic association between women and Jews, as members of
stigmatized groups."[70]

But it is the stained-glass panel titled *Rainbow Shabbat* that
will forever mark this project distinctly—if ironically—as an artifact of the ethnic revival. *Rainbow Shabbat,* as the title had to suggest to its post–Rainbow Coalition audience, lends shape and
color to the dream of a multicultural society of equals. Seated
around the Shabbat table, an ecumenical assemblage of twelve
figures roughly corresponding to the races and religions of the
world have come together peacefully for the blessing of the can-
dles. A luminous legend, rendered in Yiddish at one end of the
piece and English at the other, reads: "Heal those broken souls
who have no peace and lead us all from darkness into light." But
an ethnic-revival sensibility disturbs this scene in two respects.
First, that this is a distinctly *Jewish* Shabbat and that the Jews in
the scene occupy places of honor may bespeak a certain Jewish
chauvinism at work, an insistence on chosenness, if you will, even
amid a seeming plea for universalism. There is a certain primacy
to the Jewishness of this depiction, that is, that nicely marks the

distance Chicago had traveled since *The Dinner Party.* But second, quite suggestively, in the first edition of the book that accompanied *The Holocaust Project,* the Yiddish inscription at the far left end of *Rainbow Shabbat* appears upside down, a misconstruing of the "mother tongue" that rearticulates precisely the distance from "authentic" Jewishness—the "less than nothing" about Judaism Chicago had inherited from her parents—that her roots trip is meant to redress.[71]

Nonetheless, Chicago's feminist intervention in European history is an important one, as is her impulse to rearticulate traditional Judaism through the prism of feminism. Here her thinking joins another broad current in second-wave feminism. Letty Cottin Pogrebin's choice, for instance, to invoke the Biblical Deborah right alongside the historical Golda Meir in her book *Deborah, Golda, and Me* indicates that the feminist conception of heritage took in more than just the struggles of the grandmothers and the mothers in the Old and New World ghettos; it took in religious orthodoxy as well, and the dim antiquities of biblical narrative and Talmudic law.

Perhaps some people would be less celebratory of traditional religious forms than Chicago was in *Rainbow Shabbat.* While doing research for a bat mitzvah sermon, Pogrebin herself had discovered just how little she knew about the biblical women of Jewish lore, despite her ten years in afternoon Hebrew school and two years at the Yeshiva of Central Queens. "If the 'sages' were so smart," she now wondered, echoing the challenge that secular historians like Weinberg and Seller were posing within the academy, "why didn't they think to ask who the women were and what they were doing while the men were chronicling their own achievements? I question whether any man ought to be called a great thinker if the other half of the Jewish people slips his mind." Or, as Paula Rothenberg recalls, "Repeated trips to the synagogue taught me firsthand that separate most certainly was not equal— even before the Supreme Court handed down *Brown v. Board of Education*."[72]

Liberating Theology

In 1971 the Catholic theologian Mary Daly became the first woman to deliver a sermon in Harvard Memorial Church, the chapel of the Harvard Divinity School. Her theme, "The Women's Movement: An Exodus Community," reached its crescendo when Daly led those present in an exodus from the church in protest against "the crushing weight" of a patriarchal religious tradition that had long told women that they "do not even exist." "We cannot really belong to institutional religion as it exists," she said. "Singing sexist hymns, praying to a male god breaks our spirit, makes us less than human." The 1971 exodus was a critical step in Daly's own journey from being a staunch feminist critic *within* the church—a position first spelled out in *The Church and the Second Sex* (1968)—to articulating what she later called a fully "post-Christian" feminist theology and politics. She underwent a "dramatic/traumatic change of consciousness," in her words, "from 'radical Catholic' to post-christian feminist," a transformation that required her to abandon the "misplaced hope" of ever reconciling her impossible, dichotomous identity as a "Catholic feminist." By 1975 Daly had concluded that "a woman's asking for equality in the church would be comparable to a black person's demanding equality in the Ku Klux Klan."[73]

Daly's exodus and her dawning "post-Christian" consciousness may not have been typical of the developing relationship between established religions and their feminist congregants, but it did dramatize a critique that was becoming increasingly important for both American religion and American feminism in ensuing decades. By the late 1970s and 1980s similar discontents within both Church and Temple had generated a range of feminist projects in addition to Daly's post-Christian protests, including various efforts aimed at *reforming* the Church and rescuing it for feminist principles from within (both at the institutional level, in the struggle for women's ordination, for instance, and at the level of theology and ritual, in sustained critiques of the patriarchal terms of established "god-language" and ceremony). "We *are* church," declared Marjorie Tuite, in a defiance quite distinct from Daly's exodus. "We are coming out as church." Activist Catholic theologians like Tuite and Elisabeth Schussler Fiorenza coined the notion of "Women-Church," or *ecclesia of women,* to make a stand for "sisterhood" that might capture the Church rather than abandon it.[74] Still others turned away from traditional religions in favor of egalitarian religious structures and forms more hospitable to the feminist impulse—wicca, neopaganism, "goddess" religions, and a host of other theological and organizational enterprises under the loose rubric of feminist spirituality.

Religion, of course, is not coeval with ethnicity. But historically, both the Jewish Temple and the Catholic Church have functioned largely as immigrant institutions in America. Thus in these cases the religious dimension of feminist activism, perhaps even more than the secular, has shared in the language of ethnic revival or conservation. As with the movement among secular feminists, the convergence of ethnicity and feminism had two distinct valences: the ways in which their ethnic identity positioned certain women for feminist activism; and the ways in which feminist activism was informed by an ethnic sensibility. So, for example, in tackling the question of why so many Catholic feminists would choose to stay within the Church in the first place, given "the profound and destructive character" of the conflict between feminism and the hierarchy, Rosemary Ruether concluded that many "refuse to be defined outside this particular historical church [because of] their own ethnic, historical roots in the community. For most of them this is their family, their roots." Aviva Cantor's "Jewish Women's Haggadah" (1974), an alternative book for the Passover ritual, by contrast, has less to say about how one's "roots" might prompt a feminist struggle to redefine "church" than about how one's feminist spirituality might prompt a cultivation of one's roots. The feminist Seder includes a discussion of "what Jewish identity means and how assimilation is self-oppression" before going on to the blessing of the fourth cup of wine:

> We drink this fourth and last cup of wine on this Seder night to honor our Jewish sisters who are struggling to find new ways to say "I am a Jew . . ."
> We are liberating ourselves from the assimilationist dream-turned-nightmare and moving toward creating Jewish lifestyles, rediscovering our history and our traditions, our heritage and our values, and building on them and from them.[75]

Spiritual feminism, then, drew on the same energies and impulses as secular feminism: whether within Church, Temple, or the Covens and Crafts comprising their refugees, the dissenting vision of religious feminism is nearly identical to the secular in its antimodernism and its world-of-our-mothers inspiration. "The heritage, the culture, the knowledge of the ancient priestesses, healers, poets, singers, and seers were nearly lost," writes Starhawk, but the "long sleep of Mother Goddess is ended."[76] "We are all longing to go home to some place we have never been," she wrote elsewhere; "a place, half-remembered, and half-envisioned we can only catch glimpses of from time to time. Community." As in secular feminist writings in an ethnic-revival idiom, "heritage" here addresses both the disaffections of modernity ("the assimilationist dream-turned-nightmare") and the obscured history of women's consciousness and power. "The past is a mirror," asserts Z Budapest. "And the Craft presents women with their past. They look into this mirror and say, 'Look at what we did back then! We are strong.'" Indeed, Z asserts her authority as a wicca leader partly in terms of her status as an *immigrant* from, as it were, the premodern. "When I was a little girl in Hungary," she begins *The Grandmother of Time* (1989), "I often spent my holidays in the rural areas, where the spirit of the old folktales still came alive"; "these were the last days of traditional rural life in Hungary, the last days without TV." Among the most important incantations in this compendium of rituals is Z's repeated incantation, "I remember."[77]

But even if people like Aviva Cantor no less than Michael Novak and Tom Hayden were rallying and celebrating the "small platoon," one must not overlook the extent to which this movement was driven by notions of justice and injustice. Feminism, here as elsewhere, must be understood above all as a movement in relation to power. Daly questioned women's status in a church that "at the same time idealizes and humiliates" women; elsewhere, in response to Phyllis Trible's call for a "depatriarchalized"

Bible, she quipped that such a thing "would make a nice pamphlet." Schussler Fiorenza protested, "Women are not only the 'silent majority,' but we are also the '*silenced* majority' in the church." Rosemary Ruether challenged the Catholic hierarchy in the strongest possible terms, recalling Robin Morgan's denunciation of the New Left, "Goodbye to All That": "We will not raise one cent for your patriarchal church. We will not lift one finger to rescue your patriarchal system. We will not bend one knee to worship the patriarchal idol that you blasphemously insist on calling 'God.' We are not fooled."[78] In a Leadership Conference of Women Religious (LCWR) study packet intended to educate nuns in feminist concerns, another writer asserted, "The mainstream of tradition within the Catholic Church . . . is one of the most oppressive of all religious superstructures." This writer noted "a growing awareness and bonding" among women who now "refuse to subject themselves and their sisters" to such "institutionalized injustice." Nor, of course, were such denunciations and protests lacking in the Jewish feminist tradition: one of Riv-Ellen Prell's informants said of the havurah movement, "The logical response of a feminist to Judaism is to stop being Jewish."[79]

The timeline of Catholic second-wave feminism must begin with the Vatican II Council, 1962–1965, whose mingling of heightened expectation and dashed hope established it as the *Brown v. Board of Education* of the Catholic women's movement.[80] Daly and others have described the "euphoria" in the wake of Vatican II, as the Church seemed to promise a new, liberalized view of the relationship between liturgical practice and social conscience. But the promise was flawed: Mary Luke Tobin, an auditor at the Second Vatican Council, applauded the bishops' response to several movements within the Church, including "ecumenism, the people as the church, the liturgical movement, [and] religious liberty," but she noted that "acceptance of the insights of the women's movement was barely discernible." Daly later recalled one woman being barred from the altar railing during Holy Communion at a Council Mass, a sign of "a strange mentality which seems to regard half the human race as not quite human." The tension between promise and disappointment was already evident by 1965, when Sidney Callahan's book *Illusion of Eve* expressed a post-conciliar optimism about women's changing roles in the Church, even as Mary Daly published her first dissenting piece on sexism and religion in *Commonweal*. (Looking back as a post-Christian a decade later, Daly described women's initial, roseate views of Vatican II as a "baffling optimism," the very category of "Catholic feminist" as a "misplaced hope.")[81]

As in the secular movement, events gathered momentum in 1968. That year Daly published *The Church and the Second Sex*, and one of the first feminist Catholic organizations emerged, the National Assembly of Religious Women. The National Coalition of American Nuns (1969), the Center of Concern (1971), Catholics for a Free Choice (1974), and Chicago Catholic Women (1975) soon followed. In 1972 Catholics played a prominent role when women from several denominations convened at Grailville, Ohio, in a conference devoted to "Women Doing Theology"; and that year the Leadership Conference of Women Religious came out in support of the principle that all ministries be open to women, and that women actively participate in all decision-making bodies within the Church (even as Pope Paul VI declared that "true women's liberation" had to do with "that specific thing in the feminine personality—the vocation of a woman to become a mother").[82]

In 1974 Mary Lynch called thirty-one women together in Chicago to discuss women's ordination. A year later the first Women's Ordination Conference, which was to become the heart of Catholic feminism in the 1970s, convened in Detroit with more than twelve hundred women present. This movement gathered force in 1977, when, in a starkly unrepentant declaration, the Vatican asserted that the Church's exclusion of women was founded on Christ's intent and was fundamental to the Church's understanding of priesthood. A second, defiant Women's Ordination Conference in Baltimore the next year attracted two thousand participants.[83] Between the mid-1970s and the early 1980s several more feminist organizations emerged within the Church, including the Women of the Church Coalition, the National Association of Religious Women (NARW), the National Coalition of American Nuns (NCAN), the Quixote Center, Las Hermanas, the Black Sisters Conference, and the Women's Alliance for Theology, Ethics, and Ritual (WATER).

Jewish feminism developed along similar lines from the late 1960s to the early 1980s.[84] Much feminist activity emerged within the so-called Jewish counterculture (later known as the havurah movement), "an alternate to the hierarchical and often alienating structures of the traditional synagogue." The havurah was not explicitly feminist, but it was influenced by the secular feminist movement at a critical stage. The groups experimented with traditional religious forms, including the gendered aspects of Jewish ritual, liturgy, and theology.[85] In 1971 the consciousness-raising and study group Ezrat Nashim formed in New York, and the first group of articles on Jewish feminism appeared in a special issue of *Davka* magazine.

In 1972 the Jewish counterculture journal *Response* published a special issue titled "The Jewish Woman," and Ezrat Nashim issued a "Call for Change" within the structures of Conservative Judaism, including the full participation of women in observance, synagogue worship, and decision-making bodies; recognition of women as witnesses in Jewish law; women's right to initiate divorce; and women's admission to rabbinical and cantorial school. That year Sally Priesand became the first woman ordained as a rabbi by the Hebrew Union College.

In 1973 a small circle of Jewish feminists including Aviva Cantor Zuckoff and Susan Weidman Schneider launched *Lilith;* the first National Jewish Women's Conference convened; and the Ezrat Nashim member Arlene Argus founded the first women's Talmudic institute. The Jewish Feminist Organization formed in 1974, the same year the Reconstructionist Fellowship granted women full equality "in all matters of ritual" and ordained its first woman rabbi. Nineteen seventy-six saw the publication of several critical texts in Jewish feminism, including *The Jewish Woman* (based on the earlier *Response* collection), *The Jewish Woman in America, Siddur Nashim* (a book of women's prayers rendered in nonsexist language), *Blessing the Birth of a Jewish Daughter,* and the first issue of *Lilith.* In 1980 Judith Plaskow taught the first course on Jewish feminist theology at the National Havurah Summer Institute; in 1981 the Jewish feminist spirituality collective B'Not Esh held its first meeting; and in 1984 Susan Weidman Schneider published *Jewish and Female,* a compendium of wisdom, resources, and practical guidance based on centuries of Jewish tradition and about a decade of feminist networking through "the one-room *Lilith* office . . . the national address and telephone number of the growing Jewish women's movement."[86]

In both Catholic and Jewish feminism, institutional concerns

16.   *Sally Priesand, the first woman rabbi ordained in the United States, blesses a cup of wine, 1973. In both Catholic Church and Jewish Temple, the ethnic revival and second-wave feminism converged in battles over liturgy, theology, and ordination.* BETTMANN/CORBIS.

and protests were distinct from theological matters—at issue was how the Church or Temple *treated women* on the one hand, and how it *conceived God* on the other. As Judith Plaskow argued in "The Right Question Is Theological" (1983), the feminist struggle within Judaism had progressed largely on a civil rights model of "inclusion"; that is, it had been a movement "concerned with the images and status of women in Jewish religious and communal life, and with halakhic and institutional change," not with radical analyses of the origins of women's oppression in Torah itself.[87] Mary Daly's book *Church and the Second Sex*, her travails with the Church elders, and her tenure case at Boston College are the best examples of this institutional, "civil rights" brand of women's agitation within American Catholicism. With mirthful double-*entendre*, Daly recounts this exchange with Cardinal Konig of Vienna:

KONIG: So, you teach at Jesuit-run Boston College.

DALY: Yes, and they would like to get rid of me but they cannot.

KONIG: I'm not so sure about that!

It was in this vein that Cynthia Ozick observed, "the only place I'm not a Jew is in my *shul*," and Rabbi Elyce Goldstein penned the satirical protest "Ordination Blues."[88]

But the distinction between institutional life and theological orientation became blurry over time. Daly's own trajectory from *Second Sex* to her emergence as a post-Christian in *Beyond God the Father* charts the ways in which the institutional and the theological necessarily blended into each other. By the early 1980s Judith Plaskow, too, recognized at the heart of Jewish religious thought "an assumption of women's Otherness far more basic than the laws in which it finds expression."[89] In a tightly reasoned examination of Jewish unreason, Plaskow linked this "Otherness of women" both to women's lived experience of ritual and communal life *and* to the more rarified discourse of Jewish theology. The Otherness of women is given "dramatic expression in our language about God," she wrote. "Here, we confront a great scandal: the God who supposedly transcends sexuality, who is presumably one and whole, is known to us through language that is highly selective and partial." Male-derived language and imagery in reference to God "convey a sense of power and authority that is clearly male in character," at great cost both to Jewish women and to the Jewish tradition itself. As a model for community, the male-dominated prayer book becomes "testimony against the participation of women in Jewish religious life."[90]

Thus does theology ever inform—even police—the social realm of a group's everyday interactions. Susannah Heschel arrived at the same, urgent implication of the theological for the social in her luminous discussion of the Talmudic proclamation "A woman may not read from the Torah [during synagogue services] because of the honor of the congregation." At first, Heschel explains, feminists objected to the notion that "honor" depended on women's exclusion. But "only gradually did we recognize that the word at stake in the Talmudic dictum was not 'honor,' but 'congregation.' Whose honor was being respected? Did the Jewish congregation consist only of men?"[91]

This query, at once institutional *and* theological, became important for both Jewish and Catholic feminists in Mary Daly's wake. "If God is male, then the male is God," Daly had put it.

Rita Gross now wanted to know, "If we do not mean that God is male when we use masculine pronouns and imagery, then why should there be any objections to using female imagery and pronouns as well?" (But of course there is.) "If God is male, and we are in God's image," Plaskow asked, completing the loop from the male god to earthly males' godlike social standing, "how can maleness *not* be the norm of Jewish humanity? If maleness is normative, how can women *not* be Other? And if women are Other, how can we not speak of God in language drawn from the male norm?" In "Sexism and God-Language" Rosemary Radford Ruether posited religious patriarchy (for her, Christianity) as "male monotheism," a theology in which "God is modeled after the patriarchal ruling class and is seen as addressing this class of males directly, adopting them as his 'sons.'" Thus do theological questions of "God-language" quickly merge with street-level politics and the practicalities of social order: "Male monotheism becomes the vehicle of a psychocultural revolution of the male ruling class in its relationship to surrounding reality."[92]

These challenges found expression in a wide range of liturgical innovations and experiments that spoke to both the ethnic past and the religious future. "What are the new words and how will we speak who we are?" Plaskow had asked in the early 1970s. "Make an effort to remember. Or failing that, invent," the French novelist Monique Wettig had commanded, in an aphorism that enjoyed wide currency among American feminists. The variety and the ingenuity of feminist religious invention in the 1970s and after bespeak both a determination to "speak who we are" and a will to "remember" and "invent." (Even years later Marge Piercy would dedicate her volume of Jewish poems, *The Art of Blessing the Day,* to "all who may find here poems that speak to their identity, their history, their desire for ritual—ritual that may work for them.")[93]

These feminist interventions in identity, history, and ritual within both Church and Temple assumed two distinct forms: the radical revision of standing traditions, and the wholesale invention of new ones. Either enterprise could hold a great deal of power for a generation of women who had begun to question both institutional and theological norms. As Riv-Ellen Prell found among the women of the Havurah, "For the first time in their lives, many women put on prayer shawls and skull caps historically associated exclusively with men . . . Religious activities familiar to any preadolescent boy became accessible for the first time to women who were already in their twenties. These women expressed awe, pleasure, anxiety, and appreciation." After one such Torah blessing, a minyan member remarked, "I have heard people say those blessings literally hundreds of times. But as I got close to the scroll, I suddenly felt very apprehensive. Then, as I did all those things that were at once familiar and new, I felt I might cry. I was unprepared for what a moving experience I would have."[94]

For others, feminism's most portentous sacraments consisted not of incursions into traditionally male domains but of newly invented rituals that captured the creative and communal spirit of communicants *as women.* One report from the Grail, a Catholic organization that had become a focus of Catholic feminism since the 1970s, noted, "we create a lot of our own rituals and liturgies, drawing from a variety of sources, scriptural, official Roman Catholic, Jewish, other Christian traditions, African, Asian, native American, contemporary (especially contemporary women writers)." Mary Hunt, the Irish Catholic co-director of WATER, describes an ecumenical group of Jewish and Catholic women developing several new rituals, including a feminist *Succoh* ritual that entailed spending an evening in a tent, to "pass stories and reflections on their grandmothers, and their great grandmothers." By the 1980s feminist liturgical songs were widely available on tape, and new feminist ceremonial traditions—such as the bread-kneading ritual devised by Women-Church—circulated in holiday albums and calendars.[95]

In a classic roots-era recovery of lost tradition, members of Ezrat Nashim and others rediscovered Rosh Hodesh, the Jewish festival of the New Moon, which had "held unique significance for women, perhaps dating back as far as the Biblical period." Women once again began observing Rosh Hodesh, marking the day (eleven times a year) "with a special ceremony and feast, combining traditional practices associated with the holiday with additions from contemporary sources." The festival, according to one participant, "is a celebration of divine creation and of those characteristics which women share with the moon—the life cycle, rebirth, renewal." The revival of Rosh Hodesh as a women's holiday was "an occasion for speaking to the Creator and experimenting with the dialogue . . . a pause in which to thank God for creating us women."[96]

But perhaps the most energetic and prolific creator in the realm of feminist ritual was Esther Broner, whose work on the novel *Weave of Women* began as a 3 × 5 index card with the notation, "I want to make a new calendar for women and write it in elegiac prose." "What do you need for a holiday?" asks Broner. "A date, a legend, a blessing and a meal." The completed novel unfolds with as much narrative devotion to the calendar that punctuates it—

the "Ceremony of Girding for Battle," "Revenge Rites," "Holy Body Day," a "counterholiday"—as to the relationships that constitute the "weave" of the title. The spirit of the novel, indeed, of this dimension of religious feminism in general, is best summed up in the following exchange:

> "No songs have been written for this holiday."
> "We'll write one."

It was Broner who devised the "scroll of women's words": "You will make these holy by writing down the sayings of your mothers, of your women mentors or your teachers, your grandmothers, your lovers, the women of importance in your life." According to Broner, as one group of women wrote on the scroll, the paper "puckered under their tears."[97]

The most popular feminist ritual is the feminist Seder, and the most renowned of these was begun at Passover in 1976 by Broner and a group in New York now known as the Seder Sisters, including Aviva Cantor Zuckoff, Phyllis Chesler, Letty Cottin Pogrebin, Naomi Nimrod, and Gloria Steinem.[98] Over the years participants have included Bella Abzug, Andrea Dworkin, Grace Paley, Naomi Wolf, Marilyn French, Amy Goodman, Caroline Heilbrun, Susan Brownmiller, and Judith Plaskow, among others. The feminist Seder has been the subject of a BBC documentary, a Pacifica Radio segment, and Esther Broner's book *The Telling* (1993). The Seder Sisters have also excerpted their *Women's Haggadah* in *Ms.* magazine. "On this night," says Pogrebin, "we become ourselves. We speak with grammar of the feminine plural and invoke the *Shechina* [in Jewish mystical literature, the feminine presence of God] . . . On this night we give [woman's] story equal time." Both the power and the dissenting spirit of the feminist Seder are captured in its revision of the "Four Questions" (the Seder's most significant liturgical moment, traditionally an exchange between the youngest male present and the—always male—Seder leader):

> Why is this Haggadah different from traditional Haggadot? Because this Haggadah deals with the Exodus of Women.

> Why have our mothers on this night been bitter? Because they did the preparation but not the ritual. They did the serving but not the conducting. They read of their fathers but not of their mothers.

> Why on this night do we dip twice? Because of the natural and unnatural cycles of blood: our monthly bleedings; the blood spilled by war.

> Why on this night do we recline? We recline on this night for the unhurried telling of the legacy of Miriam.[99]

Many sects, crafts, or covens under the loose rubric of "non-traditional" religious feminisms resonated with Jewish or Catholic feminism. Such groups encompassed a range of beliefs and practices, and not a few hybrids. Wicca, for example, is rooted in witchcraft and magic. Goddess spirituality harks back to the matrifocal cultures of "Old Europe," which, according to writers like Riane Eisler, Marija Gimbutas, and Charlene Spretnak, contrasted sharply with the warlike Indo-European invaders who imposed an order ruled by patriarchal chieftains. More important

than the specific orientation of any of these groups, however, is
the interplay and intellectual exchange among them. Aside from
Carol Christ and Judith Plaskow's influential and ecumenical anthologies *Womanspirit Rising* and *Weaving the Visions,* perhaps
Donna Steichen's antifeminist tract *Ungodly Rage* (1991) is the
most thorough effort extant to trace the linkages between secular
feminism, liturgical or theological feminism, and the more experimental "new age" spiritualisms of the goddess, pagan, or wicca
movements. With great care and alarm, Steichen documents the
various spaces where secular figures like Gloria Steinem and
Robin Morgan, theologians like Mary Daly, Judith Plaskow,
and Elisabeth Schussler Fiorenza, and self-proclaimed witches
and pagans like Starhawk and Zsuzsanna Budapest have come together.[100]

It was in becoming post-Jewish or post-Christian that many
women found their way to witchcraft or the Goddess in the first
place. Twelve of the forty-nine nuns and ex-nuns interviewed
for *Lesbian Nuns: Breaking Silence* (1985) had become involved
in wicca.[101] ("We all come from the Goddess," wrote Charlene
Spretnak, a refugee from Roman Catholicism, "and to Her we
shall return like a drop of rain flowing to the ocean.")[102] "The
concept of a religion that worshipped a Goddess was amazing and
empowering," Starhawk explains. "Raised Jewish, I had been very
religious as a child and had pursued my Jewish education to an
advanced level . . . I had never heard the word *patriarchy,* but I
sensed that the tradition as it stood then was somehow lacking in
models for me as a woman and in avenues for the development of
female spiritual power."[103] Naomi Goldenberg, too, found her way
to paganism while groping toward a feminist revision of Judaism.
"Judaism has many links with paganism," she argued. "I think the

study of paganism and the effort to look at Jewish goddesses and their relationship to Canaanite figures in early Jewish history will help us to loosen up Judaism . . . [and] to see other possibilities for rituals that could incorporate women more profoundly, rituals that are more ancient than those we practice now."[104]

As Goldenberg's comments suggest, for some women an interest in nontraditional spiritualities could lead *back* to established religion: "Witchcraft led me back to Judaism," comments Ryiah Lilith. "I decided to search for a group of Witches. Instead, I found a group of Jewish women."[105] A close intellectual and spiritual relationship thus exists between feminist projects outside the Temple or Church, like Starhawk's, and projects within, like Ezrat Nashim's, Women-Church's, or the Grail's. The intellectual convergence among these diverse political and spiritual enterprises lies in what Starhawk calls the *acrostic eye.* "The essence of Witchcraft, and of political feminism," she writes, "is acrostic vision: We look at our culture and our conditioning from another angle, and read an entirely different message. Acrostic vision is uncomfortable; it sets us at odds with everything we have been taught."[106]

The extent to which spiritual feminism was compatible with secular feminism is striking, as is the connection between the emergent feminism in mainstream religions and the more experimental spiritualisms embodied by goddess feminism or wicca. When Mary Daly was first "terminated" by Boston College's Jesuit administration in 1969, members of WITCH (Women's International Terrorist Conspiracy from Hell) turned out in numbers to put a hex on the college. When a thousand women packed a BC auditorium to protest Daly's denial of tenure six years later, the highly secular political leader Robin Morgan ("a Jewish apostate," by her own description) inaugurated the proceedings.[107] Elisabeth Schussler Fiorenza, for her part, recalls ending her remarks at the first (Catholic) Women's Ordination Conference in Detroit by borrowing a secular slogan from Morgan: "Sisterhood *is* powerful," she assured, "when it is impelled by the dream of the *ekklesia* of women that inspires our struggle for ministry in the discipleship of equals." And if Kate Millett was wont to refer to the movement's secular practice of Consciousness Raising as an "arcane sacrament," Sister Marjorie Tuite and others would reciprocally borrow from CR in their leadership training packet for emergent Catholic feminists, "'How to' Skills with a Feminist Perspective" (1984). The kit, distributed by the National Assembly of Religious Women and clearly patterned on the CR model, guided group participants in "consciously and politically" sharing "herstories," and in scouring their religious heritage for "cultural sexism and patriarchalism." Starhawk, meanwhile, saw CR as "a process based on sound magical principles," the coven as "a Witch's support group, [a] consciousness-raising group."[108]

Likewise, though Daly refers to "the massively passivizing effects . . . of New Age style 'Goddess Spirituality,'" still, in refusing "reconciliation with the father," she posits radical feminism itself as "affirming our original birth, our original source, movement, surge of living." Talk of witches, paganism, matriarchs, and goddesses is not far behind: again citing Robin Morgan, Daly expresses the hope "that more feminists will give to the history of witches 'the serious study that it warrants, recognizing it as part of our entombed history, a remnant of the Old Religion which predated all patriarchal faiths and which was a Goddess-worshipping, matriarchal faith.'"[109] In 1976 Daly addressed a conference of more than 1,300 priestesses and witches in Boston. By the late

1970s and early 1980s anthologies and conferences with titles like *The Politics of Women's Spirituality* and *Womanspirit* could comfortably include religious-spiritual feminists like Daly, Schussler Fiorenza, Rosemary Ruether, and Judith Plaskow right alongside pagan priestesses and witches like Starhawk and Zsuzsanna Budapest, as well as figures mainly associated with the secular women's movement, such as Gloria Steinem and Adrienne Rich. Some, like Phyllis Chesler, shuttled quite easily between one realm and another; others—notably Robin Morgan and Judy Chicago—blended the themes of secular political struggle, ethnic heritage, Goddess feminism, and witchcraft throughout their work.[110]

Two areas highlight this shared vision among secular, religious, and wiccan or neopagan feminists: the symbology of the witch, and the patterns of revised or invented ritual. The highly secular group WITCH, for example, took as its motto the line from *I Samuel*, 15:23, "For rebellion is as the sin of witchcraft." According to one Washington, D.C., flyer, WITCH represented "a total concept of revolutionary female identity," seizing on the image of the witch as a symbol of women's power, women's rebellion, and women's martyrdom. Mary Daly saw witchcraft as a religious tradition and witch-burning as a chapter in the long history of Christian oppression of women. And yet her rendition of the witch comported easily with more secular versions: "*Hag* is from an Old English word meaning harpy, witch," she noted. "It also formerly meant: 'an evil or frightening spirit.' (Lest this sound too negative, we should ask the relevant questions: 'Evil' by whose definition? 'Frightening' to whom?) A third archaic definition of *hag* is 'nightmare.' (The important question is: Whose nightmare?)" Distinction must be made between those, like WITCH, who seized on the coven as a usable symbol of women-centered politics, and those wiccan believers for whom the Craft is not a metaphor but a *practice*. But, as observers like Margot Adler and Cynthia Eller have noted, the gray area between these polar positions in American feminism is immense.[111]

The resonance among these diverse feminisms is even more evident in the rich area of feminist ritual. "There are new ways of talking about God/Goddess," Gloria Steinem told the Seder Sisters in 1990. "The Goddess was one, whole. She has been broken, torn apart. It is up to us to put her together, to have wholeness, a unity in the universe." In Jewish and Catholic feminism, as in nontraditional spiritual feminisms, the recovery of the "wholeness" that Steinem spoke of would involve a celebration of women's collectivity and struggle. Margot Adler describes a neopagan ritual on Staten Island in which each woman "took a sip, then dipped her fingers into the wine and sprinkled a few drops into the air and onto the floor," invoking a particular goddess, giving thanks, or expressing a personal or collective desire. But most of all the recovery of wholeness would involve a ritual acknowledgment of history, a recovery of past heroines and spiritual ancestors. Just as Esther Broner exhorts in the feminist Seder, "Give us our name. Name our genealogy," so one of Starhawk's wiccan rituals includes a segment during which members of the coven "sing the names of those who have done this work of changing consciousness before us." In a description of a wiccan "bonding ritual," Starhawk writes of a "Tree of Generations":

> The earth is the body of our ancestors. It is our grandmothers' flesh, our grandfathers' bones. The earth sustained the generations that gave birth to us. As we draw on their power . . . as

we feel it rise through the roots in our feet and through the
base of our spines, let us speak the names of our ancestors—of
the ones who came before us, of the heroines and heroes who
inspire us.[112]

Here we find ourselves back at Ellis Island pier, where women
like Meredith Tax, Elizabeth Ewen, and Sydney Stahl Weinberg
had retrieved a gallery of heroines from the world of their mothers. Recall "the promise the land whispered" to Starhawk's immigrant grandparents, or her "witch of Jewish heritage" chanting the
name of a "Hebrew goddess." For many practitioners, Goddess
feminism and wicca represent a post-Christian or post-Jewish
spirituality, but are they post-*ethnic?* Or are they rather *hyper-
ethnic?* The ethnic-revival dimension of feminist spirituality is
readily discernible. "For cultural feminists with European familial
roots," writes Charlene Spretnak, "the archaeological record in-
dicating the patriarchal shift in Old Europe is particularly en-
grossing." Among the wiccans in the United States, according to
Margot Adler, are "scores . . . calling themselves 'Irish traditionalist,' 'Welsh traditionalist,' 'Scots traditionalist,' 'Greek traditionalist,' and so on . . . The 'tradition' of these covens is often the heritage of literature and scholarship related to the pre-Christian
beliefs of a particular people. Those who are drawn to a particular
'traditionalist' coven are often those whose ancestry is in that tradition and who are searching for their own culture."[113]

Werner Sollors has noted that "in the Christianized context
of the English language, the word 'ethnic' (sometimes spelled
'hethnic') recurred, from the 14th through the 19th centuries,
in the sense of 'pagan, heathen, non-Christian.'" Here, in this lit-
tle-known rivulet of the ethnic revival, the archaic and modern

meanings of "ethnicity" reconverge. Thus Adler's discussion of modern-day witchcraft and the wiccan revival is peppered with phrases like, "Her roots are Scots and Welsh, and the main family magical traditions come from her father's side"; "she described the teachings of her Irish immigrant grandmother . . ."; "despite being partly Jewish, [he had] grown up in an 'Irish sort of a ghetto'"; "When Z was sixteen the Hungarian uprising occurred and she became a political exile . . . 'I knew a lot of pagan customs that my country had preserved.'"[114]

Most striking in this connection is Adler's "Interview with a Modern Witch," Sharon Devlin, "an American of Irish descent" whose engagement with the supernatural, like her engagement with the political, is deeply tinged in a Gaelic revival sensibility: "What I actually am," explains Devlin, "is an offshoot of Paganism and early Irish Christianity. I follow beliefs which formed the basis of the Culdee Church . . . the only true union of Paganism and the real teachings of Christ; it was brutally stamped out by the papacy." The Irishness—even the Irish nationalism—of Devlin's paganism recalls the proto-nationalism of the ribbon societies in early modern Ireland: "one of the things about the old Witches," she says with approval, *they protected their community from oppression to the greatest of their ability.* Devlin's dictum that "if you ain't a threat, you ain't worth much" represents a motto that Mary Daly could easily understand—as could Kate Millett and Mary Doyle Curran (and, for that matter, the Berrigans and Tom Hayden). Her interview ends in "an Irish national liberation story associated with Biddy Early, the greatest of all Irish Witches."[115]

Z Budapest is at once more and less invested in questions of "heritage" than other wiccan or neopagan writers. She is less invested in that she can be almost cavalier in her espousal of the notion that "this religion is improvisation. There is no one way to contact the Goddess"; and more in that her commitment to the Old Religion *is* her version of the roots trip. "Let's look at our own heritage," urges this descendant of Hungarian witches, meaning—evidently—"our" European heritage. "We know more about Native American shamanism than our own. We have honorable spiritual roots, so let's reclaim them!" "Take a look at visiting folk dance groups from Hungary, Poland, Bulgaria, Russia or Yugoslavia," Z urges. "You will see how the principles of Old Nature Religion are acted out in sacred dances which survived centuries of persecution." Chapter 10 of *The Holy Book of Women's Mysteries,* "Masika's Book of Life: A Hungarian Heritage," is devoted to Z's mother and to her legacy: "out of the fertile field of Hungarian Pagan culture comes the *Book of Superstitions,* grown from religious, ethnic, cultural and individual roots unlike any other, and indicative of my own roots." "I am the last branch of an 800-year-old family tree," Z explains, "although I consider myself the first on the tree of the New World."[116]

The rich, competing, and often corresponding religious activities that came so strikingly into view around the time of Mary Daly's "exodus," then, flowed into—but also *out of*—the "world of our mothers" dimension of secular feminism.

To note the ethnic texture of second-wave feminism is, admittedly, to assume a peculiar angle of vision. Shulamith Firestone and Geraldine Ferraro? The Ellis Island accents that might unify a group as diverse as Betty Friedan, Kate Millett, Melanie Kaye/ Kantrowitz, Gloria Steinem, Mary Daly, and Kathie Sarachild, for instance, collapse many distinctions that were bitterly defended within the movement—distinctions between socialists and liberals, activists and academics, the reformers of NOW and the revolutionaries of WITCH, radical feminists and cultural feminists.

But this angle of vision does restore a significant dimension of what it meant in these years to "speak feminism," in Robin Morgan's phrase. As Susan Gubar affirms, it was "precisely the category of alterity [which is operative in anti-semitism] and the consequences of its attendant stereotypes" that formed the basis for her "feminist investigations of women's situations in male-dominated societies." Jane Gallop writes that her Jewishness bequeathed "a 'negative' identity" of being "set apart from a larger culture"—"an internal alien" yet "proudly not Christian." This aspect of her faith resonated with her "theoretical positions and . . . implicit definition of woman as proudly not a man."[117] It is thus neither incidental nor insignificant that, having examined the strictures of girlhood, the beauty ideal, and romantic love in *Memoirs of an Ex-Prom Queen*, Alix Kates Shulman would next turn her attention to Jewish women's history in *To the Barricades;* or that Esther Broner would shuttle from women's history (in *Her Mothers*) to ritual (in *Weave of Women* and *The Telling*); or that Judy Chicago would find her way from the concept of "women's heritage" to an embrace of *Jewish* heritage. In this way the intellectual weave of American feminism became, in part, a weave of ethnic sensibilities, laments, assertions, celebrations, and sensitivities.

"So what do we mean when we say we 'speak feminism'?" asks Robin Morgan. "It's nothing so sentimental . . . as presuming our differences don't exist. But it's nothing so cowardly . . . as overemphasizing them to the point of justifying not engaging each other across them":

Feminism itself dares to assume that, beneath all our (chosen or forced) diversity, we are in fact much the same—yet the *ways* in which we are similar are not for any one woman or group of women to specify, but for all of us, collectively, to explore and define—a multiplicity of feminisms. In other words, our experience as female human beings in a patriarchy may be the same, but our *experiences of that experience* differ.[118]

Since the 1980s, the division between white women and women of color consumed the most attention and energy when it came to explicating patriarchy and its "differently experienced similarities." But in its often subtle but nonetheless formative ethnic accents white feminism had been attuned to a principle of pluralist solidarity from the outset. For people like Morgan ("a European American, a white, apostate Jew"), "speaking feminism" had long supposed a certain sensitivity to the particularities within the universal. The attempts at multiracial coalition in the 1980s and 1990s (whether under the banner of Third World feminism, global sisterhood, or Women's WORLD) owed many of their solidarities and their most stubborn obstacles to this white ethnic style of "speaking feminism": Jewish/Irish/Greek/Italian/Polish might modify "white" to the extent that it eased an empathy and a solidarity with women of color; but so could Jewish/Irish/Greek/Italian/Polish perspectives lead to an obtuseness on the underlying realities of whiteness and white privilege themselves. "What Chou Mean We, White Girl," asks Lorraine Bethel. "Dear Ms Ann Glad Cosmic Womoon, / We're not doing that kind of work any more / educating white women / teaching colored herstory 101."[119]

Chapter Seven

Whose America
(Who's America)?

I am convinced that beneath our blundering conflicts as a heterogeneous national population there are two pivotal questions: Whose country is this, anyway? And who or what is "an American"?

—June Jordan,
new "Foreword" to
Civil Wars (1995)

The roots motif in American culture has never again been quite as conspicuous as it was in the 1970s, a decade that opened with *Fiddler on the Roof,* then passed through *Roots, The World of Our Fathers,* and the heritage projects of the bicentennial, before rolling down the curtain with *The Harvard Encyclopedia of American Ethnic Groups.* But neither has heritage talk lost its purchase on national consciousness. Multiculturalism and the culture wars captured attention only in the 1980s and 1990s, but both descend directly from that emotive juncture in American life when black became beautiful and people of all backgrounds and colors began to "take back their names," including white neoconservatives like Irving Kristol and Nathan Glazer, white student radicals like Tom Hayden, and white feminists like Judy Chicago and Mary Daly. American culture has traveled from dawning diversity consciousness to full-blown diversity madness ("the united colors of Benetton")—even, in the language of today's education-speak, to "diversity fatigue."

But as a set of genuine political concerns as well as a site of significant contestation, diversity claimed public attention at a very particular moment in the nation's history. Though the United States remains a "people of plenty" when gauged by global statistics on earnings and consumption, the decades since 1960—beginning with fiscal crises, gas shortages, recession, tax revolt, and deindustrialization—have been characterized by a politics of scarcity rather than a politics of abundance. In retrospect, one readily discerns Americans' "collective wince," as a perceived "national decline" became the steady backbeat in the rhythms of civic discussion: the Kennedy assassination (1963); the Watts uprising and later urban rebellions across the country (1965–1968); the Tet offensive, the King and RFK assassinations, the Chicago police riot (1968); the oil crisis and Watergate (1973); the fall of South Vietnam (1975); and the Iran hostage crisis (1979).[1]

The celebratory mood of the nation's bicentennial dissipated fairly quickly. Jimmy Carter warned in his inaugural address that "even our great Nation has its recognized limits . . . we can neither answer all problems nor solve all problems." Later in his presidency, in what became known as the "malaise speech," he asserted that "all the legislation in the world can't fix what's wrong with America." History had revealed a "fundamental threat to

American democracy" in the form of "a crisis of confidence . . . We see this crisis in the growing doubt about the meaning of our own lives and in the loss of unity of purpose for our Nation." By the early 1980s *Time* magazine was reporting on the "Gathering Gloom for Workers." American students, unaccustomed to pronouncements of official pessimism, found themselves reading from a popular U.S. history textbook that now ended with a subsection titled "A Cloudy Horizon." Overall Americans endured five recessions between the 1960s and the end of the century, as the nation fitfully adjusted to what one analysis terms a "postlabor economy."[2]

The chastening signs of national decline constituted the backdrop against which plural American identities took shape and were contested in the era of identity politics and emergent culture wars. Ethnic pride might provide some solace in a time of general malaise, for one thing. But more important, in the last decades of the twentieth century, as Americans ventured answers to June Jordon's crucial questions, "Whose country is this, and who or what is 'an American'?" the stakes were perceived to be so high precisely because of this discomfiting sense of decay. The question "Whose country?" assumed much of the urgency surrounding the question of just what, exactly, the country was to become; the ethnocentric lament "Why can't they be like us?" tapped the unsettling power of the question "Why can't we be like we once were?" From the productions of popular culture like *Rising Sun*, *Rambo*, and *Falling Down*, to Americans' increasingly heated debates over contemporary immigration and education policy, ethnoracial categories came more and more frequently into play around questions of national destiny. Lamentations that the United States risked some kind of ruin tended to borrow multiculturalism's cast of characters in assigning blame—Third World immigrants, Afrocentrists, feminists, the "underclass," Spanish speakers and bilingual educators, Japanese investors and importers, and rappers.

Frank white supremacism is no longer voiced as readily as it once was—mainstream politicians no longer speak openly of a particular group's "fitness for self-government," for instance. But white primacy persists. Its expression in post-1960s political culture does not consist of a loud and proud trumpeting of white superiority, but it is nonetheless buttressed by a gallery of imagined Others whose shortcomings are conceived in both racial and civic terms. This demonizing iconography includes the familiar imagery of black criminality and a dangerous black "underclass." It also includes two distinct versions of the "perpetual foreigner,"—one Asian, the other Latino—denizens whose presence in the United States remains forever unnaturalized. When one is Asian American, according to the poet Janice Mirikitani, the "right" answer to the question "Where are you from?" is always China, Japan, or Korea, never "Lodi / Minneapolis / Chicago."[3] For Latinos, the white, English-speaking republic remains a foreign country in perpetuity. *"To me, the border is no longer located in a geopolitical site,"* writes the performance artist Guillermo Gómez-Peña, *"I carry the border wherever I go. I also find new borders wherever I go. In fact, there is a border right now. Can you feel it?"*[4]

The persistent, naturalized whiteness of the white republic has been evident in both isolated tragedies and broad, national currents in late-twentieth-century America. The 1982 murder of the Chinese American Vincent Chin by two unemployed auto workers who mistook him for a foreigner—and a Japanese foreigner at that—perhaps says it best: the rage of American insecurity turned outward on the "foreigner," though preconceptions of the "foreign" rested less on the facts of the case than on the presumption of America as still a "white man's country."[5] A decade later in *Rising Sun* (1992) Michael Crichton set out to "document" the extent to which Americans had surrendered their country to Japanese economic interests. Critics may have mocked Crichton's marriage of potboiler with polemic (the book is "somewhere between *Uncle Tom's Cabin* and *Reefer Madness*," said one critic), but his central economic and political ideas—that trade is warfare and that America is losing—were generally taken quite seriously, and never more so than when critics took the time to refute them. In the novel Crichton assumed the rhetorical pose of the undaunted bearer of news that Americans would prefer not to know; but as the *Boston Globe* noted, "every day the newspaper tells us this is exactly what Americans want to know. That's why *Rising Sun* is already a bestseller."[6] Crichton's Manichaean tale of U.S.-Japanese warfare was so resonant, that is, first, because it depicted a racialized struggle for control of this "white" nation whose stakes and whose colors (as it were) mimicked the dire imagery that had characterized discussion of both foreign policy and immigration since the Vietnam War and the post-1965 immigration; and second, because it validated a thesis of national decline that had been haunting the popular imagination for some twenty years—notwithstanding the United States' enduring status as a superpower, and notwithstanding the rosy-hued interlude of Ronald Reagan's "morning in America."

But if the "they" in American discourse are a congeries of racialized criminals, perpetually foreign denizens, foreign investors, and competing laborers (and, later, potential terrorists), who in popular white estimation represents the "we"? Who figures as the "my" of "get out of my country"? The answer, in large part, lies in the consecration of Ellis Island, in the demographic alchemy of *Grease, Yentl, Moonstruck,* or *Titanic,* in the image of the immigrant ghetto that has been so warmly seized on by polemicists of both the left and the right. "Chevotarevich?" an officer questions the Christopher Walken character in *The Deer Hunter.* "Is that a Russian Name?" "No," he replies adamantly. "It's American." Establishing the Americanness—indeed, the prototypical Americanness—of the white ethnic is perhaps the most significant ideological work of *The Deer Hunter* (1978), a lavish rendering of stereotypical Asian villainy, to be sure, but also of the *New York Times*'s 1976 pronouncement that "white ethnics" constituted "the largest segment of Middle America."[7] That the prototypical "white" of late-twentieth-century imagination claimed an immigrant heritage (denoting relatively recent arrival, underdog credentials, and innocence in white supremacy's history of conquest and enslavement) is reflected across the culture, from the everyman status of Claude Bukowski in *Hair* (1969), to the comedian Chris Rock's dissenting account (c.2000) of the typical ethnic disavowal of whiteness:

BLACK MAN: Hey, you cracker!

WHITE MAN: I'm not a cracker, I'm Rumanian.

BLACK MAN: OK, you *Rumanian* Cracker!

One variation on this sociological theme has claimed a great deal of attention in public discussion: the realm of "Black-Jewish relations," a "special relationship" presumed to consist of historically unique patterns of alliance and betrayal.[8] But Black-Jewish relations represent only the most conspicuous instance of a more general pattern of confrontation, alliance, or conflict involving, at the symbolic level, "Ellis Island whiteness" on the one hand, and people of color on the other. This is not to argue that Black-Jewish relations have no history of their own, or that Jewishness has no currency in the United States distinct from other European ethnicities (on the contrary, when Minnesota farmers suffer foreclosure, they do not rail about a conspiracy of *Irish* bankers).

But setting aside emotional claims on both sides, Black-Jewish relations illustrate something quite significant about how "whiteness" is figured in post–Civil Rights, post–ethnic revival political culture. We have witnessed the symbolic currency of Ellis Island whiteness many times over—Patrick Moynihan's reliance on the normative Italian family in constructing the "pathological" black family; narratives of white victimization like *Rocky;* Tom Hayden's deployment of Irishness in solidarity with other colonized peoples. In its sociology of whiteness, the familiar terrain of Black-Jewish relations represents not a singular instance but a pervasive paradigm: white ethnics are (or have been) "like" people of color in their minority status on the American scene; thus a "special" understanding is presumed at the outset. Moreover, in some quarters the differences in status that do exist become cause either to lament African Americans' shortcomings from one side of the color line or to decry white ethnics' betrayal of their "roots" on the other.

The shaded whiteness at play in narratives of alliance, betrayal, or mutual disappointment unites Black-Jewish relations with Spiro Agnew's bootstrap homilies on the self-reliant Greek immigrant, preached to black leaders in the wake of Baltimore's 1968 rioting; Dick Gregory's caustic remarks on America's Irish police force, whose forebears had once served as the white man's

"injun"; white ethnics' trade-union jostling with blacks and Latinos for the crumbs of a postindustrial economy; or Martin
Scorsese's ambivalent depiction of Irish-Black relations in *The
Gangs of New York*.[9] Each of these examples rests on an interpretation of race, ethnicity, and history replete with assertions of
"natural" alliance, "natural" conflict, solidarity, prior right, competition, or betrayal. Each emerges from and evokes a complex past,
as Jennifer Guglielmo has said, "of collaboration, intimacy, hostility, and distancing" among America's nonwhites on the one hand
and its non-Nordic, underdog whites on the other.[10]

This ideological current has been especially portentous in a
country conceived as a "nation of immigrants"—where the ~~roots~~
routes of white ethnicity are not simply the stuff of literal family
history, but stand in for whiteness itself in the nation's public
symbolism and its most deeply held civic religion. The Ellis Island myth of origins constitutes a persistent undercurrent in U.S.
political discourse—a riptide whose pull may only occasionally
roil the surface, but whose power beneath has decisively influenced Americans' collective experience and their language of collectivity. According to national survey data from 1986 and 1992,
for instance, 76.1 percent of white Americans either "agreed" or
"strongly agreed" with the statement, "Irish, Italians, Jewish and
many other minorities overcame prejudice and worked their way
up. Blacks should do the same without any special favors." This
figure is significantly higher than even the 62.3 percent who felt
that the "history of slavery" and "being discriminated against"
had created unique obstacles to African-American mobility. In a
survey of white Indianapolis—not exactly the Lower East Side—
the corresponding numbers were 76.8 percent and 50.9 percent,
respectively.[11] The white "we" of America's we-and-they language

of racialized contest, in other words, has largely jettisoned the Pilgrim and the pioneer, drawing instead on the self-congratulatory social fables of those more recent white arrivals who first made land at Hoboken Pier. Even many years after *Roots*, this particular legend of American whiteness continues to texture public images of the nation, its origins, its newest immigrants, and its possibilities for cross-racial understanding.

Up from Steerage

Kennedy made the first presidential roots trip; Nixon supplemented his "southern strategy" with an explicit white ethnic appeal (hence Spiro Anagnostopoulos); and Reagan, the Irishman nicknamed "Dutch," turned Novak's unmeltable ethnics into "Reagan Democrats." But no presidential candidate ever made more of his immigrant heritage than Michael Dukakis. Public attention in the late 1980s briefly assumed the form of a Dukakis Fest—*Newsweek* dubbed 1988 the "year of the Dukakii"—as Michael pounded on the theme of his immigrant Greek heritage in his run for the White House, and cousin Olympia was celebrated for her role in the ethnic romance *Moonstruck*.[12] Though the fest was brief indeed, its ethnic undertones are worth pausing over, because without them there is no comprehending the more memorable political icon from the moment, the African-American convict Willie Horton. The 1988 presidential election was a morality play straight out of *The Rise of the Unmeltable Ethnics*.

Dukakis's extraordinary emphasis on his Ellis Island pedigree was prefaced three times over—once by Geraldine Ferraro's vice presidential candidacy in 1984, again by the Statue of Liberty gala in 1986, and yet again by his cousin's film *Moonstruck* in 1987. Ferraro had never made quite as much of her Italian-American

17.   "Welcome home to Ballyporeen, Mr. President." Ronald Reagan's "re-turn" to Ireland in June 1984. CORBIS.

background as others did. Though the *Washington Post* described one of her congressional fundraisers as "an Italian wedding," and though on the stump she occasionally appealed to Italian pride (her candidacy, she said, had redressed a state of affairs where "the only image of Italian women" was the Prince Spaghetti lady on TV), finally she fell to an odd combination of anti-Italian stereotypes (her family's alleged ties to "organized crime") and Catholics' own aloofness from her perceived feminism.[13] But in a prescient piece in the *Washington Post*, Michael Barone analyzed the 1984 election as a "battle for Ellis Island"—a joust not only for the "ethnic vote" but for the very symbolism of America and what was best about it:

> What's important in 1984 is not how each ticket appeals to specific ethnic groups, but which is more successful in appealing to the Ellis Island tradition generally. For most Ameri-

cans, Ellis Island is a living memory—not something they experienced themselves, but something they have heard about
from parents or grandparents, part of the family lore and tradition. They know that the people before them came over
with nothing, often not even knowing English. They know
that they worked, more hours a day than most Americans today can imagine; they struggled, in living and working conditions most Americans today would not tolerate for a minute.
They lived in smelly, tiny, airless apartments, endured the
prejudice of others. And they succeeded, in spite of it all.

In Barone's view, the election hinged on which party could best
harness "the Ellis Island tradition"—Republicans, whose version
stressed the adopted country's beneficent soil of "free enterprise,"
or Democrats, whose "compassionate government" had rightly
stepped in to protect the underdog, "starting with the response to
the Triangle Fire."[14]

The 1984 election went to Reagan, of course; as Barone himself had acknowledged, the president, "who grew up as an Irish-
American in mostly Yankee Dixon, Ill., understands Ellis Island."
(Recall Reagan's roots trip to Ballyporeen.) But in "The Battle
for Ellis Island," Barone had identified an important economy of
symbols, a potent consensus on who the "representative" American was and whose familial saga was most revealing of the national character. Reagan would cash in on the "orgy of sentimentality" for the Statue of Liberty Centennial in 1986, but Ellis
Island symbolism might just prove more usable still when the
Democrats set out to repackage American liberalism for the 1988
election.[15]

But first the nation paused to appreciate the performances of

*18. Feminism meets ethnic politics, Columbus Day, 1984: Italian-Ameri-
can vice presidential candidate Geraldine Ferraro at the head of the
procession with New York mayor Edward Koch (arms upraised),
ticketmate Walter Mondale, and Governor Mario Cuomo.
BETTMANN/CORBIS.*

the Greek Olympia Dukakis and the Armenian-Cherokee Cher
(Cherilyn Sarkisian) in *Moonstruck*, Norman Jewison's Hollywood love note to ethnic Italianness. Although there were indeed
some "real" Italians on the set (Vincent Gardenia, Danny Aiello,
and Nicolas Cage), Jewison's casting of Dukakis and Cher conveys quite a lot about the put-on variety of Italianness that was on
display here. When Loretta Castorini hears an old woman tell a
story, in dramatic pitch and thick Old World accent, of the curse
she has put on her sister's plane (which happens to carry Loretta's
fiancé as well), the younger woman replies coolly, "I don't believe
in curses." The old woman glares back at her, "Neither do I." In
Moonstruck, although everybody is superstitious, nobody really
believes in curses or in anything else that carries an ounce of cul-

tural specificity (Loretta rolls her eyes in exaggerated impatience as Johnny Camarieri talks about the importance of *famiglia*); and it is precisely this weightless, emptied version of Italianness that the film relies on in constructing its more generic (Greek? Armenian?) ethnic romance.

Jewison was not the first director to borrow on Greek or Armenian talent to fill an Italian role. Olympia Dukakis may have gotten her start playing "the Spirit of Young Greece" in local Red Cross pageants as a child, but Greek roles had been sparse ever since. "If your name is Olympia Dukakis, that's it, bang," she said. "You play Italians." (Indeed, Dukakis had played one of the TV spaghetti ladies from whom Ferraro rescued Italian womanhood in 1984.)[16] But in this case Jewison's casting suits the film's self-conscious construction of a role-play Italianness. In its playful exploration of two families' infidelities and betrayals—and, not least, the disregard for patriarchal authority—the film winks at the popular Francis Coppola–Richard Gambino versions of Italian-American social codes as mere fabrications, and it puts forward a new fabrication in their place. Nonetheless, *Moonstruck* is no less loving of ethnic particularity, for all that; in this film to be "ethnic" is more charming and more meaningful than to be an unmarked WASP (a judgment made clear in the emptiness and pretension of the film's few WASP characters). *Moonstruck* celebrates ethnicity as the most critically important and resonant of hollow signifiers.

The stage was set, then, for a presidential candidate with immigrant parents named Panos and Euterpe. The Dukakis campaign began in earnest on Oscar night, when, statuette held aloft, Olympia ended her acceptance speech, "OK, Michael, let's go!" thus offering encouragement from one Greek playing the generic immigrant to another. As Dukakis's campaign biographers put it, "his family's immigrant saga" quickly became "the central theme of his campaign—its heart and soul." "He emphasized it at even the briefest campaign stops and spun it out with growing detail for groups of Greek Americans. In large part, it is, as he claims, the story of America, the classic tale of poor immigrants who came here in search of a better life and found it."[17]

Dukakis was the first whole-hearted candidate for a "nation of immigrants," and the first genuine ethnic revival candidate as well. The governor "virtually wallows" in his heritage, the *Washington Post* reported, an apparent effort to win back the "traditional white ethnic base" that Democrats had lost to the "son of the Irish named Ronald Reagan." Dukakis adopted Neil Diamond's song "America" (from *The Jazz Singer*) as his campaign anthem; so pronounced did the ethnic theme in the campaign become that *Saturday Night Live*'s Jon Lovitz (a Jew playing a Greek playing everyethnic) parodied the stump speech, "I come from the little people. The little, swarthy people." "Inherent in [Dukakis's] message," wrote his campaign biographers, "is the emphasis that an immigrant past is a common denominator among all Americans. (Once, when an American Indian challenged this view of history, Dukakis replied that the Indian's own ancestors had immigrated over the Bering Strait.)"[18]

The national media could never quite resist the ethnic angle in this campaign. "After decades of quiet assimilation, the nation's one million Greek-Americans are exerting political power this election year as never before. It is a new chapter in America's melting-pot story," said the *Los Angeles Times*. "The people whose ancestors invented democracy now are a critical base of support for a leading contender for the Democratic nomination." *Newsday* ran a feature story titled "Roots, Dukakis Style," in which the journal wondered, "If the Massachusetts governor gets to the White House, will his ancestral villages in Greece and Turkey become tourist centers?" And when Dukakis and his mother "returned" to Ellis Island aboard *Liberty II*, cameras rolled greedily and network producers gushed over the "great shot" that the occasion afforded.[19]

Like Italianness in *Moonstruck*, Greekness here was more a motif than an actual substance. Flanked by a campaign triumvirate consisting of John Sasso, Nick Mitropoulos, and Jack Corrigan (Italian, Greek, and Irish), and ever accompanied by his wife, Kitty (Jewish), Dukakis fashioned himself into what Garry Wills called "the common denominator of immigrant aspiration, a kind of Everyethnic, ecumenical and assimilated." "We all know that many Americans have come to this country with nothing—nothing but hope," intoned Olympia at the Democratic National Convention. "Well, today one of their sons stands before you with the opportunity to be president of the United States."[20] Thus did his Greekness render Dukakis the symbolic son of "many Americans," and then the symbol of American "hope" itself.

His campaign took him to Italian pastry shops, Irish pubs, and Polish Constitution Day parades; he was feted by "little girls in the crimson velvet, gold-embroidered costumes of Eastern European peasants." As for Kitty, "No Jewish audience was left unreminded of her roots." "I can't help but think of my grandparents as I look out at you," she told one audience. "They were born in a shtetl outside of Kiev." Nor did Michael Dukakis eschew this emergent pan-ethnicity, even as he tried to accent his "authentic" Greekness: "Those of you who are of Polish descent, or Irish descent or Italian descent or whatever," he said, "are proud of your traditions and your culture, as am I." His was a celebration, quite precisely, of the "whatever": at a Polish parade in Cleveland he described himself as "a symbol for ethnic communities all over America."[21]

The ethnic accents of the Dukakis campaign might have been expected to play best in cities like New York and Boston, where many ethnic enclaves survived and where local political cultures had preserved voters' ethnic identifications. But ultimately this tactic came to be, not Dukakis's Eastern strategy, but his "American strategy." "No Greek dwarf can carry east Texas," said Texas Republican Charlie Wilson—a sound enough assumption, until Dukakis carried Wilson's own district in the state primary. As the *Globe* reporter David Nyhan wrote, "Iowa's Chickasaw County is about as far from Greece and Ellis Island as you can get." But in Nyhan's view, it was Dukakis's "little homily on the son-of-immigrants theme" by which he "began whittling himself into a semblance of a national candidate." Indeed, working with focus groups in North Carolina, Texas, Alabama, and Florida, Dukakis's southern coordinator found that "most Southerners . . . said all Americans are immigrants . . . They were almost insulted [by the idea] that Southerners would not vote for him because he's from Greek immigrants." One supporter at a rally in North Carolina said, "My great-granddaddy was German . . . He had the same belief as this fella [Dukakis]—work hard, nail it down, don't expect something for nothing. Now this fella, he's like that. He's solid." Nick Mitropoulos, Dukakis's right hand man, commented, "I see it hit home in almost every audience we're in."[22]

Soon after this formula had secured the nomination, Dukakis aide John Sasso predicted that the Bush campaign would try to paint Dukakis "in alien colors," though at the time he could not have known precisely what those "colors" would turn out to be.[23] As early as the New Hampshire primary, opponents had been trying to undermine Dukakis's blood-coursing Greek appeal by portraying him as a mere "manager, a technocrat"; more than one observer had noted that he seemed staid for a hot-blooded Mediterranean. "Zorba, he ain't," Morton Kondracke averred; well, maybe "Zorba the clerk," quipped the comedian Mark Russell. Most damning was Garry Wills's characterization in *Time* magazine: "The '60s were torn with passion, from the death of Kennedy through the civil rights and anti-war demonstrations, culminating for Boston in the great anti-busing struggle in the early 1970s. Michael Dukakis' great cause in this decade was no-fault automobile insurance."[24]

Even some Greek Americans wondered whether Dukakis had exploited his Greek heritage "to soften his technocrat image." ("He's like no Greek I ever met," remarked the editor Peter Pappas.) If Dukakis's ethnic awakening on a "voyage of discovery" to Greece in the magical year 1976 made his the perfect roots story, it also raised suspicions of his authenticity. Even the beloved Reagan had aroused cynicism by his ostentatious roots trip to Ballyporeen. Now James Jatras, a Senate aide, was circulating an open letter that denounced Dukakis as a "pagan," an "apostate," and a Greek "imposter" who "attacks our Church and attacks Christ." A favorite joke in Massachusetts, meanwhile, was, "I knew Dukakis before he was Greek."[25]

But Dukakis's Ellis Island approach posed a real problem for George Bush. As the *Washington Post* noted, Bush found himself "burdened with a patrician, establishment image" that was only augmented by the Dukakis campaign's celebration of the "everyethnic." Catholic voters in particular saw in Bush "the Yankee elite who did not welcome their immigrant ancestors with either covered dishes or open arms." (Bush also tended to make matters worse for himself, as when, on a visit to the very high school made famous by the can-do spirit of Edward Olmos's film *Stand and Deliver,* he implied that Mexican Americans need not think about college: "We need the people who do the hard physical work in our society," he said, in what he apparently thought a tribute to the Mexican contribution.)[26]

But as David Nyhan recognized, it was not just his patrician bearing but his actual WASPness that posed the biggest problem for Bush. Ironically, in the era of *Moonstruck,* Nyhan explained, "the WASP is the most thoroughly denigrated, widely denounced, unfairly maligned ethnic stereotype in America . . . Symbolizing, as they do, wealth and privilege, breeding and manners, ultimate advantage and superiority, WASPs attract all the psychological rocks and bottles we like to throw in the direction of the ruling class." If some, like a letter writer from Swampscott, Massachusetts, thought Dukakis "small and insignificant" ("like Columbo"), Nyhan still recognized a peculiar cachet in this circumstance of descending from the little (swarthy) people. Describing Dukakis's childhood pilgrimages to Haymarket, a large, open-air fruit and vegetable market in Boston, in the loving tones of antimodern romance, Nyhan wrote:

It was a chaotic place, of sweaty vendors, braying carters, babushkaed old ladies in basic Italian black. The air was filled with sounds of bartering, gypsy curses, the rank smells of sawdust, blood, rotting fruit. People argued in fractured English and a dozen stranger tongues over paper bags filled with dusty, spotted, fly-specked produce. This was not your basic cellophane-wrapped accurately-weighed-and-measured suburban supermarket scene . . . Those of us who were close to immigrant stock never realized how this ritual returning to our roots sometimes made more assimilated Americans envious.[27]

This is what George Bush was up against, and throughout the summer of 1988 his victory was in doubt. Michael Barone, who had enunciated the parties' "Battle for Ellis Island" four years earlier, now offered one possible solution to Bush's dilemma: "Michael Dukakis has had great success running as the 1980s version of the classic American archetype of the Immigrant. George Bush, running behind, would do well to run as the 1980s version of another classic American archetype, the Pioneer." But Meg Greenfield more astutely identified the weakness in the Dukakis strategy, and more closely understood the road that would carry Bush to victory. "The lore of the late 19th- and early 20th-century immigrant—Ellis Island, pushcarts, slums—has become the East Coast equivalent of the log-cabin, poor farm-boy upbringing and the rest of that Americana unavailable to so many people with exotic surnames," she acknowledged. Greenfield did not dismiss Dukakis's immigrant saga as "wholly a campaign contrivance," having experienced firsthand, "as a descendant of poor and persecuted 1880s immigrants . . . that their hold on one's emotions and imagination is powerful." But distance itself seemed the key. Greenfield went on to identify "two sides to this impulse to glorify a relatively recent immigrant heritage." One is "morally smug, or at least self-congratulatory," she noted. "It puts distance between me and the . . . dispossessed people of today"; and the other is "more empathetic and imaginative, seeing a connection between us and a moral connection to help." Dukakis's great theme "can be used to include or exclude."[28]

Whereas Dukakis hoped to draw on the inclusive impulses of the Ellis Island saga, Bush would thrive on the *ex*clusive. If the Dukakis campaign was taking a page from Michael Novak's book *Unmeltable Ethnics,* then the Bush campaign would take another —the page, perhaps, where Novak admitted, "ethnics think they are better people than blacks." In early July, while "politely tipping his hat to [Dukakis's] Greek heritage," as the *Washington Post* put it, Bush promised "to spend the next four months blasting away at Dukakis and competing for the votes of what Bush called 'ethnic America.'" It was here that Bush brought up "prison furloughs for convicted murderers" (along with "gun control, abortion, school prayer . . . 'neighborhood values,' and big government").[29] And it was here that the figure of William ("Willie") Horton came into play.

In searching the Dukakis record for five or six simple, easy-to-understand issues, Bush associate James Pinkerton came upon local coverage of a case in which a (black) convicted murderer, on temporary release as part of the Massachusetts prison furlough program, had reportedly raped a white woman. Many details of the *Lawrence Eagle-Tribune*'s coverage, which the Bush campaign popularized, were later called into question. But as Pinkerton told strategist Lee Atwater, "The more people who know who Willie Horton is, the better off we'll be."[30] Over the course of the summer, indeed, about as many Americans who knew about Dukakis's humble Greek origins came to know "who Willie Horton is." In a post-mortem after the election, *The Nation* would name Horton "Bush's Most Valuable Player."[31]

There are three dimensions to the Republicans' deployment of Horton's image. One concerns the political culture's centuries-old images and myths of black bestiality, and especially of the black rapist. Indeed, the Bush strategy elevated Horton "from street criminal to monstrous folk villain," David Anderson writes, and in so doing the campaign borrowed a brand of racialized villainy scripted during Reconstruction and long since familiar. "Let us begin by conceding that Bush himself is not a racist," wrote Michael Kinsley. "But he's also not an idiot, and the nuances of Hortonism are not subtle. Perhaps Bush has seen 'The Birth of a Nation.'"[32] Hence the ever-present visage of Horton throughout the last months of the campaign—paired with the narrative of the black rapist and his white victim—resonated with a universe of images that was already in place and in which social meanings were already fixed. "You can't find a stronger metaphor . . . for racial hatred in this country than a black man raping a white woman," Susan Estrich later told Atwater.[33]

The second dimension of the Bush campaign's use of Horton played into the 1980s discourse of race and criminality that characterized public discussion of the Central Park jogger case, for instance. As David Anderson has written, Americans were introduced to Horton at a moment when they were already feverishly concerned about a very particular "pattern" or type of criminality. Anderson defines the pattern as consisting of five elements: crimes that were (1) "luridly violent," against (2) "innocent" victims who were (3) "middle-class, usually white" and who had been (4) chosen "entirely at random" by (5) a perpetrator who already had "some history of involvement with the criminal justice system," but who had gone free for one reason or another. In the context of the 1980s, writes Anderson, any crime that included four of these five elements "invariably stirred broad outrage and often provoked a political reaction."[34] Horton's was just such a crime, and Dukakis would be second only to Horton himself in bearing the brunt of the outrage.

The third dimension of the Bush strategy involved destabilizing the mythic certitudes of Dukakis's *Greekness* while simultaneously borrowing stereotypes of blackness for the Willie Horton ads. "The campaign," writes Anderson, "would turn on a battle for the definition of Dukakis, not Bush," and over the course of the summer the image of Willie Horton did most of the defining. Standard ethnic refrains may have been suitable to counter Bush's early attack on Dukakis's stance on the Pledge of Allegiance in public schools: "My parents came to this country as immigrants," replied Dukakis. "They taught me that this was the greatest country in the world . . . [and] nobody's going to question my patriotism." But the figure of Willie Horton posed a very different problem: though furlough programs of the sort in question were common across the country, Horton and the furlough issue effectively transformed Dukakis from one of "the people"— a status that his steerage iconography had confirmed—into one of those "Civil Rights establishment" technocrats whom Michael Novak and others had long insisted "the people" ought to fear most. Citizens against Unsafe Society (CAUS), one of the anti-Dukakis groups that mobilized around the furlough issue, ran a "Judge for Yourself" TV commercial, in which the governor's technocratic liberalism was challenged in on-camera interviews with CAUS activists Maureen Donovan and Vivianne Ruggiero, prosecutor Michael Stella, and State Representative Larry

Giordano.[35] That *this* rendition of "the people"—here, aggrieved victims of both New Class and "underclass"—derived from the same Ellis Island template as Dukakis's "little people" proved insurmountable.

The point here transcends Dukakis's failed moment in 1988. Dukakis may have burned up the steerage appeal as a centerpiece for presidential campaigning for some time to come, but his immigrant iconography continues to hold a place in Americans' collective imagination, as evidenced by the popularity of the movies *Angela's Ashes* and *The Gangs of New York*, or the nation-of-immigrants pieties of Rudy Giuliani's post-9/11 tract *Leadership*. The Ellis Island saga surfaces as a political instrument in the new millennium, for example, whenever the issue of slavery reparations comes up. When the Chicago City Council voted on a pro-reparations resolution, Alderman Brian Doherty objected that "the constituents of [my] Northwest Side ward are, by and large, the descendants of people who immigrated to the United States after slavery had ended. They should not be forced to pay for wrongs committed by others."[36] This defense would become a standard argument against reparations, not only from Chicago's Northwest Side but from the nation at large. Point 4 of David Horowitz's "Ten Reasons Why Reparations for Slavery Is a Bad Idea—and Racist Too" notes that "two great waves of immigration occurred after 1880 and then after 1960. What logic would require [these newcomers] . . . to pay reparations to American blacks?" Elsewhere, Horowitz deploys the theme of immigration not only as a demographic circumstance that complicates reparation beyond workability, but—like Glazer and others before him—as a Eurocentric, view-from-steerage account of how America really *ought* to be understood and appreciated:

As a Jew, I know that whatever injustices my people have suffered in this country, America is the best, freest and safest
place for Jews to live in the entire world. As a Jew I owe a debt
to America for giving me the opportunities and the freedoms
I have and for creating a society that is the paragon of tolerance compared to any other place I know. It is my opinion that
black Americans—who are richer, freer and safer in America
than they would be anywhere else on earth—should feel the
same way.[37]

This "should" turned out to be wildly controversial. Horowitz seemed surprised that such a notion would spark disagreement (missing, perhaps, the echo between his argument and the
nineteenth-century assertion that blacks were "better off" in the
United States—even under a regime of slavery—than in Africa).
But in fact his argument contains its own rebuttal: in claiming
that "the GNP of black America makes the African-American
community the tenth most prosperous 'nation' in the world," Horowitz begs the question, why such disparity between this "tenth"
nation and *white* America, which ranks significantly higher?[38]

Horowitz's opposition to reparations, of course, is closely related to a broader engagement with the so-called culture wars of
recent decades, in which, as Horowitz writes, "'tenured radicals'
have waged a ferocious assault on America's conception of itself as
a beacon of freedom." His own conception of that "beacon of
freedom" aligns him with the Dukakis of 1988. Horowitz is absolutely clear about where that conception originates: "Academic
leftists have created a vast corpus of social theory that . . . reinter-
prets the narrative of American freedom as a chronicle of race and
class oppression. A nation conceived in liberty is newly described

as 'a nation conceived in slavery.' A 'nation of immigrants' becomes a nation of victims."[39]

Encounters with "Discovery"

Before there were European steerage passengers, there were European explorers—before there was Columbo, there was Columbus, no? Columbus Day is a fitting holiday for a "nation of immigrants," in both the inclusive and exclusive renderings of that conceit. Italian Americans might explain their attachment to the holiday and their penchant for parades in ecumenical terms, as when one parade-goer told a reporter, "We are honoring the immigrants. We are celebrating the courage of a navigator in search of a new land . . . for people who came to this country with no shoes and made something of themselves." The president of the National Italian American Foundation asserted, "We look at [Columbus] as the father of all immigrants who paved the road for people around the world in search of freedom, justice and economic opportunity."[40] And yet, the Indian rights activist Leonard Peltier would write from his jail cell, "My own personal story can't be told . . . [without going] back to that darkest day in all human history: October 12, 1492, when our Great Sorrow began." In this sense the Mexican-American writer Richard Rodriguez, uncomfortably astride the hyphen, described himself as "an enemy of the history that had otherwise created me." Celebratory renditions of North American history like those that characterize Columbus Day represent "the European version—the stag version" of the New World pageant.[41]

Columbus Day had been steeped in ethnic politics from the very beginning—ethnic politics was in fact the very point. The first Columbus Day was observed in Colorado in 1907, a "pride" festival for immigrants who had begun arriving in the state in the 1880s to work the mines and railroads; the first parade was intended to counteract anti-Italian stereotypes.[42] People of color, meanwhile, had developed very different ideas about the holiday. On the one hand were those who marked October 12 as *el Dia de la Raza* ("the day of the race"), a celebration of encounter as the beginning of the *mestizaje* that became modern-day Latinismo. In this view, the impact Columbus made on the New World "was wholly Iberian in character; it had nothing to do with Italy, which did not even exist as a nation at the time." Though the encounter may have been brutal initially, still "it was with [Columbus's] arrival on this continent that Latin America was born."[43] In this respect celebrants of *el Dia de la Raza* were posed directly in opposition to Italian Americans and their claims for the meaning of Columbus's voyage.

But so were they arrayed against a second position within the Latino community and among other people of color: that Columbus's voyage signified neither the laudable "spread of civilization" nor the breaking of a few eggs for the omelet of *mestizaje*, but conquest pure and simple. (Christopher Hitchens once called the Chicago offices of Louis Farrakhan for an interview, and when told to call back Monday, he said, "Isn't that Columbus Day?" "Not for us it ain't," was the terse reply.) "No sensible Indian would celebrate Columbus Day," argued George Horse Capture; "not for the discovery of the continent by some foreigner." "We're not anti-Italian," explained Bobby Castillo of the International Indian Treaty Council. "But when we see people honoring Christopher Columbus, it's the same as what Jewish people see when they see people honoring Adolf Hitler." Ward Churchill concurred that the "celebration of Columbus and the European conquest . . . he set off is greatly analogous to celebration of the glories of Nazism and Heinrich Himmler."[44]

The quincentenary of the Columbus voyage in 1992 loosed the passions all around. According to Suzan Shown Harjo, the coordinator of a group called the 1992 Alliance, although the holiday had always been hard to take ("For Native people, this half millennium of land-grabs and one-cent treaty sales has been no bargain"), Columbus Day had dwindled in American attention to little more than "a good shopping day." But now, as the anniversary approached, "an obscene amount of money will be lavished . . . on parades, statues and festivals," she lamented. "Funny hats will be worn and new myths born. Little kids will be told big lies in the name of education." In response, she promised, no one should be surprised by "Native people who mark the occasion by splashing blood-red paint on a Columbus statue here or there. Columbus will be hanged in effigy as a symbol of the European invasion, and tried in planned tribunals." Dissenting views like Harjo's gained ground. In 1992 the Minneapolis City Council adopted a resolution stating that Columbus's "so-called discovery" of America had resulted in genocide, enslavement, and the violation of native nations' sovereign rights, and Berkeley changed the name of Columbus Day to "Indigenous People's Day." The National Council of Churches, too, condemned the "invasion" as a "precursor to genocide and enslavement of native peoples," and counseled that Columbus Day be observed with penitence.[45]

Italian Americans' hagiographic mood for the holiday—so hard won—would not die easily even amid the gathering dissent. Nor had the holiday become for them anything like a mere "shopping day": Italian-American communities across the country had developed an array of public pageants, celebrations, and rituals to mark the day and to honor Italian greatness. San Franciscans held a beauty pageant to crown an iconic "Queen Isabella": the band played a tarantella as contestants introduced their families to the crowd in Italian (as part of the competition); the winner, once crowned, would (oddly) proceed to the beach to greet Columbus. In St. Louis the community held a "Miss Italian St. Louis pageant," while Houston mounted a Noche de las Americas gala and ball, whose historical pageant, though billed as a "Hispanic gala," included Italian, Irish, Polish, and Jewish revelers. Participants decried "attempts to turn [Columbus] into the world's greatest genocide artist." "The man discovered America. Can't we leave it at that?" one celebrant wanted to know. New York parades featured Italian-American celebrities, often in evocative pairings like Joe DiMaggio and Gina Lollobrigida (New York City, 1991) or Tommy Lasorda and Sophia Loren (Albany, 1990).[46]

Several incidents warned of a coming conflict as 1992 approached, including the defacement of Columbus statues all over the country, and the Minneapolis resolution prescribing celebrations that would recognize native cultures. Philadelphia witnessed a row between one Italian-American civic group, which wanted to change the name of Delaware Avenue to Christopher Columbus Boulevard ("a fitting honor"), and a group of American Indians who thought it "an insult to honor the man who . . . encouraged the rape, torture and enslavement of the Indians." Protests for the quincentenary proper got off to an early start, when eight Native Americans stepped off a plane in Italy and planted a staff of eagle feathers on the tarmac, having "discovered" the country. When armed security guards rushed out and ordered the group off the runway, James Yellowbank noted caustically, "we should have done that to Columbus."[47]

Protests gathered in 1992, though not always in the same

whimsical vein. John Sanchez, of the Ohio Center for Native American Affairs, declared "a day of mourning for Native Americans." "While Columbus didn't actually insert the sword in the millions of people who died," Sanchez stated, "he started the process of enslavement, murder, disease, pollution and racism that came after exploration and conquest . . . To us he's Hitler." "No one honors Hitler or any other despot in history," added Russell Means, a leader in the American Indian Movement (AIM), "so why should they honor Columbus?" Columbus Day festivities in Denver were cancelled in response to Native Americans' vow to disrupt them. As "would-be marchers, many wearing Italian folk costumes," retreated to the state capital, Native-American protesters led by Means rallied at Denver's Civic Center, amid a burned-out mock Indian village consisting of 100 charred teepee frames in commemoration of the invasion. Revising the Reagan-era protest slogan "U.S. Out of Central America," placards at the demonstration now read, "U.S. Out of North America." Protesters in Berkeley enjoyed a performance of an opera by White Cloud Wolfhawk titled *Get Lost (Again) Columbus;* in New York protesters stenciled "Genocide Avenue" in red on the street corners up and down Columbus Avenue; in Boston protesters distributed photographs of Christopher Columbus standing next to an Indian, with the caption, "Which one is the savage?" The *Los Angeles Times* filed this report on the San Francisco reenactment of the Columbus voyage:

> Like Columbus, Cervetto will be met upon his arrival today by American Indians. Unlike Columbus, he will also be met by members of the Bay Area Coalition for Reproductive Rights, the Lesbian Committee to Support Women Political Prisoners, the Anarchist-Communist Coalition, the General

Union of Palestinian Students, Queers for Cuba, and other groups that have vowed to protest the event.[48]

Indeed, Columbus was greeted at Aquatic Park by a small regatta and 2,000 protesters, and a "peace navy" of 5 boats summoned by AIM succeeded in turning him away, back to the Old World of Scoma's Restaurant from whence he had come. Later in the afternoon the parade was beset by protesters decrying the pageantry as "a glamorization of genocide" and chanting, "No Columbus Day, No Hitler Day," and "Five hundred years of rape and hate—what have we got to celebrate?"[49]

The lessons of the quincentenary are many. Some were quick to declare the seeming victory of a "politically correct" interpretation of Columbus. *Time* ran an obituary for the old-school narratives of American history under the title, "Hail Columbus, Dead White Male." Others clung to those narratives just as tenaciously. Charles Krauthammer (not exactly a *Mayflower* surname) asserted that "the Columbian legacy has created a civilization that we ought not, in all humble piety and cultural relativism, declare to be no better or worse than that of the Incas. It turned out better. And mankind is better for it. Infinitely better. Reason enough to honor Columbus and bless 1492."[50]

But perhaps the most powerful messages lurked between the lines. The media tended to depict this contest as a clash between "parade-goers" on the one hand and "activists" on the other, for instance, forgetting the important civics lesson embedded in the history of Columbus Day itself, that "parade-goers" are merely activists who have won. Much press coverage thus naturalized the old-school point of view and kindled the Columbus mythology, even if showing "sensitivity" to the protesters. When the *Los Angeles Times* wrote of those Indians and Latinos who were "protesting what they term the genocide of their people," for instance, few people probably paused to imagine the ramifications of a parallel construction that would posit Jews' establishing a Holocaust Museum, say, as a desire to commemorate "what they term the genocide of their people."[51]

The general press was content to endorse the Columbus-as-hero legend by reporting endlessly on whites' (usually Italian-Americans') stupefaction that Columbus himself was taking the heat for 500 years of European expansionism, without ever looking into Columbus's actual career. For the American media it really was as simple as "in 1492 Columbus sailed the ocean blue." After sailing the ocean blue, however, Columbus returned in 1493 with an invasion force of 17 ships; he installed himself as viceroy and governor of the Caribbean islands; he established a base on the island of Espanola (now Hispaniola), instituting policies of enslavement and systematic extermination that reduced the indigenous Taino population from roughly 8 million to 3 million; he required all Tainos over the age of 14 to supply "a hawk's bell of gold" to the crown every three months, or else have their hands cut off and be left to die. Columbus's contemporary chronicler, Bartolome Las Casas, wrote that the Spaniards believed that American Indians, like Africans, lacked souls. "It was upon such profoundly racist ideas that Christopher Columbus grounded his policies as the first governor of the new Spanish empire in America," Ward Churchill declares in "Deconstructing the Columbus Myth."[52] American discussion, truncated by the unexamined presumption that these hot-headed "activists" were reacting to the explorer's *voyage itself*, remained oblivious to Columbus's career as a colonial ruler.

Popular discussion suffered, too, as a result of the narrow, Eurocentric outlook that most white Americans share, that genocide is only genocide if it is carried out by a goose-stepping German army. As Churchill wrote of Columbus's colonial policies in Espanola, "In the end, all practical distinctions between Columbus and Himmler—at least those not accounted for by differences in available technology and sociomilitary organization—evaporate upon close inspection." The U.S. Holocaust Museum on the Washington, D.C., mall was dedicated in 1993, only one year after the Columbus quincentenary. Peter Novick notes with some irony, "It was American Jews' wealth and political influence that made it possible for them to bring to the Mall in Washington a monument to their weakness and vulnerability. Those who remained weak and vulnerable—who were oppressed here rather than there—lacked the wherewithal to carry off such a venture."[53]

Thus, two distinctly *ethnic* viewpoints (Italians' "home-making" myth of Columbus and Jews' proprietary claim on "genocidal" victimhood) became enmeshed in the Columbus Day debates and finally came to characterize "white" thinking on the subject. Though dominant perceptions of the Columbus legend have no doubt undergone significant revision in recent decades, both the Italian-American view of the voyage as a kind of immigrant journey and the Jewish-American view that there has "really" been only one *genocide* in human history have become naturalized in American discussion. This grafting of white ethnic sensibilities onto the very question of European expansionism—which is, after all, the historic meaning of the Columbus voyage—begins to convey the larger portent of the seismic shift from the popular Pilgrim-and-Founding-Fathers national legend to the more recent conception of a "nation of immigrants." Though anything but *supremacist,* whiteness remains supreme.

A vintage 1990s, radical interpretation of the Columbus voyage fuses the strands of an earlier ethnic revivalism. The "paradise" of Kirkpatrick Sale's Columbian jeremiad, *The Conquest of Paradise* (1990), descends directly from the antimodernism and the search for "alternatives to the dead hand of Western corporate imperialism" that had informed Sale's book *Human Scale* (1980) and his preface to *Small Is Beautiful* (1989). The "new localism" of these works, in turn, points back to his book *SDS* and to figures like Tom Hayden. The "rejection of authority," "the rise of separatism," and "the resurgence of localism" from that era all issue in Sale's contention, as the quincentenary approached, that Europeans might have found "salvation" in the New World, had they recognized it "in the integrative tribal ways, the nurturant communitarian values, the rich interplay with nature that made up the Indian cultures."[54]

But the real poet laureate of Columbus Day conflict is Robert Viscusi, whose work *Oration upon the Most Recent Death of Christopher Columbus* (1992) consists of thirty-three cantos in meditation on the historical twists and turns by which one era's hero had so decisively turned villain—how it happened that Columbus had "lived five hundred years in the character of a god / [but] once he died / he acquired a new nature as a limit." Viscusi wrote the poem in response to the controversies at Brooklyn College, where an umbrella group of Latino associations had spoken out against Columbus Day. He meant the poem to convey Italian Americans' "complex feelings on that occasion." His introductory remark, like the poem itself, is keen to the ironic revolutions of history by which one group of downtrodden peasants and their descendants had seized on a heroic symbol whose very "heroism" signaled torture and dispossession to a second group of downtrodden peasants and *their* descendants:

> hearing the pain of the many peoples who suffered in the European expansion into the western hemisphere, we were not only sympathetic, but we also recognized the sound of our own history. We did not feel ourselves to be conquistadores. Rather, we remembered the bitterness of the Italian revolution or Risorgimento . . . 25 million Italians were to leave Italy to live elsewhere in the world. When Italians parade in New York, they are remembering these dispossessed ancestors of theirs.[55]

Although some people surely bristle at Viscusi's notion that "innocent victims of innocent crime / abuse us wherever we dream," still, among the whirl of Columbian panegyrics and anti-Columbian diatribes his *Oration* remains the most catholic in its sensibilities. These victims of "innocent crime," the quatrain concludes, write "their signatures all across time / and all that we wanted to seem." *Wanting to seem* is a rendition of Columbian idolatry that Ward Churchill or Russell Means would likely be more comfortable with than the Knights of Columbus. And so, on the one hand, Viscusi evokes the difficult history of Italian-American degradation in North America, noting that nineteenth-century Americans loved Columbus even while despising the flesh-and-blood Italians who were daily arriving at Castle Garden: "he was the *right* kind of Italian / not like these dirty dagoes / and guineas and wops." Yet on the other hand, he rejects the frankly imperialist visions that have attached to Columbus,

Americans' impulse periodically to "paint him up and fill him with gas / and march him around like a gun." He likewise resists the Eurocentrism that typically attends the story of Columbus's greatness:

> people sort of get used to america
> they built an entire way of life
> based upon stock market fluctuations
> destroying whole cities on the toss of the dice
> poisoning lakes that had been alive for twenty thousand years
> eating people forests whole oceans in order to test an hypothesis
> meanwhile condemning the aztecs for practicing human sacrifice
> and bragging about how they had taken the places of cannibals
> and calling this america[56]

If Viscusi's Columbus Day represents what multiculturalism strives to become, so does it point back to the same "rejection of authority" and "resurgence of localism" that had patterned Kirkpatrick Sale's book *Conquest of Paradise.* "We paraded in the name of Columbus," wrote Viscusi. "Tomorrow we may use some other name. But the history of need and of courage we celebrate will continue to march." This "burden of ancient sorrows" that Italian Americans carry with them, "along with so many others, belongs to the history of the many peoples in this hemisphere, as it belongs to us."[57]

Alien Nation

If the idea of a nation of immigrants is so sacred in national discourse, surely today's immigrants must be greeted with open arms? Discussion of immigration in America has historically been bifurcated between an economic debate regarding immigration's impact on American business and labor, and a civic debate over whether immigrants represent a sound addition to the U.S. polity. In the 1920s, for instance, a civic argument framed in the racialized terms of immigrants' "unfitness for self-government" seemed to carry the day. Certainly the legislation of 1924 derived its system of racialized quotas from the civic line of argument. But that legislation in fact owed its political triumph to an economic realignment, as circumstances shifted after World War I. (Business, which had supported immigration throughout the 1910s, now favored restriction for reasons of its own, and restrictionism finally became law.)[58]

Since 1965, Americans have mounted a similar, two-tiered debate: anyone simply listening in these years, during which restrictionism has occasionally reached fever pitch on civic grounds, would be surprised to find the steady, incrementally increasing liberalism of policy itself. From the Hart-Celler Act (1965) onward, every policy adjustment until the U.S.A. Patriot Act has resulted in more, not fewer, incoming immigrants. Moreover, as in the 1920s, the driving logic has been economic, notwithstanding an escalating civic furor over "the browning of America," as *Time* magazine indelicately put it. California's Proposition 187, the bestseller status of Peter Brimelow's book *Alien Nation* (1992), or the high public profile of figures like Patrick Buchanan and Pete Wilson do mark something significant in the tenor of popular sentiment in this period—jealous protection of American jobs, public services, and even the English language has resulted in increasingly shrill anti-immigrant invective. In poll after poll, majorities ranging from 55 to 73 percent have responded that current levels of immigration are "too high." Policy itself, meanwhile, speaks to a winning pro-immigration coalition whose primary concern has been economic rather than civic. Thus, as Douglas Massey and his colleagues recently concluded, "Throughout the twentieth century the United States has arranged to import Mexican workers while pretending not to"; "politicians and public officials have persistently sought ways of accepting Mexicans as workers while limiting their claims as human beings." On close inspection, this is what George W. Bush's seemingly "liberal" proposal of 2004 promised as well: if the plan would indeed open the way for more Mexicans to take their place as laborers in the American economy, it had relatively little to say about legal protections, rights, privileges, and their place in the body politic.[59]

Even as economics continues to drive public policy, however, this civic discussion remains important. If economic circumstances were to result in a more restrictive policy, the *civic* terms of discussion would likely supply the formulae and logical frameworks for restrictive legislation, just as in the 1920s. Immigration policy tends to express some preference for certain peoples over others, and though cruel nineteenth-century phrases like "fitness for self-government" have fallen from fashion, still such preferences typically follow a civic logic of which groups are most likely to make "good neighbors" and "good Americans." This civic plane of discussion, then, outfits Americans with their sense of proper "Americanness" and of "America" itself, at once articulating and patrolling imaginative boundaries in a way that informs political stances and undertakings of all sorts. In the wake of the first World Trade Center bombing and even more so after 9/11, concerns about terrorism redirected public attention from immigration's purported rising "tides" to its infiltrating "cells," from the

nation's "uncontrolled borders" to its vulnerable "security perime-
ters." But even the harshest imperatives of the U.S.A. Patriot Act
did not fundamentally alter the long-term relationship between
the economic and the civic dimensions of the immigration question; nor, in fact, did the introduction of potential terrorism into
the civic debate fundamentally alter the ongoing, racialized discussion of "good" and "bad" immigrants.

When it comes to such civic assessments of the good and the
bad, America's romance with the immigrant of yore looms large.
"We are a nation of immigrants," said Peter Rodino, during a 1975
debate over refugee policy, "and when we reject our humble foreign origins, we will have ended our reason for being as a nation."
But if America "is a nation of immigrants," wrote an immigration
commission during the reign of President Jimmy Carter's politics
of scarcity, "it is one no longer, nor can it become a land of unlimited immigration." And yet, wrote Arthur Schlesinger, Jr., "America has so long seen itself as the asylum for the oppressed and
persecuted . . . that any curtailment of immigration offends something in the American soul."[60] On the first anniversary of 9/11,
even as his administration developed unprecedented powers to
detain noncitizens in the name of Homeland Security, Bush hon-
ored the nation's immigrant heritage by choosing Ellis Island as
the site for his commemorative speech.[61]

John F. Kennedy reaped some unintended consequences in his
reliance on the "nation of immigrants" conceit to sell a liberal immigration policy. The legislation that finally passed in 1965 resulted in immigration rates that were dramatically higher than in
the preceding period, but whose perceived "difference" in results
from the historic European waves of 1845–1924 was startling to
many. But even so, the decades-long civic debate on immigration

and diversity that ensued was all but dominated by the myths about, and the romance with, European immigration that held sway in post–ethnic revival America.

Immigration, thought Kennedy, had "infused the nation with a commitment to far horizons and new frontiers, and thereby kept the pioneer spirit of American life, the spirit of equality and of hope, always alive and strong."[62] Kennedy's vision was fundamentally assimilationist, to be sure. But it was not the Anglo-Saxon conformist vision that had enjoyed hegemony in the years since the 1920s; nor did it partake of the massive ethnological erasures which that model had typically entailed. Rather, in Kennedy's "nation of immigrants," a core, centuries-old Anglo-Saxon greatness had been periodically reinvigorated by impressive waves of arrivals who, though non–Anglo-Saxon, recognized and reaffirmed that greatness, and reimagined a common national destiny.

But *A Nation of Immigrants* was fundamentally Eurocentric nonetheless, just as the ensuing Kennedy-Johnson policy reforms were Eurocentric in intent. During his sentimental visit to Ireland just months before his death, Kennedy remarked, "When my great-grandfather left here to become a cooper in East Boston, he carried nothing but a strong religious faith and a strong desire for liberty. If he hadn't left, I would be working at the Albatross Company across the road."[63] Kennedy's language captures the romance that colored public discussion for years to come—his proprietary relationship to immigration ("my great-grandfather"); his depiction of migration as an individualized saga of almost incomprehensible fortitude ("he carried nothing . . ."); and his juxtaposition of himself with his ancestor as a way of marking upward mobility ("if he hadn't left . . ."), thereby proving the greatness of both "America" *and* "my great-grandfather."

"The Irish" warrant their own, titled subsection of three pages in Kennedy's narrative, and "The Germans" get nearly five. "Oriental immigration," by contrast, gets one paragraph and Mexicans and Puerto Ricans share but one short one. But even more striking than the distribution of Kennedy's attentions is his tone of description. "The Irish," for example, though discriminated against at first, climbed "gradually, rung by rung" up the social and economic ladder, eventually getting fully to "demonstrate their abilities of self-expression, of administration and organization." "The Germans" were "hardworking and knowledgeable," and almost every state in the Union profited from their intellectual and material contributions." "The Scandinavians" contributed their hardy physicality and know-how and "an intimate knowledge of animal husbandry." Italians, "bolstered by their adherence to the church [and] the strength of their family ties," overcame many prejudices in order to contribute to American cultural life. Poles brought their dogged aspiration; Jews, their intellectual talents.[64]

Non-European groups, by contrast, do not conform to this narrative template of unique contributions. (Japanese Americans did "restore our perspective" on the Orient by their valor during World War II; but by the subtleties of Kennedy's syntax this hardly rates as a "contribution" on par with, say, the dairy industry.) The "immigrants" who composed Kennedy's "nation of immigrants" were unquestionably European, despite his occasional gestures toward broader inclusivity. And indeed, whenever Kennedy enumerated those peoples unfairly closed out by U.S. immigration policy—and envisioned the immigration of a future, postreform era—his mind was drawn not to Asia, the Caribbean, or the Americas, but to Europe. His most thorough discussion of the quota system's backlogs mentioned only "Poland," "Italy," "Greece," "Hungary," and "the Baltic states" by name.[65]

These patterns of attention would mean little, were they merely idiosyncratic on Kennedy's part. But both his attachments and his omissions have been broadly shared across American political culture in the ensuing years. The debate over the 1965 immigration bill itself was a debate among "harsh" Eurocentrists (who opposed the reform bill) and "mild" Eurocentrists (who—in a logic inherited from Kennedy—supported it). Speaking for the harsh Eurocentrists, Senator Sam Ervin argued that "there is a rational basis and a reasonable basis to give preference to Holland over Afghanistan, and I hope I am not entertaining a highly iniquitous thought when I entertain that honest opinion." The worst charge of discrimination that could be leveled at the standing law, he remarked, "is that it discriminates in favor of the people who made the greatest contribution to America." In his defense of the bill, on the other hand, Edward Kennedy averred in mild Eurocentric tones that "the ethnic pattern of immigration under the proposed measure is not expected to change as sharply as the critics seem to think."[66]

But in fact it did. By the 1990 census not only had overall immigration swelled beyond its pre-1965 levels (the foreign-born population in the 1990 census reached some 19.7 million, up from 9.7 million in 1960), but the sources of immigration had also shifted. By the early 1990s Europe was contributing less than 15 percent of the overall immigration—that is, roughly 85 percent of the nearly one million immigrants arriving in 1992, to take a case, hailed from Asia, Africa, Oceania, South America, the Caribbean, and the Americas. Mexico had become the single largest sending country, accounting for more immigrants per year than the whole of Europe. Moreover, of the top ten sending countries, only one—Ireland—was European; the other nine were Jamaica, the Dominican Republic, El Salvador, Mexico, Haiti, Vietnam, Cuba, the Philippines, and Taiwan. Or, as Mike Davis has recently put it, by the year 2000 U.S. Latinos represented the fifth largest "nation" in Latin America.[67] This shift has represented something of a shock to the system in a political culture where, by myth, legend, and impressive consensus, the word "immigrant" has long meant "European."

Ironically, nativist thinking in a settler democracy like the United States must somehow consecrate previous waves of immigration even as it laments the arrival of the most recent immigrants. Immigration as a general principle is beyond reproach, that is, since immigration itself is the bedrock of the republic (and since nativist commentators almost always trace their own origins to some imported ancestor). The very terms of nativist comment must suggest some basis for embracing the millions who have arrived before; since 1965 this has often meant duplicating the standard epic of "good" European immigration and implying some distance between these "huddled masses" and more recent ones.

Few anti-immigrant polemicists have been as unabashed as Edward Abbey, who in 1988 called for a halt to "the mass influx" of "hungry, ignorant, unskilled, and culturally-morally-genetically impoverished people." But much public commentary has pivoted on the slightly subtler notion of "assimilability." As Samuel Francis wrote in *Chronicles* in 1990, "the process of becoming a real member of a living society is somewhat more complicated than translating advertising slogans into Japanese or Swahili." It requires both the predilection and the capacity for assimilation on the immigrants' part, qualities on which Europe has presumably cornered the market. Such thinking held sway even before the ethnic revival had romanced the European immigrant and prompted a contrast between pre-1924 and post-1965 immigration. In a statement before the House during the immigration debates of 1964, one speaker raised the question of who is, and who is not, "most readily assimilable" to American life. He predicted a "collapse of morale [*sic*] and spiritual values if nonassimilable aliens of dissimilar ethnic background and culture" were to "overturn the balance of our national character." Who exactly these "nonassimilable" groups might be became clear when he explained that, because of their current "population explosions," India, Asia, and Africa "could naturally be expected to take full advantage of such an increased quota opportunity."[68]

The "assimilability" of the prototypical European, then, turns out to be indispensable to our understanding of the new, non-European immigrants and their prospects. One common line of argument poses U.S. nationality as a "family" of consanguine Europeans: writing in *Chronicles* in 1989, Thomas Fleming described America as an assemblage of fellow citizens who, "like members of a family . . . prefer each other's company and will sacrifice for the common good, not because they think their family or nation is superior to every other, but simply because it is theirs." There is "an American story," he concludes, "that is primarily a saga of enterprising men and women who came from Europe." "The word 'nation,'" added Peter Brimelow in *Alien Nation*, ". . . intrinsically implies a link by blood. A nation in a real sense is an extended family." Inasmuch as left-tilting discussions of U.S. diversity underestimate this European consanguinity, Brimelow argues, they fully miss the point of the post-1965 departure from "family"—tradition: "As late as 1960, nearly 90 percent of the U.S. population was European . . . Americans who take this 'nation of immigrants' stuff too seriously tend to assume that they cannot share a common ethnic heritage. But this is false—at least it was until the Great Wave of Third World immigration."[69]

Brimelow was later chagrined that the racial dimension of *Alien Nation* got so much press. But a close reading of the book indicates just how critical racial presumptions were to Brimelow's concepts of both the post-1965 newcomers and the national tradition they threatened to disrupt. "Just as when you leave Park Avenue and descend into the subway," he had written, "when you enter the INS waiting rooms you find yourself in an underworld that is not just teeming but is also almost entirely colored." "Color," in Brimelow's political logic, is exactly why it is so portentous that America "is going to have to share its future, and its land, with a very large number of people who, as of [1965], were complete strangers. Foreigners. Aliens." This sudden influx of "aliens" would be for the nation "like suddenly replacing all the blood in a patient's body." Hence Brimelow's urgency: "just as the American nation was made with unusual speed, so it is perfectly possible that it could be unmade," and though Brimelow might deny the charge of racism, throughout *Alien Nation* it is *race* that causes America's "unmaking." As *Time* magazine had it, "White Americans are accustomed to thinking of themselves as the very picture of their nation," and the "'browning of America' will alter everything in society, from politics and education to industry, values and culture."[70]

Patrick Buchanan took this argument even further in *The Death of the West* (2001), whose eugenic outlook is carried in the subtitle, *How Dying Populations and Immigrant Invasions Imperil Our Country and Civilization.* In dwelling so deeply on questions of reproduction, *The Death of the West* is *Alien Nation* with a more pronounced antifeminist element. "In America, the places prepared for the forty million unborn lost since *Roe v. Wade* have been filled by the grateful poor of Asia, Africa, and Latin America. As Europeans forego children, the places prepared for them, too, will be occupied by strangers."[71] But like Brimelow's, Buchanan's argument rests on the presumption that there are "deep differences in attitudes toward America between old immigrants from Ireland, Italy, and Eastern Europe, and today's immigrants from Mexico." Given the number of Mexican arrivals, "we need to understand the differences between the old immigrants and the new." Buchanan is here to help us: "History and experience teach us that different races are far more difficult to assimilate"; and "unlike the immigrants of old, who bade farewell forever to their native lands when they boarded ship," today's immigrants are intent on "creating a Hispanic culture," becoming a "nation within a nation." Buchanan looks wistfully back to the pre-1965 era, when "President Eisenhower sent illegal aliens packing in Operation Wetback and apologized to no one for defending U.S. borders." Rather than leave our national fate to chance border crossings, "Americans alone should decide whether and when our national family should be enlarged."[72]

Closely akin to this trope of a familial U.S. nationality based on European ancestry is the cultural-geographical construction of a grand "European tradition" that unites all white ethnic groups just as surely as it excludes those from Asia, Africa, and the Americas. As one writer put it in *The Conservative Review*, "there is no evidence that the European tradition can or will be transmitted to immigrants of African, Asian and Hispanic origin."[73] Likewise Lawrence Auster, in *The Path to National Suicide*, relied on common tradition as a means of consecrating the earlier waves of U.S. immigration even while deploring the present one: the immigrants of the 1880s–1920s "had much in common with the earlier Americans; the fact that they were of European descent and came from related cultures within Western civilization made it relatively easy for them to assimilate into the common sphere of civic habits and cultural identity."[74]

But this European tradition is a recent and uncertain fabrication, and such assessments of Italian or Irish or Yiddish immigrants' perceived kinship arose only after a century's hindsight and a few generations of distance from the Old World. Indeed, in the late nineteenth and early twentieth centuries American commentators most often sounded remarkably like Lawrence Auster in their assessments of these incoming Europeans. According to New York's school superintendent at the turn of the century, "The majority of people who now come to us have little akin to our language; they have little akin to our mode of thought; they have little akin to our customs; they have little akin to our traditions." Senator Henry Cabot Lodge found in the European immigrants "races most alien to the body of the American people"; they "do not promise well for the standard of civilization of the United States." The Superintendent of the Census saw them as "beaten men from beaten races" who "have none of the ideas and aptitudes which fit men to take up readily and easily the problem of self-care and self-government." Even the respectable *New York Times* characterized these newcomers as "unwashed, ignorant, unkempt, childish semi-savages," bemoaning the swarming presence of the "hatchet-faced, sallow, rat-eyed young men of the Russian Jewish colony."[75]

The first maneuver in recent nativist thinking has been to forget the contemporary reception of European immigrants and the full-blown crisis they represented; the next has been to canonize their traits and their virtues. As Nancy Foner writes, "An elaborate mythology has grown around immigration at the turn of the century, and perceptions of that earlier migration deeply color how the newest wave is seen." Here the loving, sometimes epic imagery of ethnic-revival cultural production comes into full play—*Fiddler on the Roof,* the below-decks scenes from James Cameron's blockbuster *Titanic,* the History Channel's *Ellis Island,* and the massive photo installation at Ellis Island itself. In memory, the "beaten men from beaten races" have become clean and moral and hugely striving; they have become joint-stock holders in a unified "European tradition"—they have become, in a word, "America." It is this pan-European notion of white ethnicity that allowed Buchanan—radically forgetful of the degree of difference that his own Celtic forebears presented to the Anglo-Saxon republic generations ago—to muse on the relative assimilability of "Englishmen" and "Zulus" in a diatribe against the new immigration.[76] It is this pan-European notion of white ethnicity, too, that allowed an *immigrant,* the Forbes editor Peter Brimelow, to pen the most vociferous nativist tract of the 1990s.

The New Americans (2001) by Michael Barone, the very commentator who had identified the 1984 election as a "battle for Ellis Island," is a softer version of this Eurocentric commentary on immigration. On the face of it *The New Americans* is far more charitable than either *Death of the West* or *Alien Nation.* Indeed, Barone's is a self-consciously *anti*nativist tract, arguing without a great deal of nuance that today's immigrants are really no different from yesterday's—"We've Been Here Before."[77] Here again European immigration supplies the benchmark experience by which these "new Americans" will be judged, though Barone sees more similarity than contrast. He rightly observes that the language with which many Americans are today interpreting the Third World migration is precisely the racialized and alarmist language employed in decrying the "unassimilable" arrivals from Ireland, Italy, Russia, and Greece a few generations ago. In Barone's scheme, indeed, these correspondences can be traced with some specificity: in the structural features of their experience and in their group profiles, today's African Americans resemble yesterday's Irish, today's Latinos resemble yesterday's Italians, and today's Asians resemble yesterday's Jews.

But while Barone's argument so self-consciously opposes contemporary nativism, the villains of the piece are not *nativists*—in fact, prominent figures like Brimelow receive no mention. As in the earlier writings of neoconservatives like Glazer, rather, the villain is the liberal establishment, whose misguided policies (affirmative action, bilingual education, multiculturalism) have retarded the natural assimilative processes by which yesterday's immigrants were eventually made over. Despite the similarities so lovingly traced between European and Third World migrations, at bottom *The New Americans* is merely Glazer's "ethnic pattern" dressed up in the language of antinativism. Although Barone does describe "discrimination" as a salient part of the history of peoples of color in the United States, he refuses to entertain whiteness as a relevant feature of the European experience. Indeed, Barone banishes the notion of white primacy by stating, incredibly, that in the founders' early vision, "anyone could become an American. The nation would welcome newcomers of all backgrounds—there were no restrictions on immigration then." The "free white persons" clause in naturalization law, on the books from 1790 to 1952, escapes his notice. Some might regard this as a restriction.[78]

But the punch line of *The New Americans* comes when Barone

calculates how long it took for the European groups to become fully incorporated into American life, then guesses how long it might take for each of the new groups: adjustment and incorporation took "120 years" for the Irish and "eighty years" each for Italians and Jews. There is great cause for hope, then, since by Barone's mathematics African Americans' "mass migration" began only sixty years ago; "with luck" Latinos' incorporation "will take less than eighty years"; and Asians "may take considerably less than eighty years." The only racial problems in America, in other words, are "the racial quotas, preferences, and set-asides" that "nurture a sense of racial grievance and strengthen the habit of mind that the system is so fundamentally unfair as to ease any obligation to obey its rules."[79] The system does start to seem fairer, one must concede, if the African-American presence in the United States dates from 1940. Then the timetables of European assimilation appear still to be operative, and all that is needed is less liberal interventionism and more patience on the part of those non-European newcomers who expect so much before their fair portion of melting-pot time is up.

Amid one of the more fevered moments in the immigration debate, Mandy Patinkin appeared as the resident "alien" Sangia Solenz-Ahh in Graham Baker's science fiction thriller (from which Brimelow would cop his title) *Alien Nation* (1988). A few film industry referents are worth noting here: one is Patinkin's association with the cinema of ethnic diversity—as Allessandro the Cabbie in *Night of the Juggler*, Tateh in *Ragtime*, Paul Isaacson in *Daniel*, and Avigdor in *Yentl* (he would later narrate *History of Ellis Island* for the History Channel). Another is the thinly veiled relationship between science fiction and immigration in the 1980s and 1990s, beginning, perhaps, with *Blade Runner*'s depiction of melting-pot Los Angeles as some kind of putrid global chowder (1982). In addition to *Alien Nation*, whose plot of assimilating newcomers renders its immigration commentary most obvious, films like *Arrival* and *Arrival II*, *Species*, and *Men in Black* reference Mexico or the Southwestern desert in ways that cannot fail to conjure then-current obsessions with "illegal aliens." (*Men in Black* opens with a scene at the border, in which an intergalactic alien is disguised as a smuggled Mexican.)[80] But it was Patinkin as Sangia Solenz-Ahh who delivered one of the genre's most arresting observations on diversity and American democracy. "You . . . are very curious to us," he tells his human friend, amid America's great experiment in "assimilating" a shipload of alien slaves like himself who have crashed in the California desert:

> You invite us to live among you in an atmosphere of equality that we have never known before; you give us ownership of our own lives for the first time and you ask no more of us than you do of yourselves. I hope you understand how special you are in this—how unique a people you . . . are. Which is why it is all the more painful and confusing to us that so few of you are capable of living up to the ideals you set for yourselves.

Of course this is not science fiction. Sangia Solenz-Ahh's confusion points, not just to our all-too-human tendency to fall short of ideals, but to the warring impulses of U.S. political culture. This is not simply a "nation of immigrants" but also a "gatekeeping" nation. Its exclusivity has been carried out across a long history by diverse mechanisms of patrol like the 1790 naturalization law, the Black Codes, the Chinese Exclusion Act, the Asian

19.   Construction projects for "a nation of immigrants" (I): scaffolding around the Statue of Liberty during the massive restoration project, July 1984. ROBERT MAASS/CORBIS.

20. *Construction projects for "a nation of immigrants" (II): a worker pulls wire mesh into place on the "Tortilla Curtain," a galvanized steel fence intended to keep undocumented Mexican nationals from crossing the border (1979). Americans' consensus on the exclusion of Mexicans has been intricately entangled with the popular imagery of the Ellis Island era as representing the nation's "good" immigration.* STEPHANIE MAZE/CORBIS.

Barred Zone, the Johnson Reed Act, "Operation Wetback," and, most recently, "Operation Gatekeeper" (San Diego), "Operation Rio Grande" (Brownsville), "Operation Safeguard" (Nogales), and "Operation Hold the Line" (El Paso).[81] But in the decades since the bicentennial celebration of "heritage" and the concurrent militarization of the U.S.-Mexican border, the trope of the "nation of immigrants"—though common shorthand for the national tradition of inclusion—has largely become the central trope of gatekeeping itself. Nothing hinders white Americans' even-handed acceptance of Third World immigration quite as stubbornly as the mythic, lavishly celebrated, and thus thoroughly naturalized icon of the European steerage passenger as the text-book definition of the word "immigrant."

Yours in Struggle

Whose tradition? Whose gates? Whose America? Perhaps no political community in the United States has grappled with these questions as vigorously and openly as American feminists. And none attributes such large shares of both its success and its failure in cross-race communication to the Ellis Island accents that emanate from the white side of the color line. In *Union Square* (1988), the second volume of Meredith Tax's historical fiction of Lower East Side radicalism, heroine Sarah Levy becomes involved in the cause of the Scottsboro boys, nine black teenagers charged with raping a white woman on an Alabama freight train in 1932. "The way those boys had been pulled off a train reminded her so much of the way Jews had been treated in Russia"; "The South is just like Russia before the revolution," Levy would conclude her soapbox orations." But if the Scottsboro case allows Tax to explore the political resonances between blackness and Jewishness, so does she take the occasion to reflect on Jewishness as a social location of whiteness and privilege as well. After one of her radical speeches, Levy is approached by a black woman who remembers her from the Triangle Shirtwaist Factory years before. Euletha Jones had been a washroom attendant at the factory (she could not work as an operator because "the Jewish and Italian girls would object"). Now, some twenty years later, she chides Levy and reveals to her the cost of her racism. In overlooking Euletha Jones, Levy had missed an ally of considerable significance: "Sometimes I would say to myself, If that white girl would just talk to me . . . I could tell her who was wavering, who was ratting. But you never knew I was alive." Levy is horrified and transfixed by this tale of her own racism. "Maybe you can learn," Jones offers. "Plenty can't."[82]

There was more than just a dash of presentism in Tax's depiction of this troubled exchange between Levy and Jones. By the 1980s the relationship between white feminists and women of color had become a matter of some moment; and—as portrayed in *Union Square*—the subtly shaded sense of not-quite-whiteness among Jews and other white ethnics could be both a great obstacle and a great asset to interracial coalition. If, like Levy, they saw Alabama as "just like Russia," so did their subtle disavowal of full whiteness hinder white ethnic women's reckoning with their share in power and privilege. One activist confessed that, having marched with Father Groppi for open housing, she wrote herself out of the "white" in "white privilege": "when I heard women of color speaking of white privileges, I mentally inserted the word 'male': 'white male privileges.'"[83]

Thus the solidarities of ethnic attachment could sometimes disrupt, at other times foster, the allegiances of sisterhood across ethnic or racial lines. In a keynote address at the New Jewish Agenda's national convention in 1985, Adrienne Rich advocated the hard work "of turning Otherness into a keen lens of empathy." "Like Black and other dark-skinned people," she argued, "Jews and women have haunted white Western thought as Other, as fantasy, as projected obsession." Jewishness here became a basis— indeed, *the* basis—for interethnic, interracial solidarity and for an anti-imperialist feminist politics. Rich's philosophy of coalition-building, at once ethnically introspective and broadly ecumenical, was embodied in her citation of Hillel's famous three questions

("If I am not for myself, who will be for me? / If I am only for myself, what am I? / If not now, when?") and her addition of a fourth, "If not with others, how?" On the other hand, however, stunned by the perceived indifference of the women's movement to issues of anti-semitism and its outright hostility to Israel, Elly Bulkin could conclude, "Sometimes 'the other' actually is 'the enemy.'"[84] In either case the language of ethnic particularity and attachment textured the women's movement, as white second-wave feminism haltingly conjoined womanist, *mujerista,* and Third World feminisms.

We can chart the rise of Third World feminism in the United States from the early 1970s to the early 1980s by the crystallization of significant organizations and conferences—the National Chicana Conference and Hijas de Cuauhtemoc (1971), the National Black Feminist Organization (1973), the Combahee River Collective, Women of All Red Nations, and Mexican American Women's National Association (1974), the Organization of Pan Asian American Women (1976), the Third World Lesbian and Gay Conference (1979), Kitchen Table Women of Color Press (1980), and the National Alliance for American Third World Women (1982). These same years also saw the publication of many pathbreaking political and literary works, including Toni Cade's *The Black Woman* (1970), the Combahee River Collective Statement (1977), Lorraine Bethel and Barbara Smith's *Conditions: Five, the Black Women's Issue* (1979), Gloria Anzaldua and Cherrie Moraga's *This Bridge Called My Back* and bell hooks' *Ain't I a Woman* (1981), Gloria Hull, Patricia Bell Scott, and Barbara Smith's *But Some of Us Are Brave* (1982) and Alice Walker's *The Color Purple* and *In Search of Our Mothers' Gardens* (1982, 1983).[85]

The Third World voice in feminism presented, not only a

competing theoretical synthesis of race, class, and gender that would complicate the antipatriarchal analysis of Redstockings, New York Feminists, or Bread and Roses, but a critique of *white feminism* as well. "Black feminism is not white feminism in blackface," wrote Audre Lorde—a formulation that carried as much portent for white women as it did for men of all races; a truly inclusive women's movement would require, in addition to an energetic approach to the task of building bridges, a reconsideration and restructuring of white feminist *logic*.[86] As the Third World critique of white feminism took shape, two interlaced issues became central. First was the question of racialized *perspective*, the ways in which white feminists presumed to speak from a "universal" women's point of view. Within the context of the Moynihan Report and its lingering fallout, to take one example, black feminists were hardly as enthusiastic as white for the project of critiquing "the family," though white feminists took their own view as one of the givens of a "universal," antipatriarchal politics. The question arises, wrote Toni Cade, "how relevant are the truths, the experiences, the findings of white women to Black women? . . . I don't know that our priorities are the same, that our concerns and methods are the same, or even similar enough so that we can afford to depend on this new field of experts (white, female). It is rather obvious that we do not."[87]

Second was the question of racialized power itself—how whiteness functioned within the American women's movement, how power was constituted and deployed, and the ways in which the movement's cross-racial syncretism sometimes looked more like appropriation than cooperation. Elena Olazagasti-Segovia noted that within the Latina community, "the word *feminism* is associated with the struggles of white middle-class Anglo women." For

Latina onlookers, the question is "not What are [white women] complaining about? but Why are they complaining at all?" Given white women's position of relative privilege, "for Hispanic women the invitation of Anglo women to join their movement sounds as suspicious as the song of the sirens." *Essence* editor Ida Lewis, too, looked on the women's movement as "basically a family quarrel between white women and white men." As in all family disputes, "outsiders always get shafted when the dust settles."[88]

The difficult exchange between Audre Lorde and Mary Daly on Daly's book *Gyn/Ecology* in 1979 was paradigmatic of the rising Third World dissension from "white" feminism. In her "Open Letter to Mary Daly," Lorde moved bitingly from the relatively simple issue of exclusivity and omission (Daly's exclusions, Lorde wrote, "dismissed my heritage and the heritage of all other non-european women") to the more complicated and fraught issue of power relations within feminism. If Daly had missed the rich African heritage in her discussion of the Goddess, Lorde noticed, she had not similarly omitted Africa and Africans when it came to condemning patriarchal practices—in this case, genital mutilation. Not only had Daly thus portrayed African tradition in unwavering negativity, but worse, she had drawn on Lorde's own work in doing so. For Lorde this raised two troubling questions—one regarding this specific instance of appropriation ("[you] misused my words . . . to testify against myself as a woman of Color") and the other regarding white practices of appropriation in general ("Did you ever read my words," or did you merely plunder them in order to "support an already conceived idea"?). Lorde went on to decry Daly's assumption that white women's "herstory and myth" are the sole resource for all women to call on, and that nonwhite women "are noteworthy only as decorations, or examples of female victimization." "Should the next step be war between us," she asked, "or separation? Assimilation within a solely western European herstory is not acceptable."[89]

Here the power differentials of race loom largest. Moreover, as Lorde's choice of the word "assimilation" suggests, the stakes for a feminist coalition are high. "The oppression of women knows no racial or ethnic boundaries, true," Lorde concedes, "but that does not mean it is identical within those differences." It is this sense of "differences" that white feminists must become more alert to, because any failure of sensitivity or vision along these lines will inadvertently serve white supremacy: white feminism's patterns of inclusion and exclusion, attentiveness and neglect not only replicate the white-over-nonwhite dynamic of the culture at large, but actually add to the burden borne by women of color. Elsewhere Lorde explained,

> Women of today are still being called upon to . . . educate men as to our existence and our needs. This is an old primary tool of all oppressors to keep the oppressed occupied with the master's concerns. Now we hear that it is the task of women of Color to educate white women—in the face of tremendous resistance—as to our existence, our differences, our relative roles in our joint survival. This is a diversion of energies and a tragic repetition of racist patriarchal thought.[90]

Later that same year, in an address for Muriel Rukeyser Day at Sarah Lawrence College, Alice Walker similarly criticized prominent white feminists for their failures of imagination. "I have no theory to offer of Third World female psychology in America," Phyllis Chesler had said. "As a white woman, I'm reluctant and unable to construct theories about experiences I haven't had." This reluctance and inability, Walker now averred, would indeed denote a striking poverty of mind and spirit; but white feminists had in fact constructed lavish theories about the lives and works of Charlotte and Emily Brontë, for instance, however inexperienced they were with nineteenth-century Yorkshire.[91] This particular reluctance and inability, evidently, begins only at the color line.

Walker finds a similar failure of the white imagination in Judy Chicago's exhibit *The Dinner Party*. Having been astonished, on reading Chicago's earlier autobiography, that "she knew nothing of black women painters[,] not even that they exist," Walker was "gratified therefore to learn that in 'The Dinner Party' there was a place 'set,' as it were, for black women." But what Walker found in the setting for Sojourner Truth was troubling:

> All the other plates are creatively imagined vaginas (even the one that looks like a piano [Trotula] and the one that bears a striking resemblance to a head of lettuce [Aspasia] . . .) The Sojourner Truth plate is the only one in the collection that shows—instead of a vagina—a face. In fact, *three* faces. One weeping (a truly cliché tear), which "personifies" the black woman's "oppression," and another, screaming (a no less cliché scream), with little ugly pointed teeth, "her heroism," and a third, in gimcracky "African" design, smiling; as if the African woman, pre-American slavery, or even today, had no woes.[92]

While others critiqued the essentialism implied by Chicago's decision to portray women by this series of vaginas in the first place, Walker questioned Chicago's single departure from that motif. "It occurred to me that perhaps white women feminists, no less than white women generally, cannot imagine black women have vaginas. Or if they can, where imagination leads them is too far to go." The "too far" that Walker contemplated here has to do, not with vaginas directly, but with the children who pass through them in birth and with the inequities those children cannot fail to conjure for the white feminist, the guilt they cannot fail to produce. The white woman—feminist or not—"knows black children are to have less in this world so that her children, white children, will have more (in some countries, all)." "Better then," concludes Walker, "to deny that the black woman has a vagina. Is capable of motherhood. Is a woman."[93]

Here, as elsewhere, as Third World feminisms came increasingly into open conflict with "white" feminism, many of the white women involved were, quite self-consciously, Ellis Island whites. Discussions of both perspective and power relations within the women's movement were heavily inflected by the various ethnic identities at play on the white side of the divide, even if women of color tended to conflate such differences under the rubric of "white" or "Anglo." Again and again as women confronted one another across the color line over issues of exclusion, appropriation, or the contours of "herstory and myth," their exchanges were textured by the very particular assumptions attaching to whiteness among ethnics for whom modifiers like "Jewish" were often more salient than whiteness itself. "Though white women might experience the pain of oppression," wrote Chela Sandoval, "they also experience the will-to-power."[94] By "oppression" and "power" here, Sandoval undoubtedly intended *gender* oppression and *racial* power. But a share in white power and yet a perception of not-quite-white vulnerability were twinned conditions among white ethnics in post-"revival" American political culture.

Audre Lorde to the contrary, for example, Mary Daly had not exactly seen her work as aligned with whiteness. Indeed, in later editions of *Gyn/Ecology* her acknowledgment of Lorde's critique follows directly on her tribute to the "women of Ireland, that Treasure Island which I recognize deeply as the wellspring of my Background, my ancestral home." Having gone from analyses of Indian suttee, Chinese footbinding, and African genital mutilation, to European witchburnings and Nazi medicine, Daly no doubt felt that she had done her part for diversity in *Gyn/Ecology*. She never intended the book as an exhaustive "compendium of goddesses" anyway, she objected. But as others have noted, an "ethics of cross-cultural borrowing" had already complicated such discussions within American feminism, as intellectual and political influence across the color line shaded so easily toward appropriation. Moreover, "the phrase 'the Goddess' tends, in a racist society, to be corrupted—at least implicitly—into 'the White Goddess,'" even if an Irishwoman like Daly might subtly count herself among the Others.[95]

In addition to these exchanges between Lorde and Daly or between Walker and Judy Chicago, a number of important confrontations between Third World and white feminists have been similarly structured by white ethnics' tacit claims to Otherness or their perceived disavowals of a share in whiteness and white privilege. One thinks also of Angela Davis and Valerie Smith's critique of "the black rapist" in Susan Brownmiller's book *Against Our Will*; Chela Sandoval or Barbara Smith's criticism of the ease with which Jewish women "make the shift from examining their role as racist oppressors, to focusing solely on their position as victims of oppression"; or Sondra O'Neale's assertion that Jews had no right to speak of oppression or marginality since, unlike blacks, they could "choose to pass."[96] As bell hooks wrote of Madonna's appropriation of blackness in *Like a Prayer*, it is a sign of white privilege itself "to be able to 'see' blackness and black culture from a standpoint where only the rich culture of opposition black people have created in resistance marks and defines us . . . White folks who do not see black pain never really understand the complexity of black pleasure." Such cross-racial tensions persist even within "third-wave" feminism, whose Third World participants still wonder whether feminism is "just a 'white thing'"; whose gallery of "white superstar feminists" is still dominated by figures like Steinem (and for whom even "lipstick feminism" conjures Camille Paglia and Madonna); and whose discussions of "internalized oppression, the body, and race" are still vulnerable to takeover by talk of the "Jewish nose."[97]

It is not surprising that so many of the conflicts between Third World feminists and white feminists involved Jewish women, given the profile of white feminism, its cartography of notoriety, and the breadth, depth, and emotional turbulence of that vortex called "Black-Jewish relations." As Jeffrey Melnick argues, the very idea of "Black Jewish relations" is so inescapable precisely because it has a teleology of its own already in place. "There are no 'free' associations in this field of activity," writes Melnick; "say 'Old Testament' and the only possible match is 'inspiration for the Spirituals.' Say 'Civil Rights' and you get 'Goodman, Schwerner, and Chaney.' Say 'Ocean Hill/Brownsville' and then say goodnight."[98]

We can make two crucial observations in the present context: one is that the notion of "Black-Jewish relations" is a male project, rarely intended to conjure the relations between bell hooks and Tilly Olsen, between Audre Lorde and Adrienne Rich, between Barbara Smith and Elly Bulkin, or between Alice Walker and Gloria Steinem (or, for that matter, between Walker and *either* Muriel Rukeyser or Judy Chicago). The other point is that, while "Black-Jewish dialogue" within American feminism sometimes replicated the patterns of failure, misunderstanding, and betrayal often attributed to Black-Jewish relations among men, it has frequently overcome them. This fact hints at the suspicious character of the standard script of "Black-Jewish relations," but more important, the typical focus on the "fractured" (male) alliance has caused a certain impoverishment, since, as Melanie Kaye/Kantrowitz points out, "The women's movement is ahead of the mixed left in communication between blacks and Jews."[99]

Among the most significant entries in *this* realm of "Black-Jewish relations" was *Yours in Struggle* (1984), a volume of essays on anti-semitism and racism that grew out of exchanges between Elly Bulkin and Barbara Smith in the early 1980s. There was at once a combative and a nesting relationship between emergent "Jewish feminism" of the 1980s (that is, a feminism that actively accents its connection to Jewishness) and Third World feminism: "Jewish women have challenged non-Jewish women, including non-Jewish women of color, to recognize our anti-Semitism and in the process of building their movement Jewish women have also looked to Third World feminists for political inspiration and support." This dual relationship of confrontation and support is extremely complex. Smith (who is African American) claims to be "terrorized" by her relationships with Jewish women, but through them she has also seen that "people who are not the same" can get along and can work together for political change.[100]

Whence the terror? Not only in the *confrontation* between Jewish and Third World feminisms, ironically, but also in the nesting: "I saw how the feminism of women of color helped to lay the groundwork for Jewish feminists to name themselves, often without acknowledgement," writes Smith. In naming themselves as specifically Jewish, many downplayed the significance of their skin privilege and failed to acknowledge their own capacity for racism. If the historical entanglements of racism and anti-semitism had indeed "made us practical and ideological allies," Jewish racism and black anti-semitism "have just as surely made us view each other as enemies." While Smith recognizes the shared "feeling tone" that Melanie Kaye/Kantrowitz describes as existing between blacks and Jews, and while she agrees with Cherrie Moraga that Jews may constitute "a colored kind of white people," still she resents any attempts to portray racism and anti-semitism as parallel. Too often, in Smith's view, Jewish women lay claim to Third World identity by disavowing their whiteness, ignoring the historically portentous fact that "being visibly white in a racist society has concrete benefits and social-political repercussions."[101] Social location and angle of vision are everything. In response to Kaye/Kantrowitz's wish for a button that says, "Pushy Jew Loud Pushy Jew Dyke," Smith cautions that this proud affirmation "makes me wince," having been "'pushed' around by all kinds of white people."[102]

In her own entry in *Yours in Struggle,* Elly Bulkin charts the rise of Jewish feminism in two strands: one is rooted in specifically Jewish pursuits such as the creation of Ezrat Nashim (1971), the *off our backs* issue on Jewish women (1972), the establishment of the Jewish Feminist Organization (1974), and the appearance of *Lilith* (1976). The other, far more diffuse, strand is an intellectual temper deriving from the example of "a broad-based Third World feminist movement in this country." Bulkin cites the Combahee River Collective's "Black Feminist Statement" (1977) as especially influential: "Our politics evolve from a healthy love for ourselves, our sisters, and our community which allows us to continue our struggle and work," that document announced. "We believe that the most profound and potentially the most radical politics come directly out of our own identity, as opposed to working to end somebody else's oppression." Bulkin makes common cause with women of color in their shared "history of assimilation and reclamation," and in the decision "to celebrate one's identity."[103]

But common cause is made shaky by two facts: first, "the precariousness of Jewish existence" is not at all obvious to most people of color in the white-over-black setting of the United States; second, there *is* after all such a thing as white privilege. Bulkin's father had immigrated from Ukraine and had obtained "the schooling that would qualify him for the life-long civil service job he secured at a time when the newspapers were allowed to specify 'Christian'—and 'white'—in their employment ads." Bulkin understands that her political arguments "have a flimsy foundation if I am not totally clear that neither his achievements nor my own just flowed 'naturally' from our individual abilities and fortunes, if I am not prepared to recognize, analyze, and understand how race *has* affected my class prerogatives."[104]

In addition to the dangers of whites' overlooking their own privileged whiteness, however, Bulkin identifies equally dangerous obstacles to cross-racial coalition-building in women of color's failure to reckon with the oppressive specificities of white ethnic identity. One is the potential for a "competition of oppressions," which may lead to the conclusion that white-over-black oppression is more worthy of attention than anti-semitism or any other variety. Another danger is that a "scarcity theory of political struggle" can lead to the "false assumption" that one must choose which of the oppressions to combat, "that one cannot choose to oppose both." Bulkin seconds Melanie Kaye/Kantrowitz's contention that "there is no contradiction between being a proud Jew and a fighter against racism. I fight against racism because I am a Jew; because my Jewish parents taught me to hate injustice and cruelty; and because I know danger when I smell it." At moments one suspects that she would also share Kaye/Kantrowitz's protest, at a women's conference in which Jewish women were urged not to meet as Jews, that "this is divisive, that Jews are 'really' white; or 'really' European."[105]

Such disavowals of full whiteness die hard, especially among women for whom ethnic identity—whether Jewish, Italian, or Irish—is so thoroughly entwined, not only with feminist consciousness, but indeed with antiracism itself. For Starhawk, Adrienne Rich, and many others, the outsider status gleaned from ethnicity has been critical to the development of an antiracist white feminism. Starhawk's version of witchery, for example, rests squarely on an analysis of "our economic and political systems" that enabled a critique not only of modernity but of imperialism. The quest for community—Starhawk's version of the "small platoon"—led to the conclusion that "perhaps it is time for all of us to reconsider our loyalties." In her case this reconsideration unfolded in ethnoracial terms: the roots of wicca "go back to the pre-Judeo-Christian tribal religions of the West, and it is akin in spirit, form, and practice to Native American and African religions." The whiteness of the Judeo-Christian God "legitimizes the rule of whites over those with dark skin . . . Women and people of color (among whom I include Jews) are not present in the top levels of the hierarchies that wield power-over." The Judeo-Christian metaphor of light and dark as good and evil "perpetuates racism"; it once "legitimized pogroms against dark-haired Jews, and gave a religious justification for the conquest and enslavement of Africans, Native Americans, and other dark-skinned people." To be a modern witch, then, is "to identify with nine million victims of bigotry and hatred and to take responsibility for shaping a world in which prejudice claims no more victims."[106]

Adrienne Rich, too, described her struggle as she inhabited two warring dimensions of Jewish social identity: "the Jew as radical visionary and activist who understands oppression firsthand, and the Jew as part of America's devouring plan in which the persecuted, called to assimilation, learn that the price is to engage in persecution." Acknowledging that she identified as woman first and Jew second, but nonetheless that, "if Jews had to wear yellow stars again, I, too, would wear one," Rich determined that in political life "every aspect of my identity will have to be engaged." Along with other white feminists, she had long been wrestling "with the meanings of white identity in a racist society and how an unexamined white perspective leads to dangerous ignorance, heart-numbing indifference, and complacency." As a Jew, she had explored "the meanings of Jewish identity from a feminist perspective. A natural extension of all of this seemed . . . the need to examine not only racial and ethnic identity, but *location* in the United States of North America"—not just the interiority of one's self-definition or psyche, but one's political and historical relationship to the forces of imperialism, for example, and the structures of white supremacism. Like Starhawk, Bulkin, and others, she built her antiracism directly atop the foundation of her Jewishness.[107]

An important strand of this discussion between Jewish women and women of color has been the long-running controversy over Israeli-Palestinian conflict—the same geopolitical situation, indeed, that prompted a specifically Jewish brand of New Left radicalism in the first place. The discourses of civil rights and of Jewish identity diverged sharply after 1967, when the African-American canon of liberatory narratives set aside the Mosaic legend of Exodus in favor of the contemporary plight of displaced Palestinians. Jews, meanwhile, saw in the Middle East a newly posed threat of being "driven into the sea." In feminist conferences from Mexico City (1975) to Copenhagen (1980) to Milwaukee (1985), rifts opened up between those for whom "Zionism is racism" and those for whom, as Bella Abzug said in Copenhagen, "Zionism . . . is a liberation movement for a people who have been persecuted all their lives." Indeed, for Letty Cottin Pogrebin, "when a black friend refused to sign the petition protesting the Zionism-is-racism resolution . . . I was forced to recognize that the politics of identity had displaced the ideology of universal sisterhood in the Women's Movement."[108]

Two essays by Alice Walker provide a poignant measure of this change in reference points, and the meaning of that change for "Black-Jewish relations." In 1967, addressing the question of why there were no black hippies, Walker offered this glancing comment on Israel: "While the hippies are 'tripping,' Negroes are going after power, which is so much more important to their survival and their children's survival than LSD and pot. Everyone would be surprised if the Israelis ignored the Arabs and took up 'tripping' and pot smoking. In this country we are the Israelis."[109] Important here is not only the language of mutual identity—"we are the Israelis"—but also the bedrock judgment that, in the calculus of Middle East power relations, the Israelis' situation resembled that of American blacks. By 1983, although Walker still noted a "bond between Jewish and black women that grows out of their awareness of oppression and injustice," the political sands of the Middle East had shifted. In response to a Jewish friend's assertion that Israel "*needed*" the Golan Heights to protect itself from enemy shelling, Walker had to wonder, "But doesn't that land belong to people?"

> "They're not doing anything with it," he replied.
>
> I thought: I have a backyard I'm "not doing anything with." Does that give you the right to take it?
>
> He continued telling me the glories of Israel, but I found it hard to listen: Crazy Horse, Lame Deer, and Black Elk stoppered my ears. He sounded like a typical American *wasichu* (a Sioux word for white men, meaning fat-takers) to me. It seemed only incidental he was a Jew.

Walker goes on to describe the shift in her own—and, she surmises, most blacks'—sympathies from Israelis to Palestinians "to keep faith with our own ancestors."[110]

Reading the pro-Israeli responses of Jewish feminists like Pogrebin was for Walker "like reading nineteenth-century European history and seeing the word 'colonialism' [only] once or twice." The attempted "universalism" of American feminism for her begins to creak and falter, that is, precisely at that point where the United States' history as a settler democracy is eclipsed behind either a nation-of-immigrants approach to diversity or the (related) figure of Israel as a marker of *Jewish* persecution: "Jewish feminists will have to try to understand people of color's hatred of imperialism and colonialism: we have lost whole continents to the white man's arrogance and greed, and to his white female accomplice's inability to say no to stolen gold, diamonds, and furs."[111]

Jewish feminist thought, of course, has not been monolithic throughout the decades-long cycle of crises from the invasion of Lebanon through two Intifadas. As if in response to Walker, for instance, Bulkin confessed that, though in her teaching she had often used George Orwell's essay on Morocco "with indignation at the white Europeans who could not *see* a country's brown-skinned inhabitants," nonetheless when she visited Israel, she "failed to see in any meaningful way its Arab inhabitants." What struck Bulkin most about her so-called growth in consciousness was "how far it lagged behind what I had learned about people of color in the United States and in some other parts of the world [when it came to the issue of Israel]." Adrienne Rich, too, openly feared "the extent to which both Americans and Israelis, in their national consciousness, are captives of denial. Denial, first, of the existence of the peoples who, in the creation of both nations, have been swept aside, their communities destroyed, pushed into reservations and camps, traumatized by superior might calling itself destiny." As against the Zionist allegiances of Abzug or Pogrebin, Andrea Dworkin decries the "testosterone-driven identity" of the Israeli state, as manifest in its domination of women and its degradation of Palestinian Arabs, and she wonders "what distinguishes a Jewish state from an apartheid state?"[112]

These very interpretations of "domination" and "degradation" have been impossible for many Jewish feminists to accept, given the depth with which Israel has become entwined with Jewish American identity, and given, too, the depth of the Third Worldist protest against it. Pogrebin saw the "Zionism is racism" resolution of the international women's conference in Mexico City as an "ambush." Though she might "wish for a world of universalist values and deemphasized differences," she states that she "would no longer tolerate a Women's Movement in which Jews are the only group asked to relinquish their own interests while other women were allowed to push their private agendas, and subvert feminist ideals when it suited them."[113] "If feminists can understand why history entitles lesbians to separatism, or minorities and women to affirmative action, we can understand why history entitles Jews to 'preferential' safe space," she declared. "To me, Zionism is simply an affirmative action plan on a national scale," given "virtually every country's record of treating us as surplus citizenry." In the wake of the conference in Copenhagen, which had adopted a resolution "to purify Palestine of the Zionist presence," even Elly Bulkin was "hard pressed indeed to feel anything but that 'they' want me dead." (After twenty years of such struggle, Phyllis Chesler would complain, "It's almost as if the feminist world has become a wholly owned subsidiary of the PLO.")[114]

Feminist debates over the Middle East have never simply been about the Middle East; they have also been about how diverse women see the world and how they locate themselves within it. The problem for American feminists, Mirtha Quintanales wrote in reference to her own immigrant status, is "how to reconcile these different kinds of 'primary emergencies': race and culture?" But as Cherríe Moraga concluded after one confrontation between Jewish women and women of color, "We don't have to be the same to have a movement, but we *do* have to be accountable for our ignorance. In the end, finally, we must refuse to give up on each other." For the most part—and this is truer of American feminists than it is of any other political community in the country—they have not given up on each other. Much of this important collaborative work has taken place well outside of what Zillah Eisenstein calls "the legitimized liberal sector" of U.S. feminism—that is, it has taken place among radical, socialist, lesbian, and Third World feminists.[115] If feminists have looked on one another across the color line with feelings of resentment or betrayal—even, perhaps, as "the enemy"—they have nonetheless persisted in talking. As the New Left fragmented into a congeries of left publics, feminism remained multiracial and multivocal; it also remained rooted in the politics of social location and "identity" in such a way as to hold firm to its attempted reconciliation of diverse women's "primary emergencies."

The successes of American feminism, such as they are, derive in large part from the accomplishments of women of color when it comes to theorizing difference and power. But they also derive from the egalitarian impulses that white feminism continues to draw from its roots-era proposition that "our heritage is our power." This is not to say that "white feminism" is coeval with the feminism of white ethnics; nor is it to say that multiculturalism of the "roots" variety among whites is the only brand going. But the daughters and granddaughters of Ellis Island have introduced an important element into feminist antiracism: Adrienne Rich's "politics of *location*," Elly Bulkin's refusal of a "scarcity theory of struggle," Robin Morgan's "skeleton key" of cross-racial empathy, and Starhawk's prodding that the time has come "to reconsider our loyalties." All derive from a moment of introspection and heritage-hunting. "Do we think Jews can be safe within a white supremacist society?" asks Melanie Kaye/Kantrowitz. "I do not. I believe, along with a great many other Jews, that a color/class barrier means injustice, and our culture teaches us to pursue justice. I also believe that . . . race hate will never exclude us."[116]

Such "skeleton key" efforts at cross-racial alliance are not the sole province of Black-Jewish relations, although African-American and Jewish writers have been prolific on the subject. Indeed, universalism through particularity is precisely what Joann Nash Eakin, for example, had in mind when she wrote that her own politics "have their roots in the social, political, and economic commitments of my Norwegian immigrant forebears, some of whom were involved in the shaping and forming of the populist movement in the nineteenth century." On her commitment to a feminist coalition among white and Third World women, she wrote, "I have moved from the prairie to the world, carrying with me in that journey all that has formed me from my growing up days on the prairies of Minnesota and North Dakota."[117] For all its limitations, this progressive tendency "from the prairie to the world" is among the roots era's most significant, if neglected, legacies.

"My immigrant forebears." In the dominant culture this has easily been the least challenging and most pleasing conception of America's diversity in the making. "The land bridge from Asia" makes for a sweeter story than the Trail of Tears. But perhaps the outsider status of the immigrant is also especially resonant in the era of globalization. Indeed, elastic labor frontiers, porous borders, the awesome mobility of capital, and the weakening—or the abdication—of the nation-state as a guarantor of citizens' rights vis-à-vis *trans*national aggregations of corporate power have extinguished the proprietary sense of national belonging that earlier generations regarded as a birthright. Social change of the sort that has characterized the years of the culture wars, too, may lead combatants on all sides to feel that—like immigrants—they hold no title to the political culture as they find it. Call it Homeland Insecurity.

The simultaneous appearance in 2003 of Phyllis Chesler's book *The New Anti-Semitism* (in which she regrets that her fellow activists on the left "embrace all ethnicities and demonize only one: mine") and Philip Jenkins's book *The New Anti-Catholicism* (whose subtitle identifies this as *The Last Acceptable Prejudice*) signifies several different things, only one of which is that bigotry endures.[118] Another is the widespread siege mentality in the United States, in which one's distance from the established center is perceived as being so great that "pariah" seems more apt a descriptor than mere "outsider." Another, perhaps, is the havoc that the heritage crusades and the culture wars have wreaked on our very conceptions of the underdog or the victim. This may be a "nation of immigrants," that is, in being a nation of nearly 300 million people who all feel, in one way or another, that they are forced to adapt to someone else's standards more or less against their will. Hence the "sore winner" posture of victorious conservatism—just the most recent chapter in a culture war that has raged since the advent of neoconservatism and the "identity left."

But Chesler and Jenkins notwithstanding, for the moment the children and grandchildren of Ellis Island do inhabit the false universal subject position in this "nation of immigrants." "When my grandfather . . . left Italy, over a hundred years ago, he set sail for America with only $20 in his pocket," writes Rudy Giuliani.

"He left his family, his home, everything that was familiar and safe. He saw the obstacles that faced him: a treacherous journey across a dangerous ocean, coming to a place whose language he didn't understand." Like so many before him, Giuliani here makes the turn outward from the iconic ancestor to the exalted nation that the ancestor chose:

> Rudolfo and millions of others . . . were guided by an idea. America, the land of the free and the home of the brave, this very special place. It was an idealized vision, undoubtedly romanticized. But by coming here, my forebears and so many others gave something back to America, making it even more special, because they worked hard to make this country better, fairer, more prosperous for themselves and their children.

We are a "secular religion," Giuliani avers. "We believe in ideas and ideals. We're not one race, we're many; we're not one ethnic group, we're everyone; we don't speak only one language, we're all of these people."[119]

This nationalist strain in the "nation of immigrants" romance was even more pronounced when Giuliani made his U.N. pitch for world support a few days after 9/11:

> There is no nation, and no city, in the history of the world that has seen more immigrants, in less time, than America . . . Each of your nations has contributed citizens to the United States and to New York. I believe I can take every one of you someplace in New York City where you can find someone from your country, someone from your village or town, that speaks your language and practices your religion.[120]

"Getting shot!" added a Latino line cook, to a burst of edgy laughter, at the New York deli where I chanced to see Giuliani's televised speech. In this multiracial gathering of chance onlookers, the cook's subversive addition could not fail to evoke the Abner Louima, Amadou Diallo, and Patrick Dorismund police brutality cases in Giuliani's New York; to some, it probably also referenced the anxious anti-Arab atmosphere that had descended since 9/11. This protest hurled against the TV screen, like the tense racial times in New York both before and after the attack on the twin towers, underscored just how critical "my forebears" turn out to be in constructions, like Giuliani's, of the nation as consisting of "every race, religion, and ethnicity"—"everyone."

Here, then—in Giuliani's law-and-order nationalism, Viscusi's hope, Chesler's distrust, Dukakis's liberalism, Robin Morgan's universalizing and yet particularizing radicalism, Cimino's populism and also his orientalism—are the shoals of Ellis Island, a pattern of shallows and sands representing two contrary traditions in the politics of national belonging: in conjuring the nation, its diversity, and the possibilities for community, many have found this an apt place to wade ashore; but so, too, have many others run aground. The Ellis Island myth is not just a popular motif but a fully *structuring* motif, however subtle, in public discussion of Americanism, its requisites, its most treasured properties.

"All over the nation," writes Melanie Kaye/Kantrowitz, "our children are watching / to see / who we become."[121] In 1976 Americans made best sellers of *Roots* and *World of Our Fathers*. They marked their nation's bicentennial with myriad projects devoted to "heritage"—they marched in ethnic parades, revived ethnic voluntary associations, established ethnic festivals and museums dedicated to the grandeur of diverse American pasts. They refurbished Ellis Island as a site of lavish sentimentality. But, in persistent conceptions of the "foreign" and in the emergent language of black criminality and the "underclass," some also painted civic virtue exclusively in shades of white. Some spoke of contemporary immigration as a surreptitious but perilous "invasion"; the federal government commenced to militarize the U.S.-Mexican border.[122] *Whose America?* The question has haunted U.S. political life for a quarter century and more, as the diversity-loving heritage project merged with the idioms of white primacy in an increasingly uneasy "nation of immigrants."

Coda: Ireland at JFK

The country is in a very delicate condition. They're facing some sort of revolution as their culture pulls apart. I'll say it here, now. Somebody has to say it: beef up the borders. Get new Border Patrol agents on the line, and be ever vigilant. There will be a new onslaught of foreign-speaking strangers that we can no longer support. There is no more room in the lifeboat, and their ways are not our ways . . .

New hordes of Québécois and Canadians are going to sneak into Vermont and Maine.

—Luis Alberto Urrea,
By the Lake of Sleeping Children (1996)

Everybody knows exactly what is meant by the words "illegal alien." Indeed, until 9/11 one group in particular had so dominated public concern that INS officials took to referring to immigrants from all other nations under the blanket term "OTM"—"Other Than Mexican." Twenty years after John F. Kennedy addressed the admiring throngs in Galway on the special affinities between Irishness and Americanness, Americans quietly began to note—positively, for the most part—a new wave of immigration from the Emerald Isle. The immigration happened to be illegal, though no one seemed to mind terribly. Beginning in about 1982 a new generation of Doughertys and Flahertys and Ryans began to disembark at JFK and Logan airports, their intentions to stay and work in the United States safely tucked in their six-month tourist visas. They arrived by the thousands—as many as thirty thousand settling in Boston and fifty thousand in New York within the first few years of the new wave—and this when the political culture at large was in full mobilization around the "crisis" represented by illegal immigration.[1] The fact that Americans organized to aid the undocumented Irish at a time when "control of our borders" was among the nation's chief concerns says a great deal about our national life beyond the melting pot. "Because of my color," says Guadalupe Avila, "I think I will never be an American." By contrast, the new Irish, as the *New York Times* put it, were "Illegal, but Not Alien." This was a "white" country after all, and the Irish disembarking at JFK Airport were learning that fact as surely as were the Mexicans at the border near El Paso or Nogales.[2]

In a 1989 article on illegal Irish immigration titled "The Re-Greening of America" (which has an entirely different ring from "the browning of America," one notes), *Time* described with some ambivalence the travails of the estimated 100,000 Irish newcomers. On the one hand, "the U.S. immigration act of 1965 discriminated against the Irish and other Europeans" through a system of preferences that inadvertently favored Asian and Latino immigration. The "amnesty" program of the 1986 immigration reform, too, had largely passed by the new Irish, as the residency requirement for amnesty was slightly longer than most of them had been in the United States. Thus the illegal Irish were victims, unfairly relegated to a harsh and fearful life in the shadows. "Like their more numerous Hispanic and Asian counterparts," the article stated, "the undocumented 'new Irish' switch jobs often, worry about the costs of sickness without Medicaid, and can do little but gnash their teeth when family crises occur in their homeland, because to leave the U.S. might mean never to return."[3]

But on the other hand, this article also seemed to ask, just how sorry can we feel for them? Unlike "the flood of Third World immigrants, the Irish come with advantages: white skin, good education, a knowledge of the language and a talent for politics that would make Boston's legendary Mayor James Michael Curley beam with pride." And political connections—or at least sentimental connections. Boston's Mayor Raymond Flynn announced that "the welcome mat is out" for Irish aliens, and he created a special office to provide them with legal aid. In New York, Ed Koch assured the undocumented Irish that they had "nothing to fear in utilizing fully the services [of the city]," and he granted $30,000 to establish a counseling hotline. These benefits came in addition to the initiatives of the Catholic Church, Irish-American politicians, the Irish-American press, and political groups like the Irish Immigration Reform Movement, including the publication of *A Guide for the New Irish in Chicago, Emigrating USA*, New York City's official "Guide for Irish Immigrants," and Boston's *Guide for the New Irish*. The Archdiocese of Boston, meanwhile, operated a special Irish Pastoral Center to attend to the social and legal needs of the illegal Irish, modeled after the Archdiocese of New York's Project Irish Outreach; Cardinal O'Connor urged a special presidential amnesty for all undocumented Irish.[4]

The social and political weave of Flynn's "welcome mat" is what the *Irish Echo* editor Ray O'Hanlon had in mind when he later noted, "The Irish were fast becoming the most officially briefed and municipally accepted lawbreakers on the North American continent." At the national level various proposals emerged to encourage higher rates of immigration from Europe —all favoring the Irish and all, ironically, articulated in the language of enhancing "diversity": Joe DioGuardi's bill allowing for "a new wave of Irish immigration that will again result in a better United States"; Ted Kennedy and Alan Simpson's proposal "to facilitate immigration from countries in Western Europe" (by awarding 54,000 visas according to a point system favoring, among other things, English competency, though this provision was ultimately defeated); Brian Donnelly's visa program, in which the Irish won 3,500 of the first 10,000 visas; the so-called Berman lottery, in which the Irish won 40 percent of the first 10,000 visas; and Bruce Morrison's "regional diversity" provision, whose inclination toward the peoples of Western Europe led one commentator to describe it as "virtual amnesty to all the illegal Irish immigrants in the country."[5]

For the moment, however, *Time* magazine was having a hard time deciding whether this was a story of victimization or of unfair advantage. But in a sense, the popular story of Irish victimization *was* the Irish immigrants' unfair advantage. Mayor Koch, for example, urged President-elect Bush to declare an executive amnesty on behalf of the Irish, who endured "pain, anguish, and inequalities" while "languishing in a troubling limbo." A *Wall Street Journal* article on the new Irish in 1987 concluded, in the first-person voice of the young illegal immigrant, "Listen, dad, I don't feel that I'm doing anything illegal. I'm trying to make a future for myself." When he launched his special municipal programs for aiding the illegal Irish, Mayor Flynn cited Boston's "special relationship to Ireland."[6]

Such sentiments have not translated particularly well into Spanish or Chinese. It is difficult to imagine an argument evoking the "special relationship" between Los Angeles and Mexico, for instance; and setting aside the issue of popular empathy with immigrants' endurance of "pain, anguish, and inequalities," even the degree of individuation carried in the phrase, "Listen, dad," has been absent in most U.S. media coverage of migration from Mexico and the "Third World." Indeed, in these accounts immigrant subjectivity is more often effaced behind aquatic metaphors of massive and uncontrollable *volume:* "Immigration Law Is Failing to Cut Flow from Mexico"; "U.S. Plans a Ditch in California to Stem the Flow of Illegal Aliens"; "Wave of Immigrant Children Strains Schools and Housing"; "wave of Latin American immigrants now flooding Texas, California and Florida"; "Tide of Illegal Aliens Headed for the U.S."; "Amnesty Law Is Seen as Failing to Slow Alien Tide."[7] When the *Golden Venture* ran aground carrying a desperate cargo of "illegal" Chinese immigrants in 1993, the columnist A. M. Rosenthal was more or less alone in his call to "let them in" and to "honor those heroes from China, those men and women who sought the beautiful land." By nightfall, immigration officials had "put them in handcuffs, sent them to distant prisons and made sure they did not see any lawyers."[8]

By contrast, press coverage of the "new Irish" gave voice to that "emotional sense of loss in the collective Irish soul" for the Emerald Isle's demographic hemorrhage, or bemoaned the fact that "over 100,000 have now hawked their dream to America like millions of Irish before them." If the Irish immigrants could not become naturalized in the legal sense, at least the Irish *presence* was rendered "natural" in the cultural sense. "It's part of the Irish identity to become an American citizen," explained the *Times*. "It's easy to slip into the culture." In 1986 only 1,839 Irish were admitted legally as permanent residents, but another 98,188 arrived on temporary visas (no one knows how many were to overstay and "slip into the culture"). In the wake of the Immigration Reform and Control Act, too, "surprising numbers of Irish, British, Italian, and other Europeans who overstayed tourist visas" claimed amnesty, including "thousands of Poles" in Chicago alone. In the early 1990s, New Yorkers were taken aback to find that their state had "more illegal Italians and Israelis than illegal Chinese," though nothing in media coverage or public debate had ever suggested such a trend.[9] The story of the undocumented Irish was not about taking American jobs or draining American social services; like other "invisible aliens" from Europe, the new Irish claimed national attention for a time, but never as a source of civic concern.

In *Black Hole, Green Card* (1994), an exploration of the new, global Ireland of the late twentieth century, Fintan O'Toole noted the odd convergence of a well-worn American nostalgia with an emergent Irish social reality in a place called the Tipperary Inn in Montauk, at the far eastern tip of Long Island. Rather sad and tattered, the Tipperary Inn is decorated in maps of Ireland—genealogical maps, literary maps, maps whose towns and territories are indicated in Gaelic—an almost generic expression of American attachment to some (imagined) homeland. "If you're Irish," writes O'Toole,

> There is something surreal about the way Ireland, or a version of Ireland, can be a holiday destination even in New York state. You can visit a little bit of Ireland without ever leaving America.

What is even more surreal is that you visit America without ever really leaving Ireland. Every shop, every bar, every hotel in Montauk seems to be staffed by young Irish people. You walk in feeling hip in your shades and shorts, only to be asked in familiar tones: "What's the weather like at home?" You have to think for a moment where home might be when a whole generation seems to be over here.[10]

With the backward glance of its Irish décor and the forward look of its new Irish staff, the Tipperary Inn captures the theme of "where home might be" more overtly and honestly than is usually the case. But in the era of ethnic reverie on the one hand and globalization on the other, such musings on "home" have textured the public discussion of a wide range of concerns. Since the 1990s, of course, the entire debate over immigration has been respun according to new and pressing questions of terrorism and national security. One report in 1993 concluded that New Yorkers' anti-immigration sentiment was on the rise, in part in response to the first World Trade Center bombing: 85 percent of those surveyed said that immigration "had been good in the past," though "only 40% thought current immigration to be a good thing." Further, 55 percent "thought illegal immigrants to be a terrorist threat, and 82% of the American-born and 68% of the foreign-born . . . said they believed the trade center bombing in February would not have occurred if controls over immigration had been tighter."[11] Indeed, in the post-9/11 world the "OTM" of immigration and naturalization discourse might well be taken to mean "Other Than Muslim."

In a discussion of the LA8, a group of seven Palestinians and one Kenyan arrested on shaky evidence as a terrorist cell in 1987, the legal scholar David Cole noted, "Had the government sought to deport a similarly situated group of white immigrants allegedly associated with the Irish Republican Army (IRA), the popular outcry would have almost certainly been more substantial. Over the course of the LA8 case, Irish immigrants and citizens living here actively and notoriously supported the IRA, yet the INS never sought to deport a single person for association with the IRA, or for seeking to raise money for its illegal activities," though it did "seek to deport persons accused of engaging in actual terrorist acts." "Because the Palestinians were more easily portrayed as 'other,'" concluded Cole, "the government could treat them in ways that it certainly could not have treated citizens, and probably could not have treated many white immigrants."[12]

It was thus altogether fitting that during the Concert for New York in the wake of 9/11, among the most straightforward and well-received expressions of outraged Americanism was the firefighter Michael Moran's exhortation, "Osama bin Laden, you can kiss my royal Irish ass!" Like JFK's "return" to Ireland and William Shannon's pluralistic portrait of a distinct and unmelted Irish-America in 1963, the racial valences of the discourse of "terrorism" signal a widespread understanding that to emphasize and even to celebrate the hyphen is not to diminish individuals' "Americanism," but rather, as Shannon put it, "to show what kind of Americans they are."[13] But as David Cole's attention to the racialized patterns of antiterrorism suggest, and as George W. Bush's visit to Ellis Island for the first anniversary of 9/11 affirms, it must be the right kind of hyphen. Such patterns in our collective sense of naturalized Americanness should command the strictest attention, as should the mythology of the "nation of immigrants" that binds them. These more than anything else constitute the historical weave of that hypnotic political ideal, *America.*

Notes

Acknowledgments

Index

Notes

Introduction

1. Paul Kivel, *Uprooting Racism: How White People Can Work for Racial Justice* (Philadelphia: New Society Publishers, 1996), p. 10.
2. Marcus Lee Hansen, "The Third Generation in America" [1938], reprinted in *Commentary*, Nov. 1952, pp. 494, 495; Werner Sollors, *Beyond Ethnicity: Consent and Descent in American Culture* (New York: Oxford University Press, 1986), pp. 215, 214–221.
3. Sollors, *Beyond Ethnicity*, p. 214; Will Herberg, *Protestant—Catholic—Jew* [1955] (New York: Anchor, 1960), p. 186.
4. Jonathan Rieder, *Canarsie: The Jews and Italians of Brooklyn against Liberalism* (Cambridge, Mass.: Harvard University Press, 1985), p. 206. Compare Roy Rozenzweig and David Thelan, *The Presence of the Past: Popular Uses of History in American Life* (New York: Columbia University Press, 1998), pp. 118, 137.
5. Lawrence Levine, *The Opening of the American Mind: Canons, Culture, and History* (Boston: Beacon Press, 1996), pp. 118, 132.
6. Peter Schrag, "The Decline of the WASP" [1970], in Peter Rose, *Nation of Nations: The Ethnic Experience and the Racial Crisis* (New York: University Press of America, 1972), p. 184.
7. There is an uncredited recording of this speech, probably dating from early 1967, in the collection at WBAI, New York. On this same theme see also James Baldwin, *The Fire Next Time* [1963] (New York: Vintage, 1993), p. 60.
8. *New York Times*, Aug. 30, 2004, p. P8.
9. Quoted in Sheng-Mei Ma, *The Deathly Embrace: Orientalism and Asian American Identity* (Minneapolis: University of Minnesota Press, 2000), p. 155.

1. Hyphen Nation

1. Maurice Hennessy, *I'll Come Back in the Springtime: John F. Kennedy and the Irish* (New York: Ives Washburn, 1966), p. 39.
2. *New York Times*, May 7, 1963, p. 35; June 27, 1963, p. 1; June 28, 1963, p. 3.

3. *New York Times,* June 27, 1963, p. 13.

4. Hennessy, *I'll Come Back,* pp. v–vi.

5. Will Herberg, *Protestant—Catholic—Jew* [1955] (New York: Anchor, 1960), p. 20.

6. Hennessy, *I'll Come Back,* pp. 85–86.

7. Ibid., pp. 40, 49; *New York Times,* June 29, 1963, p. 2.

8. *New York Times,* June 30, 1963, p. 3.

9. William Shannon, *The American Irish: A Political and Social Portrait* (New York: Collier, 1963), p. vi.

10. *New York Times,* June 4, 1984, p. A8; Lou Cannon, *Ronald Reagan: The Role of a Lifetime* (New York: Touchstone, 1992), p. 463.

11. *New York Times Book Review,* Jan. 2, 1977, section 7, p. 2.

12. "Assimilation Blues," *Time,* Jan. 26, 1976, p. 71; "A New World Found, An Old Culture Lost," *Business Week,* Feb. 16, 1976, p. 11; *Christian Science Monitor,* July 23, 1976, p. 23; "Heritage of the Ghetto," *The Nation,* March 27, 1976, p. 373.

13. Michael Novak, "The New Ethnicity" [1974], in *Unmeltable Ethnics: Politics and Culture in American Life* (New Brunswick: Transaction, 1995), p. 347; Irving Howe, *World of Our Fathers: The Journey of the East European Jews to America and the Life They Found and Made* (New York: Simon and Schuster, 1976), p. 632.

14. Stokely Carmichael and Charles Hamilton, *Black Power: The Politics of Liberation in America* (New York: Random House, 1967), p. 49; Myron Kuropas, *Ukrainian American Citadel: The First Hundred Years of the Ukrainian National Association* (Boulder: East European Monographs, 1996), p. 532.

15. Michael Staub, *Torn at the Roots: The Crisis of Jewish Liberalism in Postwar America* (New York: Columbia University Press, 2002), pp. 200, 201.

16. Michael Novak, *The Rise of the Unmeltable Ethnics: Politics and Culture in the Seventies* (New York: Macmillan, 1971), p. xx; Melanie Kaye/Kantrowitz, "To Be a Radical Jew in the Late Twentieth Century," in *The Issue Is Power: Essays on Women, Jews, Violence, and Resistance* (San Francisco: Aunt Lute, 1992), p. 109; Lillian Rubin, *Families on the Fault Line: America's Working Class Speaks about the Family, the Economy, Race, and Ethnicity* (New York: Harper, 1994), p. xiv and *passim.*

17. Micaela di Leonardo, "White Ethnicities, Identity Politics, and Baby Bear's Chair," *Social Text* (Winter 1994), p. 175; Philip Gleason, "American Identity and Americanization," in William Petersen et al., *Concepts of Ethnicity* (Cambridge, Mass.: Belknap Press of Harvard

University Press, 1980), pp. 134–135; Jonathan Rieder, *Canarsie: Brooklyn's Italians and Jews against Liberalism* (Cambridge, Mass.: Harvard University Press, 1985); Richard Krickus, *Pursuing the American Dream: White Ethnics and the New Populism* (New York: Anchor, 1976), pp. 351–398.

18. Jerald Podair, *The Strike That Changed New York: Blacks, Whites, and the Ocean Hill–Brownsville Crisis* (New Haven: Yale University Press, 2002), p. 126; see esp. pp. 123–133 on New York Jews' "journey to unambiguous white identity" during the crisis. Rieder, *Canarsie*, p. 73.

19. Anne Roiphe, *Generation without Memory: A Jewish Journey in Christian America* (New York: Simon and Schuster, 1981), p. 11. On modernity and political identity, see also Paul Gilroy, *Against Race: Imagining Political Culture beyond the Color Line* (Cambridge, Mass.: Belknap Press of Harvard University Press, 2000), p. 106.

20. Horace Kallen, "Democracy versus the Melting-Pot," [1915], in Horace Kallen, *Culture and Democracy in the United States* (New York: Liveright, 1924), p. 84.

21. Braverman in Ursula Huws, *The Making of a Cybertariat: Virtual Work in a Real World* (New York: Monthly Review Press, 2003), p. 24. For a useful political critique of this "small is beautiful" brand of anti-modernist anticapitalism, see Doug Henwood, *After the New Economy* (New York: New Press, 2003), pp. 159–169.

22. Michael Novak, "Pluralism in Humanistic Perspective," in Peterson et al., *Concepts of Ethnicity*, p. 35; David Lowenthal, *The Heritage Crusade and the Spoils of History* (Cambridge: Cambridge University Press, 1998), pp. xv, 81–82; Arthur Waskow, "Judaism and Revolution Today," in Jack Nusan Porter and Peter Dreier, eds., *Jewish Radicalism: A Selected Anthology* (New York: Grove, 1973), p. 15; David Riesman, *The Lonely Crowd: A Study of the Changing American Character* [1950] (New Haven: Yale University Press, 1989); William Whyte, *The Organization Man* (New York: Simon and Schuster, 1955).

23. Celeste Ray, *Highland Heritage: Scottish Americans in the American South* (Chapel Hill: University of North Carolina Press, 2001), pp. 7, 8, 69 (see esp. chap. 3 on the relationship among ethnicity, anti-modernism, and "community"); Henry Miller, *The Air Conditioned Nightmare* (New York: New Directions, 1970); "East Village Other," in Aniko Bodroghkozy, *Groove Tube: Sixties Television and the Youth Rebellion* (Durham: Duke University Press, 2001), p. 40; Roiphe in Richard Gambino, *Blood of My Blood: The Dilemma of the Italian-Americans* [1974] (Toronto: Guernica, 1998), pp. 354–355.

24. David Mamet, "The Disappearance of the Jews" [1982], in *The Old Neighborhood* (New York: Vintage, 1998), pp. 18–19. See also Ray, *Highland Heritage*, pp. 189–194; Paul Breines, *Tough Jews: Political Fantasies and the Moral Dilemma of American Jewry* (New York: Basic, 1990).

25. E. Anthony Rotundo, "Wonderbread and Stagots: Italian American Manhood and *The Sopranos*," in Regina Berreca, ed., *A Sitdown with the Sopranos* (New York: Palgrave, 2002), p. 74; Kallen, "Democracy versus the Melting-Pot"; Theodore Roosevelt, "The Strenuous Life" [1899], in *The Strenuous Life* (New York: Review of Reviews, 1910).

26. Compare Herbert Gans, "Symbolic Ethnicity: The Future of Ethnic Groups and Cultures in America," *Ethnic and Racial Studies* (Jan. 1979), esp. pp. 8–13; and Matthew Frye Jacobson, *Special Sorrows: The Diasporic Imagination of Irish, Polish, and Jewish Immigrants in the United States* (Cambridge, Mass.: Harvard University Press, 1995), pp. 217–243.

27. Alan Dershowitz, *Chutzpah* (Boston: Little Brown, 1991), p. 80. See also Melvin Urofsky, *We Are One! American Jewry and Israel* (Garden City: Anchor/Doubleday, 1978).

28. Michael Funchion, ed., *Irish American Voluntary Organizations* (Westport: Greenwood Press, 1983); Michael Dobkowski, ed., *Jewish American Voluntary Organizations* (Westport: Greenwood Press, 1986); Kuropas, *Ukrainian American Citadel*; Donald Pienkos, *PNA: A Centennial History of the Polish National Alliance of North America* (Boulder: East European Monographs, 1984); Lubomyr Wynar, *Encyclopedic Directory of Ethnic Organizations in the United States* (Littleton, Colo.: Libraries Unlimited, 1975), pp. 157, 236, 324.

29. Donna Gabaccia, *We Are What We Eat: Ethnic Food and the Making of Americans* (Cambridge, Mass.: Harvard University Press, 1998), p. 183.

30. George Lipsitz, "The Meaning of Memory: Family, Class, and Ethnicity in Early Network Television Programs," in Lynn Spigel and Denise Mann, eds., *Private Screenings: Television and the Female Consumer* (Minneapolis: University of Minnesota Press, 1992), pp. 71–77; David Marc, *Comic Visions: Television Comedy and American Culture* (New York: Blackwell, 1997), pp. 80–81; David Zurawik, *The Jews of Prime Time* (Lebanon, N.H.: Brandeis University Press, 2003), pp. 51–57, 224–225; Vincent Brook, *Something Ain't Kosher Here: The Rise of the "Jewish" Sitcom* (New Brunswick: Rutgers University Press, 2003), p. 45; Todd Gitlin, *Inside Prime Time* (New York: Pantheon, 1983), p. 185. See also Jonathan Pearl and Judith Pearl, *The Chosen Image:*

Television's Portrayal of Jewish Themes and Characters (Jefferson, N.C.: McFarland, 1999).

31. Zurawik, *Jews of Prime Time*, p. 84; Herman Gray, *Watching Race: Television and the Struggle for Blackness* (Minneapolis: University of Minnesota Press, 1995), p. 79.

32. Arthur Schlesinger, Jr., *The Disuniting of America: Reflections on a Multicultural Society* (New York: Norton, 1993); Dinesh D'Sousa, *Illiberal Education: The Politics of Race and Sex on Campus* (New York: Free Press, 1998); Richard Bernstein, *Dictatorship of Virtue: How the Battle over Multiculturalism Is Reshaping Our Schools, Our Country, and Our Lives* (New York: Vintage, 1995); Lynne V. Cheney, *American Memory: A Report on the Humanities in the Nation's Public Schools* (Washington, D.C.: Government Printing Office, 1998); Herbert Kliebard, *Changing Course: American Curriculum Reform in the Twentieth Century* (New York: Teachers College Press, 2002).

33. David Hollinger, *Post-Ethnic America: Beyond Multiculturalism* (New York: Basic, 1995), pp. 51–77. Such universalism was briefly challenged in the 1940s. See Carey McWilliams, *Brothers under the Skin* (Boston: Little Brown, 1942); Louis Adamic, *Nation of Nations* (New York: Harper, 1944).

34. Ashley Montagu, "What Every Child and Adult Should Know about 'Race,'" in *Education* (Jan. 1946), pp. 262–264; *Race: Man's Most Dangerous Myth* (New York: Columbia University Press, 1942); Elazar Barkan, *The Retreat from Scientific Racism: Changing Conceptions of Race in Britain and the United States between the World Wars* (Cambridge: Cambridge University Press, 1992).

35. John Hajduk, "Tin Pan Alley on the March: Popular Music, World War II, and the Quest for a Great War Song," *Popular Music and Society* (Dec. 2003).

36. Lloyd Warner and Leo Srole, *The Social Systems of American Ethnic Groups* (New Haven: Yale University Press, 1945), p. 294; Herberg, *Protestant—Catholic—Jew*, pp. 38, 20, 23.

37. Nathan Glazer and Daniel Patrick Moynihan, *Beyond the Melting Pot: The Negroes, Puerto Ricans, Jews, Italians, and Irish of New York City* [1963] (Cambridge: MIT Press, 1971); Novak, *The Rise of the Unmeltable Ethnics;* Thomas Sowell, *Ethnic America: A History* (New York: Basic, 1981), p. 4.

38. Stephen Steinberg, *Turning Back: The Retreat from Racial Justice in American Thought and Policy* (Boston: Beacon, 1995), p. 24, pp. 21–49.

39. Maureen Dezell, *Irish America Coming into Clover: The Evolution of a*

People and a Culture (New York: Doubleday, 2000), p. 200. On race and ethnicity, see esp. Richard Alba, *Ethnic Identity: The Transformation of White America* (New Haven: Yale University Press, 1990); Yen Le Espiritu, *Asian American Panethnicity: Bridging Institutions and Identities* (Philadelphia: Temple, 1992); Felix Padilla, *Latino Ethnic Consciousness: The Case of Mexicans and Puerto Ricans in Chicago* (South Bend: Notre Dame, 1985); Mary Waters, *Black Identities: West Indian Immigrant Dreams and American Realities* (Cambridge: Harvard University Press, 1999).

40. Mary Waters, *Ethnic Options: Choosing Identities in America* (Berkeley: University of California Press, 1990); Alba, *Ethnic Identity,* pp. 316, 312.

41. John F. Kennedy, *A Nation of Immigrants* [1958] (New York: Harper and Row, 1964), p. 58.

42. Gary Nash, Charlotte Crabtree, and Ross Dunn, eds., *History on Trial: Culture Wars and the Teaching of the Past* (New York: Knopf, 1997), p. 54; Peter Novick, *That Noble Dream: The "Objectivity Question" and the American Historical Profession* (Cambridge: Cambridge University Press, 1988), pp. 339–340.

43. Oscar Handlin, *The Uprooted: The Epic Story of the Great Migrations That Made the American People* (Boston: Little Brown, 1951), p. 3; Novick, *Noble Dream,* pp. 469–521. The Immigration and Ethnic History Society was founded in 1965 "to promote the study of the history of immigration to the United States and Canada from all parts of the world . . . ; to promote study of ethnic groups in the United States, including regional groups in the United States, Native-Americans, and forced immigrants; and to promote understanding of the processes of acculturation and of conflict." (Mission statement, *Journal of American Ethnic History.*) Early presidents included Moses Rischin, John Higham, Rudolph Vecoli, and Victor Greene.

44. Rudolph Vecoli, "Ethnicity: A Neglected Dimension of American History," in Herbert Bass, ed., *The State of American History* (Chicago: Quadrangle, 1970), pp. 71–72, 75, 80, 83, 84; Rudolph Vecoli, "The *Contadini* of Chicago," *Journal of American History* 51:3 (1964), pp. 404–417.

45. Rudolph Vecoli, "The Resurgence of American Immigration History," *American Studies International* (Winter 1979), pp. 46, 55, 54–62, 47–48.

46. Ibid., p. 62. See also Linda Symcox, *Whose History? The Struggle for National Standards in American Classrooms* (New York: Teachers Col-

lege Press, 2002), pp. 76–80; Joyce Appleby, Lynn Hunt, and Margaret Jacoby, *Telling the Truth about History* (New York: Norton, 1994), pp. 291–302; Eric Foner, *Who Owns History? Rethinking the Past in a Changing World* (New York: Hill and Wang, 2002), pp. 149–166; Jonathan Zimmerman, *Whose America? Culture Wars in the Public Schools* (Cambridge, Mass.: Harvard University Press, 2002).

47. Immigration History Research Center flyer (c.1970s), in the author's possession. My gratitude to Werner Sollors.

48. Frances Fitzgerald, *America Revised: History Schoolbooks in the Twentieth Century* (Boston: Atlantic Monthly Press, 1979), pp. 63, 21.

49. Ibid., pp. 99–100, 82.

50. Stephan Thernstrom, Ann Orlov, and Oscar Handlin, eds., *Harvard Encyclopedia of American Ethnic Groups* (Cambridge, Mass.: Belknap Press of Harvard University Press, 1980), pp. v, ix; Thomas Dublin, ed., *Becoming American, Becoming Ethnic: College Students Explore Their Roots* (Philadelphia: Temple University Press, 1996).

51. Alex Haley, *Roots: The Saga of an American Family* (New York: Dell, 1976), p. 729.

52. *Time*, March 28, 1977, p. 54; Haley, *Roots*, p. 729.

53. The *Times'* universalistic assessment now appears on the flyleaf of the paperback.

54. Neilson cited in John Higham, "Current Trends in the Study of Ethnicity in the United States," *Journal of American Ethnic History*, 2:1 (1982), p. 5; *Time*, March 28, 1977, p. 43, set the viewership at 130 million.

55. Haley, *Roots*, p. 707.

56. This assessment, too, appears on the flyleaf.

57. Haley, *Roots*, p. 715. Linda Williams has argued, "What *Roots* did for its African-American readers and viewers is . . . not unlike what blackface and a song about 'Mammy' in *The Jazz Singer* did for Jews: it offered identification with an exoticized blackness, ennobled through suffering, whose actual purpose, however, was ultimately to forge an *assimilated* American identity." Linda Williams, *Playing the Race Card: Melodramas of Black and White from Uncle Tom to O.J.* (Princeton: Princeton University Press, 2002), p. 230.

58. *Newsweek*, July 4, 1977, p. 30.

59. *Time*, March 28, 1977, p. 43; A. Richard Rizzo, "Interviewing Italian Americans about Their Life Histories," *Italian Americana* 3:1 (1976), p. 99; "The Boom in Ancestor Hunting," *Christian Science Monitor*, March 21, 1977; *Newsweek*, July 4, 1977, pp. 26, 38; Gilbert Doane,

Searching for Your Ancestors: The How and Why of Genealogy (Minneapolis: University of Minnesota Press, 1973); Jeanne Eddy Westin, *Finding Your Roots* (New York: Ballantine, 1982); Dan Rottenberg, *Finding Our Fathers: A Guidebook to Jewish Genealogy* (New York: Random House, 1977); George Everton, *The Handy Book for Genealogists* (Logan, Utah: Everton Publishers, 1971). On the "quest for ancestors," see also Ray, *Highland Heritage,* pp. 80–84.

60. "The Boom in Ancestor Hunting," *Christian Science Monitor,* March 21, 1977; *Newsweek,* July 4, 1977, pp. 26, 30; Lowenthal, *Heritage Crusade,* p. 16. Visit the website at www.ancestry.com.

61. *Newsweek,* July 4, 1977, p. 26; Marilyn Halter, *Shopping for Identity: The Marketing of Ethnicity* (New York: Schocken, 2000), p. 30; Ray, *Highland Heritage,* pp. 127–152; Lowenthal, *Heritage Crusade,* pp. 9–10. Of these American throngs who continually "sightsee the shtetl," novelist Jonathan Safran Foer caustically wrote in the first person of a Ukrainian tour guide, "I had the opinion that Jewish people were having shit between their brains" because they paid "very much currency in order to make vacations *from* America *to* Ukraine." Jonathan Safran Foer, *Everything Is Illuminated* (Boston: Houghton Mifflin, 2002), pp. 60, 3. For a more sympathetic treatment, see Anne Paolucci, "Back in the Old Country," in Helen Barolini, *The Dream Book: An Anthology of Writings by Italian American Women* (New York: Schocken, 1985), p. 314.

62. Philip Roth, *Portnoy's Complaint* [1967] (New York: Random House, 1994); Michael Arlen, *Passage to Ararat* (New York: Penguin, 1975); *Madonna Ciao Italia: Live from Italy* (Warner Reprise Video, 1988); Michael Kalafatas, *The Bellstone: The Greek Sponge Divers of the Aegean: One American's Journey Home* (Hanover: Brandeis University Press, 2003). See also Erica Jong, *Fear of Flying* [1973] (New York: Signet, 2003); Alice Carey, *I'll Know It When I See It: A Daughter's Search for Home in Ireland* (New York: Clarkson Potter, 2002); Maria Laurino, *Have You Always Been Italian?* (New York: Norton, 2000), pp. 77–99; Robert Viscusi, *Astoria* (Toronto: Guernica, 1995); Wendy Wasserstein, "Poles Apart," in *Shiksa Goddess (or: How I Spent My Forties)* (New York: Vintage, 2001), pp. 159–164.

63. Tom Hayden, *Reunion: A Memoir* (New York: Collier, 1988), p. 433. See also Paddy Logue, ed., *Being Irish* (Dublin: Oak Tree Press, 2000).

64. Arlen, *Passage to Ararat,* p. 290. See also Ellen Willis, "Next Year in Jerusalem" [1976], in *Beginning to See the Light: Pieces of a Decade* (New

York: Alfred A. Knopf, 1981); John Gregory Dunne, *Harp* (New York: Simon and Schuster, 1989), ch.26.

65. Howard Jacobson, *Roots Schmoots: Journeys among Jews* (Woodstock, N.Y.: Overlook Press, 1993), pp. 9–10, 500, 501.

66. Halter, *Shopping for Identity*, p. 79.

67. Donald Pienkos, *One Hundred Years Young: A History of the Polish Falcons of America, 1887–1987* (Boulder: East European Monographs, 1987), p. 230; Pienkos, *PNA*, p. 196; Kuropas, *Ukrainian American Citadel*, p. 638.

68. Dobkowski, *Jewish American Voluntary Organizations*, pp. 641–653, 401; Funchion, *Irish American Voluntary Associations*, pp. 283–292; Lubomyr Wynar, *Encyclopedic Directory of Ethnic Organizations in the United States* (Littleton, Colo.: Libraries Unlimited, 1975). Wynar identifies seventy-three diverse ethnic organizations that were founded between 1960 and 1975, including the American Committee for Irish Studies (1960), the Omaha Czech Club (1960), the Irish American Cultural Institute (1962), Estonian House (1965), Thanks to Scandinavia (1965), the American Croatian Cultural and Educational Society (1965), the Norwegian Torsk Club (1966), the Slovak American Cultural Center (1967), the Armenian Cultural Association (1967), the Magyar Communion of Friends (1967), Jews for Urban Justice (1967), the Icelandic Association (1968), the Association of Young Italians (1969), the Association for Jewish Studies (1969), the Hungarian American Cultural Foundation (1969), the Latvian Heritage Foundation (1969), the Carpatho-Russian Literary Association (1970), the United Irish Cultural Center of San Francisco (1971), the German Family Society (1973), the National Jewish Resource Center (1974), and the Greenwood Lake Gaelic Cultural Society (1975).

69. Lubomyr Wynar and Lois Buttlar, *Guide to Ethnic Museums, Libraries, and Archives in the United States* (Kent: Program for the Study of Ethnic Publications, 1978), pp. 131–132, 141, 206–207, 220, 322, 314–315; see also Nancy Frazier, *Jewish Museums of North America: A Guide to Collections, Artifacts, and Memorabilia* (New York: Wiley and Sons, 1992).

70. Halter, *Shopping*, pp. 153, 80; Frazier, *Jewish Museums*, pp. 28–31; Aaron Lansky, *Outwitting History* (New York: Algonquin, 2004).

71. *Fortune*, Aug. 20, 1984, p. 10; Brook, *Something Ain't Kosher*, p. 103.

72. Hasia Diner, *Lower East Side Memories: A Jewish Place in America* (Princeton: Princeton University Press, 2000), pp. 96–97.

73. Ibid., pp. 112–118, 119, 122–123, 91. *Schmaltz* is chicken fat, table-ready as a condiment to be poured over a dish.

74. Thernstrom et al., *The Harvard Encyclopedia of American Ethnic Groups*, pp. 343–344.

75. Gabaccia, *We Are What We Eat*, p. 193; John Bodnar, *Remaking America: Public Memory, Commemoration and Patriotism in the Twentieth Century* (Princeton: Princeton University Press, 1992), pp. 236–244.

76. "The Boom in Ancestor Hunting," *Christian Science Monitor*, March 21, 1977; Joseph Wytrwal, *Behold the Polish Americans!* (Detroit: Endurance Press, 1976), p. 600; *New York Times*, April 14, 1976, p. 1.

77. Barbara Kirshenblatt-Gimblett, *Destination Culture: Tourism, Museums, Heritage* (Berkeley: University of California Press, 1998), pp. 149–150.

78. *New York Times*, April 7, 1976, p. 1; April 9, 1976, p. 1; April 10, 1976, p. 10. The "ethnic purity" fracas in 1976 merely continued the urban struggles over school desegregation and busing that had been roiling since the 1960s. On the conflicting and explosive interpretations of the word "community" in these contests, for example, see Podair, *The Strike That Changed New York*, pp. 21–47. *Richard Pryor: The Anthology, 1968–1992*, Warner Bros. Records Inc., 2001.

79. *Washington Post*, July 4, 1986, p. A15; July 7, 1986, p. A1; July 5, 1986, p. D1; *Los Angeles Times*, July 3, 1986, p. 1; July 7, 1986, p. 1; May 22, 1986, p. 2; F. Ross Holland, *Idealists, Scoundrels, and the Lady: An Insider's View of the Statue of Liberty–Ellis Island Project* (Urbana: University of Illinois Press, 1993), pp. 223, 224; *New York Times*, Nov. 15, 1986, p. 34; June 29, 1986, p. 44.

80. *New York Times*, Oct. 27, 1986, p. B3; Oct. 30, 1986, p. C14.

81. Nestor Rodriguez, "The Social Construction of the U.S.–Mexican Border," in Juan Perea, ed., *Immigrants Out! The New Nativism and the Anti-Immigrant Impulse in the United States* (New York: New York University Press, 1997), p. 233.

82. *New York Times*, Nov. 13, 1954, p. 20; Barbara Blumberg, *Celebrating the Immigrant: An Administrative History of the Statue of Liberty National Monument, 1952–1982* (New York: Institute for Research in History, 1985), p. 98; *New Republic*, Jan. 4, 1964, p. 21.

83. Judith Smith, "Celebrating Immigration History at Ellis Island," *American Quarterly* 44:1 (March 1992), p. 82. The phrase "recreational immigrants" is Barbara Kirshenblatt-Gimblett's (*Destination Culture*, p. 177).

84. Blumberg, *Celebrating the Immigrant*, p. 97.

85. *Public Papers of the Presidents,* Lyndon Johnson, 1965 (Washington, D.C.: Government Printing Office, 1966), p. 1038.
86. Holland, *Idealists, Scoundrels, and the Lady,* pp. 80, 157.
87. Ibid., pp. 10, 2, 244, 78, 242; Henry James, *The American Scene* [1906] (n.l.: New American Library, 1993), pp. 425–427.
88. Holland, *Idealists, Scoundrels, and the Lady,* pp. 157–162, 84.
89. *Los Angeles Times,* June 8, 1986, part 6, p. 1.
90. *New York Times,* Dec. 16, 1963, movie section; John Bodnar, "Symbols and Servants: Immigrant America and the Limits of Public History," *Journal of American History* 73:1 (June 1986), p. 140; Holland, *Idealists, Scoundrels, and the Lady,* pp. 245–246.
91. Smith, "Celebrating Immigration History," p. 85.
92. Bodnar, "Symbols and Servants," pp. 138, 150, 151.
93. David Brownstone, Irene Franck, and Douglass Brownstone, *Island of Hope, Island of Tears* [1979] (New York: Barnes and Noble, 2000), p. 3.
94. Bonnie Honig, *Democracy and the Foreigner* (Princeton: Princeton University Press, 2001), pp. 74, 75, 84.
95. Holland, *Idealists, Scoundrels, and the Lady,* p. 224; *New York Times,* Oct. 16, 1986, p. B10; May 30, 1986, p. 1; June 29, 1986, p. 44. Ironically, some of the most bitter protests came from Irish and Italian groups, who resisted the dilution of Ellis Island's history through these gestures toward broader inclusion. Holland, *Idealists, Scoundrels, and the Lady,* p. 216.
96. Blumberg, *Celebrating the Immigrant,* p. 101; Kirshenblatt-Gimblett, *Destination Culture,* p. 180; Guillermo Gómez-Peña, *Dangerous Border Crossers: The Artist Talks Back* (New York: Routledge, 2000), p. 70.
97. Vivian Gornick, *Fierce Attachments* (Boston: Beacon Press, 1987), p. 47.
98. *New York Times,* April 14, 1976, op-ed; Wytrwal, *Behold! The Polish Americans,* p. 595.

2. Golden Door, Silver Screen

1. David Zarawik, *The Prime Time Jews* (Hanover, N.H.: Brandeis University Press, 2003), pp. 15, 62–71; Todd Gitlin, *Inside Prime Time* (New York: Pantheon, 1983), pp. 184–186; Vincent Brook, *Something Ain't Kosher Here: The Rise of the "Jewish" Sitcom* (New Brunswick: Rutgers University Press, 2003), pp. 47–48. Brook credits Michael Elkin, "Jews on TV: From 'The Goldbergs' to 'Hill Street's' Cops," *Jewish Exponent,* June 28, 1985, p. 25; J. Hoberman and Jeffrey Shandler, eds., *Entertaining America: Jews, Movies, and Broadcasting* (Prince-

ton: Princeton University Press, 2003), pp. 47–76; Paley quoted in David Halberstam, *The Powers That Be* (New York: Dell, 1980), p. 50.

2. As a start. Just beyond the horizon of ethnic blockbusters like *The Godfather* is a raft of minor ethnic classics *(The Angel Levine, Mac, Lost in Yonkers, School Ties, Mermaids, Glengarry Glen Ross, Slums of Beverly Hills)*. There are gangster films *(Bugsy, Lepke, Mean Streets, Once Upon a Time in America, Billy Bathgate, The Untouchables, Mobsters, Miller's Crossing, Hoodlum, Bella Mafia, Casino, Suicide Kings, Bound)* and gangster comedies *(The Gang That Couldn't Shoot Straight, Prizzi's Honor, Married to the Mob, Wise Guys, Analyze This, Analyze That)*. There are cop and detective films *(Serpico, V. I. Warshawski, Homicide, A Stranger among Us)*, boxing films (the *Rocky* series, *Raging Bull, Rocky Marciano*), films of labor organization and radicalism *(F.I.S.T., The Molly Maguires, Blue Collar, The Way We Were, Reds, Norma Rae)*; show biz films *(Enter Laughing, The Producers, Lenny, A Star Is Born, Zelig, Mr. Saturday Night, Private Parts)*; sex work films *(Midnight Cowboy, Jade, Showgirls, Claire Dolan, American Virgin)*; films of delusion *(Dementia 13, Where's Poppa?, The King of Comedy)*; and dance films and musicals *(Funny Lady, Finian's Rainbow, The Jazz Singer, Fame, Yentl, Flashdance, Chicago)*. There are love stories *(The Heartbreak Kid, Annie Hall, Crossing Delancey, Torch Song Trilogy, Baby It's You, Jungle Fever, Mystic Pizza, The Bridges of Madison County, Kissing Jessica Stein)* and nostalgic love notes to the old neighborhood *(Italianamerican, Brighton Beach Memoirs, Radio Days, Avalon, Liberty Heights)*. There are films of the ethnic ghetto *(A Bronx Tale, Do the Right Thing, Southie, Summer of Sam)* and films of mobility *out* of the ghetto *(Broadway Bound, Next Stop Greenwich Village, Staying Alive, The Godfather Part III)*. There are cartoons *(American Pop, An American Tail)*, films of the American West *(The Frisco Kid, Blazing Saddles, Heaven's Gate, Far and Away)*, Catskills resort movies *(Dirty Dancing, A Walk on the Moon)*, road films *(My Cousin Vinny, Stranger Than Paradise)*, and bowling movies *(Kingpin, The Big Lebowski)*. There are films about Jewish-American Princesses *(Goodbye Columbus, Heartburn, Private Benjamin)* and films about matrimony *(Polish Wedding, My Big Fat Greek Wedding)*. Which still leaves treatments of the postwar refugee *(The Pawnbroker, Harold and Maude, Sophie's Choice)*, the Cold War refugee *(Moscow on the Hudson)*, and explicit treatments of departure, migration, and resettlement *(America America, The Godfather Part II, Hester Street, Ragtime, Green Card)*. There are also a number of "Old World" films of presumed interest

to American ethnics-in-diaspora *(Cast a Giant Shadow, The Hiding Place, Masada, Voyage of the Damned, Michael Collins, Schindler's List, Riverdance, The Pianist).*

3. See, for example, Lee Lourdeaux, *Italian and Irish Filmmakers in America: Ford, Capra, Coppola, and Scorsese* (Philadelphia: Temple University Press, 1990); Lawrence Friedman, *The Cinema of Martin Scorsese* (New York: Continuum, 1999), pp. 20–38; Jack Hunter, *Robert De Niro: Movie Top Ten* (London: Creation, 1999); Hoberman and Shandler, *Entertaining America;* Joe Eszterhas, *Hollywood Animal* (New York: Knopf, 2004), pp. 142–164.

4. Examples of the group-based approach include Randall Miller, ed., *The Kaleidoscopic Lens: How Hollywood Views Ethnic Groups* (Englewood, N.J.: Ozer, 1980); Les Keyser and Barbara Keyser, *Hollywood and the Catholic Church* (Chicago: Loyola University Press, 1984); Hoberman and Shandler, *Entertaining America;* Thomas Ferraro, *Feeling Italian and the Art of American Culture* (New York: New York University Press, 2005).

5. Bruce Curtis, "Aspects of Sitcom," in Jim Cook, ed., *Television Sitcom* (London: BFI, 1982), p. 9.

6. Video packaging, *Once Upon a Time in America,* Warner Home Video, 1991.

7. Hasia Diner, *Lower East Side Memories: A Place in America* (Princeton: Princeton University Press, 2000), pp. 79–80.

8. Allon Schoener, *Portal to America: The Lower East Side, 1875–1925* (New York: Holt Rinehart, 1967), preface, n.p.

9. Diner, *Lower East Side Memories,* p. 80.

10. A fair sampling includes John F. Kennedy, *A Nation of Immigrants* [1958] (New York: Harper and Row, 1964); Moses Rischin, *The Promised City: New York's Jews, 1870–1914* (New York: 1962); Jacob Riis, *How the Other Half Lives* [1890] (New York: Hill and Wang, 1971); Schoener, *Portal to America;* Irving Howe, *World of Our Fathers* (New York: Harper, 1976); Ronald Sanders, *The Downtown Jews: Portrait of an Immigrant Generation* (New York: Dover, 1969); Center for Migration Studies, *Images: A Pictorial History of Italian Americans* (New York: Center for Migration Studies, 1981); Joseph Byron, *New York Life at the Turn of the Century in Photographs* (New York: Dover, 1985); Pamela Reeves, *Ellis Island: Gateway to the American Dream* (New York: 1998); David Brownstone, Irene Franck, and Douglass Brownstone, *Island of Hope, Island of Tears* [1979] (New York: Barnes and Noble, 2000). The photographic canon includes Edwin Levick's

crowded steamer; Lewis Hine's Italian family on an Ellis Island ferry; Joseph Byron's deck of the *USS Pennland;* an anonymous shot of the *USS Westernland;* Lewis Hine's Italian family with bundles and valises; various almost identical depictions of the Ellis Island medical examination; Underwood and Underwood's Ellis Island eye exam; anonymous overhead shots of immigrants waiting to be processed in the Great Hall at Ellis Island; crowded street scenes of the Lower East Side, usually either Hester or Mullberry Street; various Riis and Hine depictions of immigrant children at work; and numerous sweatshop scenes.

11. Deborah Dash Moore and David Lobenstine, "Photographing the Lower East Side: A Century's Work," in Hasia Diner, Jeffrey Shandler, and Beth Wenger, eds., *Remembering the Lower East Side* (Bloomington: University of Indiana Press, 2000), pp. 30–34; Marin Stange, *Symbols of Ideal Life: Social Documentary Photography in America, 1890–1950* (New York, 1989), p. 1.

12. Moore and Lobenstine, "Photographing the Lower East Side," p. 30; Alan Trachtenberg, *Reading American Photographs: Images as History* (New York: Hill and Wang, 1989), pp. 164–230.

13. Video packaging, *Once Upon a Time in America;* Stange, *Symbols of Ideal Life,* p. 2.

14. Moore and Lobenstine, "Photographing the Lower East Side," pp. 34–35.

15. Adrian Martin, *Once Upon a Time in America* (London: British Film Institute, 1998), p. 31; Moore and Lobenstine, "Photographing the Lower East Side," p. 28; Marita Sturken, *Tangled Memories: The Vietnam War, the AIDS Epidemic, and the Politics of Remembering* (Berkeley: University of California Press, 1997), p. 90.

16. David Lubin, *Titanic* (London: British Film Institute, 1999), pp. 116–121.

17. Stanley Creen, *Hollywood Musicals Year by Year,* 2nd ed. (Milwaukee: Hal Leonard, 1999).

18. *Newsweek,* Nov. 15, 1971, p. 114; Joel Samberg, *Reel Jewish* (Middle Village, N.Y.: Jonathan David, 2000), p. 11.

19. *New York Times,* Nov. 28, 1971, pp. 178, 179; *Newsweek,* Nov. 15, 1971, p. 114.

20. Rick Altman, *The American Film Musical* (Bloomington: Indiana University Press, 1987), p. 32.

21. Ibid., p. 33. Alberto Sandoval Sanchez, "*West Side Story:* A Puerto Rican Reading of 'America,'" in Clara Rodriguez, ed., *Latin Looks: Im-*

ages of Latinas and Latinos in the U.S. Media (Westview: Westview Press, 1997), pp. 164–179.

22. Eric Lott, *Love and Theft: Blackface Minstrelsy and the American Working Class* (New York: Oxford University Press, 1995); Jeffrey Melnick, *A Right to Sing the Blues: African Americans, Jews, and American Popular Song* (Cambridge, Mass.: Harvard University Press, 1999); Michael Rogin, *Blackface, White Noise: Jewish Immigrants in the Hollywood Melting Pot* (Berkeley: University of California Press, 1996); W. T. Lhamon, Jr., *Raising Cain: Blackface Performance from Jim Crow to Hip Hop* (Cambridge, Mass.: Harvard University Press, 1998); Michael Alexander, *Jazz Age Jews* (Princeton: Princeton University Press, 2003); William Williams, *'Twas Only an Irishman's Dream: The Image of Ireland and the Irish in American Popular Song Lyrics, 1800–1920* (Urbana: University of Illinois Press, 1996); Annemarie Bean, James Hatch, and Brooks McNamara, eds., *Inside the Minstrel Mask: Readings in Nineteenth-Century Blackface Minstrelsy* (Hanover: Wesleyan University Press, 1996).

23. As Chris Messenger notes, when Mario Puzo had Michael and Kay go to see *Carousel* in *The Godfather,* he was citing "American popular culture's most renowned melting pot entertainment, the American musical with its class, racial, and ethnic lines always highlighted, then recontained in moral statements." *The Godfather and American Culture: How the Corleones Became "Our Gang"* (Albany: State University of New York Press, 2002), pp. 118–119.

24. Bernard Schwartz, *Behind Bakke: Affirmative Action and the Supreme Court* (New York: New York University Press, 1988), p. 13.

25. Schwartz, *Behind Bakke,* p. 14; Joel Dreyfuss and Charles Laurence III, *The Bakke Case: The Politics of Inequality* (New York: Harcourt Brace Jovanovich, 1979); Howard Ball, *The Bakke Case: Race, Education, and Affirmative Action* (Lawrence, Kan.: University of Kansas Press, 2000); Peter Wood, *Diversity: The Invention of a Concept* (San Francisco: Encounter, 2003), pp. 99–145.

26. Schwartz, *Behind Bakke,* pp. 18, 22, 23; *Allan Bakke v. Regents of the University of California,* 18 Cal 3d 34; 45 USLW 3570.

27. Schwartz, *Behind Bakke,* pp. 71, 72, 89, 128, 148.

28. See, for example, Ronald Formisano, *Boston against Bussing: Race, Class, and Ethnicity in the 1960s and 1970s* (Chapel Hill: University of North Carolina Press, 1991); Alan Lupo, *Liberty's Chosen Home: The Politics of Violence in Boston* (Boston: Beacon, 1988); J. Anthony Lucas, *Common Ground: A Turbulent Decade in the Lives of Three American*

Families (New York: Vintage, 1986); Paul Kleppner, *Chicago Divided: The Making of a Black Mayor* (Chicago: Northern Illinois University Press, 1985).

29. Kermit the Frog's claim to fame, a song called "It's Not Easy Bein' Green," itself represented Children's Television Workshop's commentary on whiteness at the dawn of the "multicultural" era.

30. Mary Ten Thor et al., *The Bakke Symposium* (Sacramento: Uncommon Lawyers' Workshop, 1977), p. 171.

31. David Remnick, *King of the World* (New York: Random House, 1998), p. 25.

32. *Los Angeles Times*, Nov. 14, 1999, Calendar, p. 5.

33. Ibid., Nov. 17, 1999, Sec F, p. 1; *Chicago Sun-Times*, Dec. 10, 1999, weekend plus, p. 37; *Daily News*, Nov. 15, 1999, p. 33.

34. David Mamet, *The Old Religion* (New York: Free Press, 1997); Jeffrey Melnick, *Black-Jewish Relations on Trial: Leo Frank and Jim Conley in the New South* (Jackson: University of Mississippi Press, 2000).

35. Mary Waters, *Ethnic Options: Choosing Identities in America* (Berkeley: University of California Press, 1990).

36. From *Erin Brockovich; Working Girl; Mystic Pizza; My Cousin Vinny; A Walk on the Moon; Fargo;* and *The Jazz Singer*, respectively.

37. Arthur Laurents, *West Side Story* [1957] (New York: Dell, 1965), p. 137.

38. Rachel Buff, *Immigration and the Political Economy of Home: West Indian Brooklyn and American Indian Minneapolis* (Berkeley: University of California Press, 2000), pp. 38–39.

39. David Thompson and Ian Christie, eds., *Scorsese on Scorsese* (London: Faber and Faber, 1989), p. 48.

40. Jeff Young, *Kazan: The Master Director Discusses His Films* (New York: Newmarket, 1999), p. 277.

41. Gerald Mast, "Woody Allen: The Neurotic Jew as American Clown," in Sarah Blacher Cohen, ed., *Jewish Wry: Essays on Jewish Humor* (Detroit: Wayne State University Press, 1987), pp. 131–133.

42. Quoted in Brook, *Something Ain't Kosher*, p. 82.

43. Ethan Coen, "Introduction," in Ethan Coen and Joel Coen, *Fargo* (London: Faber and Faber, 1996), pp. ix–x.

44. Ibid., p. x.

3. Old World Bound

1. Of course one might point back to the success of Philip Roth's *Goodbye, Columbus* (1959), Bernard Malamud's *The Assistant* (1957), Saul Bellow's *Adventures of Augie March* (1953), and even back to the wild

popularity of Betty Smith's *A Tree Grows in Brooklyn* (1943)—here again one begins to chafe at the very term "revival."

2. John Higham, "Introduction," in Abraham Cahan, *The Rise of David Levinsky* [1917] (New York: Harper, 1960), p. xii.

3. Bernard G. Richards, "Abraham Cahan Cast in a New Role," in Abraham Cahan, *Yekl, the Imported Bridegroom and Other Stories* (New York: Dover, 1970); Mary Antin, *The Promised Land* [1912] (New York: Penguin, 1997); Morris Rosenfeld, *Songs from the Ghetto* (Boston: Small, Maynard, 1900); Finley Peter Dunne, *Mr. Dooley in the Hearts of His Countrymen* (Boston: Small, Maynard, 1899); Israel Zangwill, *The Melting Pot* [1908] (New York: Macmillan, 1914).

4. On the longer history of "ethnic literature" in the United States, see esp. Werner Sollors and Marc Shell, eds., *Multilingual America: Transnationalism, Ethnicity, and the Languages of American Literature* (New York: New York University Press, 1998); Werner Sollors and Marc Shell, eds., *A Multilingual Anthology of American Literature* (New York: New York University Press, 2000); Werner Sollors, *Beyond Ethnicity: Consent and Descent in American Culture* (New York: Oxford University Press, 1988); William Boelhower, *Through a Glass Darkly: Ethnic Semiosis in American Literature* (New York: Oxford University Press, 1987); Jules Chametzky, *Our Decentralized Literature: Cultural Mediations in Selected Jewish and Southern Writers* (Boston: University of Massachusetts Press, 1987); Mary Dearborn, *Pocahontas' Daughters: Gender and Ethnicity in American Culture* (New York: Oxford University Press, 1987); Magdalena Zaborowska, *How We Found America: Reading Gender through East European Narratives* (Chapel Hill: University of North Carolina Press, 1995); Laura Browder, *Slippery Characters: Ethnic Impersonators and American Identities* (Chapel Hill: University of North Carolina Press, 2000).

5. Samuel Ornitz, *Haunch, Paunch and Jowl* [1923] (New York: 1969), p. 68; Cahan, *Rise of David Levinsky*, p. 530.

6. Harry Mark Petrakis, *A Dream of Kings* (New York: Random House, 1966), pp. 3–4.

7. Ibid., pp. 83, 107–108.

8. Ibid., pp. 10, 134.

9. Ibid., pp. 116, 16, 105, 26.

10. Ibid., p. 132.

11. Anne Halley, "Afterword," in Mary Doyle Curran, *The Parish and the Hill* [1948] (New York: Feminist Press, 1986), p. 260.

12. On the "American Wake" see Kirby Miller, *Emigrants and Exiles: Ire-*

land and the Irish Exodus to North America (New York: Oxford University Press, 1985); Thomas Gallagher, *Paddy's Lament, Ireland 1846–1847: Prelude to Hatred* (New York: Harvest, 1987).

13. Curran, *Parish and the Hill,* pp. 2–3, 68.

14. Ibid., pp. 2, 49.

15. Ibid., pp. 49, 95–96.

16. Ibid., pp. 97, 27.

17. Ibid., pp. 25, 77.

18. Mario Puzo, *The Fortunate Pilgrim* [1964] (New York: Bantam, 1985), pp. 143, 252, 185, 242. Compare Thomas Ferraro, *Feeling Italian and the Art of American Culture* (New York: New York University Press, 2005), chap. 4.

19. Werner Sollors, "Literature and Ethnicity," in Stephen Thernstrom, ed., *The Harvard Encyclopedia of American Ethnic Groups* (Cambridge, Mass.: Harvard University Press, 1980), p. 663.

20. Puzo, *Fortunate Pilgrim,* pp. 83, 129–130.

21. Ibid., p. 61. On the specifically "ethnic" dimension of the rising postwar suburb, see esp. Rosalyn Baxandall and Elizabeth Ewen, *Picture Windows: How the Suburbs Happened* (New York: Basic, 2000), pp. 108–109, 131, 233.

22. Puzo, *Fortunate Pilgrim,* pp. 185, 37, 193, 100.

23. Michael Harrington, "Afterword," in Mike Gold, *Jews without Money* [1930] (New York: Avon, 1965), pp. 232, 233.

24. Ibid., pp. 232–233.

25. In *Blood of My Blood,* Richard Gambino included a chapter titled "The Problem of the Mafia Image," and plaintive references to *The Godfather* pepper the book throughout. A recent collection of essays on "the real Italian American experience" carries the title *Beyond the Godfather* (1997). Here Gambino laments that "one film producer responded sincerely to the idea of an Italian American *Roots,* 'It's been done . . . *The Godfather.*'" But what exactly is a "crime family"? Gambino wants to know. Richard Gambino, *Blood of My Blood: The Dilemma of the Italian-Americans* [1974] (Toronto: Guernica, 1998); Kenneth Ciongoli and Jay Parini, eds., *Beyond the Godfather: Italian American Writers on the Real Italian American Experience* (Hanover, N.H.: University Press of New England, 1997), pp. 278, 279.

26. Mary Waters, *Ethnic Options* (Berkeley: University of California Press, 1990), p. 142. On the allure of the Italian family, see also *New York Times,* March 1, 1970, sec. VI, p. 22.

27. Mario Puzo, "Choosing a Dream: Italiana in Hell's Kitchen," quoted

in Chris Messenger, *The Godfather and American Culture: How the Corleones Became "Our Gang"* (Albany: State University of New York Press, 2002), p. 54.

28. Gambino, *Blood of My Blood*, p. 309; Messenger, *Godfather and American Culture*, p. 39. On the *famiglia* values appeal, see Nick Browne, *Francis Ford Coppola's The Godfather Trilogy* (Cambridge: Cambridge University Press, 2000), pp. 88–90, 170–171.

29. Daniel Patrick Moynihan, *The Negro Family: The Case for National Action* (Washington, D.C.: Government Printing Office, 1965).

30. *New York Times*, June 5, 1965, p. 1; June 6, 1965, editorial; July 19, 1965, p. 1; July 30, 1965, p. 29; Aug. 27, 1965, p. 13; Oct. 26, 1965, p. 20; Nov. 25, 1965, p. 52; Nov. 28, 1965, sec. VI, p. 60; Dec. 2, 1965, p. 41; Dec. 5, 1965, p. 1; Dec. 12, 1965, pp. 43, 74; Dec. 17, 1965, p. 22; *New Republic*, July 24, 1965, p. 4; *Wall Street Journal*, Aug. 16, 1965, p. 1, and Nov. 30, 1965, p. 1; *New Yorker*, Sept. 11, 1965, p. 116; *Nation*, Nov. 22, 1965, p. 38; *Commonweal*, Sept. 17, 1965, p. 649, and Oct. 15, 1965, p. 47; *America*, Oct. 30, 1965, p. 492, and Feb. 25, 1967, p. 269; *Christian Century*, Dec. 15, 1965, p. 1531; *Newsweek*, Aug. 22, 1966, p. 41, and Dec. 6, 1965, p. 38; *Dissent*, March/April 1966, p. 133; *Time*, Sept. 9, 1966, p. 21; *New York Review of Books*, Oct. 1965; *Look*, May 17, 1966, p. 27; *New York Times Magazine*, Sept. 11, 1966, p. 24; *National Review*, Aug. 8, 1967, p. 842; *Harper*, Aug. 1967, p. 6; *Life*, Nov. 3, 1967, p. 72; *Science*, Aug. 23, 1968, p. 756; *Science News*, Oct. 19, 1968, p. 393. On the long-term relationship between race, patriarchy, and "family values," see Ruth Feldstein, *Motherhood in Black and White: Race and Sex in American Liberalism, 1930–1965* (Ithaca: Cornell University Press, 2000).

31. Mario Puzo, *The Godfather* [1969] (New York: Signet, 1978), p. 288.

32. Ibid., pp. 37, 145, 171, 238, 275, 361, 363.

33. Richard Alba, *Ethnic Identity: The Transformation of White America* (New Haven: Yale University Press, 1990), p. 316.

34. Philip Roth, *Goodbye, Columbus* [1959] (New York: Vintage, 1987), p. 90; June Sochen, "From Sophie Tucker to Barbra Streisand: Jewish Women Entertainers as Reformers," in Joyce Antler, ed., *Talking Back: Images of Jewish Women in American Popular Culture* (Hanover, N.H.: Brandeis University Press, 1998), pp. 75–77; Sarah Blacher Cohen, "The Unkosher Comediennes: From Sophie Tucker to Joan Rivers," in Sarah Blacher Cohen, ed., *Jewish Wry: Essays on Jewish Humor* (Detroit: Wayne State University Press, 1987), esp. pp. 115–123; Gerald Mast, "Woody Allen: The Neurotic Jew as American Clown," in Cohen, *Jewish Wry*, p. 130; Alix Kates Shulman, *Memoirs of an Ex-*

Prom Queen [1969] (New York: Penguin, 1997); Marge Piercy, *Small Changes* [1973] (New York: Ballantine, 1997); Mary Gordon, *The Company of Women* (New York: Ballantine, 1980); Marilyn French, *The Women's Room* (New York: Simon and Schuster, 1977); Michael Flamini, "'Pa cent' Anni, Dr. Melfi': Psychotherapy in the Italian American Community," in Regina Berreca, *A Sitdown with the Sopranos: Watching Italian American Culture on TV's Most Talked-about Series* (New York: Palgrave, 2002), pp. 113–127.

35. Beth Bailey, *Sex in the Heartland* (Cambridge, Mass.: Harvard University Press, 1999), pp. 15, 16, 17, 13–44.

36. Ibid., p. 16.

37. Margot Adler, *Heretic's Heart: A Journey through Spirit and Revolution* (Boston: Beacon, 2003), p. x.

38. Bailey, *Sex in the Heartland,* 45–74; quotation from p. 50.

39. Philip Roth, *Portnoy's Complaint* [1967] (New York: Vintage, 1994), pp. 118–119.

40. Riv-Ellen Prell, *Fighting to Become Americans: Assimilation and the Trouble between Jewish Women and Jewish Men* (Boston: Beacon, 1999), p. 210; Charlotte Baum, Paula Hyman, and Sonya Michel, *The Jewish Woman in America* (New York: Plume, 1975), pp. xii–xiii.

41. Roth, *Portnoy's Complaint,* p. 98.

42. Matthew Frye Jacobson, *Special Sorrows: The Diasporic Imagination of Irish, Polish, and Jewish Immigrants in the United States* (Cambridge, Mass.: Harvard University Press, 1995), pp. 103–105; Susan Kress, "Women and Marriage in Abraham Cahan's Fiction," *Studies in American Jewish Literature,* 3 (1983), pp. 26–39; Leslie Fiedler, *Fiedler on the Roof* (Boston: David Godine, 1991), p. 12.

43. Roth, *Portnoy's Complaint,* pp. 145, 146–147.

44. Ibid., pp. 216–217, 209.

45. Ibid., pp. 216–217, 218, 235.

46. Ibid., pp. 253, 254, 258, 259.

47. Ibid., p. 265.

48. Ibid., pp. 266, 268, 271.

49. Erica Jong, *Fear of Flying* [1973] (New York: Signet, 2003), pp. 436, 201. The *New York Review of Books* is quoted on the cover.

50. Ibid., pp. 25, 138.

51. Ibid., pp. 201, 208.

52. Ibid., pp. 19, 73, 74.

53. Ibid., pp. 75, 76, 29–30, 84.

54. Ibid., pp. 84, 85, 196, 86.

55. Ibid., pp. 37, 38, 39.

56. Ibid., pp. 320, 351; Betty Friedan, *The Feminine Mystique* (New York: Norton, 1963), p. 282 ff.

57. Judith Krantz, *Sex and Shopping: Confessions of a Nice Jewish Girl* (New York: St. Martin's, 2001); Kate Simon, *Bronx Primitive: Portraits of a Childhood* [1982] (New York: Penguin, 1997); Alix Kates Shulman, *Memoirs of an Ex-Prom Queen* [1969] (New York: Penguin Books, 1997); Camille Paglia, "Madonna—Finally a Real Feminist," and Joyce Millman, "Primadonna," in Adam Sexton, ed., *Desperately Seeking Madonna* (New York: Delta, 1993), pp. 53–57, 167–169; Ann Brooks, *Postfeminisms: Feminism, Cultural Theory, and Cultural Forms* (New York: Routledge and Kegan Paul, 1997), pp. 147–162; Michelangelo Signorile, *Queer in America: Sex, the Media, and the Closets of Power* [1993] (Madison: University of Wisconsin Press, 2003), pp. 18–35; Vincent Brook, *Something Ain't Kosher Here: The Rise of the "Jewish" Sitcom* (New Brunswick: Rutgers University Press, 2003), pp. 154–163; Jeffrey Eugenides, *Middlesex* (New York: Picador, 2002).

58. See, for example, the *New York Times,* March 18, 1991, p. B1; March 21, 1991, p. A23; Jan. 25, 1992, p. 22; Feb. 19, 1992, p. B2; Feb. 29, 1992, p. L23; March 6, 1992, p. B3. On the controversy in Boston, see the *New York Times,* March 6, 1992, p. B3; March 14, 1992, p. 6.

59. *New York Times,* March 15, 1991, p. A32; Jan. 25, 1992, p. 22; March 17, 1992, p. A24.

60. Peter Novick, *The Holocaust in American Life* (New York: Houghton Mifflin, 2000).

61. Haim Chertok, *Stealing Home: Israel Bound and Rebound* (New York: Fordham University Press, 1988), pp. 8, 64–65.

62. Alan Dershowitz, *Chutzpah* (Boston: Little Brown, 1991), p. 7.

63. Meir Kahane, *Time to Go Home* (Los Angeles: Nash, 1972), pp. 100–101, 260, 279; Meir Kahane, *Our Challenge* (Radnor, Penn.: Chilton, 1974), p. 113; Meir Kahane, *Uncomfortable Questions for Comfortable Jews* (Secaucus, N.J.: Lyle Stuart, 1987), p. 324.

64. Chertok, *Stealing Home,* p. 64; Janowitz quoted in Saul Bellow, *To Jerusalem and Back: A Personal Account* (New York: Viking, 1976), p. 166; Letty Cottin Pogrebin, *Deborah, Golda, and Me: Being Female and Jewish in America* (New York: Crown, 1991), pp. 213, 155; Melvin Urofsky, *We Are One! American Jewry and Israel* (Garden City: Anchor Doubleday, 1978), p. 392.

65. Bellow, *To Jerusalem and Back,* p. 135.

66. Dershowitz, *Chutzpah,* pp. 234–235; Philip Roth, *The Counterlife*

(New York: Penguin, 1988), p. 180. See also Tony Kushner and Alisa Solomon, *Wrestling with Zion: Progressive Jewish-American Responses to the Israeli–Palestinian Conflict* (New York: Grove, 2003); Paul Breines, *Tough Jews: Political Fantasies and the Moral Dilemma of American Jewry* (New York: Basic, 1990); Irena Klepfisz, *Dreams of an Insomniac: Jewish Feminist Essays, Speeches, and Diatribes* (Portland: Eighth Mountain Press, 1990), pp. 129–131.

67. Melanie Kaye/Kantrowitz, "In the Middle of the Barbeque She Brings up Israel," in *My Jewish Face and Other Stories* (San Francisco: Spinster–Aunt Lute, 1990), p. 228.

68. Kaye/Kantrowitz, "In the Middle of the Barbeque," p. 231. See also Kushner and Solomon, *Wrestling with Zion.*

69. Pogrebin, *Deborah, Golda, and Me,* p. 147; Roth, *The Counterlife,* pp. 166–167.

70. Roth, *The Counterlife,* p. 125, echoing Ellen Willis, "Next Year in Jerusalem" [1976], in *Beginning to See the Light: Pieces of a Decade* (New York: Alfred A. Knopf, 1981), pp. 261–292.

71. Roth, *The Counterlife,* pp. 124–125.

72. Ibid., pp. 259, 260.

73. Philip Roth, *Operation Shylock: A Confession* (New York: Simon and Schuster, 1993), p. 158.

74. Ibid., pp. 81, 193. Alfred Dreyfus was a French officer charged with treason. His trial in the 1890s became the occasion for an outpouring of anti-semitism in Western Europe. His plight (and, by extension, the vulnerability of all Jews) in its turn became an important element of the argument for Jewish statehood advanced by Theodore Herzl, the chief architect of modern Zionism.

75. Roth, *Operation Shylock,* p. 388.

76. Kaye/Kantrowitz, "The Woman in Purple," in *My Jewish Face,* p. 172.

77. Henry Roth, *Call It Sleep* [1934] (New York: Avon, 1964), p. 9.

78. Walter Allen, "Afterword," in Roth, *Call It Sleep* [1934] (New York: Avon, 1971), p. 442.

79. Henry Roth, *Mercy of a Rude Stream* (New York: Picador USA, 1994), pp. 66, 161.

80. Henry Roth, *A Diving Rock on the Hudson* (New York: Picador USA, 1995), pp. 46–47.

81. Henry Roth, *From Bondage* (New York: Picador USA, 1996), p. 106; Roth, *Diving Rock,* p. 70.

82. Roth, *From Bondage*, p. 29, italics in original.
83. Ibid., pp. 29, 67, italics in original.
84. Ibid., p. 69, italics in original; Roth, *Mercy of a Rude Stream*, pp. 201–202; Mario Materassi quoted in Robert Weil, "Afterword," in Henry Roth, *Requiem for Harlem* (New York: St. Martin's, 1998), p. 277.

4. The Immigrant's Bootstraps

1. Nathan Glazer and Daniel Patrick Moynihan, *Beyond the Melting Pot* [1963] (Cambridge: MIT Press, 1970), p. xcvii; Will Herberg, *Protestant—Catholic—Jew: An Essay in American Religious Sociology* [1955] (New York: Anchor, 1960), p. 20.
2. Glazer and Moynihan, *Beyond the Melting Pot*, p. 26. For Glazer's earliest experimentation with this idea, see "America's Ethnic Pattern: 'Melting Pot' or 'Nation of Nations'?" *Commentary*, 15:4, April 1953, pp. 401–408. Lila Corwin Berman, "Presenting Jews: Jewishness and America, 1920–1965," Ph.D. dissertation, Yale University, 2004.
3. Irving Kristol, "The Negro Today Is Like the Immigrant of Yesterday" [1966], in Peter Rose, *Nation of Nations* (Washington, D.C.: University Press of America, 1972), pp. 197–210.
4. Rogers Smith, *Civic Ideals: Conflicting Visions of Citizenship in U.S. History* (New Haven: Yale University Press, 1999); Gary Gerstle, *The American Crucible: Race and Nation in the Twentieth Century* (Princeton: Princeton University Press, 2002); Matthew Frye Jacobson, *Whiteness of a Different Color: European Immigrants and the Alchemy of Race* (Cambridge, Mass.: Harvard University Press, 1998), and *Barbarian Virtues: The United States Encounters Foreign Peoples at Home and Abroad, 1876–1917* (New York: Hill and Wang, 2000).
5. Compare, for example, Gunnar Myrdal, *An American Dilemma: The Negro Problem and Modern Democracy* [1944] (New York: Transaction, 1996), or Gordon Allport, *The Nature of Prejudice* [1953] (New York: Perseus, 1988), against Stokely Carmichael and Charles Hamilton, *Black Power: The Politics of Liberation in America* [1967] (New York: Vintage, 1992); Ronald Takaki, *Iron Cages: Race and Culture in Nineteenth-Century America* (New York: Oxford University Press, 1979); or Michael Omi and Howard Winant, *Racial Formation in the United States: From the 1960s to the 1990s*, 2nd ed. (New York: Routledge, 1994).

6. Mary Waters, *Ethnic Options: Choosing Identities in America* (Berkeley: University of California Press, 1990).

7. Nathan Glazer, "White Noise," *New Republic,* Oct. 12, 1998, pp. 44, 46; Kristol, "The Negro Today," p. 207.

8. Mark Gerson, *The Neoconservative Vision: From the Cold War to Culture Wars* (New York: Madison Books, 1997), p. 272.

9. Michael Lind, *Up from Conservatism: Why the Right Is Wrong for America* (New York: Free Press, 1996), pp. 15–96; Angela Dillard, *Guess Who's Coming to Dinner Now? Multicultural Conservatism in America* (New York: New York University Press, 2002). On the emergence of neoconservatism from the ranks of the left, see Irving Kristol, *Reflections of a Neoconservative: Looking Back, Looking Ahead* (New York: Basic, 1983), pp. 3–13; Peter Steinfels, *The Neoconservatives: The Men Who Are Changing America's Politics* (New York: Simon and Schuster, 1979), pp. 25–48; and the "Generational Perspectives" of Martin Peretz and Norman Podhoretz in Peter Collier and David Horowitz, eds., *Second Thoughts: Former Radicals Look Back at the Sixties* (New York: Madison, 1989), pp. 171, 193.

10. Kevin Phillips, *The Emerging Republican Majority* (New Rochelle: Arlington House, 1969), pp. 461, 471; Garry Wills, *Nixon Agonistes: The Crisis of the Self-Made Man* (New York: Mentor, 1969), pp. 247–251, 257–272.

11. Lind, *Up from Conservatism,* p. 128.

12. Stefano Luconi, *From Paesani to White Ethnics: The Italian Experience in Philadelphia* (Albany: State University of New York Press, 2000), p. 144; Marlene Pomper, ed., *The Election of 1976: Reports and Interpretations* (New York: David McKay Co., 1977), p. 61; Marlene Michaels Pomper, ed., *The Election of 1980: Reports and Interpretations* (Chatham, N.J.: Chatham House, 1981), p. 71; Marlene Michaels Pomper, ed., *The Election of 1984: Reports and Interpretations* (Chatham, N.J.: Chatham House, 1985), pp. 67–69; Gerald Pomper et al., *The Election of 1988: Reports and Interpretations* (Chatham, N.J.: Chatham House, 1989), pp. 133–134; Gerald Pomper et al., *The Election of 1992: Reports and Interpretations* (Chatham, N.J.: Chatham House, 1993), pp. 138–139; Steven Cohen and Robert Kapsis, "Religion, Ethnicity, and Party Affiliation in the U.S.: Evidence from the Pooled Electoral Surveys, 1968–1972," *Social Forces,* 56 (1972); Joan Fee, "Religion, Ethnicity, and Class in American Electoral Behavior," in William Crotty, ed., *The Party Symbol: Readings on Political Parties* (San Francisco: W. H. Freeman, 1980). Although the samples become very small when numbers

are broken out for specific ethnicities, still there is a wonderful electoral portraiture in Virginia Sapiro, Steven Rosenstone, and the National Election Studies, *1948–1998 Data File* [dataset] (Ann Arbor, Mich.: University of Michigan, Center for Political Studies, 1999). Figures for 2004 were not yet available as this book went to press, though preliminary assessments suggest that Bush's victory fit the long-term pattern of combined pluralities in the Catholic and blue-collar votes.

13. Thomas Byrne Edsall and Mary Edsall, *Chain Reaction: The Impact of Race, Rights, and Taxes on American Politics* (New York: W. W. Norton, 1992), pp. 60, 72–73; William Prendergast, *The Catholic Voter in American Politics: The Passing of the Democratic Monolith* (Washington, D.C.: Georgetown University Press, 1999), pp. 149–169. See also Stefano Luconi, "Frank L. Rizzo and the Whitening of Italian Americans in Philadelphia," in Jennifer Guglielmo and Salvatore Salerno, eds., *Are Italians White? How Race Is Made in America* (New York: Routledge, 2003), pp. 177–191; Samuel Friedman, *The Inheritance: How Three Families and the American Political Majority Moved from Left to Right* (New York: Simon and Schuster, 1996), esp. Part III; Richard Krickus, *Pursuing the American Dream: White Ethnics and the New Populism* (New York: Anchor, 1976), pp. 253–304; Sandy Zipp, "The New Ethnicity: The Culture and Politics of the Nation and Identity in the Cities of the 1970s," unpublished seminar paper in the author's possession.

14. Dillard, *Guess Who's Coming to Dinner Now?*, pp. 141, 142.

15. Ibid., p. 144.

16. Dan Carter, *From George Wallace to Newt Gingrich: Race in the Conservative Counterrevolution, 1963–1994* (Baton Rouge: Louisiana State University Press, 1996), p. 13. See also Luconi, *Paesani to White Ethnics*, pp. 144–145.

17. Phillips, *Emerging Republican Majority*, p. 470. See also Nathan Glazer, *Affirmative Discrimination: Ethnic Inequality and Public Policy* [1975] (Cambridge, Mass.: Harvard University Press, 1987), pp. 168–195; Edsall and Edsall, *Chain Reaction*.

18. Michael Novak, *The Rise of the Unmeltable Ethnics* (New York: Macmillan, 1971), p. 63.

19. Ibid., pp. 166, 237.

20. Ibid., pp. 293, 294–295.

21. Ibid., pp. xx, 71, 5, 301.

22. Jacobson, *Whiteness of a Different Color*, esp. Chaps. 2 and 3.

23. Novak, *Rise of the Unmeltable Ethnics*, pp. 166–167.

24. Ibid., pp. 72, 35.

25. Gary Dorrien, *The Neoconservative Mind: Politics, Culture, and the War of Ideology* (Philadelphia: Temple University Press, 1993), pp. 136–137; Irving Kristol, *Neoconservatism: The Autobiography of an Idea* (New York: Free Press, 1995), pp. 442, 454; Gertrude Himmelfarb, *One Nation, Two Cultures: A Searching Examination of American Society in the Aftermath of Our Cultural Revolution* (New York: Vintage, 2001), p. 79.

26. Joseph Dorman, *Arguing the World: The New York Intellectuals in Their Own Words* (New York: Free Press, 2000), pp. 1–24 and *passim*. To this group, Michael Lind adds those conservatives like Peter Brimelow and Arianna Stassinopoulos Huffington—in an earlier incarnation—who are themselves recent immigrants: the "immicons" (Lind, *Up from Conservatism*, pp. 83–84). See also Seth Foreman, *Blacks in the Jewish Mind: A Crisis of Liberalism* (New York: New York University Press, 1998), pp. 97–134.

27. Nathan Glazer, "Negroes and Jews: The New Challenge to Pluralism" [1964], in Norman Podhoretz, ed., *The Commentary Reader: Two Decades of Articles and Stories* (New York: Atheneum, 1967), pp. 397, 398.

28. Michael Staub, *Torn at the Roots: The Crisis of Jewish Liberalism in Postwar America* (New York: Columbia University Press, 2002), p. 151.

29. Kristol, *Neoconservatism*, p. 49.

30. Norman Podhoretz, "My Negro Problem—And Ours" [1963], in Podhoretz, *Commentary Reader*, pp. 376, 377, 381.

31. Ibid., pp. 382, 383.

32. Ibid., p. 387.

33. Glazer, *Affirmative Discrimination*, pp. 6, 7.

34. Ibid., pp. 3–32, 28, 29.

35. Ibid., p. xii; Dorman, *Arguing the World*, pp. 162–163. For a trenchant critique of Glazer's "ethnic pattern," see Ronald Takaki, "Reflections on Racial Patterns in America," in Ronald Takaki, ed., *From Different Shores: Perspectives on Race and Ethnicity in America* (New York: Oxford University Press, 1987), pp. 26–37. As late as 1997 Charles Murray continued to argue that the antidiscrimination measures of the 1964 Civil Rights Act could not be *proven* to have been necessary, since both anti-Irish and anti-semitic discrimination had faded away earlier in the century without the help of such legislation. *What It Means to Be a Libertarian: A Personal Interpretation* (New York: Broadway Books, 1997), pp. 84–87.

36. Glazer, *Affirmative Discrimination,* pp. 194, 201.

37. Peter Berger and Richard John Neuhaus, *To Empower People: From State to Civil Society* [1977] (Washington, D.C.: American Enterprise Institute, 1996), pp. 158 (emphasis in original), 160, 161.

38. This divergence was later corrected, when Novak and his colleagues at the American Enterprise Institute convened a symposium to discuss the policy implications of Berger's work. As the historian Gary Dorrien wryly notes, this symposium's accomplishments included a redefinition of the concept of "mediating structures" so spacious as to take in "such 'human scale' enterprises as General Dynamics and Exxon." Indeed, writes Dorrien, "The only megastructure worth worrying about, it turned out, was the state." Dorrien, *Neoconservative Mind,* p. 311; Richard Viguerie, *The Establishment vs. the People: Is a New Populist Revolt on the Way?* (Chicago: Regnary Gateway, 1983). As Gerald Horne argues, the right's "attack on government" was from the very start "in effect, an attack on blacks," so central were New Deal and Great Society programs to these discussions. *Fire This Time: The Watts Uprising and the 1960s* [1995] (New York: Da Capo, 1997), p. 15.

39. Dorrien, *Neoconservative Mind,* p. 265.

40. Glazer, *Affirmative Discrimination,* pp. 188–189.

41. Berger and Neuhaus, *To Empower People,* pp. 167, 205, 109.

42. Ibid., pp. 202, 203, 208.

43. Ibid., p. 51.

44. Nathan Glazer, *The Limits of Social Policy* (Cambridge, Mass.: Harvard University Press, 1988), p. 7.

45. Bruce Schulman, *The Seventies: The Great Shift in American Culture, Society, and Politics* (New York: Da Capo, 2002), p. 204.

46. Ronald Formisano, *Boston against Bussing: Race, Class, and Ethnicity in the 1960s and 1970s* (Chapel Hill: University of North Carolina Press, 1991), pp. 3, 35. See also Alan Lupo, *Liberty's Chosen Home: The Politics of Violence in Boston* (Boston: Beacon, 1988); J. Anthony Lucas, *Common Ground: A Turbulent Decade in the Lives of Three American Families* (New York: Vintage, 1986); Ellen Bigler, *American Conversations* (Philadelphia: Temple University Press, 1999); Paul Kleppner, *Chicago Divided: The Making of a Black Mayor* (Chicago: Northern Illinois University Press, 1985); Jerald Podair, *The Strike That Changed New York: Blacks, Whites, and the Ocean Hill–Brownsville Crisis* (New Haven: Yale University Press, 2002).

47. Formisano, *Boston against Bussing,* p. 183; Jonathan Rieder, *Canarsie:*

New York's Italians and Jews against Liberalism (Cambridge, Mass.: Harvard University Press, 1986), pp. 113, 121, 206–207, 79.

48. Bigler, *American Conversations,* pp. 117, 97, 81.

49. Marc Dollinger, *Quest for Inclusion: Jews and Liberalism in Modern America* (Princeton: Princeton University Press, 2000), p. 203; Curt Flood and Richard Carter, *The Way It Is* (New York: Trident, 1971), pp. 23–24.

50. Edsall and Edsall, *Chain Reaction,* p. 277; Maureen Dezell, *Irish America Coming into Clover: The Evolution of a People and a Culture* (New York: Doubleday, 2000), p. 158; Malcolm X with Alex Haley, *The Autobiography of Malcolm X* [1964] (New York: Ballantine, 1997), p. 201.

5. I Take Back My Name

1. James Miller, *Democracy Is in the Streets: From Port Huron to the Siege of Chicago* (Cambridge, Mass.: Harvard University Press, 1987), p. 318.

2. Sol Stern, "My Jewish Problem—and Ours" [*Ramparts,* 1971], in Jack Nusan Porter and Peter Dreier, eds., *Jewish Radicalism: A Selected Anthology* (New York: Grove, 1973), p. 351.

3. Marla Brettschneider, "Introduction" in *The Narrow Bridge: Jewish Views on Multiculturalism* (New Brunswick: Rutgers University Press, 1996), pp. 5–8.

4. Michael Novak, *Unmeltable Ethnics: Politics and Culture in American Life* [reprinted and expanded edition of the 1971 book] (New Brunswick: Transaction, 1995), p. xvi.

5. Stephen Whitfield, "Rethinking the Alliance between Blacks and Jews," in Marc Lee Raphael, ed., *"Jewishness" and the World of "Difference"* (Williamsburg: William and Mary Department of Religion, 2001), p. 87; Isaac Deutscher, *The Non-Jewish Jew and Other Essays* (New York: Oxford University Press, 1968), pp. 26–27. As the former student activist and now progressive rabbi Michael Lerner complains, in many cases it has been precisely those Jewish elders who most opposed their children's involvement in left politics who now trot out the argument that "we did everything for blacks . . . but now they aren't one bit grateful." Michael Lerner, *Jewish Renewal: A Path to Healing and Transformation* (New York: Harper, 1994), p. 8. See also the essays collected in Raphael, ed., *"Jewishness" and the World of "Difference,"* esp. Marc Dollinger, "'Is It Good for the Jews?' Liberalism

and the Challenges of the 1960s," pp. 8–25; Jeffrey Melnick, "Rattling the Cage of Black-Jewish Relations," pp. 50–64; and Whitfield, "Rethinking the Alliance," pp. 78–93.

6. Arthur Schlesinger, Jr., *The Disuniting of America: Reflections on a Multicultural Society* (New York: W. W. Norton and Co., 1998), p. 47; Novak, *The Rise of the Unmeltable Ethnics* (New York: Macmillan, 1971), p. 336.

7. Quoted in Gertrude Himmelfarb, *One Nation, Two Cultures* (New York: Knopf, 1999), p. 16. See Rick Margolies, "On Community Building," in Priscilla Long, ed., *The New Left: A Collection of Essays* (Boston: Extending Horizons, 1969), pp. 355–375. Compare James Farrell's concept of "personalism" on the left, in *The Spirit of the Sixties: The Making of Postwar Radicalism* (New York: Routledge, 1997), esp. pp. 5–19.

8. Miller, *Democracy Is in the Streets*, p. 124; Doug Rossinow, *The Politics of Authenticity: Liberalism, Christianity, and the New Left in America* (New York: Columbia University Press, 1998), p. 5; and Howard Brick, *Age of Contradiction: American Thought and Culture in the 1960s* (Ithaca: Cornell University Press, 1998), pp. 1–22, 98–123210.

9. Novak, *Rise of the Unmeltable Ethnic*, pp. 290, 271, 136. See also David Colburn and George Pozzetta, "Race, Ethnicity, and the Evolution of Political Legitimacy," in David Farber, ed., *The Sixties: From Memory to History* (Chapel Hill: University of North Carolina Press, 1994), pp. 119–148, esp. 130–138.

10. Novak, *Rise of the Unmeltable Ethnics*, pp. 165, 208, 206, 77.

11. Ibid., pp. 206, 82.

12. Ibid., pp. 270, 199.

13. Ibid., pp. 288, 311.

14. Jim Sleeper and Alan Mintz, eds., *The New Jews* (New York: Vintage, 1973), pp. 4–5, 15, 13.

15. Stern, "My Jewish Problem—and Ours," p. 370; Aviva Cantor Zuckoff, "The Oppression of America's Jews," in Porter and Dreier, *Jewish Radicalism*, pp. 34–35, 45; Robert Greenblatt, "Out of the Melting Pot, into the Fire," in Sleeper and Mintz, eds., *The New Jews*, p. 38.

16. Constance Curry, *Deep in Our Hearts: Nine White Women in the Freedom Movement* (Athens: University of Georgia Press, 2000), pp. 3, 4.

17. Ibid., pp. 256–261. Compare Lawrence O'Rourke, *Geno: The Life and Mission of Geno Baroni* (New York: Paulist Press, 1991), pp. 71–99.

18. Porter and Dreier, *Jewish Radicalism,* pp. xv, xxi; Jonathan Kaufman, *Broken Alliance: The Turbulent Times between Blacks and Jews in America* (New York: Simon and Shuster, 1988), p. 93. See also Melanie Kaye/Kantrowitz, "Stayed on Freedom: Jew in the Civil Rights Movement," in Brettschneider, *Narrow Bridge;* Seymour Martin Lipset, "The Activists: A Profile," in Daniel Bell and Irving Kristol, eds., *Confrontation: The Student Rebellion and the Universities* (New York: Basic, 1969); Dollinger, *Quest for Inclusion,* esp. chaps. 7 and 8; Rebecca Klatch, *A Generation Divided: The New Left, the New Right, and the 1960s* (Berkeley: University of California Press, 1999), pp. 37–58; Elly Bulkin, "Left Leanings," in Elly Bulkin, Minnie Bruce Pratt, and Barbara Smith, *Yours in Struggle: Three Feminist Perspectives on Anti-Semitism and Racism* (Ithaca: Firebrand, 1984), pp. 120–124; and Debra Schultz, *Going South: Jewish Women in the Civil Rights Movement* (New York: New York University Press, 2001).

19. Schultz, *Going South,* p. 41; Stanley Rothman and S. Robert Lichter, *Roots of Radicalism: Jews, Christians, and the New Left* (New York: Oxford University Press, 1982), p. 81; Marge Piercy, "The Grand Coolie Damn," in Robin Morgan, ed., *Sisterhood Is Powerful: An Anthology of Writings from the Women's Liberation Movement* (New York: Vintage, 1970), pp. 424, 425, and *passim.* Paul Buhle argues that in the social and political crucible of 1960s Madison, Wisconsin, Jews "became less Jewish" and gentiles "became *more* Jewish," but that the overall fusion approximated "the spirit of an otherwise near-vanished secular *Yiddishkayt* embracing both radical politics and radical culture." *History and the New Left: Madison, Wisconsin, 1950–1970* (Philadelphia: Temple University Press, 1990), p. 8.

20. Porter and Dreier, *Jewish Radicalism,* p. xx; Melanie Kaye/Kantrowitz, "Stayed on Freedom," p. 105; Schultz, *Going South.*

21. Richard Flacks, "The Liberated Generation: An Exploration of the Roots of Student Protest," *Journal of Social Issues,* July 1967, and "Who Protests: A Study of Student Activists," in Julian Foster and Durwood Long, eds., *Protest: Student Activism in America* (New York: 1970); Miller, *Democracy Is in the Streets,* p. 185; Wini Breines, *Community and Organization in the New Left, 1962–1968: The Great Refusal* [1989] (New Brunswick: Rutgers University Press, 1982), pp. 14–15.

22. Vivian Gornick, *The Romance of American Communism* (New York:

Basic, 1977), p. 27. See also Margot Adler, *Heretic's Heart: A Journey through Spirit and Revolution* (Boston: Beacon, 2003).

23. Schultz, *Going South*, p. 1; see also Paul Cowan's comments in Michael Staub, *Torn at the Roots: The Crisis of Jewish Liberalism in Postwar America* (New York: Columbia University Press, 2002), p. 87. Jeffrey Kaplow describes himself as "'American born,' but brought up to identify with the stings and arrows to which [East] European flesh is heir." Buhle, *History and the New Left*, p. 58. This is a common theme in 1960s memoirs, dotting the pages, for example, of Becky Thompson, *A Promise and a Way of Life: White Antiracist Activism* (Minneapolis: University of Minnesota Press, 2001), and Cheryl Lynn Greenberg, ed., *A Circle of Trust: Remembering SNCC* (New Brunswick: Rutgers University Press, 1998). A peculiar and not especially approving variant of this interpretation is developed in "Radical Jews: The Dilemmas of Marginality," in Rothman and Lichter, *Roots of Radicalism*, pp. 80–145.

24. Schultz, *Going South*, p. 158; Kaye/Kantrowitz, "Stayed on Freedom," p. 107; Paul Lauter, "Strange Identities and Jewish Politics," in Jeffrey Rubin-Dorsky and Shelley Fisher Fishkin, eds., *People of the Book: Thirty Scholars Reflect on Their Jewish Identity* (Madison: University of Wisconsin Press, 1996), p. 43; Porter and Dreier, *Jewish Radicalism*, p. xxxvii.

25. Todd Gitlin, *The Sixties: Years of Hope, Days of Rage* (New York: Bantam Doubleday, 1987), pp. 25, 26, 84; George Lipsitz, "Don't Cry for Me, Ike and Tina," in *American Studies in a Moment of Danger* (Minneapolis: University of Minnesota Press, 2001), p. 295. Compare Gitlin's remarks in Dorman, *Arguing the World*, p. 134.

26. Kaye/Kantrowitz, "Stayed on Freedom," p. 111; "To Be a Jewish Radical in the Late Twentieth Century," in *The Issue Is Power: Essays on Women, Jews, Violence and Resistance* (San Francisco: Aunt Lute, 1992), p. 77.

27. Lerner, *Jewish Renewal: A Path to Healing and Transformation* (New York: Perennial, 1995), pp. 61, 66; Arthur Waskow, "Judaism and Revolution Today," in Porter and Dreier, *Jewish Radicalism*, p. 12; Danny Goldberg, *Dispatches from the Culture Wars: How the Left Lost Teen Spirit* (New York: Mirimax, 2003), p. 51. Waskow's first Freedom Seder was in 1969. See Staub, *Torn at the Roots*, pp. 163–169, and chap. 2 on this strand of the prophetic tradition in Judaism.

28. Sleeper and Mintz, *New Jews*, p. 15.

29. Doug McAdam does not weigh in on this question directly, but in

"Biographical Roots of Activism" he does note that most student activists seemed not to be rebelling against their parents, but rather "to be acting in accord with values learned at home"—leaving only the question of whether the operative values here were primarily religious or secular. *Freedom Summer* (New York: Oxford University Press, 1988), p. 49. Compare Rothman and Lichter, *Roots of Radicalism*, who posit that this was the case for Jewish radicals but not for Christian radicals.

30. Sleeper and Mintz, *New Jews*, p. 6; Porter and Dreier, *Jewish Radicalism*, pp. xxiii–xxiv. On the Jewishness of Jerry Rubin and Abbie Hoffman, see also John Downton Hazlett, *My Generation: Collective Autobiography and Identity Politics* (Madison: University of Wisconsin Press, 1998), pp. 50–51, 65–66.

31. Abbie Hoffman, *The Autobiography of Abbie Hoffman* [1980] (New York: Four Walls Eight Windows, 2000), pp. 107, 14, 15. Hoffman also identifies Mark Rudd as "a member in good standing of the International Jewish Conspiracy," even though, "like me, his Russian roots had been sanitized by some border guard at Ellis Island" (p. 139).

32. Porter and Dreier, *Jewish Radicalism*, pp. xi, xxxii–xxxiii, xliii, lii. On the organizations and publications of "the Jewish left," see pp. 378–389. On the Cornell Seder, see Murray Polner and Jim O'Grady, *Disarmed and Dangerous: The Radical Life and Times of Daniel and Philip Berrigan, Brothers in Religious Faith and Civil Disobedience* (Boulder: Westview, 1998), pp. 222–223. On the *havurot* and the Jewish counterculture, see esp. Riv-Ellen Prell, *Prayer and Community: The Havurah in American Judaism* (Detroit: Wayne State University Press, 1989); Sleeper and Mintz, *The New Jews;* and Sharon Strassfeld and Michael Strassfeld, *The Second Jewish Catalog* (Philadelphia: Jewish Publication Society of America, 1976). Quoted phrases on the *havurah* in Prell, *Prayer and Community*, pp. 80, 83.

33. Dollinger, *Quest for Inclusion*, p. 221; Porter and Dreier, *Jewish Radicalism*, pp. 231–242, xxiv–xxv; Staub, *Torn at the Roots*, pp. 128–132, quotation from p. 130; Lauter, "Strange Identities and Jewish Politics," p. 44. On the Jewish romance with Israeli might in the wake of the Six Day War, see also Paul Breines, *Tough Jews: Political Fantasies and the Moral Dilemma of American Jewry* (New York: Basic, 1990).

34. Porter and Dreier, *Jewish Radicalism*, pp. xxiv–xxv; Clayborne Carson, *In Struggle: SNCC and the Black Awakening of the 1960s* (Cambridge, Mass.: Harvard University Press, 1981), pp. 266–272; Sara Evans, *Personal Politics* (New York: Vintage, 1980), p. 197; McAdam, *Freedom*

Summer, pp. 180–181; Abe Peck, *Uncovering the Sixties: The Life and Times of the Underground Press* [1985] (New York: Citadel, 1991), pp. 66–67; Edward Bacciocco, Jr., *The New Left in America: Reform to Revolution, 1956–1970* (Stanford: Hoover Institution, 1974), pp. 99–108.

35. Itzhak Epstein, "Open Letter to the Black Panthers" [1969], in Porter and Dreier, *Jewish Radicalism*, p. 69. On the shifting Civil Rights perspective on the Middle East, see Melani McAlister, *Epic Encounters: Culture, Media, and U.S. Interests in the Middle East, 1946–2000* (Berkeley: University of California Press, 2001), pp. 84–124.

36. M. J. Rosenberg quoted in Porter and Dreier, *Jewish Radicalism*, p. xlviii. On student responses to Israel, see also Sleeper, *New Jews*, pp. 56–99. Prell, *Prayer and Community*, p. 86.

37. Waskow, "Judaism and Revolution Today," p. 21.

38. Prell, *Prayer and Community*, pp. 96–97; Porter and Dreier, *Jewish Radicalism*, p. xli; Marc Zborowski and Elizabeth Herzog, *Life Is with People: The Culture of the Shtetl* (New York: Schocken, 1971).

39. Arthur Waskow, *Seasons of Our Joy: A Celebration of Modern Jewish Renewal* (New York: Bantam, 1982); Lerner, *Jewish Renewal*; Marge Piercy, *The Art of Blessing the Day: Poems with a Jewish Theme* (New York: Knopf, 2000); Judy Chicago, *The Holocaust Project: From Darkness into Light* (New York: Viking, 1993); Melanie Kaye/Kantrowitz, *My Jewish Face and Other Stories* (San Francisco: Spinster–Aunt Lute, 1990).

40. Dollinger, *Quest for Inclusion*, p. 201.

41. Robert Greenblatt, "Out of the Melting Pot, into the Fire" (1970), in Sleeper and Mintz, *The New Jews*, p. 41; Alan Mintz, "Along the Path to Religious Community," in Sleeper and Mintz, *The New Jews*, p. 33.

42. Debbie D'Amico, "To My White Working-Class Sisters," in Barbara Crow, ed., *Radical Feminism: A Documentary Reader* (New York: New York University Press, 2000), p. 522; Susan Brownmiller, *In Our Time: Memoir of a Revolution* (New York: Dell, 2000), p. 65.

43. Tom Hayden, *Irish on the Inside: In Search of the Soul of Irish America* (London: Verso, 2001), p. 105; Tom Hayden, *Reunion: A Memoir* (New York: Collier, 1988), p. 433. Horowitz quoted in E. J. Dionne, *Why Americans Hate Politics* (New York: Touchstone, 1991), p. 89.

44. Paul Lyons, *New Left, New Right, and the Legacy of the Sixties* (Philadelphia: Temple University Press, 1996), p. 67.

45. Nathan Glazer, *We Are All Multiculturalists Now* (Cambridge, Mass.: Harvard University Press, 1997), p. 7.

46. Breines, *Community and Organization*, p. 16; Richard Rorty, *Achieving Our Country: Leftist Thought in Twentieth-Century America* (Cambridge, Mass.: Harvard University Press, 1999), pp. 76–77; Gitlin, *Twilight of Common Dreams: Why America Is Wracked by Culture Wars* (New York: Henry Holt, 1995), pp. 100–101.

47. Jerald E. Podair, *The Strike That Changed New York: Blacks, Whites, and the Ocean Hill–Brownsville Crisis* (New Haven: Yale University Press, 2002), p. 34.

48. David Yamane, *Student Movements for Multiculturalism: Challenging the Curricular Color Line in Education* (Baltimore: Johns Hopkins University Press, 2001), pp. 14, 17–18.

49. William Van DeBurg, *New Day in Babylon: The Black Power Movement and American Culture, 1965–1975* (Chicago: University of Chicago Press, 1992), p. 66; Jonathan Zimmerman, *Whose America? Culture Wars in the Public Schools* (Cambridge, Mass.: Harvard University Press, 2002), pp. 107–129.

50. The best-known critics include Dinesh D'Sousa, *Illiberal Education: The Politics of Race and Sex on Campus* (New York: Free Press, 1991); Alan Bloom, *The Closing of the American Mind* (New York: Touchstone, 1988); Richard Bernstein, *Dictatorship of Virtue: How the Battle over Multiculturalism Is Reshaping Our Schools, Our Country, and Our Lives* (New York: Vintage, 1995).

51. Rhett Jones, "From Ideology to Institution: The Evolution of Africana Studies," in Johnnella Butler, ed., *Color Line to Borderlands: The Matrix of American Ethnic Studies* (Seattle: University of Washington Press, 2001), pp. 113–149, 129; Rudolph Vecoli, "The Resurgence of American Immigration History," *American Studies International*, Winter 1979, p. 62.

52. Mark Naison, *White Boy: A Memoir* (Philadelphia: Temple University Press, 2002), p. 173. See also Sydney Stahl Weinberg, "The World of Our Fathers and the World of Our Mothers," *American Jewish History*, 88:4 (Dec. 2000), pp. 548–549. On the struggle for Italian-American Studies at the City University of New York, see Joseph Scelsa, "The 80th Street Mafia," in A. Kenneth Ciongoli and Jay Parini, eds., *Beyond the Godfather: Italian American Writers on the Real Italian American Experience* (Hanover, N.H.: University Press of New England, 1997), pp. 293–310.

53. Porter and Dreier, *Jewish Radicalism*, pp. xxxv–xxxvi; Bob Goldfarb, "Klal Israel," in Brettschneider, *Narrow Bridge*, p. 58.

54. Arthur Schlesinger, Jr., *The Disuniting of America: Reflections on a*

Multicultural Society (New York: W. W. Norton and Co., 1998), pp. 98–104; Novak, "Introduction" to *Unmeltable Ethnics*, pp. xiii, xvi; Troy Duster, "They're Taking Over! And Other Myths about Race on Campus," in Michael Berube and Cary Nelson, *Higher Education under Fire: Politics, Economics, and the Crisis of the Humanities* (New York: Routledge, 1995), pp. 276–283.

55. John Wilson, *The Myth of Political Correctness: The Conservative Attack on Higher Education* (Durham: Duke University Press, 1995), pp. 80–81.

56. Lawrence Levine, *The Opening of the American Mind* (Boston: Beacon, 1997), pp. xvii–xviii, 100; Theodore Gross, *A Nation of Nations: Ethnic Literature in America* (New York: Free Press, 1971), p. xiii.

57. Werner Sollors, "Proposal for an Ethnic Studies Project at Columbia University," Nov. 1975. Memorandum in the author's possession. Many thanks to Werner Sollors.

58. Lauter, "Strange Identities and Jewish Politics," pp. 40, 41, 42.

59. Shelley Fisher Fishkin, "Changing the Story," in Rubin-Dorsky and Fishkin, *People of the Book*, pp. 61, 62.

60. Robin Morgan, *Saturday's Child: A Memoir* (New York: W. W. Norton, 2000), p. 24; Susan Gubar, "Eating the Bread of Affliction," in Rubin-Dorsky and Fishkin, *People of the Book*, pp. 30, 36 (n.44). Such "skeleton-key" allegiances constitute a pervasive theme in Thompson, *A Promise and a Way of Life*.

61. Maria Mazziotti Gillan and Jennifer Gillan, *Unsettling America: An Anthology of Contemporary Multicultural Poetry* (New York: Penguin, 1994), pp. 380–381. See also Maria Mazziotti Gillan and Jennifer Gillan, *Identity Lessons: Contemporary Writing about Learning to Be American* (New York: Penguin, 1999).

62. Gillan, *Unsettling America*, pp. 380–381, 384.

63. Yamane, *Student Movements for Multiculturalism*, pp. 99–101, 104; Sara Horowitz, "The Paradox of Jewish Studies in the New Academy," in David Biale, Michael Galchinsky, and Susannah Heschel, eds., *Insider/Outsider: American Jews and Multiculturalism* (Berkeley: University of California Press, 1998), pp. 116–129, quotation from p. 125; George Yudice, "Neither Impugning nor Disavowing Whiteness Does a Viable Politics Make: The Limits of Identity Politics," in Christopher Newfield and Ronald Strickland, eds., *After Political Correctness: The Humanities and Society in the 1990s* (Boulder: Westview, 1995), pp. 255–285.

64. Robert Rhoads, *Freedom's Web: Student Activism in an Age of Cultural*

Diversity (Baltimore: Johns Hopkins University Press, 1998), p. 72; Tom Hayden, ed., *Irish Hunger: Personal Reflections on the Legacy of the Famine* (New York: Rinehart, 1998), p. 287.

65. Hayden, *Irish Hunger*, pp. 283, 286–289.
66. Ibid., p. 273.
67. Ibid., p. 283.
68. Ibid., p. 289, emphasis in original.
69. Hayden, *Irish on the Inside*, p. 285.
70. Ibid., p. 145.
71. Robert Greenblatt, "Out of the Melting Pot, into the Fire," in Sleeper and Mintz, eds., *The New Jews*, p. 40. Lyons, *New Left, New Right, and the Legacy of the Sixties*, is particularly useful on the shared impulse behind the left and the right's "images of beloved communities that appeared to establish harmonies between antinomian and communitarian traditions" (p. 5). See also Rebecca Klatch, *A Generation Divided: The New Left, the New Right, and the 1960s* (Berkeley: University of California Press, 1999), pp. 213–215.
72. Gitlin, *Twilight of Common Dreams*, pp. 103, 126.
73. Michael Novak, *The Guns of Lattimer* [1978] (New Brunswick: Transaction, 1996), dedication, p. xiii (p. xviii in 1978 ed.).
74. Ibid., pp. xvii, xviii, xxiii, xxiv, 246.
75. Stanley Lieberson, *A Piece of the Pie: Blacks and White Immigrants since 1880* (Berkeley: University of California Press, 1980; Micaela di Leonardo, "White Lies, Black Myths: Race, Rape, and the Underclass," *Village Voice*, Sept. 22, 1992, pp. 29–36; Karen Brodkin, *How Jews Became White Folks and What That Says about Race in America* (New Brunswick: Rutgers University Press, 2000). For similar commentary on the structural interventions of the New Deal versus "white ethnic pluck," see also Paula Rothenburg, *Invisible Privilege: A Memoir about Race, Class, and Gender* (Lawrence: University of Kansas Press, 2000), and Hayden, *Irish on the Inside*, p. 81.
76. Brodkin, *How Jews Became White Folks*, pp. 50–52.
77. Micaela di Leonardo, "White Fright," *Village Voice*, May 18, 1993, p. 40.

6. Our Heritage Is Our Power

1. Robin Morgan, "Goodbye to All That" [1970], in Rosalyn Baxandall and Linda Gordon, eds., *Dear Sisters: Dispatches from the Women's Liberation Movement* (New York: Basic Books, 2000), p. 57.
2. Debbie D'Amico, "To My White Working-Class Sisters," in Alexan-

der Bloom and Wini Breines, eds., *Takin' It to the Streets: A Sixties Reader* (New York: Oxford University Press, 1997), p. 522.
3. Ibid., pp. 520, 524.
4. Robin D. G. Kelley, "'This Battlefield Called Life': Black Feminist Dreams," in *Freedom Dreams: The Black Radical Imagination* (Boston: Beacon, 2002), p. 150.
5. Elisabeth Schussler Fiorenza, "In Search of Women's Heritage," in Judith Plaskow and Carol Christ, eds., *Weaving the Visions: New Patterns in Feminist Spirituality* (San Francisco: HarperSanFrancisco, 1989), pp. 34–35.
6. Ibid., p. 35; Marianna De Marco Torgovnick, *Crossing Ocean Parkway: Readings by an Italian American Daughter* (Chicago: University of Chicago Press, 1996); Meredith Tax, *Rivington Street* (New York: William Morrow, 1982); Meredith Tax, *Union Square* [1988] (Champaign: University of Illinois Press, 2001); Helen Barolini, *Umbertina* [1984] (New York: Feminist Press, 1999); Elisabeth Schussler Fiorenza, *Discipleship of Equals: A Critical Feminist Ekklesia-Logy of Liberation* (New York: Crossroad, 1993); Elisabeth Schussler Fiorenza, *In Memory of Her: A Feminist Theological Reconstruction of Christian Origins* (New York: Herder and Herder, 1994); Aviva Cantor Zuckoff, "The Lilith Question," *Lilith*, 1:1 (Oct. 31, 1976), p. 3; Charlene Spretnak, *Lost Goddesses of Early Greece* (Berkeley: Moon Books, 1978); Marija Gimbutas, *Goddesses and Gods of Old Europe, 6500–3500 B.C.: Myths and Cult Images* (Berkeley: University of California Press, 1990); Riane Eisler, *The Chalice and the Blade: Our History, Our Future* (San Francisco: HarperSanFrancisco, 1987). In 1977 Alice Bloch wrote in *Dyke* magazine, "I hope to join with other Jewish lesbians to develop rituals that would flow from our womanhood, our lesbianism, and our Jewish roots." "Scenes from the Life of a Jewish Lesbian" [1977], in Susannah Heschel, ed., *On Being a Jewish Feminist* (New York: Schocken, 1995), p. 174.
7. E. M. Broner, "Honor and Ceremony in Women's Rituals," in Charlene Spretnak, ed., *The Politics of Women's Spirituality: Essays on the Rise of Spiritual Power within the Feminist Movement* (New York: Anchor, 1982), p. 238; Shulamith Firestone, *The Dialectic of Sex: The Case for Feminist Revolution* [1970] (New York: Bantam, 1971), p. 215. See also Lesley Hazelton, "Israeli Women: Three Myths," in Heschel, *On Being a Jewish Feminist*, pp. 65–87.
8. Naomi Wolf, *Promiscuities: The Secret Struggle for Womanhood* (New York: Fawcett, 1997), p. 111. Elaine DeLott Baker offers yet a third

variation on the feminism-kibbutz theme: "I attribute the fundamental shift in awareness of myself as a woman to the juxtaposition of my experiences with gender equality in the progressive atmosphere of the kibbutz, where it was a given, and the presence of gender discrimination in a civil rights community that declared itself to be egalitarian." Constance Curry et al., eds., *Deep in Our Hearts: Nine White Women in the Freedom Movement* (Athens: University of Georgia Press, 2002), p. 279.

9. Helen Barolini, "Introduction" and "Looking for Mari Tomasi," *Chiaroscuro: Essays of Identity* (Madison: University of Wisconsin Press, 1997), pp. vii, 62. Compare Sandra Gilbert, "Life with (God)Father," in Regina Berreca, ed., *A Sitdown with The Sopranos* (New York: Palgrave, 2002), pp. 11–26.

10. Vivian Gornick, "The Next Great Moment in History Is Theirs" [1969], in *Essays in Feminism* (New York: Harper and Row, 1978), p. 11; compare Robin Morgan, *Saturday's Child: A Memoir* (New York: Norton, 2001), p. 108. Marge Piercy, "The Ram's Horn Sounding," in *The Art of Blessing the Day: Poems with a Jewish Theme* (New York: Knopf, 2000), p. 174.

11. Mary Daly, "New Intergalactic Introduction" to *Gyn/Ecology: The Metaethics of Radical Feminism* [1978] (Boston: Beacon, 1990), p. xxx; Starhawk, *Dreaming the Dark: Magic, Sex, and Politics* (Boston: Beacon, 1982), p. 93; Laura Levitt, *Jews and Feminism: The Ambivalent Search for Home* (New York: Routledge, 1997), p. 151.

12. Alice Echols, *Daring to Be Bad: Radical Feminism in America, 1967–1975* (Minneapolis: University of Minnesota Press, 1989), p. 5; Donna Steichen, *Ungodly Rage: The Hidden Face of Catholic Feminism* (San Francisco: Ignatius, 1991), p. 156; Gloria Steinem, *Outrageous Acts and Everyday Rebellions* (New York: Henry Holt, 1995), p. 231; E. M. Broner and Naomi Nimrod, *The Telling: Including the Women's Haggadah* (San Francisco: HarperSanFrancisco, 1994), pp. 105, 165. See also Mary Jo Weaver, *New Catholic Women: A Contemporary Challenge to Traditional Religious Authority* [1986] (Bloomington: Indiana University Press, 1995), p. 38; Annie Lally Milhaven, *Inside Stories: Thirteen Valiant Women Challenging Today's Church* (Mystic, Conn.: Twenty-Third Publications, 1987), p. 168; Naomi Wolf, *The Beauty Myth: How Images of Beauty Are Used against Women* (New York: Anchor, 1991), p. 21; Wendy Chapkis, *Beauty Secrets: Women and the Politics of Appearance* (Boston: South End, 1986), p. 5.

13. Schussler Fiorenza, "The Ethics and Politics of Liberation: Theorizing the Ekklesia of Women," in *Discipleship of Equals*, pp. 335, 336.

14. A photograph of the 1978 rally by Bettye Lane is reprinted on the cover of Rachel Blau DuPlessis and Ann Snitow, eds., *The Feminist Memoir Project: Voices from Women's Liberation* (New York: Three Rivers Press, 1998).

15. Francine Zuckerman, ed., *Half the Kingdom: Seven Jewish Feminists* (Montreal: Vehicule, 1992); Kesselman cited in Melanie Kaye/Kantrowitz, "Stayed on Freedom: Jew in the Civil Rights Movement and After," in Marla Brettschneider, ed., *The Narrow Bridge: Jewish Views on Multiculturalism* (New Brunswick: Rutgers University Press, 1996), p. 115. To take the list of prominent Jewish feminists a little further: Bella Abzug, Jesse (Kantor) Bernard, Esther Broner, Kim Chernin, Phyllis Chesler, Judy Chicago, Nancy Chodorow, Nancy Cott, Lillian Faderman, Susan Faludi, Jane Gallop, Linda Gordon, Vivian Gornick, Susan Gubar, Caroline Heilbrun, Florence Howe, Melanie Kaye/Kantrowitz, Grace Paley, Marge Piercy, Judith Plaskow, Letty Cottin Pogrebin, Ruth Rosen, Vivian Rothstein, Eve Kosofsky Sedgwick, Meredith Tax, Naomi Weisstein, and Ellen Willis.

16. For examples of Jewish exceptionalism, see Joyce Antler, *The Journey Home: How Jewish Women Shaped Modern America* (New York: Schocken, 1998); Susan Gubar, "Eating the Bread of Affliction: Judaism and Feminist Criticism," in Jeffrey Rubin-Dorsky and Shelley Fisher Fishkin, eds., *People of the Book: Thirty Scholars Reflect on Their Jewish Identity* (Madison: University of Wisconsin Press, 1996), pp. 15–36; Anne Roiphe, *Generation without Memory: A Jewish Journey in Christian America* (New York: Simon and Schuster, 1981), p. 148. The non-Jewish roster of Ellis Island–descended luminaries includes Patricia Mainardi, Carol Giardina, Michela Griffo, Helen Barolini, Marianna De Marco Torgovnick, Micaela di Leonardo, Barbara Zanotti, Sandra Gilbert (Italian); Jane O'Reilly, Liz O'Sullivan, Mary Daly, Sally Cunneen, Mary Jo Weaver, Marjorie Tuite, Joyce O'Brien (Irish); Irene Peslikis, Karen Kollias, Lynda Benglis, Mary Grigoriadis (Greek); Barbara Mikulski, Mari Jo Buhle (Polish); Florika (Romanian); and Maureen Mrizek (Slavic).

17. Melanie Kaye/Kantrowitz, "To Be a Radical Jew in the Late Twentieth Century" [1984–1985], in *The Issue Is Power: Essays on Women, Jews, Violence and Resistance* (San Francisco: Aunt Lute, 1992), pp. 92, 104. This same spirit suffuses Melanie Kaye/Kantrowitz and Irena

Klepfisz, eds., *The Tribe of Dina: A Jewish Women's Anthology* (Boston: Beacon, 1986).

18. Kate Millett, *Flying* (New York: Ballantine, 1974), pp. 172, 356.

19. Milhaven, *Inside Stories*, pp. 115, 113–114.

20. Adrienne Rich, "If Not with Others, How?" [1985], in *Blood, Bread, and Poetry: Selected Prose* (New York: Norton, 1986), p. 202. See also Adrienne Rich, "Split at the Root: An Essay on Jewish Identity" (1982), in *Blood, Bread, and Poetry*, esp. pp. 120–123.

21. Betty Friedan, *The Feminine Mystique*, pp. 37, 305, 282 ff; see also Daniel Horowitz, *Betty Friedan and the Making of the Feminine Mystique: The American Left, the Cold War, and Modern Feminism* (Amherst: University of Massachusetts Press, 1998), pp. 22–23, 205, 218.

22. Amy Stone, "Friedan at Fifty-Five: From Feminism to Judaism," *Lilith* 1:1 (1976), p. 11; Antler, *Journey Home*, p. 267; Friedan, *Feminine Mystique*, p. 398; Alix Kates Shulman, *Memoirs of an Ex-Prom Queen* [1969] (New York: Penguin Books, 1997), p. 22.

23. Friedan, *Feminine Mystique*, pp. 294, 351–352; Sally Cunneen, *Sex: Female; Religion: Catholic* (New York: Holt, Rinehart and Winston, 1968), p. 22; Antler, *Journey Home*, p. 260.

24. Ruth Rosen, *The World Split Open: How the Modern Women's Movement Changed America* (New York: Penguin, 2001), p. 93; Vivian Gornick, "Woman as Outsider," in Vivian Gornick, ed., *Woman in Sexist Society: Studies in Power and Powerlessness* (New York: Mentor, 1971), p. 136; Judy Chicago, *The Holocaust Project: From Darkness into Light* (New York: Viking, 1993), p. 78.

25. Blu Greenberg, "Feminism: Is It Good for the Jews?" and "A Yeshiva Girl among the Feminists" [c. 1970s], in Blu Greenberg, *On Women and Judaism: A View from Tradition* [1981] (Philadelphia: Jewish Publication Society, 1998), pp. 4, 28.

26. Micaela di Leonardo, *Varieties of Ethnic Experience: Kinship, Class, and Gender among California Italian-Americans* (Ithaca: Cornell University Press, 1984), p. 116; Louise DeSalvo, "A Portrait of the *Puttana* as a Middle-Aged Woolf Scholar," in Carol Ascher, Louise DeSalvo, and Sara Ruddick, eds., *Between Women: Biographers, Novelists, Critics, Teachers, and Artists Write about Their Work on Women* [1984] (New York: Routledge, 1993), pp. 35, 36; Daniella Gioseffi, "A Bicentennial Anti-Poem for Italian-American Women," in Helen Barolini, *The Dream Book: An Anthology of Writings by Italian American Women* (New York: Schocken, 1985), p. 382; Vivian Gornick, *Fierce Attachments* (Boston: Beacon Press, 1987), p. 5. This is not to say that intra-

ethnic gender arrangements necessarily weakened a woman's attachment to her ethnic group. See, for instance, Louise DeSalvo, "Color: White / Complexion: Dark," in Jennifer Guglielmo and Salvatore Salerno, eds., *Are Italians White? How Race Is Made in America* (New York: Routledge, 2003), pp. 17–28.

27. Torgovnick, *Crossing Ocean Parkway*, pp. 39, 25, 104; Helen Barolini, "Reintroducing *The Dream Book*," in *Chiaroscuro*, p. 159; Julien Murphy, "Coming Out of Catholicism," in Barbara Zanotti, ed., *A Faith of One's Own: Explorations by Catholic Lesbians* (Trumansberg, N.Y.: Crossing Press, 1986), p. 84.

28. Curry, *Deep in Our Hearts*, p. 173.

29. Kate Millett, *Sexual Politics* [1971] (New York: Ballantine, 1978), p. 25.

30. Kate Millett, *Mother Millett* (London: Verso, 2001), pp. 163, 244; Hasia Diner, *Erin's Daughters in America: Irish Immigrant Women in the Nineteenth Century* (Baltimore: Johns Hopkins University Press, 1983), pp. 20–21, 58. The gendered antagonisms of ethnic group life sometimes became far sharper than a generalized disgust with "oppressive macho culture," cutting right to the core of a given group's self-definition and common interests. Affirmative action, for example, which theoretically pitted the principle of "group" rights against "women's" rights (as if women do not also belong to groups) was one arena where this conflict became most vivid. Susan Weidman Schneider, *Jewish and Female: Choices and Changes in Our Lives Today* (New York: Touchstone, 1984), p. 492; *Jewish News of Greater Phoenix*, Feb. 20, 2002, at jewishaz.com/jewishnews/980220/affirmative.shtml; Robert Entman and Andrew Rojecki, *The Black Image in the White Mind: Media and Race in America* (Chicago: University of Chicago Press, 2000), pp. 107–124, 115; Abraham Lavender, *Ethnic Women and Feminist Values: Toward a "New" Value System* (New York: University Press of America, 1986), pp. 38–39.

31. Sonya Jason, "The Liberation of a First Generation Slovak-American Woman," in Edith Blicksilver, ed., *The Ethnic American Woman: Problems, Protests, Lifestyle* (Dubuque: Kendall/Hunt, 1978), p. 195; Wolf, *Promiscuities*, p. 111.

32. Maria Frangis, "An Ancient Heritage in a New World," in Blicksilver, *Ethnic American Woman*, p. 45.

33. Elizabeth Haiken, *Venus Envy: A History of Cosmetic Surgery* (Baltimore: Johns Hopkins University Press, 1997), pp. 10, 91, 177; Rhonda Lieberman, "Jewish Barbie," in Norman Kleeblatt, ed., *Too Jewish? Challenging Traditional Identities* (New Brunswick: Rutgers Univer-

sity Press and the Jewish Museum, 1996), p. 108; Ophira Edut, "Bubbe Got Back," in Danya Ruttenberg, *Yentl's Revenge: The Next Wave of Jewish Feminism* (Seattle: Seal Press, 2001), pp. 24–30. Significantly, Joyce Millman identifies Madonna Louise Ciccone as "Barbie's most apt pupil." Joyce Millman, "Primadonna," in Adam Sexton, ed., *Desperately Seeking Madonna* (New York: Delta, 1993), p. 53.

34. Firestone, *Dialectic of Sex*, pp. 151–152. See also Una Stannard, "The Mask of Beauty," in Gornick, *Woman in Sexist Society*, pp. 187–203; Wolf, *The Beauty Myth*; Sarah Banet-Weiser, *The Most Beautiful Girl in the World: Beauty Pageants and National Identity* (Berkeley: University of California Press, 1999), chap. 5, on Bess Myerson, the only Jewish Miss America.

35. Wini Breines, *Young, White, and Miserable: Growing up Female in the Fifties* (Chicago: University of Chicago Press, 2001), p. 96. See also Karen Brodkin, *How Jews Became White Folks* (New Brunswick: Rutgers University Press, 1998), p. 10; Maria Laurino, *Have You Always Been Italian?* (New York: Norton, 2000), esp. pp. 16–29. Esther Broner describes a character plucking and bleaching to the point of pain to "counteract" her "Mediterranean" look, though in fact "Bea's ancestors were once from the steppes of Russia." E. M. Broner, *Her Mothers* (New York: Holt Rinehart and Winston, 1975), pp. 27, 30–31. In a more radical vein, in *With the Weathermen* Susan Stern wrote of her relationship to "blond, Christian America." At one point, on the side of her house she painted "an eight-foot tall nude woman with flowing green blond hair and a burning American flag coming out of her cunt!" This represented "what I wanted to be somewhere deep in my mind; tall and blond, nude and armed, consuming—or discharging—a burning America." Quoted in Stanley Rothman and S. Robert Lichter, *Roots of Radicalism: Jews, Christians, and the New Left* (New York: Oxford University Press, 1982), p. 136. For an "ethnic" critique of the tyrannies of beauty, see also Erica Jong, *Fear of Flying* (New York: Signet, 1973). Jane Gerhard, *Desiring Revolution: Second Wave Feminism and the Rewriting of American Sexual Thought, 1920–1982* (New York: Columbia University Press, 2001), pp. 127–137, is an excellent account of this dimension in the work of Jong and Shulman, though Gerhard does not take up ethnicity explicitly.

36. DuPlessis and Snitow, *Feminist Memoir Project*, pp. 198–199; Banet-Weiser, *The Most Beautiful Girl*, p. 10; Chapkis, *Beauty Secrets*, p. 7 and

passim; Lois Banner, *American Beauty* (Chicago: University of Chicago Press, 1983), pp. 289–290; Haiken, *Venus Envy,* pp. 169–170.

37. Barbara Smith, "Between a Rock and a Hard Place," in Elly Bulkin, ed., *Yours in Struggle: Three Feminist Perspectives on Anti-Semitism and Racism* (New York: Firebrand, 1984), p. 73; Rosen, *World Split Open,* p. 159; Susan Brownmiller, *Femininity* (New York: Fawcett, 1994), p. 55.

38. Nancy Miller, "Hadassah Arms," in Rubin-Dorsky and Fishkin, *People of the Book,* pp. 155–157.

39. Melanie Kaye/Kantrowitz, "Some Notes on Jewish Lesbian Identity," Evelyn Torton Beck, *Nice Jewish Girls: A Lesbian Anthology* [1982] (Boston: Beacon, 1989), p. 40; Haiken, *Venus Envy,* pp. 182–200. See also Aishe Berger, "Nose Is a Country . . . I am the Second Generation," in Kaye/Kantrowitz and Klepfisz, *Tribe of Dina,* p. 135; Virginia Blum, *Flesh Wounds: The Culture of Cosmetic Surgery* (Berkeley: University of California Press, 2003), pp. 10, 38–39, 133, 209–210, 263; Faderman, *Naked in the Promised Land,* p. 121, and the chapter titled "My Movie Actress Nose," pp. 130–141; Roiphe, *Generation without Memory,* p. 28; Chapkis, *Beauty Secrets,* p. 127; Paula Rothenberg, *Invisible Privilege: A Memoir about Race, Class, and Gender* (Lawrence: University of Kansas Press, 2000), pp. 183–184; Riv-Ellen Prell, "Cinderellas Who (Almost) Never Become Princesses: Subversive Representations of Jewish Women in Postwar Popular Novels," in Joyce Antler, ed., *Talking Back: Images of Jewish Women in American Popular Culture* (Hanover, N.H.: Brandeis University Press, 1998), pp. 123–138. Alix Kates Shulman makes a related point in *Memoirs of an Ex-Prom Queen,* noting the heroine's "prize-winning *shiksa* profile," but later wondering, "Of what use is a gentile nose among gentiles?" Shulman, *Memoirs,* pp. 82, 91. This theme continues well on into the third wave. On the continuing contention "with East European genes," see Tobin Belzer, "On Being a Jewish Feminist Valley Girl," in Ruttenberg, *Yentl's Revenge,* pp. 181–188.

40. Tali Edut, Dyann Logwood, and Ophira Edut, "*HUES* Magazine: The Making of a Movement," in Leslie Heywood and Jennifer Drake, eds., *Third Wave Agenda: Being Feminist, Doing Feminism* (Minneapolis: University of Minnesota Press, 1997), pp. 83–84; Lisa Jervis, "My Jewish Nose," in Ophira Edut, ed., *Body Outlaws: Young Women Write about Body Image and Identity* [previously *Audiós Barbie!* 1998] (Seattle: Seal Press, 2000), p. 64.

41. Teresa de Lauretis, *Technologies of Gender: Essays on Theory, Film, and Fiction* (Bloomington: Indiana University Press, 1987), p. 3.

42. Bulkin, *Yours in Struggle,* p. 188. On assimilation, cultural retention, and the codes of gender, see also Roiphe, *Generation without Memory,* pp. 169–170, 199–200.

43. "It is easy to look backward and pluck from histories of antecedents . . . hints and influences that may have molded a human being," writes Carolyn Heilbrun in the opening of her Steinem biography. But, she warns, "in the United States, where many of us have the conviction, often accurate, that we have largely created ourselves, as well as the knowledge that our grandparents often dwelt in another country under conditions we cannot readily imagine, this concentration upon forebears can seem overdone." *The Education of a Woman: The Life of Gloria Steinem* (New York: Ballantine, 1995), p. 1.

44. Ellen Willis, "The Greening of Betty Friedan" [1981], in *No More Nice Girls: Countercultural Essays* (Hanover, N.H.: Wesleyan University Press, 1992), p. 62.

45. Ibid., p. 62.

46. Katha Pollitt, "Whose Culture?" in Susan Moller Okin, *Is Multiculturalism Bad for Women?* (Princeton: Princeton University Press, 1999), p. 27.

47. Andrea Dworkin, *Scapegoat: The Jews, Israel, and Women's Liberation* (New York: Free Press, 2002), p. ix.

48. Letty Cottin Pogrebin, *Deborah, Golda, and Me: Being Female and Jewish in America* (New York: Crown, 1991), p. 253.

49. Alice Kessler Harris, "Introduction," in Anzia Yezierska, *Bread Givers* (New York: Persea, 1975), pp. xvii, ix.

50. Meredith Tax, *Rising of the Women: Feminist Solidarity and Class Conflict, 1880–1917* (New York: Monthly Review Press, 1982); Meredith Tax, *Union Square* [1988] (Urbana: University of Illinois Press, 2001), p. 72.

51. Willis, "Letter to the Left" [1969], in Rosalyn Baxendall and Linda Gordon, eds., *Dear Sisters: Dispatches from the Women's Liberation Movement* (New York: Basic, 2001), p. 51.

52. Broner, *Her Mothers,* pp. 126, 34.

53. Ibid., p. 21.

54. Tax, *Rising of the Women,* p. 290. Kathie Sarachild, "The Power of History," in Redstockings, *Feminist Revolution* (New York: Random House, 1975), pp. 13–43, comments at length on both the problematic

and the instrumental uses to which "history" was put by the early movement.

55. Vivian Gornick, *The Romance of American Communism* (New York: Basic, 1977), pp. 258, 259; Ellen Willis, "The Family: Love It or Leave It" [1979], in *Beginning to See the Light: Pieces of a Decade* (New York: Knopf, 1981), p. 166.

56. Sydelle Kramer and Jenny Masur, eds., *Jewish Grandmothers* (Boston: Beacon, 1976), pp. xv–xvi; Rosen, *World Split Open*, pp. 205–206.

57. Ellen Messer-Davidow, *Disciplining Feminism: From Social Activism to Academic Discourse* (Durham: Duke University Press, 2002), pp. 83–84; Annelise Orlick, *Common Sense and a Little Fire: Women and Working-Class Politics in the United States, 1900–1965* (Chapel Hill: University of North Carolina Press, 1991), p. 303. On the early cultivation of Women's Studies, see also Faderman, *Naked in the Promised Land;* Florence Howe, ed., *The Politics of Women's Studies: Testimony from Thirty Founding Mothers* (New York: Feminist Press, 2000).

58. Gerda Lerner, "Placing Women in History: A 1975 Perspective," *Feminist Studies* 3, nos. 1–2 (1975), pp. 5–15; Gerda Lerner, *Why History Matters: Life and Thought* (New York: Oxford University Press, 1998), pp. 210, 201.

59. Alix Kates Shulman, *To the Barricades: The Anarchist Life of Emma Goldman* (New York: Crowell, 1971), pp. vii, 1, 159, 160–161. Similarly, see Charlotte Baum, Paula Hyman, and Sonya Michel, *The Jewish Woman in America* (New York: Plume, 1975), pp. xii–xiii; Weaver, *New Catholic Women,* pp. xxix–xxx, 18, 22–23, 24.

60. Karen Brodkin, "On the Politics of Being Jewish in a Multiracial State," unpublished manuscript in the author's possession, pp. 6–7; Brodkin, *How the Jews Became White Folks,* pp. 131–136.

61. Maxine Seller, *Immigrant Women* (Albany: State University of New York Press, 1994), pp. 6, 7. See also Donna Gabaccia, *From the Other Side: Women, Gender, and Immigrant Life in the U.S., 1820–1990* (Bloomington: Indiana University Press, 1994); Donna Gabaccia, ed., *Seeking Common Ground: Multidisciplinary Studies of Immigrant Women in the United States* (Westport: Praeger, 1992).

62. Elizabeth Ewen, *Immigrant Women in the Land of Dollars: Life and Culture on the Lower East Side, 1890–1925* (New York: Monthly Review Press, 1985), p. 13; Sydney Stahl Weinberg, *The World of Our Mothers: The Lives of Jewish Immigrant Women* (New York: Schocken, 1987), p. xiii; Sydney Stahl Weinberg, "The World of Our Fathers

and the World of Our Mothers," *American Jewish History* 88:4 (Dec. 2000), p. 550.

63. Orlick, *Common Sense and a Little Fire*, p. 1; Kathie Friedman-Kasaba, *Memories of Migration: Gender, Ethnicity, and Work in the Lives of Jewish and Italian Women in New York, 1870–1924* (Albany: State University of New York Press, 1996), pp. 1–2. See also Antler, *The Journey Home*, pp. xv, xviii.

64. Judy Chicago, *Beyond the Flower: The Autobiography of a Feminist Artist* (New York: Viking, 1996), pp. 3–5; Judy Chicago, *The Holocaust Project: From Darkness into Light* (New York: Viking, 1993), pp. 22, 26.

65. Patricia Mainardi, "Women Artists and Women's Studies," in Redstockings, *Feminist Revolution*, p. 117; Judy Chicago, *The Dinner Party: A Symbol of Our Heritage* (New York: Anchor, 1979), p. 52.

66. Chicago, *Dinner Party*, pp. 98, 65, 92–93, 202, 241–251.

67. Chicago, *Beyond the Flower*, p. 174.

68. Chicago, *Holocaust Project*, pp. 98, 10, 30–31; Chicago, *Beyond the Flower*, p. 168.

69. Chicago, *Holocaust Project*, pp. 124, 109, 110.

70. Chicago, *Beyond the Flower*, p. 201; Chicago, *Holocaust Project*, pp. 88, 91.

71. Chicago, *Holocaust Project*, plates 27–31.

72. Pogrebin, *Deborah, Golda, and Me*, pp. 139–140; Rothenberg, *Invisible Privilege*, p. 19.

73. Cynthia Eller, *Living in the Lap of the Goddess: The Feminist Spirituality Movement in America* (Boston: Beacon Press, 1993), p. 47; Mary Jo Weaver, *Springs of Water in a Dry Land: Spiritual Survival for Catholic Women Today* (Boston: Beacon Press, 1993), p. 81; Mary Daly, "Autobiographical Preface," *The Church and the Second Sex* [1968] (New York: Colophon, 1975), pp. 5, 6, 8.

74. Milhaven, *Inside Stories*, pp. 41, 57; Schussler Fiorenza, *Discipleship of Equals*.

75. Milhaven, *Inside Stories*, p. xi; Aviva Cantor, "Jewish Women's Haggadah," in Carol Christ and Judith Plaskow, eds., *Womanspirit Rising: A Feminist Reader in Religion* (New York: Harper Collins, 1979), p. 192.

76. Starhawk, "Witchcraft and Women's Culture," in Christ and Plaskow, *Womanspirit Rising*, p. 268; on the antimodernist theme, see also Merlin Stone's lament over "high-rise steel buildings, formica countertops, and electronic television screens," and her solace in, among other things, "Celtic Ireland and the Goddess Brigit." "When God Was a Woman," in *Womanspirit Rising*, pp. 120, 121.

77. Starhawk, *Dreaming the Dark,* p. 92; Margot Adler, *Drawing Down the Moon* (Boston: Beacon, 1987), p. 105; Zsuzsanna Budapest, *The Grandmother of Time: A Women's Book of Celebrations, Spells, and Sacred Objects for Every Month of the Year* (San Francisco: HarperSanFrancisco, 1989), pp. xvii–xviii. The fact that feminist antimodernism was at once related to, and arrayed *against,* the masculinist antimodernism so rampant in American culture was nicely captured in Mary Daly's identification of the ethnic-revival idol Vito Corleone as "a vivid illustration of the marriage of tenderness and violence so intricately blended in the patriarchal ideal." Daly, *Beyond God the Father* [1974] (New York: FSG, 1985), p. 16. Adrienne Rich makes a similar association in "The Anti-Feminist Woman" (1972), in *On Lies, Secrets, and Silence: Selected Prose* (New York: Norton, 1979), p. 73.

78. Weaver, *New Catholic Women,* p. 112; Judith Plaskow, *Standing Again at Sinai: Judaism from a Feminist Perspective* (San Francisco: Harper SanFrancisco, 1991), p. 14; Schussler Fiorenza, *Discipleship of Equals,* p. 251; Ruether quoted in Weaver, *Springs of Water,* p. 8.

79. Leadership Conference of Women Religious, "Focus on Women" (1975), in Rosemary Radford Ruether and Rosemary Skinner Keller, eds., *In Our Own Voices: Four Centuries of American Women's Religious Writings* (San Francisco: HarperSanFrancisco, 1995), p. 54; Mary Bader Papa, *Christian Feminism: Completing the Subtotal Woman* (Chicago: Fides/Claretian, 1981), p. 22; Riv-Ellen Prell, *Prayer and Community: The Havurah in American Judaism* (Detroit: Wayne State University Press, 1989), p. 273; Roiphe, *Generation without Memory,* p. 18.

80. Here I rely on Sidney Callahan, *The Illusion of Eve: Modern Women's Quest for Identity* (New York: Exlibris, 1965); Weaver, *Springs of Water;* Daly, *Church and the Second Sex;* Milhaven, *Inside Stories;* Schussler Fiorenza, *Discipleship of Equals;* Rosemary Ruether, "Entering the Sanctuary: The Roman Catholic Story," in Rosemary Ruether and Eleanor McLaughlin, eds., *Women of Spirit: Female Leadership in the Jewish and Christian Traditions* (New York: Simon and Shuster, 1979), p. 375; Maria Riley, *Transforming Feminism* (New York: Sheed and Ward, 1989); Ruether and Keller, *In Our Own Voices;* Rosemary Radford Ruether, ed., *Religion and Sexism: Images of Woman in the Jewish and Christian Traditions* (New York: Touchstone, 1974).

81. Mary Luke Tobin, "Foreword" to Papa, *Christian Feminism,* p. xi; Daly, *The Church and the Second Sex,* pp. 123, 11, 17, 9.

82. Daly, *Beyond God the Father,* p. 3; Milhaven, *Inside Stories,* p. 45.

83. Schussler Fiorenza, *Discipleship of Equals,* p. 104; Ruether, "Entering

the Sanctuary," pp. 379, 381; Papa, *Christian Feminism*, pp. 126–127. See also "Church Roles for Women," in Cunneen, *Sex: Female; Religion: Catholic*, pp. 130–146.

84. The following account of Jewish religious feminism derives from Ellen Umansky, "Women in Judaism: From the Reform Movement to Contemporary Jewish Religious Feminism," in Ruether and McLaughlin, eds., "Women of Spirit," p. 346; Rachel Adler, *Engendering Judaism: An Inclusive Theology and Ethics* (Boston: Beacon, 1998), esp. the "Introduction"; Sylvia Barack Fishman, *A Breath of Life: Feminism in the American Jewish Community* (New York: Free Press, 1993), pp. 1–17, 121–180; Paula Hyman, "Ezrat Nashim and the Emergence of a New Jewish Feminism," in Robert Sletzer and Norman Cohen, eds., *The Americanization of the Jews* (New York: New York University Press, 1995); Elizabeth Koltun, *The Jewish Woman: New Perspectives* (New York: Schocken, 1976); Baum, Hyman, and Michel, *The Jewish Woman in America;* Heschel, *On Being a Jewish Feminist*, "Introduction," pp. xxi–liv, esp. xxxii–xxxv; Deborah Lipstadt, "Women and Power in the Federation," in Heschel, *On Being a Jewish Feminist*, p. 152; Schneider, *Jewish and Female;* Ruether and Keller, *In Our Own Voices*.

85. Plaskow, *Standing again at Sinai*, p. 235; Prell, *Prayer and Community*.

86. Schneider, *Jewish and Female*, p. 6.

87. Judith Plaskow, "The Right Question Is Theological," in Heschel, *On Being a Jewish Feminist*, pp. 223–233. This essay is a response to Cynthia Ozick's essay "Notes Toward Finding the Right Question," *Lilith* 6 (1979). The ins and outs of this theological discussion are summed up nicely in Adler, *Engendering Judaism*.

88. Daly, *Gyn/Ecology*, p. xii; Francine Zuckerman, *Half the Kingdom: Seven Jewish Feminists* (Montreal: Vehicule, 1998), pp. 141, 75–76.

89. Plaskow, "The Right Question Is Theological," p. 224. See also Alicia Ostriker, "Back to the Garden: Reading the Bible as a Feminist," in Rubin-Dorsky and Fishkin, *People of the Book*, pp. 64–77.

90. Plaskow, "The Right Question Is Theological," pp. 227, 228. Of her brother's bar mitzvah, Anne Roiphe writes, "I have at no other day, at no other time, been that jealous of another human being. It appeared to me that he had sanctity and I had none." *Generation without Memory*, p. 142.

91. Heschel, *On Being a Jewish Feminist*, p. xi.

92. Daly quoted in ibid., p. xxi; Plaskow, "The Right Question Is Theological," p. 229; Ellen Umansky, "Creating a Jewish Feminist Theol-

ogy," in Plaskow and Christ, eds., *Weaving the Visions*, p. 190; Rosemary Radford Ruether, "Sexism and God-Language," in Plaskow and Christ, *Weaving the Visions*, p. 151. See also Rachel Adler, "And Not Be Silent: Toward Inclusive Worship," in *Engendering Judaism*, pp. 61–103; Cynthia Ozick, "Notes toward Finding the Right Question," p. 29.

93. Rachel Adler, *Engendering Judaism*, pp. xviii, 69; Marge Piercy, *Art of Blessing the Day*, dedication.

94. Prell, *Prayer and Community*, pp. 280, 281.

95. Rosemary Radford Ruether, "Women-Church: An American Catholic Feminist Movement," in Mary Jo Weaver, *What's Left: Liberal American Catholics* (Bloomington: Indiana University Press, 1999), p. 55; Milhaven, *Inside Stories*, pp. 137–138; Zuckerman, *Half the Kingdom*, p. 20.

96. Arlene Agus, "This Month Is for You: Observing Rosh Hodesh as a Woman's Holiday," in Koltun, *The Jewish Woman*, pp. 84, 89, 92.

97. Zuckerman, *Half the Kingdom*, pp. 23, 21; E. M. Broner, *A Weave of Women* (New York: Henry Holt, 1978), pp. 256, 152–154, 233–238, 256–262, 261.

98. More than thirty women's haggadot—books for the Passover ritual—were published between 1971 and 1995. See Maida Solomon, "Claiming Our Questions: Feminism and Judaism in Women's Haggadot," in Antler, *Talking Back*, pp. 220–241.

99. Broner, *The Telling*, pp. 184, 193; Seder themes over the years are enumerated on pp. 87–88. On the feminist Seder see also Pogrebin, *Deborah, Golda, and Me*, pp. 111–127.

100. Steichen, *Ungodly Rage*, esp. "Eve Reconsidered," pp. 119–191. Steichen's conclusions will strike some as extreme—her assessment of liberation theology, for example, as a case where "a theory of social revolution designed for destitute Latin American peasants [is being] used to lure middle-class North American nuns into witchcraft" (pp. 278–279). But in simply documenting the writings, the speeches, the conferences, and the convergences of figures from diverse segments of the secular and spiritual feminist movements, Steichen's historiography is invaluable. See also the "Special Section on Neo-Paganism," *Journal of Feminist Studies of Religion*, 5:1 (Spring 1989), pp. 47–100.

101. Rosemary Curb and Nancy Monahan, eds., *Lesbian Nuns: Breaking Silence* (New York: Warner, 1985). In Margot Adler's small sample, 23 percent of neopagan informants were originally Catholic, 7 percent

mixed Catholic, and 5 percent Jewish, for a total of 35 percent from the religions most solidly associated with the "new immigration." Margot Adler, *Drawing Down the Moon: Witches, Druids, Goddess-Worshippers, and Other Pagans in America Today* [1979] (New York: Penguin, 1986), p. 444. Cynthia Eller, too, notes the large proportion of refugees from these religions (in Daly's sense of the term), and remarks that some spiritual feminist workshop leaders "say that they meet more Catholic and Jewish women in the course of this work," possibly because "they have a familiarity with ritual and the use of religious symbols." *Living in the Lap of the Goddess*, pp. 41, 22–23.

102. Charlene Spretnak, *States of Grace: The Recovery of Meaning in the Postmodern Age* (New York: HarperCollins, 1991), pp. 146–147. This "return" is described in a passage on menarche (first menstruation) and a bride's prenuptial ritual.

103. Starhawk, *The Spiral Dance: A Rebirth of the Ancient Religion of the Great Goddess* [1979] (San Francisco: HarperSanFrancisco, 1999), p. 14. Similarly, Riane Eisler's treatment of the Kurgan invasion of "Old Europe" explicitly relates it to the Nazi disruption of her Austrian youth. If the Goddess-worshipping practices of pre-invasion Old Europe represent a charged and appealing heritage for modern feminists, this rendition of the invasion itself intertwines the author's distinctly *ethnic* heritage. *The Chalice and the Blade*, p. 182.

104. Zuckerman, *Half the Kingdom*, pp. 112–113. As Cynthia Eller notes, Jewish narratives and symbols have generally been incorporated into feminist spirituality more readily and widely than Christian materials. "For most Jewish women," she notes, "Judaism is not an identity that can easily be cast aside." Eller, *Living in the Lap of the Goddess*, p. 224. On the anti-semitic strains of some spiritual feminism, see Fishman, *A Breath of Life*, pp. 10–11; Annette Daum, "Blaming the Jews for the Death of the Goddess," *Lilith*, no.7 (1980).

105. Ryiah Lilith, "Challah for the Queen of Heaven," in Danya Ruttenberg, ed., *Yentl's Revenge: The Next Wave of Jewish Feminism* (Seattle: Seal Press, 2001), pp. 102, 104. For a Catholic version of this return to traditional religion, see Ruether, "Women-Church," p. 54.

106. Starhawk, *Spiral Dance*, p. 216.

107. Daly, *Gyn/Ecology*, p. xiv; Daly, *The Church and the Second Sex*, p. 11. On the compatibility between spiritual and secular feminisms, see also Charlene Spretnak, *The Politics of Women's Spirituality: Essays by Founding Mothers of the Movement* (New York: Anchor, 1982), esp.

Robin Morgan, "Prose Poem," p. 87; Phyllis Chesler, "The Amazon Legacy," pp. 97–113; Gloria Steinem, "Tales of a Reincarnated Amazon Princess," pp. 114–120; and Judy Chicago, "Our Heritage Is Our Power," pp. 152–156.

108. Schussler Fiorenza, *Discipleship of Equals*, p. 236; Millett, *Flying*, p. 112 (Millett does go on to note, however, that the term "CR" "smacks of an evangelism faintly embarrassing to a lapsed Catholic"); Marjorie Tuite et al., "'How to' Skills with a Feminist Perspective" (Chicago: National Assembly of Religious Women, 1984); Starhawk, *Dreaming the Dark*, p. 28; Starhawk, *Spiral Dance*, p. 59.

109. Daly, *Gyn/Ecology*, pp. xvi, 39, 221. On witches and the Old Religion, see esp. pp. 178–222. Morgan had already discovered Margaret Murray's work *Witch-Cult in Western Europe* by the early 1970s, and was celebrating Joan of Arc as wicca. See "Lesbian Poem," in *Monster* (New York: Vintage, 1972), p. 71. As already noted, Judy Chicago later made the witch-burnings central to her thinking about the relationship between antifeminism and anti-semitism. See *The Holocaust Project*, p. 91.

110. Adler, *Drawing Down the Moon*, p. 223. See Spretnak, *The Politics of Women's Spirituality;* Christ and Plaskow, *Womanspirit Rising*. On the affinities connecting goddess religions and wicca to the emergent feminisms within Judaism and Christianity, see also Weaver, *Springs of Water in a Dry Land*, pp. 14–22, 25–36, 76–95; Schussler Fiorenza, "Cartography of Struggle," in *Discipleship of Equals*, p. 9; Broner, *The Telling;* Broner, "Honor and Ceremony in Women's Rituals," in Spretnak, *The Politics of Women's Spirituality*, p. 238; Morgan, esp. "The Network of the Imaginary Mother," which "recalls" Dachau and also calls a roll of dead witches. In *Lady of the Beasts* (New York: Random House, 1976), pp. 63–88. See also Judy Chicago, *Beyond the Flower, The Dinner Party, The Holocaust Project*.

111. Robin Morgan, ed., *Sisterhood Is Powerful: An Anthology of Writings from the Women's Liberation Movement* (New York: Random House, 1970), pp. 538, 539, 538–553; Daly, *Gyn/Ecology*, pp. 14–15 (see also Daly's comments on Joan of Arc and "the witch within" in *Beyond God the Father*, pp. 146–149); Eller, *In the Lap of the Goddess*, esp. pp. 38–61; Adler, *Drawing Down the Moon*. See also Erica Jong, *Witches* (New York: Abradale, 1981). On the feminist symbolism of witchcraft, see also Mary Bader Papa, *Christian Feminism*, pp. 24–26; Curb and Manahan, *Lesbian Nuns: Breaking Silence*, p. 316.

112. Broner, *The Telling*, p. 136; Starhawk, *Dreaming the Dark*, pp. 31, 162;

Starhawk, "Ritual as Bonding: Action as Ritual," in Plaskow and Christ, *Weaving the Visions,* p. 327.

113. Spretnak, *States of Grace,* p. 130; Adler, *Drawing Down the Moon,* pp. 117–118; Eller, *Living in the Lap of the Goddess,* pp. 78–79.

114. Werner Sollors, "Literature and Ethnicity," in Stephen Thernstrom, ed., *The Harvard Encyclopedia of American Ethnic Groups* (Cambridge, Mass.: Harvard University Press, 1980), p. 648; Adler, *Drawing Down the Moon,* pp. 72–77.

115. Adler, *Drawing Down the Moon,* pp. 139, 145–147, 148, 149. Elsewhere Adler comments in more general terms on the ways in which wicca, in emphasizing a nonexploitative European heritage—"the old tribal/peasant heritage of Europe"—may provide practitioners with a usable past for left politics (p. 380).

116. Zsuzsanna Budapest, *The Holy Book of Women's Mysteries* [1980] (Oakland: Wingbow, 1989), pp. 227, 17, 239, 264, 270.

117. Gubar, "Eating the Bread of Affliction," pp. 24, 26.

118. Robin Morgan, "Feminist Diplomacy" [1991], in *The Word of a Woman: Feminist Dispatches* (New York: Norton, 1991), p. 278.

119. Robin Morgan, "The Politics of Silence" [1989], in *Word of a Woman,* p. 195; Lorraine Bethel, "What Chou Mean We, White Girl," *Conditions: Five* (Autumn 1979), pp. 86–92.

7. Whose America (Who's America)?

1. Bruce Schulman, *The Seventies: The Great Shift in American Culture, Society, and Politics* (New York: Free Press, 1991), p. 158; George Lipsitz, *American Studies in a Moment of Danger* (Minneapolis: University of Minnesota Press, 2001).

2. Schulman, *The Seventies,* pp. 124, 141; *Time,* Dec. 14, 1981, pp. 64–65; Bernard Bailyn et al., *The Great Republic: A History of the American People* [1977] (Lexington, Mass.: D.C. Heath, 2nd ed., 1981); Leo Chavez, *Covering Immigration: Popular Images and the Politics of the Nation* (Berkeley: University of California Press, 1999), pp. 19–20; Sidney Plotkin and William Scheuerman, *Private Interest, Public Spending: Balanced-Budget Conservatism and the Fiscal Crisis* (Boston: South End Press, 1994), p. 19. On late-twentieth-century political economy see especially Mike Davis, *Prisoners of the American Dream* (New York: Verso, 2000); Eric Schlosser, *Fast Food Nation* (New York: HarperCollins, 2002); Doug Henwood, *After the New Economy* (New York: New Press, 2003), esp. chaps. 2 and 3; Ursula Huws, *The Making of a Cybertariat: Virtual Work in a Real World* (New York: Monthly

Review Press, 2003), on the myth of the "weightless economy" and the escalating burdens of "consumption work." On the relationship between political economy and "white anxiety, anger, and alienation," see Robert Entman and Andrew Rojecki, *The Black Image in the White Mind: Media and Race in America* (Chicago: University of Chicago Press, 2000), esp. pp. 60–77.

3. Janice Mirikitani, *Shedding Silence: Poetry and Prose* (San Francisco: Celestial Arts, 1987), p. 21. Pandora Leong writes, "I've always thought that 'Why are you brown?' would be a more honest question." "Living Outside the Box," in Daisy Hernandez and Bushra Rehman, eds., *Colonize This! Young Women of Color on Today's Feminism* (New York: Seal, 2002), p. 349. See also Mia Tuan, *Forever Foreigners or Honorary Whites: The Asian Ethnic Experience Today* (New Brunswick: Rutgers University Press, 1999), pp. 40, 137; William Wong, *Yellow Journalist: Dispatches from Asian America* (Philadelphia: Temple University Press, 2001); Neil Gotanda, "Exclusion and Inclusion: Immigration and American Orientalism," in Evelyn Hu-Dehart, *Across the Pacific: Asian Americans and Globalization* (Philadelphia: Temple University Press, 2000), p. 144; Frank Wu, *Yellow: Race in America beyond Black and White* (New York: Basic, 2003), esp. pp. 79–129; Darrell Hamamoto, *Monitored Peril: Asian Americans and the Politics of TV Representation* (Minneapolis: University of Minnesota Press, 1994); Jun Xing, *Asian America through the Lens: History, Representations, and Identity* (New York: AltaMira, 1998).

4. Guillermo Gómez-Peña, *Dangerous Border Crossers: The Artist Talks Back* (New York: Routledge, 2000), p. 147. See also Ada Maria Isasi-Diaz and Yolanda Tarango, eds., *Hispanic Women, Prophetic Voice in the Church: Toward a Hispanic Women's Liberation Theology* (New York: Harper Collins, 1988); Mike Davis, *Magical Urbanism: Latinos Reinvent the U.S. Big City* (London: Verso, 2001), p. 60; Marco Portales, *Crowding Out Latinos: Mexican Americans in the Public Consciousness* (Philadelphia: Temple University Press, 2000), p. 2; Juan Gonzalez, *Harvest of Empire: A History of Latinos in America* (New York: Penguin, 2001), p. 96; Otto Santa Ana, *Brown Tide Rising: Metaphors of Latinos in Contemporary American Public Discourse* (Austin: University of Texas Press, 2002); Gloria Anzaldua, *Borderlands / La Frontera: The New Mestiza* (San Francisco: Aunt Lute, 1987), p. 243; Ian Haney-López, *Racism on Trial: The Chicano Fight for Justice* (Cambridge, Mass.: Harvard University Press, 2003), pp. 56–87; Cheech Marin,

Born in East L.A. (1985) Marin's plot pivots on the wrongful deportation and subsequent "illegal" re-entry of a U.S. citizen.

5. June Jordan, *Civil Wars: Observations from the Front Lines of America* [1981] (New York: Touchstone, 1995), p. xix. On Vincent Chin, see Helen Zia, *Asian American Dreams: The Emergence of an American People* (New York: Farar Straus Giroux, 2000), pp. 58–81; Robert Chang, *Disoriented: Asian Americans, Law, and the Nation State* (New York: New York University Press, 1999), pp. 21–26; Yen Le Espiritu, *Asian American Panethnicity: Bridging Institutions and Identities* (Philadelphia: Temple University Press, 1992), pp. 141–160; Sheng-Mae Ma, *The Deathly Embrace: Orientalism and Asian American Identity* (Minneapolis: University of Minnesota Press, 2001), pp. 76–92; Amitava Kumar, *Passport Photos* (Berkeley: University of California Press, 2000), pp. 18–19; Robert Lee, *Orientals: Asian Americans in Popular Culture* (Philadelphia: Temple University Press, 1999), p. 217.

6. Michael Crichton, *Rising Sun* (New York: Ballantine, 1992); *New York Times,* June 14, 1992, Section 2, p. 1; *Boston Globe,* Feb. 13, 1992, p. 78. *Rising Sun* provoked serious rebuttals of economic doctrine in the op-ed pages of several major journals. See the *Washington Post,* Feb. 19, 1992, p. A19; *Newsweek,* May 4, 1992, p. 82; *Los Angeles Times,* March 15, 1992, p. 95; *New York Times,* Sept. 3, 1992, p. A22; *Business Week,* Feb. 10, 1992, p. 12.

7. See John Horton, *The Politics of Diversity: Immigration, Resistance, and Change in Monterey Park, California* (Philadelphia: Temple University Press, 1995), pp. 84–85; *New York Times,* April 14, 1976. See also Michael Cimino's films *Heaven's Gate* (1981) and *Year of the Dragon* (1985).

8. Cornel West and Michael Lerner, *Jews and Blacks: A Dialogue on Race, Religion, and Culture in America* (New York: Plume, 1996); Jack Salzman et al., *Bridges and Boundaries: African Americans and American Jews* (New York: Braziller, 1992); Hasia Diner, *In the Almost Promised Land: American Jews and Blacks, 1915–1935* (Baltimore: Johns Hopkins University Press, 1977); Jeffrey Melnick, *A Right to Sing the Blues: African Americans, Jews, and American Popular Song* (Cambridge, Mass.: Harvard University Press, 1999); Seth Foreman, *Blacks in the Jewish Mind: A Crisis of Liberalism* (New York: New York University Press, 1998); Jonathan Kaufman, *Broken Alliance: The Turbulent Times between Blacks and Jews* (New York: Mentor, 1989).

9. Garry Wills, *Nixon Agonistes* (New York: Mentor, 1969), pp. 268–269; Dick Gregory, "Cowboys and Indians" [1971], *Dick Gregory at Kent State* (collectables, 1997), disc 2, track 2; Bruce Nelson, *Divided We*

Stand (Princeton: Princeton University Press, 2003); Martin Scorsese, dir., *The Gangs of New York*, 2002. See also David Roediger, "Smear Campaign: Giuliani, the *Holy Virgin Mary*, and the Critical Study of Whiteness," in *Colored White: Transcending the Racial Past* (Berkeley: University of California Press, 2002), pp. 27–33.

10. Jennifer Guglielmo, "White Lies/Dark Truths," in Jennifer Guglielmo and Salvatore Salerno, eds., *Are Italians White? How Race Is Made in America* (New York: Routledge, 2003), p. 4.

11. Entman and Rojecki, *Black Image*, pp. 23–24, 228.

12. *Newsweek*, April 25, 1988, p. 63.

13. *Washington Post*, May 20, 1982, p. C3; Geraldine Ferraro and Linda Bird Francke, *Ferraro: My Story* (New York: Bantam, 1985), pp. 230, 231–235; Geraldine Ferraro, "One Stand against Bigotry," in *Changing History: Women, Power and Politics* (Wakefield, R.I.: Moyer Bell, 1993), pp. 41–50; John McGreevy, *Catholicism and American Freedom: A History* (New York: Norton, 2003), pp. 287–288; "Italian Men," *National Review*, Nov. 2, 1984, p. 18.

14. *Washington Post*, Aug. 14, 1984, p. A19.

15. Ibid.; *New York Times*, June 4, 1984, p. A8; *Washington Post*, Sept. 25, 1988, C1.

16. *Newsweek*, April 25, 1988, p. 63; *People Weekly*, March 28, 1988, p. 45; *Washington Post*, Jan. 20, 1988, p. C1; Olympia Dukakis, *Ask Me Again Tomorrow: A Life in Progress* (New York: Harper Collins, 2003), pp. 77, 147.

17. *New York Times*, April 14, 1988, p. D26; *Newsweek*, April 25, 1988, p. 63; Dukakis, *Ask Me*, pp. 1–22; Charles Kenney and Robert Turner, *Dukakis: An American Odyssey* (Boston: Houghton Mifflin, 1988), pp. 2–3.

18. *Washington Post*, May 22, 1988, p. A7; July 23, 1988, p. A16; July 24, 1988, p. A16; *New York Times*, July 24, 1988, p. 16; Kenney and Turner, *Dukakis*, pp. 8–9. Lovitz played Dukakis on *Saturday Night Live* throughout the fall of 1988.

19. *Los Angeles Times*, April 8, 1988, p. 1; *Newsday*, July 10, 1988, p. 3; *Washington Post*, Sept. 4, 1988, p. A6. Indeed, when Olympia traveled to Greece to see where her parents had come from, she recalls, "The first thing I saw was a sign that said *The ancestral home of Michael Dukakis*." Dukakis, *Ask Me*, p. 179.

20. *Time*, July 25, 1988, pp. 24, 29; Christine Black and Thomas Oliphant, *All by Myself: The Unmaking of a Presidential Campaign* (Chester, Conn.: Globe Pequot Press, 1989), p. 173.

21. *Newsday*, April 17, 1988, p. 7; *Washington Post*, May 22, 1988, p. A7; David Nyhan, *The Duke: The Inside Story of a Political Phenomenon* (New York: Warner, 1988), p. 153.

22. Nyhan, *The Duke*, pp. 79, 120; *Los Angeles Times*, March 1, 1988, p. 16; *Washington Post*, May 22, 1988, p. A7.

23. St. Petersburg *Times*, Oct. 17, 1988, p. 10A.

24. *Macleans*, Feb. 22, 1988, p. 28; *New Republic*, June 6, 1988, p. 22; *Washington Post*, June 22, 1988, p. A23; Nyhan, *The Duke*, p. 12; *Life*, June 1988, p. 6; *Time*, July 25, 1988, p. 26.

25. Kenney and Turner, *Dukakis*, pp. 10–13; *Los Angeles Times*, April 8, 1988, p. 1; *Washington Post*, May 28, 1988, p. A12; Sept. 25, 1988, p. C1.

26. *Washington Post*, May 22, 1988, p. A7; June 7, 1988, p. A23; *New York Times*, June 6, 1988, B6.

27. Nyhan, *The Duke*, pp. 180, 256, 257, 31–32.

28. Michael Barone in *Washington Post*, June 26, 1988, p. C7; Meg Greenfield, "The Immigrant Mystique," *Newsweek*, Aug. 8, 1988, p. 76.

29. Michael Novak, *Rise of the Unmeltable Ethnics* (New York: Macmillan, 1971), p. 72; *Washington Post*, July 8, 1988, p. A4.

30. David Anderson, *Crime and the Politics of Hysteria: How the Willie Horton Story Changed American Justice* (New York: Times Books, 1995), p. 213. One critique of the *Lawrence Eagle-Tribune*'s Pulitzer Prize–winning series on Horton, for instance, characterized it as a "one-sided, sloppily reported, heat-seeking case of advocacy journalism." *Washington Journalism Review*, July–Aug. 1989, pp. 15–19.

31. Anderson, *Crime and the Politics of Hysteria*, p. 251; *Nation*, Nov. 14, 1988, p. 20. See also Tali Mendelberg, *The Race Card: Campaign Strategy, Implicit Messages, and the Norm of Equality* (Princeton: Princeton University Press, 2001).

32. Anderson, *Crime and the Politics of Hysteria*, p. 192; *Washington Post*, Oct. 27, 1988, p. A27; Oct. 30, 1988, p. 1.

33. Entman and Rojecki, *Black Image*, pp. 52–53, 92; Anderson, *Crime and the Politics of Hysteria*, pp. 30, 207. Democrats did not openly object to the racial politics of the Horton ads until late October; protests like that at Howard University, in which 1,000 students occupied a building and demanded Lee Atwater's resignation from the Board of Trustees, took place later still (*New York Times*, Oct. 24, 1988, p. A1; *U.S. News and World Report*, March 20, 1989, p. 13). For his part, Atwater claims that the Bush campaign stopped using the Horton story for "paid" advertising as soon as they discovered Horton's race. "In retro-

spect," he later said, "I'm sorry he was black, we should have used a white guy." *New York Times*, April 26, 1989, p. A24; Anderson, *Crime and the Politics of Hysteria*, pp. 217, 246.

34. Anderson, *Crime and the Politics of Hysteria*, pp. 5–8.

35. Ibid., pp. 211, 241, 162–163.

36. David Horowitz, *Uncivil Wars: The Controversy over Reparations for Slavery* (San Francisco: Encounter, 2002), pp. 10–11. On the long history of reparations as a political idea, see Robin D. G. Kelley, *Freedom Dreams: The Black Radical Imagination* (Boston: Beacon, 2002), pp. 110–134.

37. Horowitz, *Uncivil Wars*, pp. 13, 90.

38. Ibid., p. 12.

39. Ibid., p. 105.

40. *San Francisco Chronicle*, Oct. 3, 1992, p. A12; *USA Today*, Oct. 8, 1992, p. 2A. Hollywood may have subtly endorsed this view of the explorer-as-immigrant: *Christopher Columbus: The Discovery* was written by Mario Puzo and starred Marlon Brando; *1492: Conquest of Paradise* featured Gerard Depardieu, whose most recent English-language role had been as an illegal alien in *Green Card*.

41. Leonard Peltier, *Prison Writings: My Life Is My Sundance* (New York: St. Martin's Griffin, 1999), p. 50; Richard Rodriguez, *Days of Obligation: An Argument with My Mexican Father* (New York: Penguin, 1992), pp. 5, 8. See also Guillermo Gómez-Peña, Enrique Chagoya, and Felicia Rice, *Codex Espangliensis: From Columbus to the Border Patrol* (San Francisco: City Lights, 2000).

42. *Los Angeles Times*, Oct. 11, 1992, p. A16; *Chicago Sun Times*, Oct. 9, 1992, p. 3; Matthew Frye Jacobson, *Barbarian Virtues: The United States Encounters Foreign Peoples at Home and Abroad, 1876–1917* (New York: Hill and Wang, 2000), p. 203; Orm Overland, *Immigrant Minds, American Identities: Making America Home, 1870–1930* (Champaign-Urbana: University of Illinois Press, 2000), chap. 2.

43. *New York Times*, Nov. 4, 1989, Final Section, p. 24; *St. Petersburg Times*, Oct. 3, 1990; *Los Angeles Times*, Oct. 12, 1989, p. 7. See also "Columbus Day 1992: Will Latin Americans Celebrate the Anniversary or Denounce It as Marking '500 Years of Sin'?" *St. Petersburg Times*, Sept. 23, 1989, p. 2E; "Columbus Day or Dia de la Raza?" *Los Angeles Times*, Oct. 12, 1989 (*Nuestro tiempo* edition), p. 7. On *mestizaje* see also Haney-López, *Racism on Trial*, pp. 218–220.

44. *London Independent*, Feb. 3, 1991, Sunday Review Section, p. 26; *Boston Globe*, Oct. 14, 1991, p. 38; *San Francisco Chronicle*, March 5,

1992, p. A13; Ward Churchill, "Deconstructing the Columbus Myth," in *A Little Matter of Genocide: Holocaust and Denial in the Americas, 1492 to the Present* (San Francisco: City Lights, 1997), p. 81.

45. Suzan Shown Harjo, "I Won't Be Celebrating Columbus Day," *Newsweek*, Sept. 1, 1991, p. 32; *Minneapolis Star Tribune*, April 25, 1992, p. 1B; *USA Today*, Oct. 8, 1992, p. 2A; *Los Angeles Times*, Oct. 4, 1990, p. 4.

46. *Los Angeles Times*, Oct. 11, 1992, p. A3; *San Francisco Chronicle*, Sept. 26, 1990, p. E14; *St. Louis Post-Dispatch*, Oct. 6, 1990; *Houston Chronicle*, Oct. 14, 1991, p. 4. On Houston's ecumenical tradition, see also *Houston Chronicle*, Oct. 11, 1992, p. 22; *Newsday*, Oct. 15, 1991, p. 85; *USA Today*, Oct. 13, 1992, p. 3A.

47. *Minneapolis Star Tribune*, April 25, 1992, p. 1B; *USA Today*, Oct. 8, 1992, p. 2A; *Newsday*, Oct. 15, 1991, p. 85; *New York Times*, Aug. 25, 1991, p. 27; James Yellowbank quoted in *Chicago Sun-Times*, Oct. 9, 1992, p. 3.

48. *USA Today*, Oct. 8, 1992, p. 2A; *Washington Post*, Oct. 11, 1992, p. A11; *Los Angeles Times*, Oct. 11, 1992, pp. A16, A3; *New York Times*, Oct. 12, 1992, p. B7; Oct. 11, 1992, p. 18.

49. *San Francisco Chronicle*, Oct. 12, 1992, p. A1; Oct. 3, 1992, p. A12; *Washington Post*, Oct. 11, 1992, p. A11.

50. Charles Krauthammer, "Hail Columbus, Dead White Male," *Time*, May 27, 1991, p. 74.

51. *Los Angeles Times*, Oct. 12, 1992, p. A3.

52. Churchill, "Deconstructing the Columbus Myth," pp. 85–88.

53. Ibid., pp. 84, 88; Peter Novick, *The Holocaust in American Life* (New York: Houghton Mifflin, 1999), pp. 194–195. People "who were oppressed here rather than there" refers in this instance to African-American slaves.

54. Kirkpatrick Sale, *The Conquest of Paradise: Christopher Columbus and the Columbian Legacy* (New York: Plume, 1990), p. 368; Kirkpatrick Sale, "Preface to the 1989 Edition," in E. F. Schumacher, *Small Is Beautiful: Economics as if People Mattered* [1973] (New York: Harper and Row, 1989), p. xx; Kirkpatrick Sale, *Human Scale* (New York: Coward, McCann, and Geoghegan, 1980), pp. 429–442; Kirkpatrick Sale, *SDS* (New York: Random House, 1973).

55. Robert Viscusi, *An Oration upon the Most Recent Death of Christopher Columbus* (West Lafayette, Ind.: Bordighera, 1993), p. 8; "Preface" (no page number).

56. Ibid., pp. 14, 2, 7, 12.

57. Ibid., "Preface" (no page number).

58. Michael LeMay, *From Open Door to Dutch Door* (New York: Praeger, 1987); Jacobson, *Barbarian Virtues*, pp. 217–218.

59. David Heer, *Immigration in America's Future: Social Science Findings and the Policy Debate* (Boulder: Westview, 1996), pp. 209–210; Douglas Massey, Jorge Durand, and Nolan Malone, *Beyond Smoke and Mirrors: Mexican Immigration in an Era of Economic Integration* (New York: Russell Sage, 2002), p. 105; Juan Perea, ed., *Immigrants Out! The New Nativism and the Anti-Immigrant Impulse in the United States* (New York: New York University Press, 1997); David Reimers, *Unwelcome Strangers: American Identity and the Turn against Immigration* (New York: Columbia University Press, 1998); Peter Schuck, *Citizens, Strangers and In-Betweens: Essays on Immigration and Citizenship* (Boulder: Westview Press, 1998); David Abraham, "American Jobs but Not the American Dream," *New York Times*, Jan. 9, 2004, p. A19; Bush's address on immigration, *New York Times*, Jan. 8, 2004, p. A28; Kevin Phillips, *American Dynasty: Aristocracy, Fortune, and the Politics of Deceit in the House of Bush* (New York: Viking, 2004), pp. 117–118.

60. Cheryl Shanks, *Immigration and the Politics of American Sovereignty, 1890–1990* (Ann Arbor: University of Michigan Press, 2001), pp. 192, 216; William Dudley, *Immigration: Opposing Viewpoints* (San Diego: Greenhaven, 1990), p. 67; Heer, *Immigration in America's Future*, p. 202.

61. *New York Times*, Sept. 12, 2002, p. 1; Sheldon Rampton and John Stauber, *Weapons of Mass Deception: The Uses of Propaganda in Bush's War on Iraq* (New York: Penguin, 2003), p. 38. See also David Cole, *Enemy Aliens: Double Standards and Constitutional Freedoms in the War on Terrorism* (New York: New Press, 2003).

62. John F. Kennedy, *A Nation of Immigrants* [1958] (New York: Harper and Row, 1964), pp. 99–100.

63. Ibid., p. 10.

64. Ibid., pp. 41, 43, 50, 51–58.

65. Ibid., pp. 58, 109–110, 149–150.

66. Lawrence Auster, *The Path to National Suicide: An Essay on Immigration and Multiculturalism* (Fairfield, Va.: AICF, 1991), pp. 19–20, 12; Richard Alba and Victor Nee, *Remaking the American Mainstream: Assimilation and Contemporary Immigration* (Cambridge, Mass.: Harvard University Press, 2003), p. 176.

67. Heer, *Immigration in America's Future*, pp. 28–29, 152; Alba and Nee, *Remaking the American Mainstream*, pp. 174–214; Davis, *Magical Urbanism*, p. 15.

68. Dudley, *Immigration: Opposing Viewpoints,* pp. 173–174, 68, 58, 60, 59.

69. Dudley, *Immigration: Opposing Viewpoints,* p. 69, emphasis added; Peter Brimelow, *Alien Nation: Common Sense about America's Immigration Disaster* (New York: Perennial, 1996), pp. 203, 206.

70. Brimelow, *Alien Nation,* pp. 28, 48, 208, 203. In an elaborate, graphed discussion of shifting demographics (pp. 62–64), Brimelow likens the growing nonwhite population to a military "pincer" movement, the declining white population and the growing Latino population to "closing the pincers."

71. Patrick Buchanan, *The Death of the West: How Dying Populations and Immigrant Invasions Imperil Our Country and Civilization* (New York: St. Martins, 2002), p. 97. That this competition was understood in some quarters in the eugenic terms of an earlier generation's "race suicide" became clear when John Tanton, the founder of the Federation of American Immigration Reform (FAIR), commented on Latino fecundity: "Can *homo contriceptivus* compete with *homo progenitiva* if borders aren't controlled? Or is advice to limit ones [*sic*] family simply advice to move over and let someone else with greater reproductive powers occupy the space?" Linda Chavez, *Out of the Barrio: Toward a New Politics of Latino Assimilation* (New York: Basic, 1992), p. 92; Richard Lamm and Gary Imhoff, *The Immigration Time Bomb: The Fragmenting of America* (New York: Dutton, 1986), p. 93.

72. Buchanan, *Death of the West,* pp. 124–126, 208, 228, 236.

73. Dudley, *Immigration: Opposing Viewpoints,* pp. 239, 240; Glenn Dumke, "Preface," in Nathan Glazer, *Clamor at the Gates* (New York: Institute for Contemporary Studies, 1985), no page number.

74. Auster, *Path,* p. 45; Samuel Huntington, "The Hispanic Challenge," *Foreign Policy,* March/April, 2004 (www.foreignpolicy.com).

75. Nancy Foner, *From Ellis Island to JFK: New York's Two Great Waves of Immigration* (New Haven: Yale University Press, 2000), p. 206; Cheryl Shanks, *Immigration and the Politics of American Sovereignty, 1890–1990* (Ann Arbor: University of Michigan Press, 2001), pp. 55–95; Jacobson, *Whiteness of a Different Color,* pp. 77, 72, 184.

76. Foner, *From Ellis Island to JFK,* p. 2; *Newsweek,* Dec. 23, 1991, p. 17.

77. Michael Barone, *The New Americans: How the Melting Pot Can Work Again* (Washington, D.C.: Regnery, 2001), pp. 275–279.

78. Ibid., p. 3.

79. Ibid., pp. 64, 148, 248, 114, 192, 274, 112.

80. Jeffrey Melnick and Rachel Rubin, *Immigrants and American Popular Culture* (New York: New York University Press, forthcoming).

81. Erika Lee, *At America's Gates: Chinese Immigration during the Exclusion Era, 1882–1943* (Chapel Hill: University of North Carolina Press, 2003), pp. 19–46, 249. On the creation of the "illegal alien" and the portent of that category for U.S. citizenship, see esp. Mae Ngai, *Impossible Subjects: Illegal Aliens and the Making of Modern America* (Princeton: Princeton University Press, 2004).

82. Meredith Tax, *Union Square* [1988] (Urbana: University of Illinois Press, 2001), pp. 241, 242–244.

83. Ellen Pence, "Racism—A White Issue," in Gloria Hull, Patricia Bell Scott, and Barbara Smith, eds., *All the Women Are White, All the Blacks Are Men, But Some of Us Are Brave: Black Women's Studies* (New York: Feminist Press, 1982), p. 45; bell hooks, *Feminism Is for Everybody: Passionate Politics* (Boston: South End, 2000), esp. pp. 55–60; bell hooks, *Killing Rage: Ending Racism* (New York: Owl, 1995), pp. 98–107, 184–196; Jo Carillo et al., "And When You Leave, Take Your Pictures with You: Racism in the Women's Movement," in Cherrie Moraga and Gloria Anzaldua, eds., *This Bridge Called My Back: Writings by Radical Women of Color* (New York: Kitchen Table, 1981), pp. 63–106; Ellen Willis, "Sisters under the Skin? Confronting Race and Sex" [1982], in *No More Nice Girls: Countercultural Essays* (Hanover, N.H.: University Press of New England, 1992), pp. 101–116; "Roundtable Discussion: Racism in the Women's Movement," *Journal of Feminist Studies in Religion*, 4:1 (Spring 1988), pp. 94–114; Gloria Anzaldua, ed., *Making Face, Making Soul: Haciendo Caras—Creative and Critical Perspectives by Women of Color* (San Francisco: Aunt Lute, 1990), esp. pp. xv–xxvi, 3–71.

84. Adrienne Rich, "If Not with Others, How?" [1985], in *Blood, Bread, and Poetry: Selected Prose* (New York: Norton, 1986), pp. 203, 209; Elly Bulkin, "Hard Ground: Jewish Identity, Racism, and Anti-Semitism," in Elly Bulkin, Minnie Bruce Pratt, and Barbara Smith, *Yours in Struggle: Three Feminist Perspectives on Anti-Semitism and Racism* (Ithaca: Firebrand, 1984), p. 181.

85. Becky Thompson offers a useful timeline of these developments in *A Promise and a Way of Life: White Antiracist Activism* (Minneapolis: University of Minnesota Press, 2001), appendix. Patricia Hill Collins, *Black Feminist Thought: Knowledge, Consciousness, and the Politics of Empowerment* (New York: Routledge, 2000); Toni Cade, *The Black Woman* (New York: Signet, 1970); Hull, Bell-Scott, and Smith, *Some of Us Are Brave*; Anzaldua and Moraga, *This Bridge Called My Back*; bell hooks, *Ain't I a Woman: Black Women and Feminism* (Boston:

South End, 1981); Chandra Talpade Mohanty, Ann Russo, and Lourdes Torres, eds., *Third World Women and the Politics of Feminism* (Bloomington: Indiana University Press, 1991).

86. Audre Lorde, "Sexism: An American Disease in Blackface" [1979], in *Sister Outsider: Essays and Speeches* (Freedom, Calif.: Crossing, 1984), p. 60. Emily Erwin Culpepper, "New Tools for the Theology: Writings by Women of Color," *Journal of Feminist Studies in Religion*, 4:2 (Fall 1988), p. 45; Alice Echols, *Daring to Be Bad: Radical Feminism in America, 1967–1975* (Minneapolis: University of Minnesota Press, 1989), pp. 292–293; Ann Brooks, *Postfeminisms: Feminism, Cultural Theory, and Cultural Form* (New York: Routledge and Kegan Paul, 1997), pp. 13–25.

87. Collins, *Black Feminist Thought*, p. 77; Toni Morrison, "What the Black Woman Thinks about Women's Lib," *New York Times Magazine*, Aug. 22, 1971; Hazel Carby, "White Woman Listen! Black Feminism and the Boundaries of Sisterhood," in Centre for Contemporary Cultural Studies, *The Empire Strikes Back: Race and Racism in '70s Britain* (London: Hutchinson, 1982), p. 217; Toni Cade, Introduction to *The Blackwoman* [1970], in Barbara Crow, ed., *Radical Feminism* (New York: New York University Press, 2000), pp. 424–425.

88. Elena Olazagasti-Segovia in Ada Maria Isasi-Diaz, "*Mujeristas:* Who We Are and What We Are About," *Journal of Feminist Studies in Religion*, 8:1 (Spring 1992), p. 110; Morrison, "What the Black Woman Thinks about Women's Lib," p. 454. See also Ada Maria Isasi-Diaz and Yolanda Tarango, *Hispanic Women: Prophetic Voice in the Church* (San Francisco: Harper and Row, 1988).

89. Lorde, "An Open Letter to Mary Daly" [1979], in *Sister Outsider,* pp. 68, 69. See Mary Daly, *Gyn/Ecology: The Metaethics of Radical Feminism* [1978] (Boston: Beacon, 1990).

90. Ibid., p. 70; Lorde, "The Master's Tools Will Never Dismantle the Master's House" [1979], in *Sister Outsider,* p. 113. Compare bell hooks, "Overcoming White Supremacy: A Comment," in *Killing Rage,* p. 193.

91. Alice Walker, "One Child of One's Own: A Meaningful Digression within the Work(s)" [1979], in *In Search of Our Mothers' Gardens: Womanist Prose* (New York: Harcourt Brace Jovanovich, 1983), p. 372.

92. Ibid., p. 373.

93. Ibid., pp. 373, 374.

94. Sandoval, "Feminism and Racism," p. 64.

95. Daly, *Gyn/Ecology,* p. xxx; Cynthia Eller, *Living in the Lap of the God-*

dess (Boston: Beacon, 1995), pp. 74–82; "Roundtable Discussion: Racism in the Women's Movement," *Journal of Feminist Studies in Religion* (Spring 1988), p. 110. Eller cites a similar controversy at the 1990 National Women's Studies Association meeting over the appropriation of Native-American spirituality by white middle-class feminists of the movement (pp. 75–76). See also "Special Section on Appropriation and Reciprocity in Womanist/Mujerista/Feminist Work," in *Journal of Feminist Studies in Religion,* 8:2 (Fall 1992), pp. 91–122.

96. Angela Davis, "Rape, Racism, and the Myth of the Black Rapist," in *Women, Race, and Class* (New York: Random House, 1983), pp. 178–182; Valerie Smith, "Split Affinities: The Case of Interracial Rape," in Marianne Hirsch and Evelyn Fox Keller, eds., *Conflicts in Feminism* (New York: Routledge, 1990), p. 274. Compare Brownmiller's treatment of "the black rapist" on the one hand and the rape of Jewish women in pogroms on the other. *Against Our Will: Men, Women, and Rape* (New York: Fawcett, 1975), pp. 121–124, 210–255. Chela Sandoval, "Feminism and Racism: A Report on the 1981 National Women's Studies Association Conference," in Anzaldua, *Making Face, Making Soul,* p. 58; Barbara Smith, "Between a Rock and a Hard Place: Relationships between Black and Jewish Women," in Bulkin, Pratt, and Smith, *Yours in Struggle,* p. 79; O'Neale cited in Laura Leavitt, "Feminist Dreams of Home," in *Jews and Feminism: The Ambivalent Search for Home* (New York: Routledge, 1997), p. 111.

97. bell hooks, "Madonna: Plantation Mistress or Soul Sister?" in *Black Looks: Race and Representation* (Boston: South End Press, 1992), pp. 157, 158. See also the essays in Hernandez and Rehman, *Colonize This!,* Rebecca Hurdis, "Heartbroken," p. 287; Adriana Lopez, "In Praise of Difficult Chicas," pp. 126–127; Siobhan Brooks, "Black Feminism in Everyday Life," pp. 112–113.

98. Jeffrey Melnick, "Rattling the Cage of Black-Jewish Relations," in Marc Lee Raphael, ed., *"Jewishness" and the World of "Difference" in the United States* (Williamsburg: William and Mary, 2001), p. 51.

99. Melanie Kaye/Kantrowitz, "To Be a Radical Jew in the Late Twentieth Century," in *The Issue Is Power: Essays on Women, Jews, Violence, and Resistance* (San Francisco: Aunt Lute, 1992), p. 126. See also bell hooks, "Keeping a Legacy of Shared Struggle," in *Killing Rage,* pp. 204–225, and Martha Ackelsberg, "Toward a Multicultural Politics: A Jewish Feminist Perspective," in Marla Brettschneider, ed., *The Narrow Bridge: Jewish Views on Multiculturalism* (New Brunswick: Rutgers University Press, 1996), pp. 89–104.

100. Smith, "Between a Rock and a Hard Place," pp. 67, 68. This essay is also reproduced in Barbara Smith, *The Truth That Never Hurts: Writings on Race, Gender, and Freedom* (New Brunswick: Rutgers University Press, 1998), pp. 132–153.

101. Smith, "Between a Rock and a Hard Place," pp. 67–68, 69, 79, 72, 73, 75. See Evelyn Torton Beck: "the attempt to include anti-Semitism in discussions of racism is rejected [within the feminist movement] and sometimes met with a sense of outrage that Jews are trying to take over *again*." "Why Is This Book Different?" in Evelyn Torton Beck, ed., *Nice Jewish Girls: A Lesbian Anthology* (Watertown: Persephone, 1982), p. xix.

102. Smith, "Between a Rock and a Hard Place," p. 76.

103. Bulkin, "Hard Ground," pp. 98–99, 106. The Combahee River Collective "Black Feminist Statement" is collected in Hull, Scott, and Smith, *But Some of Us Are Brave*, pp. 13–22.

104. Bulkin, "Hard Ground," pp. 110, 115.

105. Ibid., pp. 139, 140; Melanie Kaye/Kantrowitz, "Some Notes on Jewish Lesbian Identity," in Beck, *Nice Jewish Girls*, p. 37.

106. Starhawk, *Dreaming the Dark*, pp. 137, 134, xii, 6, 21; Starhawk, *The Spiral Dance*, pp. 31–32.

107. Adrienne Rich, "Split at the Root" [1982], in *Blood, Bread, and Poetry*, pp. 120, 122, 123; Adrienne Rich, "North American Tunnel Vision" [1983], in *Blood, Bread, and Poetry*, p. 162.

108. Letty Cottin Pogrebin, *Deborah, Golda, and Me: Being Female and Jewish in America* (New York: Crown, 1991), pp. 157, 276.

109. Alice Walker, "The Civil Rights Movement: What Good Was It?" [1967], in *In Search of Our Mothers' Gardens*, p. 128; McAlister, *Epic Encounters*, pp. 84–124.

110. Alice Walker, "To the Editors of *Ms.* Magazine" [1983], in *In Search of Our Mothers' Gardens*, pp. 347–349.

111. Ibid., pp. 350, 354, 353; Smith, "Between a Rock and a Hard Place," pp. 82–83.

112. Bulkin, "Hard Ground," p. 163; Rich, "If Not with Others, How?", p. 205; Andrea Dworkin, *Scapegoat: The Jews, Israel, and Women's Liberation* (New York: Free Press, 2000), p. 207; Ellen Willis, "Is There Still a Jewish Question? Why I Am an Anti-Anti-Zionist," in Tony Kushner and Alisa Solomon, *Wrestling with Zion: Progressive Jewish-American Responses to the Israeli-Palestinian Conflict* (New York: Gravoe, 2003), pp. 226–232.

113. Pogrebin, *Golda, Deborah, and Me*, p. 161. This is a primary theme in

Phyllis Chesler, *The New Anti-Semitism: The Current Crisis and What We Must Do about It* (San Francisco: Jossey-Bass, 2003).

114. Pogrebin, *Golda, Deborah, and Me*, p. 213; Bulkin, "Hard Ground," pp. 169, 181; Chesler, *The New Anti-Semitism*, pp. 53, 155.

115. Mirtha Quintanales, "I Paid Very Hard for My Immigrant Ignorance," in Moraga and Anzaldua, *This Bridge Called My Back*, pp. 150–151; Beck, "Why Is This Book Different?" p. xxi; Zillah Eisenstein, *The Radical Future of Liberal Feminism* (Boston: Northeastern University Press, 1981), p. 230.

116. Kaye/Kantrowitz, "To Be a Radical Jew in the Twentieth Century," pp. 146–147.

117. Joann Nash Eakin, "From the Prairie to the World," in Letty Russell et al., eds., *Inheriting Our Mothers' Gardens: Feminist Theology in Third World Perspective* (Louisville: Westminster, 1988), pp. 117, 122.

118. Chesler, *The New Anti-Semitism*, p. 17; Philip Jenkins, *The New Anti-Catholicism: The Last Acceptable Prejudice* (New York: Oxford University Press, 2003). On comparative pariah status, check Chesler's treatment of feminist anti-semitism against Jenkins's chapter "The Church Hates Women," pp. 67–91.

119. Rudolph Giuliani, *Leadership* (New York: Miramax, 2002), p. xvii.

120. Ibid., pp. 184–186.

121. Melanie Kaye/Kantrowitz, "Notes of an Immigrant Daughter: Atlanta" [1981], in Beck, *Nice Jewish Girls*, p. 113.

122. Rudolfo Acuna, *Occupied America: A History of Chicanos* (New York: HarperCollins, 1981), p. 115; Otto Santa Ana, *Brown Tide Rising: Metaphors of Latinos in Contemporary American Public Discourse* (Austin: University of Texas Press, 2002); Timothy Dunn, *The Militarization of the US-Mexico Border, 1978–1992: Low Intensity Conflict Doctrine Comes Home* (Austin: University of Texas Press, 1992).

Coda: Ireland at JFK

1. *New York Times*, April 17, 1987, p. A30; Nov. 8, 1987, Sec. 4, p. 6. Reliable numbers are notoriously hard to come by for undocumented immigration. The *Irish Voice* estimated between 135,000 and 200,000 undocumented Irish nationwide in early 1988; and by 1989 the *New York Times* was reporting "as many as 30,000 illegal Irish in Boston and 100,000 in New York" alone. *New York Times*, March 13, 1988, Sec. 21, p. 16; March 17, 1989, p. A12.

2. *New York Times*, Aug. 23, 1989, p. A12; March 17, 1989, p. A12.

3. "The Re-Greening of America," *Time*, March 20, 1989, p. 30.

4. Ibid.; *New York Times,* Nov. 20, 1988, Sec. 6-II ["New York, New York"], p. 32; March 17, 1989, p. A12.

5. Ray O'Hanlon, *The New Irish Americans* (Niwot, Colo.: Roberts Rinehart, 1998), pp. 42, 70, 61–63, 57–75 *passim,* 98–109; *New York Times,* March 16, 1988, p. A14; April 10, 1988, Sec. 4, p. 5; July 13, 1989, p. A18; July 14, 1989, pp. 1, B5; Nov. 27, 1988, p. A52; June 25, 1989, Sec. 22, p. 6; March 1, 1989, p. A19; Oct. 7, 1990, p. 47; Oct. 12, 1991, p. 31; Maureen Dezell, *Irish America Coming into Clover: The Evolution of a People and a Culture* (New York: Doubleday, 2000), pp. 189–209.

6. O'Hanlon, *New Irish Americans,* p. 82; *New York Times,* Oct. 11, 1987, p. 67; Nov. 8, 1987, Sec. 4, p. 6; O'Hanlon, *New Irish Americans,* p. 53.

7. *New York Times,* April 17, 1987, p. A30; June 24, 1988, p. 1; Jan. 26, 1989, p. A12; Oct. 12, 1991, p. A7; Jan. 29, 1989, p. 1; April 10, 1989, p. A5; June 18, 1989, p. 1; Nov. 4, 1992, p. A24; Leo Chavez, *Covering Immigration: Popular Images and the Politics of the Nation* (Berkeley: University of California Press, 2001); Otto Santa Ana, *Brown Tide Rising: Metaphors of Latinos in Contemporary American Public Discourse* (Austin: University of Texas Press, 2002).

8. *New York Times,* June 7, 1993, pp. 1, B4, B5; June 8, 1993, p. A25; June 11, 1993, p. A31.

9. *New York Times,* April 17, 1987, pp. A1, A3, B1, B3; Nov. 8, 1987, Sec. 4, p. 6; May 3, 1987, p. 1; Sept. 2, 1993, p. B8.

10. Fintan O'Toole, *Black Hole, Green Card: The Disappearance of Ireland* (Dublin: New Island, 1994), p. 23.

11. *New York Times,* Oct. 18, 1993, p. B4.

12. David Cole, *Enemy Aliens: Double Standards and Constitutional Freedoms in the War on Terrorism* (New York: New Press, 2003), p. 169. On the LA8, see also David Cole and James Dempsey, *Terrorism and the Constitution: Sacrificing Civil Liberties in the Name of National Security* (New York: New Press, 2002), pp. 35–48.

13. William V. Shannon, *The American Irish: A Political and Social Portrait* (New York: Collier, 1963), p. vi.

Acknowledgments

This book began with a strong but unproved conviction that the so-called ethnic revival was both longer-lived and more deeply emplotted than common wisdom allows. On close inspection, I was convinced, it would turn out to run much deeper in American political culture and its portent would far surpass a seeming national fondness for kielbasa festivals, "Italians Do It Better" T-shirts, and Irish trivia books. This is not necessarily the most ambitious project I have ever worked on, but for a number of reasons it turned out to be the most difficult, not least because it sent me back into my own past. I am lucky to have received so much help from both friends and strangers along the way—more, certainly, than anyone is entitled to expect.

My deepest gratitude is to Werner Sollors, who walked up to me at the Massachusetts Historical Society after a presentation of this work in its earliest stages, and handed me a very fat file of newspaper clippings, magazine articles, and other 1970s ephemera relating to the ethnic revival. "It's your project now," he said. In a better world this kind of thing might happen all the time; but personally, I've only seen it this once. The loan of the material was important enough, but the gift of Werner's confidence carried me further than he knows.

A number of people read earlier versions of the manuscript from beginning to end, offering much-needed encouragement and suggestions for improvement: Alicia Schmidt Camacho, Steve Pitti, Nikhil Singh, Mark Krasovic, and Brian Herrera.

Each saw something a little bit different in the book, but together they helped me to understand it with renewed clarity. Judy Smith, Jeff Melnick, Rachel Rubin, and Robert Fleegler also read and improved individual chapters. It's a much better book for having passed through all these people's hands. Once again my experience with the editors at Harvard University Press has been that every time they touch a manuscript, it gets better. Since I hate to admit when an editor is right and I am wrong, it has been most excruciating working with Joyce Seltzer. Damn. And once again I'm grateful to Christine Thorsteinsson for her golden touch, and to Megan Glick for hers. My thanks, too, to Harvard's anonymous reviewers for their careful readings, at once generous and exacting.

My colleagues and students in American Studies, History, and African American Studies at Yale have taught me and pressed me and held me up in all sorts of ways. I'm not exactly a company man, but I can't imagine a more challenging and rewarding intellectual community. Special thanks to Jean-Christophe Agnew, Lila Corwin Berman, Jon Butler, Alicia Schmidt Camacho, Hazel Carby, Erin Chapman, Michael Denning, Johnny Faragher, Glenda Gilmore, Paul Gilroy, Megan Glick, Laura Grappo, Brian Herrera, Jonathan Holloway, Paula Hyman, Rebecca Kobrin, Mark Krasovic, Patricia Pessar, Steve Pitti, Besenia Rodriguez, Alan Trachtenberg, Laura Wexler, Bryan Wolf, and Sandy Zipp. I am also grateful to Vicki Shepard, Brenda Crocker, Janet Giarratano, and Geneva Melvin for making it possible to maintain a little sanity and concentration, even when the odds were against it. Students in my classes "The Politics and Culture of the American Color Line" and "The Formation of Modern American Culture" have tolerated more of this work than they bargained for, and they have contributed a great deal to it. The graduate students in "Race and Races in American Studies" over the years have kept me fresh for the whole scholarly enterprise.

One student I will never get the chance to repay is Shafali Lal, who came blazing across the firmament at Yale like a meteor, and then was gone. Before she died, she worked as my research assistant for a year, and she and I had many conversations about politics and "difference," some in relation to her work, some in relation to mine. More a colleague and friend than a student, she was always incisive and bold in her thinking; our talks left a major mark on this book, especially Chapters 2 and 6. (I'll always remember her this way: we are debating some interpretive point about the 1970s, she looks me squarely in the eye—I am technically one of her dissertation advisors, mind—and she says, "I can't believe you think that.") She really lit the place up while she was here.

The first piece of this research to see the light of day was an essay titled "Hyphen Nation," for Jean-Christophe Agnew and Roy Rosenzweig's book *Companion to Post-1945 America.* Throughout the process of getting that essay out, Jean-Christophe and Roy offered many important words of encouragement and criticism. It was they who really allowed me to see the potential of the subject. I was also fortunate to cross paths with Gary Gerstle at one of my very first presentations of the work. He, too, encouraged and redirected me where I needed help most. He also demonstrated an uncanny ability to bounce my own words back to me in a way that made me understand them anew. His commentary was sharp, his criticisms unabashed; but so was his critique remarkably caring. More than any other single person, Gary helped me to imagine how to do justice to this unruly topic.

I began presenting portions of this research in about 2000, and I picked up much valuable assistance and criticism along the way. My thanks to audience members at the Massachusetts Historical Society and the Organization of American Historians; the English Departments at Harvard, the University of Massachusetts at Amherst, and the University of Kentucky; the History Departments at the University of Maryland, Sussex College in Cambridge, Georgia State University, and Emory; the Religious Studies program at William and Mary; the American Studies programs at Yale and Cornell; the Geography Department at Dartmouth; and the History, Political Science, and Ethnic Studies departments at Columbia. Often the comments that stayed with me and most changed my thinking came from those who remain unknown to me. The following, happily, I can acknowledge by name: Elaine Abelson, Alan Brinkley, Mona Damosh, Marc Dollinger, Eric Goldstein, Marilyn Halter, Gordon Hutner, Tamar Jacoby, Alan Kraut, Tony Marx, Melani McAlister, Tim Meagher, Jeff Melnick, Phil Napoli, Dana Nelson, Gary Okihiro, Marc Lee Raphael, Linda Raphael, Rachel Rubin, Nick Salvatore, Sandhya Shukla, Joe Skerrit, Judy Smith, Reed Ueda, Barbara Weinstein, and Steven Whitfield.

A number of research assistants ran down materials for me over the course of this project; each brought back treasures, even on the scantest instruction, and each offered some insightful (sometimes wry) commentary along the way. My thanks to Brian Herrera, Michael Cohen, Shafali Lal, J. J. Fueser, Mandi Isaacs Jackson, and Gretchen Heefner.

Although I chose not to take the oral history route here, my inquiry into the ethnic revival—and into ethnic identity in general—has been developed in conversation with Gail Bederman,

Lila Corwin Berman, Carlo Corea, Peter D'Agostino, Catherine Eagan, Robert Fleegler, Seth Foreman, Donna Gabaccia, Jennifer Gillan, Linda Grasso, Tom Guglielmo, Ken Jacobson, Amy Kaplan, Russ Kazal, Janice Okoomian, Dave Roediger, Judy Smith, Rudy Vecoli, Robert Viscusi, David Waldstreicher, Laura Wexler, and Leo Zanderer.

This project incubated over a very long period of time—beginning, when it comes right down to it, with a college essay I was assigned in 1977 on the subject of my family's "roots." Twenty-five years' worth of influence have come into play as I've thought this through. I remain ever grateful to David Marr, Richard Jones, and David Powell, whose guidance and example I hope still shows. Dale Favier and Martha West were among the first to show me how to do the whole writing thing. Judy Smith has been an inspiration, an important mentor, and a good friend for some twenty years now; I trust she'll spot her influence infusing these pages. Many aspects of this project took me back to materials and issues I was first grappling with at Brown in the 1980s. Enduring thanks to Teresa Bill, Nan Boyd, Mari Jo Buhle, Oscar Campomanes, Ann du Cille, Jim Cullen, Kevin Gaines, Todd Gernes, Linda Grasso, Susan Hendel, Bob Lee, Bob McMichael, Rich Meckel, Joanne Melish, Kate Monteiro, Louise Newman, Janice Okoomian, Tricia Rose, Laura Santigian, Jessica Shubow, Lyde Sizer, Michael Topp, and Laurie Umansky. I benefit from their insights and their generosity even still.

As ever, I owe the most to my wife, Francesca Schwartz, who not only put up with the demands, constraints, and vicarious torments of another fat damn book, but who managed to retain her respect for me—or at least to feign it—even when she came in night after night to find me watching *Species, Yentl,* or Neil Diamond's *Jazz Singer.* (And these were some of the good ones.) One day she came in waving a copy of *Fear of Flying,* which I had left on the kitchen counter. With a wonderful, understated smile, she asked, "Is there anything you want to tell me?" She enlivens my days, and she also remains my toughest and most demanding critic. Hers is the eye I write for.

In the acknowledgment page to an earlier project I thanked my children, Nick and Tess, for teaching me the important lesson that a book is just a book. That was true at the time, and an important lesson for me then. My experience with the present project teaches that maybe a book *isn't* just a book. But Nick and Tess are still da bomb.

Finally, one cannot spend this long thinking about "roots" without reflecting an awful lot on one's own family. And so I want to thank my parents, Sarah and Jerry Jacobson, and my sisters, Carol Wright and Beth Smith, for their support and sustenance over the years. I got better than I gave. But I also want to ask: How is it, do you think, that each of us ended up with a different heritage? Just wondering.

Index

Abortion and reproductive rights, 161, 162, 187, 356
Abruzzi, 44
Academia, 31, 34, 37–40, 42, 51, 54, 63, 125, 229–230, 236, 335
Adler, Margot, 152–153, 306, 307–308
Affirmative action, 9, 98–101, 108, 182, 192, 360, 382
Africa and Africans, 43–44, 47, 68, 354, 356, 368, 370, 377, 381; and colonialism, 194, 335, 342, 378
African American migration, 178
African Americans, 8, 17, 31, 35, 36, 41–44, 56, 68, 87, 96, 98, 100–109, 112–114, 186–197, 202, 218, 231, 265, 315, 317–318, 319, 335, 359, 360, 361, 364–365; Civil Rights and, 19, 20, 21, 22, 218, 222–224; criminalization of, 148, 315, 318, 332–333, 388; feminism and, 366–374. *See also* Black-Jewish relations; Black nationalism; Black Power Movement; Reparations; Slavery
African American Studies, 229–230
Afrocentrism, 18, 230, 315
Agnew, Spiro, 214, 318, 320
Alba, Richard, 36, 150
Aleichem, Sholem, 87, 89
Ali, Muhammad, 21, 68, 101, 115
Alien Nation (Peter Brimelow), 347, 354–356, 358, 360
Alien Nation (film), 360–361
Allen, Woody, 74, 110, 126, 151
All in the Family, 31
Alternative press, 221
America America, 64, 76, 126
American Historical Association (AHA), 37, 38
Americanism, 6, 7, 8, 9, 10, 13, 15, 16, 32–33, 56, 58, 64–69, 84–85, 179–180, 240, 320, 348, 386, 387, 396
American Immigrant Wall of Honor, 8, 62–63

American Immigration Museum, 59–69
American Indian Movement (AIM), 340–341
American Pop, 78, 87, 90, 116
Ancestors and Immigrants, 37
Ancient Order of Hibernians (AOH), 162–163
Anderson, David, 332–333
Angela's Ashes, 74, 77
Annie Hall, 126, 127, 212, 213, 272, 288–289, 329–330, 344, 401n21, 445n77
Antimodernism, 23–26, 87–89, 135–137, 188, 198
Anti-Semitism, 111, 112, 117–123, 159, 160, 215, 223, 224, 235, 257–258, 267, 268, 284, 310, 366, 374, 375, 377, 385
Anzaldua, Gloria, 229, 366
Arab-Israeli War, 222, 224–225, 239
Arabs, 158, 203, 381, 387, 379
Arlen, Michael, 46–47
Armenian, 47, 50, 323
Arnie, 30, 73
Asia, 69, 352, 354, 356
Asian Americans, 35, 77, 145, 195, 204, 315, 317, 351, 359, 360, 361, 390–391
Assimilation, 3, 12, 21, 34, 38, 44, 63, 92, 93–94, 128, 133–141, 173–174, 175, 192, 193, 206, 214, 220–221, 222, 226, 236, 237, 238, 262, 263, 264, 267, 268, 269, 278, 279, 288, 289, 330, 353–354, 356, 357, 358, 359, 369, 376, 378
Assimilation in American Life, 34
Austen, Alice, 78, 80–81
Authenticity, 23, 43–44, 53, 55, 78, 123, 130, 210, 238, 285
Avalon, 75–76, 110, 127, 240

Bailey, Beth, 151–152
Bakke case, 98–101, 108
Balanchine, George, 57

Baldwin, James, 232, 399n7
Ball, Lucille, 30, 92
Ballyporeen, 16, 17, 46, 321, 322, 328
Baltimore, 76, 110–111
Barbie Doll, 264–266, 439n33
Barolini, Helen, 244, 249, 250, 270
Barone, Michael, 321–322, 330, 358–360
Baryshnikov, Mikhail, 57
Battery Park, 60
Beals, Jesse Tarbox, 79–80
Beauty, 263–267, 310, 440n35
Belfast, 35
Bellow, Saul, 28, 157
Bellstone, The, 46
Benedict, Ruth, 33
Berger, Peter, 198–200
Berlin Wall, 14
Beyond the Melting Pot, 1, 10, 49, 177–178,
    191, 195, 254
Bicentennial, 17, 53, 54–56, 313, 387
Bilingualism, 18, 203, 359, 315
Bintel Brief, 78, 80
Birmingham, 22
Black Hole, Green Card, 394–395
Black-Jewish relations, 111–115, 209, 223–
    225, 317–318, 373–377, 379–381, 384
Black nationalism, 2, 9, 207, 225, 233
Black Power, 20
Black Power Movement, 9, 20, 38, 189, 190,
    192, 207, 222, 223, 225, 240–241, 312–313
Black Woman, The, 366–367
Blade Runner, 360–361
Boas, Franz, 32–33, 35
Border (U.S.–Mexico), 315, 361–364, 388,
    390, 458n71
Borge, Victor, 68
Boston, 13, 22, 35, 140, 162, 304, 327, 328,
    329, 340, 390, 391, 393
Bread and Roses, 274, 367
Bread Givers, 30, 131, 269, 271
Breakdancing, 96, 115
Breira, 49, 224
Brice, Fanny, 86, 91, 95
Bridget Loves Bernie, 30–31, 73, 126
Brighton Beach Memoirs, 110, 127
Brimelow, Peter, 347, 354–356, 358–359, 360,
    424n36
Broadway, 58, 88, 89

Brodkin, Karen, 267–277
Brody, Jennifer DeVere, 9
Broner, Esther [E. M.], 249, 270, 272–274,
    299–300, 306, 310
Bronx Primitive, 161, 270
Brooklyn, 6, 15, 190, 193, 199, 203
Brooklyn Bridge, 31, 73
Brownmiller, Susan, 226, 253, 265, 300, 372
Brown v. Board of Education, 114, 286, 290
Brzezinski, Zbigniew, 68
Buchanan, Patrick, 347, 355–356, 358
Budapest, Zsuzsanna, 289, 302, 305, 308–
    309
Bulkin, Elly, 366, 374, 375–377, 378, 381, 382,
    383
Bureaucratization, 23
Bush, George Herbert Walker, 200–201,
    202, 204, 327–333
Bush, George W., 181, 184–185, 348–349,
    392, 396
Bush family, 8
Business Week, 18
Byelorussian-American Union, 49
Byron, Joseph, 78–80, 85

Cade, Toni, 229, 366–367
Cades, Hazel Rawson, 263–264
Cahan, Abraham, 30, 130–131, 133, 154, 171,
    175
California Supreme Court, 98–101, 108
Call It Sleep, 30, 131, 171–172
Campbell, Joseph, 32
Canarsie, 6
Cantor, Aviva. See Zuckoff, Aviva Cantor
Caribbean, 125–126, 351, 352
Carmichael, Stokely, 20, 22
Carousel, 91
Carter, Jimmy, 4, 56, 58, 185, 313, 314, 349
Castle Garden, 9, 253, 345
Catholicism, 16, 58, 107, 162, 184–186, 195,
    199, 211, 225, 255, 256, 257, 260–261, 286–
    288, 290–299, 302, 306, 321, 328–329, 385,
    391
CBS, 51, 73
Central Park jogger case, 332
Chavez, César, 68
Cheney, Lynne, 32

Cheney family, 8
Cher, 74, 323
Chernin, Kim, 269, 278–279
Chertok, Haim, 165, 166
Chesler, Phyllis, 300, 305, 369–370, 382, 385, 387
Chicago, 28, 185, 334, 337
Chicago Irish Ancestry Workshop, 44
Chicago, Judy, 8, 224, 259, 280–285, 305, 310, 313, 370–372, 374
Children's entertainment, 64, 87, 107
Chin, Vincent, 315
Chinese, 17, 19, 195, 372, 315, 393–394
Chosen, The, 30, 131
Christian Right, 183, 184, 199
Christian Science Monitor, 18, 45
Christ in Concrete, 131, 146
Chronicles, 353, 354
Church and the Second Sex, The, 286, 291, 295
Churchill, Ward, 337–338, 342–343, 345
Citizenship, 68–69, 125, 150, 179, 269, 347–348, 384, 396
Civic life and belonging, 55, 58, 63, 69, 71, 125, 126, 269
Civil Rights Act, 192, 424n35
Civil Rights Movement, 2, 9, 19–22, 207, 214–215, 216, 217, 218, 222, 223, 246
Clark, Pat, 163, 164
Class relations, 36, 70, 84–85, 94, 104, 138, 145, 182, 186–187, 212–213, 334, 388
Cold War, 13–14, 19, 65, 242
Cole, David, 395–396
Colonialism, 19, 21, 67, 194, 195, 197, 335, 336–346, 378, 380–381
Color Purple, The, 124
Columbian Quincentenary, 338–346
Columbo, 31, 73, 329, 336
Columbus, Christopher, 156, 336–346, 455n40
Columbus Day, 126, 323, 336–346
Combahee River Collective Statement, 366, 376
Commercialism and consumerism 23, 24, 25, 51, 89, 145
Conquest of Paradise, The, 344, 346
Consciousness raising, 274–275, 304
Conservatism, 180–205, 239, 385

Constitution, 68; and equal protection clause, 100
Coppola, Francis Ford, 74, 93, 244, 324
Cork, 13, 44
Cosby, Bill, 31
Cosmopolitanism, 92, 151
Costello, 31
Cotton Club, The, 87, 90, 91, 93
Counterculture, 207, 210, 216, 221, 224, 292
Counterlife, The, 167–168, 171, 174
Covens and crafts, 288–289, 300, 306
Crichton, Michael, 316
Crossing Delancey, 52, 124, 240
Cross-racial and cross-ethnic romantic "coupling," 91–93, 95, 115, 124, 155, 175, 320
Cultural production, 56
Cuomo, Mario, 51, 323
Curran, Mary Doyle, 137–141, 143, 308
Curry, Constance, 214–215, 216

Daly, Mary, 251, 286–287, 289, 291, 295–296, 302, 303, 304, 305, 308, 309, 313, 368, 372
D'Amico, Debbie, 225, 247–248
Damnable Question, The, 28
Davis, Mike, 353
Death of the West, 355–356, 358
Deborah, Golda, and Me, 270, 285
Deer Hunter, The, 74, 97, 124, 317
DeFunis v. Odegaard, 99
de Lauretis, Teresa, 266–267
Demjanjuk, John, 169–170
Democratic Party, 183–185, 322, 325–326
DeNiro, Robert, 74, 83
Desegregation, 112, 114–115, 195, 227, 408n78
Detroit, 22, 71, 148, 185, 279
Deutcher, Isaac, 209, 219
de Valera, Eamon, 12, 15
Dia de la Raza, 337
Dialectic of Sex, The, 249, 264
Diamond, Neil, 57, 325
Diary of Anne Frank, The, 31, 131, 159
Diaspora, 18, 46, 156–157, 165, 167, 169, 171
Dick Van Dyke Show, 30
di Leonardo, Michaela, 244–245, 260
Dillingham Commission Report, 39

DiMaggio, Joe, 51, 68, 339
Diner, Hasia, 52
Dinner Party, The, 281–283, 285, 370–371
Dirty Dancing, 87, 90, 91
Discrimination, 36, 99, 130, 359, 385
Disney, 87, 208
Diversity, 55, 58, 61, 177–179, 197, 204, 231, 248, 311, 384
Do the Right Thing, 115
Dover Press, 64, 79, 82
Downtown Jews, 52
Dream of Kings, A, 134–137, 140, 144, 147, 171, 176
Drescher, Fran, 31
Drugs, 114, 148, 152, 214, 379–380
D'Sousa, Dinesh, 32, 183, 209
Dublin, 12, 14, 206, 207, 236
Dublin Parliament, 15
Dukakis, Michael, 46, 185, 320, 324–331, 333–335, 387
Dukakis, Olympia, 74, 95, 320, 323–326
Dutch, 50, 93
Dworkin, Andrea, 253, 270, 300, 381
Dylan, Bob, 207, 216, 225

Eastman Kodak, 51
Ebert, Roger, 112
Ebonics, 18
Education of Max Bickford, The, 31
Education system, 203–204, 211
Eisenhower, Dwight, 60, 356
Eldridge St. Synagogue restoration, 52
Election of 1988, 320–334
Elections, 181, 183–185, 187, 188, 204, 320–334
Elementary and Secondary Education Act of 1965, 54
Ellis Island, 7, 8, 9, 16, 18, 19, 41, 51, 57, 59–69, 73, 76, 77, 78, 80, 85, 95, 164, 179, 194, 205, 218, 233, 234, 239, 243, 253, 254, 269, 307, 317, 318, 319, 358, 363, 364, 320, 321–323, 326, 327, 330–331, 334, 349, 358, 363, 369, 383, 385, 387, 388, 396, 409n95; Ellis Island Medal of Honor and, 68; restoration of, 59–69; Ellis Island Restoration Commission (EIRC) and, 61–62
Ellis Island, 31, 80, 358

English language, 2, 34, 76, 77, 315, 322, 329, 347, 357
Equal Rights Amendment, 252
Erin Brockovich, 123
Eszterhas, Joe, 74, 126
Ethnic cookbooks, 30, 58
Ethnic cuisine, 126
Ethnic Heritage Research Program, 41
Ethnic Heritage Studies Program, 5, 39, 54
Ethnic merchandizing, 5, 51, 52, 64
Ethnic Options, 36, 123
Ethnic particularism, 30, 35, 36, 51, 54, 83, 87, 132, 239, 240–241, 384, 387. *See also* Ethnic universalism
Ethnic revival, 2, 4, 56, 59–62, 66–67, 69, 74, 88, 90, 97, 115–117, 123, 130, 132, 142, 144–145, 158, 175, 181–182, 208, 237, 252, 271, 278, 279, 289, 294, 307, 318, 358
Ethnic revival in American literature/ethnic literature, 130–176, 414nn1,4
Ethnic Studies, 5, 18, 228–229, 233, 236
Ethnic tourism, 5, 45–48, 52–53, 58, 258, 267, 320, 406nn60,61
Ethnic universalism, 32–33, 36, 37, 83, 284, 324, 380, 384, 387, 403n33, 405n53. *See also* Ethnic particularism
Ethnic women's literature, 269–270
Eugenides, Jeffrey, 132
Eurocentrism, 141, 334, 343, 346, 350–358
Europe, 25, 33, 51, 58
European: culture, 40; immigration, 2, 8, 34, 36, 75; Eastern, 46, 76, 156, 173, 268, 279, 326
Everybody Loves Raymond, 31, 73
Ewen, Elizabeth, 270, 276, 279, 307
Exoticism, 43–44, 80–82, 84, 129, 175, 405n57
Ezrat Nashim, 292–293, 299, 303, 375

Faderman, Lillian, 267
Fairleigh Dickinson University, 61
Fall, The, 283–284
Fame, 87, 90, 91
Family of Man, 32, 159
Family values, 146–147, 149, 182, 186, 417n30
Fargo, 74, 124, 128–129
Farrakhan, Louis, 337

Farrell, James T., 131, 132, 232
Father Knows Best, 30
FBI, 114, 117
Fear of Flying, 131, 150–151, 152, 153, 157, 158–161, 164, 175
Female Studies I, II, and *III*, 275–276
Feminine Mystique, The, 254, 257–258, 267
Femininity, 264–266
Feminism, 8, 94, 97, 137, 187, 225, 226, 246–311, 313, 315, 321, 323, 364–384; second-wave, 8, 247–248, 253–272; Third World, 311, 366–367, 382–384
Feminist seder (Passover), 288, 300–301, 306
Feminist theology, 248, 286, 288, 292, 295–297, 298, 302
Ferraro, Geraldine, 51, 161, 254, 309, 320–321, 323, 324
Festival of American Folklife, 54, 58
Festivals, 55, 58, 125–126, 299, 387
Fiddler on the Roof, 4, 7, 18, 25, 26, 30, 73–74, 76, 82, 87–89, 90, 136, 149, 279, 312, 358
Film, 23, 53, 72–129, 132, 145, 151, 410n2
Finding Your Roots, 45
Firestone, Shulamith, 225, 246, 249–250, 253, 264, 309
Fitzgerald, Frances, 40
Flashdance, 75, 87, 90, 91, 95, 96, 97
Flower Drumsong, 86
Flynn, Elizabeth Gurley, 238, 272
Flynn, Raymond, 391–393
Folk: culture, 82, 87–89, 174–175; dancing, 3; epic, 89; knowledge, 83; life, 55, 57–58; musicals, 87
Ford, Gerald, 4, 18, 185
Fortunate Pilgrim, 134, 141–146
Fortune, 51
Fourth of July, 57, 76
Franklin, John Hope, 68
Freedom Riders, 216
Freedom Seder (Passover), 219, 221
Freedom Summer, 209, 216
French, Marilyn, 151, 254, 300
Friedan, Betty, 161, 253, 257–259, 262, 267, 268–269
Friedman-Kabasa, Kathie, 279–280
Funny Girl, 30, 74, 86, 129
Funny Lady, 87, 90, 91

Galway, 45, 389
Gangs of New York, The, 74, 129, 319
Gay rights, 162–163, 186, 187
Gays and lesbians, 117, 162, 183
Gender relations, 105–106, 142, 158, 187, 261–263, 439n30
Genealogy, 4, 15, 41, 43, 44–45, 55, 85, 249
Generation without Memory, 23
German, 37, 50, 159–160, 268, 351
Gershwin, George, 57
Ghetto, 52, 65; blackness and, 108, 117, 201; Jewish, 88, 119, 157, 164, 221, 269, 271, 285; literary representations of, 133, 134, 142, 145, 156, 157, 271, 285; white ethnic, 78, 80–82, 108, 131, 142, 145, 171–172, 182, 184, 190–191, 193, 201, 202, 204, 205, 271
Giants in the Earth, 30, 131, 137
G. I. Bill, 37, 180, 244
Gimbutas, Marija, 249, 254, 301
Ginsberg, Allen, 216, 232
Gitlin, Todd, 216, 218, 227, 241
Giuliani, Rudy, 334, 385–387
Glazer, Nathan, 1, 5, 34, 41, 177, 178–179, 180, 181, 191–192, 195–199, 201, 202, 204, 226, 313, 334, 359, 421n2
Goddess Feminism, 287, 289, 301, 302, 304, 305, 306, 307, 309, 368, 372, 444n76, 448n103
Godfather I and *II*, 30, 74, 76, 81, 116, 124, 130, 136, 146–149, 175, 415n25
Gold, Mike, 131, 132, 145–146
Goldbergs, The, 30
Goldenberg, Naomi, 302–303
Goldman, Emma, 219, 272, 274, 277
Gómez-Peña, Guillermo, 69, 315
Goodbye, Columbus, 151, 159
Goodfellas, 74
Goodman, Paul, 216, 227
Good Will Hunting, 74
Gordon, Mary, 256, 270
Gornick, Vivian, 69, 217, 250, 259, 274–275
Grassroots activism, 54–55
Gray, Herman, 31
Grease, 74–75, 87, 91, 317
Greece, 40, 46, 135, 326, 327, 328
Greek, 2, 36, 73, 83, 127, 135–137, 263, 264, 318, 320, 324–328, 331, 333
Greenblatt, Robert, 214, 225

Gregory, Dick, 318
Grodno, 45, 55
Group Rights, 19–20, 270
Guide to Ethnic Museums, Libraries, and Archives, 50
Guns of Lattimer, The, 242–243
Gyn/Ecology, 368, 372

Haley, Alex, 17, 41–44, 46, 47, 58, 69
Hamilton, Charles, 20
Handlin, Oscar, 37, 232
Handy Book for Genealogists, The, 45
Hansen, Marcus Lee, 2, 3, 9
Hansen's Law, 1, 3, 4, 45, 130, 171, 255, 280
Harjo, Suzan Shown, 338
Harlem, 68, 93, 172
Harper's, 6
Harris, William, 68
Hart-Celler Act, 347
Harvard Encyclopedia of American Ethnic Groups, 41, 51
Harvard Jewish Law Students' Association, 49
Haunch, Paunch, and Jowl, 133
Havurah, 222, 290, 292, 293, 298
Hayden, Tom, 8, 46, 216, 225, 226, 236–240, 244, 289, 308, 313, 318, 344
Heidelberg, 159–161
Herberg, Will, 14, 34
"Heritage Hunt" board game, 46, 58
Her Mothers, 270, 273–274, 310
Hero with a Thousand Faces, 32
Higham, John, 37, 130, 175
Himmelfarb, Gertrude, 182, 191
Hine, Lewis, 78–80, 82, 84, 85
Hippies, 379–380; aesthetic of, 25, 220
Historic neighborhoods, 56
History (written), 5, 10, 15, 32, 36–42, 54, 62–63, 66, 125, 196, 241, 248, 271–280, 285, 310
Hitler, Adolph, 119, 337, 340, 341
Hoffman, Abbie, 216, 220–221, 430n31
Hoffman, Dustin, 111
Hofstadter, Richard, 40
Holland, F. Ross, 65
Hollywood, 4, 15, 17, 33, 73–76, 86, 88, 92, 93, 95, 116, 123, 175, 455n40

Hollywood war movies, 33
Holocaust, 4, 31, 159
Holocaust Museum, 342, 343
Holocaust Project, The, 224, 282–283, 285
Homeland Security, 349
Homicide, 117, 120, 122–123, 129
Homophobia, 163
hooks, bell, 366, 373, 374
Horton, William (Willie), 320, 331–333, 454n33
"House I Live In, The," 57
Howe, Irving, 17, 18, 20, 52, 80, 244
Howells, William Dean, 131
How the Other Half Lives, 39, 79
Hungarian, 50, 83, 126, 309
Hungary, 23
Hyphen-nation/alism, 9, 10, 75

Iacocca, Lee, 62
Iconography of immigration, 75–77, 92, 115
Illegal aliens, 361, 389–396, 463n1
Images of Liberty, 64
Immigrant Reform and Control Act, 394
Immigrants, 2, 7, 8, 9, 10, 13, 17, 18, 37, 40–41, 57, 64, 65, 66, 68, 76–85, 124, 128–129, 131–132, 145, 178, 182, 189, 193, 195, 196, 197, 198, 200, 201, 203, 204, 205, 214, 225, 243, 244, 247, 250, 251, 253, 254, 258, 268, 269, 271, 272, 273, 275, 278, 279, 281–282, 289, 308, 315, 318, 320, 325–330, 333, 337, 346–364, 382, 384, 385–386, 390–396
"Immigrants Still," 58
Immigrant Women in the Land of Dollars, 270, 279
Immigration History Research Center, 40, 63
Immigration History Society, 38, 63
Immigration policy, 346–364, 390, 392
In America, 74
"Indigenous People's Day," 338
Individualism, 65–66, 205
Industrialization, 81, 129
In My Mother's House, 269, 278–279
Inouye, Daniel, 68
In Search of Liberty, 64
"In the Middle of the Barbeque She Brings Up Israel," 166–167, 170

Intifada, 166, 170, 381
Iran Hostage Crisis, 313
Ireland, 11, 12, 13, 14, 15, 16, 25–28, 46, 61, 77,
137, 163, 164, 207, 236, 238–239, 262, 321,
353, 389, 390, 392–396
Irish, 14–17, 46, 183, 236–239, 319, 351,
409n95; assimilation of, 2, 12, 13, 137–141,
205–207, 214, 261–262, 377; Catholics,
162, 185, 256, 261, 299; immigrants, 37,
258, 308, 318, 320, 325, 390–396, 463n1;
organizations of, 49, 162–163. *See also*
Kennedy, John F.
Irish Hunger, The, 46, 236
Irish Northern Aid Commission,
(NORAID), 27, 28, 50
Irish on the Inside, 46, 236, 239
Irish "Troubles," 26, 28, 171, 225, 236
Island of Hope, Island of Tears, 66
Israel and Israeli, 28, 48, 118, 120, 156–157,
164, 165, 175, 207, 222–224, 249, 259, 262,
267, 379–380, 394; military service, 26,
170, 203; Palestinian conflict with, 379–
382; Wars of 1967–73, 26, 164–170
Italian Americana, 44
Italians, 1, 26, 46, 225, 235, 409n95, 416n25;
assimilation of, 93, 141, 264, 377; Catholics, 199, 225, 260–261; Columbus Day
and, 336–346; film representations of, 53,
76, 101, 106–107, 149, 320–321; immigrants,
2, 83, 145, 178, 183, 199, 258, 318, 323–324,
346, 351, 360, 394. *See also* Family values
Italy, 46, 53, 141–142, 385

Jackson, Jesse, 68
Jacobson, Howard, 47–48
Japanese, 19, 195, 315–316
Jazz Singer, The, 87, 90, 91, 92, 129, 325,
405n57
Jerusalem, 48, 167, 169
Jewish aesthetic, 160, 264–266, 373, 440n34,
441n39
Jewish Catalogue, The 52
Jewish counterculture, 52
Jewish Defense League, 49, 165, 207
Jewish Holocaust, 21, 164–165, 169–170, 279,
282–284
Jewish mother figure, 154–155, 157–158

Jewish Museum of New York, 78–79
Jewish nationalism, 21, 26, 164–171, 174–175,
222–223, 270
Jewison, Norman, 89, 323–324
Jews and Jewishness, 1, 33, 34, 37, 150–161,
164–170, 181, 186, 188, 190–194, 204, 207,
209, 230, 233–235, 239, 240, 244, 335, 343,
351, 357, 359, 360, 419n61, 420n74; activism, 20–22, 24, 26, 70, 214–226; culture,
48, 50, 52, 53, 73; exile of, 165–166; feminism and, 249–251, 253, 255, 257–259,
264–268, 270–287, 290, 292–299, 302–
303, 310–311, 364, 365, 371, 372–385, 435n8;
Hassidic, 121, 124; Jewish Studies, 230,
239; literature and film representations
of, 17, 18, 86, 88, 90, 92, 111, 117–123, 128,
172–175; orthodox, 77, 92, 120–121, 127,
158; radicals, 209, 216–226, 233, 236, 239,
240, 246, 428n19. *See also* Black-Jewish
relations; Zionism
Jews without Money, 131, 132, 145
JFK Airport, 389–390, 396
Johnson, Lyndon, 59–60, 350
Jong, Erica, 132, 150, 157–158, 164, 175
Jordan, June, 312, 314
Joy Luck Club, The, 18, 132
Jungle Fever, 115, 125, 129

Kallen, Horace, 23, 26
Kaye/Kantrowitz, Melanie, 21, 22, 218–219,
224, 255, 266, 267, 309, 374, 375, 377, 384,
387
Kazan, Elia, 64
Kennedy, Edward, 352
Kennedy, John F., 4, 11, 12, 13, 14, 15, 16, 36–
37, 46, 59, 61, 69, 185, 178, 232, 237, 238,
313, 320, 328, 349–352, 389
Kennedy, Joseph, 16
Kerr, Clark, 25
Kibbutz, 224, 249–250, 435n8
King, Martin Luther, Jr., 8, 185, 313
Kingston, Maxine Hong, 17
Kinsey, Alfred, 32
Kirshenblatt-Gimblett, Barbara, 55–56
Kissing Jessica Stein, 127, 161
Koch, Edward, 323, 391, 392
Kojak, 31, 73

Kristol, Irving, 178–179, 180, 181, 182, 191, 193, 202, 313

LA8 case, 395–396
Lansky, Aaron, 50–51
Latin America, 351, 352, 353, 356; and colonialism, 337
Latina/os, 35, 75, 145, 186, 315, 319, 329, 337, 342, 344, 351, 353, 356, 359, 360, 367–368, 387, 390–391
Latvian Foundation, 28, 171
Lauter, Paul, 218, 233–234
Lazarus, Emma, 8, 51, 94, 232, 253
Leadership Conference of Women Religious (LCWR), 290, 291
Leah's Journey, 52
Lee, Spike, 115
Lemlich, Clara, 272, 277
Lerner, Gerda, 254, 276, 278
Lerner, Rabbi Michael, 219, 221, 224, 426n5
Lesbianism, 260, 283, 382, 435n6
Levick, Edwin, 79, 84
Levine, Lawrence, 232, 233
Levinson, Barry, 75, 110–112
Liberalism, 19, 188, 198, 202, 205, 209, 241, 322, 333, 349, 359, 387
Liberty Heights, 110–112, 114–115
Liberty Island, 57–65, 252
Libraries, 43, 44, 51, 68
Lilith collective, 249, 293, 375
Limerick, 16
Lincoln Center, 27
Lithuania and Lithuanians, 48, 50
Little Italy, 53, 81, 125
Litvak, 48
Lonely Crowd, The, 25
Long Island, 142–144
Lorde, Audre, 367, 368, 372, 374
Los Angeles, 92, 393, 361
Los Angeles Times, 325, 340, 342
Lowenthal, David, 24
Lower East Side, 17, 23, 77, 79, 164, 319; ethnic tourism, 52–53; literary representations of, 133, 145, 364–365; Tenement Museum, 52
Lumet, Sidney, 74, 120

Madonna, 46–47, 161, 260, 373, 440n33
Madonna—Ciao Italia, 46–47
Main Street, 71
Malamud, Bernard, 159
Malcolm X, 205, 226
Mama, 30
Mambo Kings, The, 18
Mamet, David, 25, 116, 122, 279
Mann Act, 114
Masada, 6, 202
Masculinity, 26, 70, 104–106, 122, 261
McCourt, Frank, 77
Means, Russell, 340, 345
Mehta, Zubin, 58
Melting Pot paradigm, 2, 7, 10, 25, 34, 36, 41, 49, 56, 62–63, 75, 112, 325, 360, 361
Memoirs of an Ex-Prom Queen, 161, 258, 310, 441n39
Memory and nostalgia, 56, 71, 77, 129, 140, 172, 182, 394
Mercy of a Rude Stream, 146, 172–175
Mexicans, 19, 329, 336, 348, 356, 363, 390
Mexico, 197, 352, 361, 363, 382, 388, 393
Mickey Mouse, 60
"Middle America," 71, 73, 87, 155, 188, 268, 317
Middle East, 164, 183, 222–223, 379–382
Middlesex, 161
Midler, Bette, 74
Miller, Nancy, 265–266, 267
Minstrelsy, 90, 92, 123
Mitropoulos, Nick, 326, 327
Modernity and the modern, 23, 24, 26, 44, 52, 67, 70, 89, 142, 144, 188, 210, 212, 377
Montagu, Ashley, 33, 35
Montauk, 394–395
Montega, Joe, 117, 123
Montgomery, 22
Moonstruck, 74, 116, 127, 317, 320, 323–324, 326, 327
Moraga, Cherríe, 265, 366, 375, 382
Morality, 143, 150–151, 153
Morgan, Robin, 216, 235, 246, 253, 290, 302, 303, 304, 305, 310–311, 383, 387
Moynihan, Daniel Patrick, 1, 5, 7, 34, 41, 177, 191, 244, 318
Moynihan Report, 7, 148–149, 201, 367

"Multicultural conservatives," 183

Multiculturalism, 2, 8, 9, 17, 38, 124, 132, 162, 171, 175, 178, 202, 203, 208, 209–210, 226–240, 241, 242, 243, 270, 281, 284, 312, 314–315, 346, 383

Murphy, Julie, 260–261

Museums: ethnic, 50, 52, 78–79; Holocaust, 342, 343; immigration, 57, 60, 63–65

Musicals, 413n23; ethnic, 85–93; film, 89, 91, 92; folk, 87–89; show, 89–90

Muzzy, David Saville, 40

My Big Fat Greek Wedding, 71, 127–128, 129

Mystic Pizza, 116, 124

Nanny, The, 31

Nation, The, 18, 210, 331

National Assembly of Religious Women, 291–292

National Endowment for the Humanities, 39, 54

Nationalism (Old World), 26–29, 50, 164–171

National Park Service, 59, 61, 65, 68

National Yiddish Book Center, 50

Nation of Immigrants, A, 4, 16, 36–37, 61, 79, 350

"Nation of immigrants" paradigm, 36, 41, 57, 59, 67, 69, 84, 85, 178, 179, 204, 336, 343, 346, 349, 361–363, 385, 388, 396

Native Americans, 22, 25, 47, 125, 325; colonialism and, 19, 21, 195, 197, 336–346, 377–378; carnival and powwow, 126; appropriation of, 240, 460n95

Native American Studies, 38

Nativism, 238, 347, 353, 354–358, 359

Naturalization Law (1790), 2, 64, 359, 361

Nazi Germany, 32–33, 159, 164; Third Reich and, 97, 159

Nazism, 118, 217, 257, 283, 338, 343, 372

"Negro Problem," 35, 193–194

Neoconservativism, 8, 175, 180, 182, 183, 191, 194, 195–197, 202, 203, 209, 241, 313, 359, 385

Neonazism, 119, 122

Neopaganism, 153, 287, 302–303, 305, 306, 308–309

Neuhaus, Richard John, 198–200

New Age, 240

New Americans, The, 358–360

New England Historic Genealogical Society, 44

New Jersey, 142–143

New Left, 8, 49, 207–210, 213–227, 237–238, 240, 246, 257, 261, 290, 383

Newman, Pauline, 276, 277

New Right, 182, 240

New Ross, 12, 14, 15, 46, 69

Newsweek, 45, 88, 89

New World, 55–56, 68, 70, 95, 126, 131, 134, 136, 137, 139, 141, 143, 145, 269, 273, 285, 336–337, 344

New York, 13, 22, 26, 29, 48, 57, 76, 77, 78, 79, 81, 85, 100, 141–143, 162, 164, 171, 178, 183, 203, 228, 323, 327, 340, 386–387, 390, 391, 396

New York, New York, 90, 91

New York Radical Women, 265, 274

New York Times, 11, 12, 17, 28, 42, 59, 64, 71, 98, 148, 163, 357

Nixon, Richard, 46, 65, 183–184, 241, 320

Nordic supremacism, 189, 210

Normativity and "deviance," 75, 153, 155, 164, 203–204, 297

Novak, Michael, 20–22, 24, 34, 68, 180, 182, 187–191, 197–199, 201, 208–212, 214, 216, 225, 229, 231, 233, 238, 241–243, 289, 320, 331, 333, 425n38

Novick, Peter, 343

Nyhan, David, 327, 329

Ocean Hill—Brownsville strike, 227, 373, 401n18

Olazagasti-Sergovia, Elena, 367–368

Old World, 3, 25, 26, 30, 36, 43, 46, 77, 90, 95, 96, 134, 136, 137, 141, 143, 145, 164, 207, 236, 238, 247, 250, 263, 271, 273, 285, 323, 357

Once Upon a Time in America, 78, 82, 83

Operation Shylock, 169–170

Oral history, 54

"Oration Upon the Most Recent Death of Christopher Columbus," 344–346

O'Reilly, Leonora, 272, 274

Organization Man, The, 25

Otherness, 127, 134, 137, 145, 160, 296–297, 365, 372, 396
O'Toole, Fintan, 394–395
Ozzie and Harriet, 30

Pacino, Al, 74
Paglia, Camille, 161, 260, 373
Palastinians, 223, 379–382, 395–396
Palladino, Pixie, 107, 202
Parish and the Hill, The, 137, 139–142, 144, 175
Parks, Rosa, 68
Path to National Suicide, The, 356–357
Patinkin, Mandy, 360, 361
Patriarchy, 260, 261, 263, 267, 269, 271, 272, 273–274, 275, 282–283, 286, 289–290, 297, 301, 302, 304, 307, 369
Patriotism, 54, 65
Perot, Ross, 184
Petrakis, Harry Mark, 134–137, 140, 143, 145, 147, 152
Philadelphia, 101, 103 107, 108, 122
Phillips, Kevin, 183–184, 187
Photography, 78–83, 411n10
Piercy, Marge, 151, 216, 224, 250, 297
Pilgrims and pioneers motif, 76, 320, 330, 341, 343. *See also* Columbus, Christopher; Plymouth Rock
Plaskow, Judith, 295–297, 300, 302, 305
Plastic surgery, 264
Plessy vs. Ferguson, 100
Pluralism, 14, 16, 39, 41, 92, 151–152, 162, 178, 200, 208, 209, 268, 269, 311, 396
Plymouth Rock, 7, 9, 41, 60, 69, 205. *See also* Pilgrims and pioneers motif
Podhoretz, Norman, 182, 190, 191, 193–194, 232
Pogrebin, Letty Cottin, 167, 244, 246, 270, 271, 285, 300–301, 379, 380, 381–382
Poland, 23, 26, 28, 40, 46, 239
Police, 115, 119, 387
Polish, 3, 20, 28, 33, 36, 48, 49, 171, 239, 326–327, 351
Pollard spy case, 165, 169–170
Pollitt, Katha, 270–271
Populism, 8, 181–182, 184, 205
Portal to America, 52, 78, 79, 82

Port Huron Statement, 207, 210, 227, 238
Portnoy's Complaint, 18, 46, 131, 150–151, 152, 153, 161, 164, 165, 171, 175
Postindustrial order, 24, 25, 144–145
Postwar period, 37, 151–152, 163; and economy, 51
Potok, Chaim, 30
Prell, Riv-Ellen, 223, 290–298
Priesand, Sally, 293, 294
Proposition 187, 347
Proulx, Annie, 132
Pryor, Richard, 56
Psychology, psychiatry, and psychoanalysis, 150–151, 153, 157; as a literary genre, 151, 154; sexuality and, 171
Puerto Rico, 203
Puzo, Mario, 30, 132, 133, 141–144, 146–149, 152, 175

Quayle, Dan, 69

Race, 32–36, 93, 96–116, 123, 148–150, 180–181, 186–187, 188–189, 190, 192, 194, 195, 196, 197, 202, 203, 204–205, 210, 211, 212, 218, 222, 223, 229, 243, 244, 245, 264, 265, 283, 311, 315, 316, 319, 320, 331–336, 342, 347, 349, 354–356, 359, 360, 364–384, 390, 396
Radical Zionist Alliance, 20–22, 221, 239
Radio, 23, 24, 90
Radio Days, 110, 127
Raging Bull, 74, 108–110, 115,
Ragtime, 77, 78, 131, 360
Rainbow Shabbat, 283, 284–285
Random House, 64, 208
Reagan, Ronald, 16, 17, 46, 97, 108, 182, 185, 201, 205, 316, 320, 322, 325, 328, 340
Reagan Democrats, 183, 185, 187, 205, 240, 320, 321
Realism, 82, 123
Red Diaper Babies, 217
Redstockings, 226, 274, 367
Religion/religiosity, 57, 11, 153, 182, 186–187, 213, 214, 219–220, 259, 287–298, 305, 307, 308
Reparations (slavery), 9, 334–336

Republican Party, 8, 181–184, 187, 200, 204, 322, 332
Rich, Adrienne, 251, 253, 300, 302, 305, 306, 309, 365, 374, 377–378, 381, 383
Riis, Jacob, 78–82
Rise of David Levinsky, 30, 130–131, 133, 171, 175
Rise of the Unmeltable Ethnics, 34, 187–190, 208–212, 214, 225, 229, 231, 320, 331
Rising of the Women, 271–272
Rising Sun, 314, 316
Rivington Street, 52, 270
Robinson, Sugar Ray, 109
Rock, Chris, 317
Rocksteady Crew, 96
Rocky I and *II*, 17, 75, 96–98, 100–105, 107, 108, 110, 114, 115, 122, 125
Roe v. Wade, 356
Roiphe, Anne, 11, 23, 25
Rolvaag, Ole, 30, 131, 137, 232
Rome, 47
Roosevelt, Theodore, 26
Roots, 4, 6, 17, 18, 28, 31, 41–46, 279, 312
Roots Schmoots, 47
Roth, Henry, 30, 131, 132, 171, 175
Roth, Philip, 132, 150, 154, 157, 164, 166, 167–170, 175
Rubin, Jerry, 206, 216, 220
Ruether, Rosemary, 288, 290, 297, 305
Rukeyser, Muriel, 369, 374
Rumania, 23
Russia, 23, 40, 269, 364–365
Russian, 77, 88, 90, 115, 173, 357

Saint Patrick's Day, 7; New York Parade, 162–163
Sale, Kirkpatrick, 344, 346
Sanders, Ronald, 52
Sandoval, Chela, 371–372
San Francisco, 77, 340–341
Sanger, Margaret, 272, 281
Sarachild, Kathie, 254, 309
Sasso, John, 326, 327
Saturday Night Fever, 74, 87, 90, 95, 115, 124, 127
Saturday Night Live, 73, 325
Schlesinger, Arthur, Jr., 32, 210, 349

Schneiderman, Rose, 255, 272, 277
Schoener, Allon, 52, 82
Schomberg Library, 68
Schussler, Elisabeth Fiorenza, 248–249, 251, 254, 287, 290, 302, 304, 305
Schwerner, Michael, 209, 373
Science fiction, 360–361
Scorsese, Martin, 53–54, 74, 109–110, 125, 126, 319
Scottsboro case, 364
Second-wave feminism. *See* Feminism
Segregation, 56, 93, 114. *See also* Desegregation
Seinfeld, 31
Selma, 22
September 11 (2001), 334, 348–387, 389, 395, 396
Sexual Behavior in the Human Male and *Female*, 32
Sexuality, 150–164, 186, 260–261, 263, 283
Sexual Revolution, 150–153, 162
Shiksa figure, 155–156, 161, 164, 264, 266, 441n39
Shtetl, 46, 87, 88, 116, 224, 230, 320
Shulman, Alix Kates, 151, 161, 258, 276–277, 310, 441n39
Sicilians, 34, 53
Simon, Carly, 94
Sinatra, Frank, 57, 113–114
Slavery, 21, 67, 68, 178, 197, 214, 240, 338, 342. *See also* Reparations
Slavic, 2, 50
Sleeper, Jim, 213–214, 220, 222
Smith, Barbara, 265, 366, 372, 374–375
Social sciences, 32–36, 153, 178, 277
Sociology, 15, 32, 62, 38, 39, 125, 177–178
Sollors, Werner, 233, 307–308
Sopranos, The, 26, 31, 73, 151
Soviets, 26, 28, 221
Sowell, Thomas, 34–35
Spiritual Feminism, 288, 293, 301, 302, 303, 306
Spretnak, Charlene, 301, 302, 307
Srole, Leo, 33–34
Stallone, Sylvester, 74, 97, 98, 102, 122, 244
Starhawk (Miriam Simos), 251, 253, 302, 303, 304, 305, 306–307, 377, 378, 383

State (administration and power), 5, 19, 53–55, 59–69, 197–202

Staten Island, 53, 94

Statue of Liberty, 5, 8, 51, 57, 59, 60–61, 64, 65, 76, 78, 94, 251–253, 320, 322, 362

Statue of Liberty Centennial (1986), 51, 56–58, 62, 64, 68, 137, 179, 204, 320, 322; Statue of Liberty–Ellis Island Centennial Commission and, 62, 68

Staying Alive, 87, 90, 91

Steinem, Gloria, 251, 253, 300, 302, 305, 306, 309, 373, 374

Stern, Sol, 207, 214

Stieglitz, Alfred, 80, 84

Stranger Among Us, A, 120, 124

Strangers in the Land, 37

Streisand, Barbra, 74, 84

Student Nonviolent Coordinating Committee (SNCC), 209, 214, 215, 218, 223, 228, 261

Students for a Democratic Society (SDS), 46, 206, 207, 216, 218, 222, 223, 226, 236, 261

Suburbanization, 18, 23, 25, 142–144, 205, 214, 264

Summer of Sam, 115

Swedish, 2, 37, 50

Tax, Meredith, 52, 249, 270, 271–272, 274, 364–365

Television, 4, 30–31, 71, 72–73, 212, 247, 321, 324, 333

Telling, The, 300, 310

Terrorism, 348–349, 395–396

Tevye Stories, 87–88

Thanksgiving, 31, 75–76

Thernstrom, Stephan, 51

Third World, 208, 211, 229, 236, 243–244, 275; feminism, 311, 366–367, 382–384; migration, 315, 355, 359, 363, 391, 393; Zionism and, 382

Third World Liberation Front (TWLF), 228

This Bridge Called My Back, 366

Time, 4, 18, 41, 43, 44, 45, 314, 329, 341, 347, 355, 390, 392, 394

Titanic, 74, 78, 84–85, 317, 358

To Empower the People, 198, 200

To Have and To Hold, 31

To Jerusalem and Back, 28

Tonight Show, 151

Topol, Chaim, 88

Torgovnick, Marianna De Marco, 249, 260, 263, 267

To the Barricades, The Anarchist Life of Emma Goldman, 276–277, 310

Triangle Shirtwaist Factory, 21, 31, 277, 322, 364

Tribalism, 23, 117, 119, 239

Trible, Phyllis, 289–290

Tuite, Marjorie, 287, 304

Ukrainian, 20, 49, 50, 376, 406n61

"Underdog" mentality. *See* White grievance and victimology

Union Square, 364–365

University of California: Berkeley, 25, 275, 338, 340; Berkeley Free Speech Movement, 153, 216; Davis, 98–100

Uprooted, The, 37

U. S. A. Patriot Act, 347, 348

U.S. Supreme Court, 100, 286

Van Steeg, Clarence, 40

Vatican II, 290–292

Vaudeville, 90, 92

Vecoli, Rudolph, 38–39, 63, 230, 244

Vietnam War, 21, 25, 65, 97–98, 185, 213, 279, 313, 316

Viscusi, Robert, 344–346, 387

Visuality, 79, 83, 94, 116, 125, 132

Voluntary Associations, 49–50, 199–201, 221, 387

Voters and voting, 1, 181, 183–185, 187, 188, 204, 325, 327, 422n12

Walker, Alice, 366, 369–372, 374, 379–380, 381

Wallace, George, 187, 205

Warner, Lloyd, 33–34

Washington Post, 57, 321, 325, 328, 331

Waskow, Arthur, 24, 219, 221, 224

WASP/WASPdom, 6, 7, 20, 30, 73, 74, 75, 127, 156, 165, 188–189, 210, 220, 226, 211, 264, 324, 329
Watergate, 313
Waters, Mary, 36, 123, 146
Weave of Women, 299–300, 310
Weinberg, Sydney Stahl, 276, 279, 285, 307
Welfare, 9, 65, 108, 182, 193, 202, 205
Westchester Columbus Committee, 50
West Side Story, 86, 124
White grievance and victimology, 95, 98, 101–102, 107–108, 110, 111, 175, 197, 245, 278, 318, 332; "underdog" mentality and, 97, 103, 115, 205, 319, 385
Whiteness, 2, 7, 9, 20, 22, 33–34, 35, 70–71, 74, 101, 115, 145, 186, 189–190, 197, 202, 203, 233, 243, 245, 264, 311, 315, 316, 317, 318, 319, 320, 343, 359, 364–365, 367, 368, 369, 370, 371, 372, 375, 376, 377
White privilege, 197, 210, 243, 245, 311, 359, 365, 376
White supremacy, 9, 189, 315, 369, 378
Whyte, William, 25
Wicca, 287, 289, 301, 302, 305, 306, 377
Wilbur, Richard, 58
Will & Grace, 31
Willis, Ellen, 208–209, 272, 275
Willkie, Wendell, 32
Wills, Gary, 326, 328
Winds of War, The, 31
Witchcraft, 284, 302, 303, 304–306, 308, 309, 377, 378, 447n100

Wolf, Naomi, 249–250, 262–263
Womanspirit Rising, 302, 305
Woman Warrior, 17
Women's International Terrorist Conspiracy from Hell (WITCH), 303, 305–306, 310
Women's ordination, 287, 292, 293, 294, 295
Women's Studies, 275–276
Working Girl, 93–95
World of Our Fathers, 4, 17, 18, 52, 80, 269, 312, 387
World Trade Center, 348, 395
World War II, 32–33, 35, 151, 351

X, Malcolm, 205, 226

Yekl, 131, 154
Yentl, 84–85, 87, 90, 116, 317, 360
Yezierska, Anzia, 30, 269, 271
Yiddish/Yiddishisms, 50–51, 73, 77, 111, 120, 161, 268, 283–285
Your Show of Shows, 30
Yours In Struggle, 371, 375–377

Zionism, 118–119, 159, 166–170, 174–175, 221–225, 246, 270–271, 379, 380, 381–382, 420n74
Zuckoff, Aviva Cantor, 214, 282, 288, 293, 300